Also by Marilyn Tausend

Mexico the Beautiful

(coauthor)

Cocina de la Familia

MORE THAN 200 AUTHENTIC RECIPES FROM
MEXICAN-AMERICAN HOME KITCHENS

MARILYN TAUSEND *with* MIGUEL RAVAGO

A Fireside Book

Published by Simon & Schuster

FIRESIDE
Rockefeller Center
1230 Avenue of the Americas
New York, NY 10020

First Fireside Edition 1999

FIRESIDE and colophon are registered trademarks
of Simon & Schuster Inc.

Permissions Acknowledgments begin on page 393.

Designed by Bonni Leon-Berman

Manufactured in the United States of America

3   5   7   9   10   8   6   4   2

The Library of Congress has cataloged the
Simon & Schuster edition as follows:
Tausend, Marilyn.
Cocina de la familia : more than 200 authentic recipes from
Mexican-American home kitchens / Marilyn Tausend with Miguel Ravago.
p.   cm.
1. Mexican American cookery.   I. Ravago, Miguel.   II. Title.
TX715.2.S69T38   1997
641.59'26872073—dc21   97-26979
CIP
ISBN 0-684-81818-3
0-684-85525-9 (Pbk)

To

Ed Lewis and Fredric Tausend

Without these two men in my

life this book would not be.

My father imbued me with a curiosity about all foods
and a deep respect for those who made feasts out of
meager offerings. My husband rekindled my love of
Mexico, and his influence is shown on every page.

M. L. T.

Acknowledgments

Cocina de la Familia is more a historical cooking story than a cookbook. If it were a stage production, there would be a cast of more than a hundred Mexican Americans and one Mexican Canadian to be applauded. And I do so—with all my heart. They are the voices in their own stories; I only put it in writing. The pages of this book acknowledge my gratitude to all who contributed.

My ability to interpret their recipes is built on knowledge I have gained from more than a decade of learning from innumerable cooks throughout Mexico. In so many instances when I was interviewing someone in the United States and found the person was from a specific region in Mexico, I was able to say I had been in that village or city, eaten the local dishes, and on several occasions even knew the same cooks.

Diana Kennedy opened the wonders of Mexican cooking to me, as she has done for so many. From her I learned to respect the honesty and integrity of Mexican cooking and gained an understanding of its flavor dimensions. I seldom cook a Mexican dish without heeding her many procedural admonitions. "Dearie, don't boil the cactus to death." Or, "Don't wash away all the flavor—every germ is going to perish anyway when we cook it." Thank you, Diana, for sharing your knowledge and friendship with me.

My loving thanks to Susy Torres in Puerto Angel, Oaxaca, a member of my "second family" who traveled with me during part of my research and acted as an interpreter when needed, and to Carmen Barnard, my friend and business associate in Morelia, Michoacán, who cheered me by faxing a constant stream of puns and humorous drawings, and for her unconventional wisdom.

Wherever I went, I was welcomed into the homes and lives of new and old friends. They provided me with shelter, good meals, and companionship. So thank you, Rosie and Don Price in Idaho; Claire Archibald in Oregon; Mary Jo Heavey and Lupe Peach in Washington; Mario and Diane Montaña, Rusty Mitchell in Colorado; Joe and Elena Kurstin in Florida; Angelita Espinosa in Michigan; Rick and Deann Bayless in Illinois; Shirley King in New York; Jeannaine Brookshire in Arizona; Park Kerr in Texas; Bill and Cheryl Jamison in New Mexico; and Bernadette Guitierrez, Nancy Zaslavsky, Peg Tomlinson, Kirsten West, and Kurt and Kitty Spataro in California. I want to thank you all—along with so many others who freely shared insights and information with me.

If a cookbook is to be of value, then the recipes must be accurate and easily understood.

While Miguel and I tested and tasted our way through many, many dishes before selecting the ones that became part of this collection, there was an informal coterie of cooks who for over a year diligently and repeatedly tested each recipe. I wish to express my deep appreciation to these volunteers: Renée Downey, Doris Evans, Marilyn Farrell, Albert Furbay, Joan Wickham, Allen and Suzanne Peery, Claire Archibald, Shelly Wiseman, Amy Neal, Darcy Clark, Jessica and Bill Baccus, Nancy Leushel, Kelly Martin, Maria McMahon, Jeff Pilcher, Terri Pomerenk, Rusty Mitchell, Dane and Wendy Henas, Nancy Irwin, Shirley King, David and Margaret Juenke, and Corinne Hagen.

Before I started this book, I never appreciated the role of an agent. Maureen and Eric Lasher have been indispensable, working with me for several years and through many drafts until we were all satisfied. The Lashers then found for me a publishing company with an editor, Sydny Miner, with equal enthusiasm, skill, and patience. Thank you.

I'm one of those strange creatures who write everything by hand on legal paper. My saving grace is Carole Jordan, my assistant, who for about thirty years has been deciphering my scrawl and, with the help of her mother, Gwen Jordan, a former newspaper proofreader, putting it into proper form.

I owe a special debt to Miguel Ravago, a second-generation Mexican American. For over twenty years he was the co-owner and chef of Fonda San Miguel in Austin, Texas, one of the finest Mexican restaurants in the United States. We were together when my agent and I first explored the possibility of this book, and Miguel immediately and wholeheartedly offered his invaluable assistance. *Cocina de la Familia* has been four long years aborning. Throughout this time we worked harmoniously, even though thousands of miles apart. Often both of us were preparing the same recipe at the same time and consulting back and forth by phone and fax. Miguel's vast experience in cooking savory Mexican food and his discerning testing provided me with constant assurance that we were on course.

For over a year my daughter Sara McIntyre opened the front door every day with an ungrudging and joyful *"Buenos días,* Mama," and set about washing the constant accumulation of pots and pans and cleaning up the debris from my cooking. It was the most unrewarding task of any, yet it was Sara's unending optimism that kept me going—to try just one more dish, to verify another fact, or to rewrite another page—even when I was past all desire to continue.

M.L.T.

Que bonita es la vida cuando nos da de sus riquezas.
(How beautiful life is when it gives us its riches.)

As a little boy I spent countless hours in the kitchen watching my wonderful grandmother, Guadalupe Velásquez, prepare traditional Mexican dishes while telling me old family stories from when she was a little girl in Mexico. She transmitted to me the knowledge of this great cuisine as well as the pride of my heritage. She changed my life forever. Without her riches I would never have become a chef. *Gracias, Abuelita!*

I also want to thank all my *familia*—my dear mother, Amelia Galbraith; my sister, Betty Saenz; my aunt Linda Mendivil; and my cousin Dina Mendivil Lansdell—for their contribution and encouragement, and for just being the best family in the world.

Nushie Chancellor, who gave so much of her time in testing recipes with me, who helped with her knowledge and great Mexican cooking tips, and who brought so much fun to my kitchen all the time we were working, *gracias.*

Mere words cannot express my appreciation for all the help I received from my dear friend Philippe Mercier during the preparation of this book from the beginning, and for his powerful support when I went through hard times this past year. Thanks.

And to the Mexican-American families who helped make this book, thank you all.

M.R.

Contents

Introduction

For much of the past three years I have traveled back and forth across the United States talking to hundreds of Mexican and Mexican-American cooks, hearing their stories, and collecting their recipes. Seldom were the ingredients or instructions written down, but I learned from watching, listening, and talking. *Cocina de la Familia* is the tale of these many cooks—all of whom have adapted the family dishes and traditions they remember from their past to accommodate a life considerably different from the lives of their parents and grandparents.

This is a transition that deserves to be understood. As society changes, our eating habits change. Most home cooks, whether in Mexico or anywhere else in the world, were women who did it out of necessity and not because of a creative urge. What they cooked came less from individual fancy than from knowledge passed on from generation to generation.

Today's Mexican cooks may use oil instead of lard, canned instead of fresh tomatoes, or a food processor instead of grinding on a slab of volcanic rock, but food is still the strand that ties them to their past. María, who lives and works in Sacramento, California, but whose family is from a small village near Guadalajara, says it best: "In our culture, food is much more than just nourishment. It connects us. It isn't just served at a celebration, it *is* a celebration."

It is this celebration of the food—the spirit of the country itself—that I have tried to focus on in these contemporary recipes from Mexican-American kitchens. I think it is important to stress that I use the word "contemporary" to mean real food eaten every day by Mexican-American families, whether they live in cities such as Los Angeles or Chicago, the border towns of Texas or Arizona, farming communities in the Pacific Northwest, or the isolated villages of New Mexico and southern Colorado. This is food that has its roots in the prehistoric soil of Mexico but has branched out, survived, and flourished in this modern world.

I am not Mexican by birth, heritage, or citizenship. But my relationship to the food of Mexico spans more than half a century. My father was what is called a carlot produce distributor, which means that he bought produce such as onions, potatoes, and citrus fruits from the fields and orchards, and sold them by the railroad car to wholesale buyers in Chicago and New York. By necessity, I grew up following the rhythmic cycle of the growing season throughout southern Texas, the Central Valley of California, and southern Idaho. I slept at night in hotels and motor courts, and I learned about food by sharing meals with the Mexican and Mexican-American migrant field-workers.

I must have aroused the passionate maternal nature of the Mexican women as I trailed my father around in the fields. No matter that they were living out of cars and cooking over a butane burner, they showed their compassion in the way they knew best: by having me share the flavors and textures of their foods—and lives. When I was about eleven, I think, I worked the crops with my Mexican-American friends. They showed me the fastest way to top onions for seed, to pick peaches from the top of the tree without falling off the ladder, and to weed corn without disturbing the roots. Then they shared with me their midday meal. I remember thick tortillas wrapped around a chile-pungent stew of meat, all tied together in a bandanna and left in the shade until time to eat. My hands were small, and it took many tries before I could tip the rolled tortillas just right, curling my fingers around the far end so that none of the sauce squished out and ran down my chin.

I remember one large family that seemed to be all male, every age and every size. They often brought a large red coffee can filled with slightly warm but still crispy potato cakes made with lots of springy cheese. We would pile them with a salsa made of freshly picked tomatoes so ripe that they popped open when pricked with a thumbnail. The tomatoes, a milky white onion, and very tiny, very hostile chiles were all chopped together on the lid of the can with a sharp, shiny knife. We'd eat sitting beside the irrigation ditch, kicking our feet in the slow-moving water and splashing ourselves to cool off.

I can still recall a young girl, about my age, making up a bed of old blankets in the backseat of a beat-up old Ford, then laying down a tired toddler and gently fanning him to sleep with corn leaves. One full-moon-faced woman had a new baby with her every year—always wrapped tightly in a dark-colored *rebozo* while she bent over weeding up and down the furrows. This was my first conscious sight of a nursing mother, milk dribbling out around the baby's mouth and sweat running down the woman's bare neck and chest. I admired the men with their muscular arms and would know envy when one would stop by his wife and casually stroke her neck. I watched it all, absorbing the love I felt around me. It was then, too, that I began to equate Mexican food with that unusual balance of contentment and excitement.

Decades later, after raising my own family in largely Scandinavian and Yugoslavian communities, I set out to rediscover these foods of my past. They certainly weren't being served in the Mexican chain restaurants that dotted the strip malls near where we lived. I began to wonder if they were anywhere but in my memory.

The logical place to search seemed to be in Mexico itself. And, like Columbus, I found a culinary world that I didn't know existed—one more vast and varied than I had imagined. The more my husband, Fredric, and I traveled and tasted, the happier I became.

Early on, I was lucky enough to become friends with Diana Kennedy, who is perhaps the greatest living expert on the traditional cooking of Mexico. With her guidance I began to recognize the ingredients and cooking techniques common throughout the country and, just as important, to search out and understand the divergent characteristics of regional food. I was intrigued by all of the dishes but always wondered where I could find similar ones in the United States if I didn't prepare them myself.

The answer came while I was in Oaxaca sharing a late evening meal with Emilia Arroya de Cabrera, a friend of several years. Her dining room table held a bowl—the same sun-glazed earth tones as the parched hillsides—filled with a clear broth. Tendrils from young squash plants were twisted among the submerged hunks of pale yellow corn, the kernels still attached and encircling the cob. A platter held curds of soft scrambled eggs gashed by vivid red streaks of *colorin* blossoms. There were two salsas, one red and one green, and a basket of corn tortillas, heat-freckled on the *comal*.

Emilia's mother had cooked this satisfying supper just as she prepared most of the family food. Though a simple meal, the visual contrasts of color and texture, the harmonizing tastes of fresh seasonal ingredients, and the aroma that filled the room made it very special.

After supper I sat on the couch with Aurora, one of Emilia's daughters, who had recently married a Texan. When I casually asked what she cooked in her new home, she replied, "The dishes I learned from my grandmother, of course."

"The dishes I learned from my grandmother" became the starting place for my new culinary search—one that would lead across the United States and into the kitchens of many Mexican Americans like Aurora. I set out to discover how 13 million United States citizens of Mexican heritage—those of first, second, third, and even eighth generations—were creating their traditional dishes.

I found that Mexico's indigenous ingredients—primarily corn, beans, chile, and tomatoes—continue to be the foundation of all Mexican cooking. Squash, turkey, and avocado are as important now as they were in the days when Cortés came ashore in Mexico. Equally important are rice and wheat, as well as the many types of citrus fruits and all the different livestock and their products, incorporated into the cuisine by the Spanish. In the face of both the opportunities and the restraints of today's world, what has changed is the use of time-saving equipment and products, the introduction of many other ethnic influences, and an emphasis on healthier eating.

This was a way of cooking that I wanted to learn more about and then to share. I asked these cooks for their hoarded taste memories. I ate and I cooked with them, observing how they modified the traditional foods of remembrance and wove them into the fabric of their everyday lives.

In Los Angeles I discovered an unusual chicken dish with a prune and raisin sauce; its flavor was heightened with chipotle chile and soothed by Coca-Cola. From Miami, by way of Guanajuato, came traditional rustic enchiladas together with chile-sauced chunks of carrots and potatoes. But in Detroit a more diet-conscious cook substituted bean curd, spinach, and yogurt. In Illinois, a cook added chocolate to the classic Mexican rice pudding, and mustard enhanced a shredded beef salad in El Paso. The list goes on and on.

Most of the recipes are quite simple, but even the more complex dishes—*moles* or tamales—can be made in stages. The ingredients should be easy to find unless it is an out-of-season product. In that case, a substitute will be listed.

Throughout all my journeys I discovered one consistent theme: During the many years as Mexicans became Mexican Americans, whether by annexation or by immigration, and in times of discrimination and estrangement, they kept their past alive in their homes through the stories they told and the food they cooked. Everywhere I went I saw how for most Mexican Americans the family has played a major role as a defense against an often indifferent, even hostile, society, and the family is extended to include grandparents, aunts, uncles, and cousins related by either blood or marriage. It is through this larger family that the Mexican customs and culinary heritage are being preserved.

Many experts say that home cooking is becoming obsolete. More of us have the means to eat out often or, if in a hurry, to buy already prepared foods, but then we find that these mass-produced meals rarely satisfy: They lack heart. The conditions that created the recipes in this book cannot be duplicated, but those who use the recipes will learn where the dishes originated, the history and tradition behind them, who makes and eats them now, and how to re-create the dishes in their own kitchens to enjoy with their own families.

Basic Techniques of the Mexican-American Kitchen

ROASTING, TOASTING, SEARING, AND SOURING

Most of the vibrant flavors and rustic textures of Mexican food are created using a few basic techniques that seemingly haven't changed over the centuries, whether the cook is living in Acapulco, Guerrero, or Albany, New York. There are also some useful utensils, appliances, and cooking equipment that most Mexican-American cooks find essential.

EQUIPMENT

For Grinding, Blending, and Processing Ingredients

Preparing Mexican food is extremely labor-intensive. For centuries ingredients that needed to be pulverized or roughly crushed were ground by hand in a carved-out rock *molcajete*. When the *liquadora* (blender) was introduced to Mexican cooks, it was jubilantly welcomed, and today very few kitchens in that country are without one. The heavy-duty blender quickly reduces nuts and seeds, soaked dried chiles, and tomatoes to the proper consistency for smooth sauces with the addition of just a little liquid.

The more versatile—and expensive—food processor may simplify chopping chores but doesn't take the place of a blender for pureeing. It can, though, with a brief, careful whirl of the blades, make a very satisfying salsa.

To create the chunky texture needed for salsas and guacamole, many Mexican-American cooks still grind the ingredients in a *molcajete*. This three-legged gray or black volcanic rock bowl is used as a mortar with a pestle (*tejolote/metlapíl/mano*) of the same rough-surfaced material. The small end should fit into the palm of your hand, with the wrist used to rotate it. For Estella Ríos-Lopez of El Paso, Texas, her most prized possession is the century-old *molcajete* of her great-grandmother. As another young woman in Chicago said, "Besides being awfully useful, it looks a lot more attractive on my counter than a food processor, and I can serve directly from my *molcajete*."

Look for your own *molcajete* in Mexican neighborhood stores or bring one back from a trip to Mexico. It should have the darkest possible color and very small pores. So as not to grind rock into your salsas, first put a handful of uncooked rice in the bowl and grind it to a powder with the *tejolote*. Rinse out the *molcajete* and repeat the process three or four times, until no grit can be seen mingling with the rice. Then it's ready to use.

When making a salsa, always start with the most solid ingredients first, rotating the pestle until they are pulverized, then add the softer ones and continue grinding until the mixture is of the desired consistency. The *molcajete* is also useful for grinding certain foods to a rough texture, such as the tougher-skinned dried chiles, fresh corn, or meat.

Spices wake up your sense of smell and taste, and are an indispensable element of Mexican-American cooking. To ensure a well-balanced, highly aromatic mixture it is important to use freshly ground spices. Although I still use my *molcajete* for grinding small amounts, these days I couldn't be without my electric coffee / spice grinder. The spice grinder is equally helpful for grinding nuts and seeds for *moles* and *pipianes*. If possible, don't use the same one for grinding your coffee, because the assertive taste of the spices always seems to cling. I find the best way to clean it is to finely grind one-quarter cup of white rice in the bowl, toss it out, and wipe out any remaining powder with a paper towel.

For Stirring, Cooking, Rolling, and Pressing

I don't have a heavy-duty mixer, such as a KitchenAid, with all its attachments, but I know it would be useful for beating the air into my *tamal masa*. I still rely on a smaller handheld electric beater for whipping egg whites, and I use wooden spoons and long, blunt-edged wooden spatulas for virtually everything else.

In Mexico a clay or thin metal *comal* placed over an open flame would be used for cooking tortillas, toasting dry ingredients such as seeds and dry chiles, and roasting fresh chiles, garlic, onions, and tomatoes. Most of the Mexican-American cooks I know use a griddle or heavy cast-iron skillet for these purposes.

Mexican sauces are seared over high heat, so heavy-bottomed pans are essential. I use the same ten-inch cast-iron skillet that my stepmother gave me in 1951. It's blackened and deeply crusted with, I like to think, the memories of all the best meals I've ever cooked. With such a skillet, some similar ones in smaller sizes, and a heavy cast-iron Dutch oven, you will have most of the cookware needed for preparing a *pipián* or *mole*. I also recommend many of the Spanish and Mexican earthenware *cazuelas,* which, though somewhat breakable, are ideal for cooking and serving because they heat evenly and retain the heat for a long time. An enameled cast-iron casserole with a lid is another useful and versatile type of cookware to use. For enchiladas and other tortilla dishes, shallow ceramic or earthenware baking dishes are very useful. Pyrex-brand glassware can be used, but it is not as attractive to take directly to the table.

You must have at least one big pot for beans, soups, and stews; I like to use a Mexican earthenware *olla,* a large round pot with quite a small neck opening on the top. It may just be my imagination, but I think the clay imparts a traditional taste that I favor. I also use it to make *café de olla,* a special spice-infused coffee. Almost everyone in the United States now seems to use regular metal stockpots, Dutch ovens, or large saucepans for those dishes. They may be more practical, but they're certainly not as attractive to have around.

Tamales are the only other traditional dish that requires a particular pot for cooking. You don't need to have an authentic *tamal* steamer—any big pot with a tight lid will work. I've seen a wide variety of improvisations that have steamed the tamales to the texture and consistency the cook wanted. What is needed is a perforated rack that can be propped up at least two to three inches above the bottom so that a goodly amount of water can simmer away underneath, creating steam that will envelop the tamales. For very small amounts or for reheating tamales, a perforated aluminum or bamboo steamer is perfect.

If you're planning to make your own flour tortillas, the best rolling pin to use is one at least twelve inches long, about an inch in diameter, and without handles. It is almost identical to the Italian pasta rolling pin. A metal tortilla press is useful for making your own corn tortillas. However, most Mexican-American cooks I met confessed to using premade tortillas, which are widely available.

TECHNIQUES
Roasting Fresh Chiles, Onions, Garlic, Tomatoes, and Tomatillos

Something magical happens when fresh chiles, onions, garlic, tomatoes, and tomatillos are roasted. The high heat concentrates flavors and adds texture.

Fresh Chiles

When selecting fresh chiles for roasting, look for those with the fewest indentations because they will roast much more evenly. The easiest method is to place them directly in or over the flame of a gas stove for about five minutes, turning with tongs as they char and blister on all sides. The idea is to char the skin but barely cook the flesh. The aroma is unforgettable. The chiles can be roasted on a very hot charcoal or gas grill as close to the coals as possible. As a last resort, the chiles can be broiled close to a preheated element, turning occasionally until blackened on all sides, usually about ten minutes. The chiles are usually too soft to stuff, however, but can be used for *rajas* (thin strips) or blended into sauces.

After the chiles are roasted, put them in a paper or plastic bag or in a bowl covered with a heavy kitchen towel. Let the chiles sit for about five minutes before removing the skin.

Everyone develops his or her own technique for removing the charred skin, using one's hands to rub, pick, and/or peel it away. If you are fixing many chiles or if your skin is sensitive,

x gloves or slip a plastic bag over each hand. If necessary, rinse the chiles quickly un-
and don't worry if some charred bits of chile skin remain on them. Slice open the
pending on how they are to be used, and cut and scrape out the membrane with its
seeds.

Onions and Garlic

Roast thick slices or quarters of onions directly on a grill or over medium heat on a hot griddle or heavy cast-iron skillet. I've learned from experience that it helps to line the griddle or
skillet with a layer of heavy foil so that the flesh of the onion doesn't stick to the surface.
Roast, turning from time to time, until the onion is blackened in spots and has begun to
soften, about ten minutes.

Roast garlic the same way, separating but not peeling each clove. Roast until the paper skin
is blackened, and remove when the cloves are cool enough to handle.

Tomatoes and Tomatillos

I roast my tomatoes and tomatillos (husks removed) in a heavy skillet or on a griddle over
medium heat for eight to ten minutes, turning from time to time, until the skin begins to blister and blacken and the insides become soft and oozy. Line the skillet or griddle with a layer of
foil so it is easier to save the sweet juices and add them to the tomatoes to be chopped or
pureed. I add all but the most burned skin to my soups and sauces, but that is personal choice.
I like the rustic texture.

To use the broiler, preheat it and put the rack as close as possible to the heat source. Ideally,
the tomatoes should be only an inch or so away from the heat. Line a broiler pan with foil and
roast the tomatoes until the flesh is soft and the skin is charred in patches. You will need to flip
the tomatoes over at least once.

Toasting Dry Chiles

The process of toasting dry chiles is very similar to roasting fresh ones. The difference is
that you just want to brown the chiles very lightly, enriching the natural flavor before the necessary soaking in hot water. Stem and break open the chile; scrape out the seeds, and tear the
chile into pieces. Heat a heavy skillet or griddle over medium heat and, when hot, put in the
chile pieces, skin side down. Press the chile down with a spatula for only a few seconds, turn
it over, press down again, and quickly take the chile off the heat. Be very careful not to burn
the skin, or you will have to throw the chiles out and start again. You want the chile to only
start changing its color and give off a rich, pungent aroma.

Searing Sauces

Sweetening, concentrating, and melding the often harsh and disparate flavors of ingredients used in Mexican cooking is accomplished by bringing the pureed mixtures of chiles, tomatoes, or tomatillos into contact with a very hot oil-coated surface. It is an essential technique, though a bit scary at first if you are unprepared, because the sauce erupts and spatters everything around it. But it's not hard to do.

It helps to use a heavy cast-iron skillet or Dutch oven, something with deep sides and that holds heat. I use my earthenware *cazuelas.* Warm the pot over medium-high heat, add the amount of oil or fat needed for the particular recipe, and let it heat for a brief time. Pour in the thick sauce all at once and stand back as it sputters and spews. You can lower the heat to medium, but the sauce should always continue to bubble. Stir frequently for four to five minutes, until the mixture thickens and darkens in color, then pour in the liquid that is called for in the recipe and let the sauce simmer a bit longer.

Souring Cream

True Mexican *crema* is very similar to France's crème fraîche—thick, rich, and slightly soured. Many stores carry a commercial crème fraîche that can be substituted for *crema,* though the real thing is very simple to make and will keep, refrigerated, for at least a week. An adequate substitute for most dishes that cry out for the luscious textures and the taste of the thick acidic cream is commercial sour cream slightly thinned with whole milk or half-and-half. The result works quite well to top most *antojitos,* those "little whims" or "sudden cravings," such as tacos and burritos, that are Mexico's street and market foods.

To make about one cup of Mexican *crema,* mix one cup of heavy cream (*not* ultrapasteurized) in a small bowl with one tablespoon of buttermilk or a good-quality plain yogurt with active cultures. Cover with plastic wrap that has a few holes poked in it, or a kitchen towel, and put in a warm place (about 85 degrees Fahrenheit) until the cream sets, anywhere from eight to twenty-four hours, depending on how active the culture and how pasteurized the heavy cream. When it is quite thick, stir the cream again, cover with plastic wrap, and put it in the refrigerator for about six hours or more so that it will chill and become firm. If the cream becomes too thick, it can be thinned with a little whole milk or half-and-half.

I found commercial Mexican *crema* being sold in quite a few Mexican neighborhood grocery stores. I had the opportunity to taste only a few brands, all of which appeared to have additives.

Everyday Basic Ingredients

COOKING OILS AND FATS

Use a good-quality cooking oil such as safflower or canola that has a healthy fatty acid profile and can sustain high temperatures (at least 375 degrees Fahrenheit or higher without smoking). For fritters, I like the flavor of peanut oil, and sometimes for frying tortillas, corn oil. For tamales and, once in a while, for a pot of beans, rich-tasting rendered pork lard—*not* the hydrogenated supermarket type—is the only thing that will give that traditional taste and texture (see page 291).

SUGAR

Except for desserts and baking, *piloncillo,* or unrefined sugar, is the basic sweetening used in Mexican cooking. It is formed out of boiled cane syrup that is molded into cones or bars of dark brown crystallized sugar. *Piloncillo* can be found in most supermarkets' ethnic food sections or in Mexican grocery stores. The small one-inch cones, commonly sold in the United States, weigh about one ounce, and the larger cones about seven ounces. If the sugar isn't too hard, I usually chop off what is needed, but it can also be easily dissolved in the liquid that is used in the recipe. Raw sugar or dark brown sugar can be substituted, but they do not have the same deep molasses flavor.

SALT

All salts do not have the same flavor or the same degree of saltiness. For Mexican food I prefer the more pronounced flavor of medium-grain sea salt. It is a perfect mate for the cuisine's assertive flavors; I keep mine in a salt grinder. Coarse kosher salt has a much milder flavor. The common table salt used in the United States contains additives that produce a harsh, strong taste. Because of these differences, and because many people are restricting their intake of sodium, we usually do not specify the amount of salt to use in a recipe unless it plays a crucial role in balancing the flavors of a dish. If it is a long cooking process, such as the simmering of soup, always add salt at the end because the saltiness becomes more concentrated as the liquid is reduced.

HERBS

There are six common herbs that you should not be without if you plan to do any Mexican cooking:

- *Mexican oregano:* Dried or fresh Mexican oregano has quite a different flavor from the more common Greek variety. Schilling and some other spice companies market the dried oregano leaves, and it is also often available in small cellophane packets in the ethnic food section of grocery stores or in ethnic markets.
- *Bay leaf, thyme, and marjoram:* These aromatic herbs *(hierbas de olor)*—are usually used together, either fresh or dried, in soups, stews, pickled dishes, and some cooked sauces.
- *Cilantro:* Fresh cilantro is used in dishes and as a garnish. Always look for the freshest cilantro, preferably with the roots attached, because it is highly perishable. I store mine like a bouquet, in a small glass of water in the refrigerator, and enclose the leaves loosely in a plastic bag.
- *Flat-leaf parsley or Italian parsley:* This is the only parsley that should be used in Mexican cooking and for garnishing. You may need to ask your produce manager to carry it, or you can easily grow your own, as I do.

There are many, many other herbs used regionally in Mexico. Two of the most important, epazote (page 223) and *hoja santa* (known also as *hierba santa, acuyo,* or *momo;* page 96), are ingredients in some of our recipes. For an authentic flavor, do try to locate them.

New Mexico Impressions

New Mexico is a severe land. Winter arrives early in the high arid plains that roll to a halt beside desert mountains. Windstorms come with the spring, but the green haze of leafing cottonwood trees is a sign of renewal to the generations of Spanish, Mexican, and Indian people who have made this land their home for many centuries. This is a world where the past is alive and the sacred strands of tradition still bind.

Most of the cooks I met in New Mexico shared interwoven family ties stretching back to the first decades of the 1600s. One day I tried to set up appointments with people in three different communities, only to be told over and over, "We are going to a funeral. Maybe we can get together tomorrow." I wondered at the number of deaths until someone explained it was only one. "Here we are all cousins or related to the godparents."

I can trace my family tree to before the Revolutionary War, but the family of Carmen Barnard Baca, one of my closest friends in Mexico, was living in what is now the state of New Mexico a hundred years earlier. Many of us are unaware that even before the English colonized Jamestown, Virginia, in 1607, the forebears of many Mexican Americans were a presence in the western part of the country—first as explorers and then in the 1590s as early colonists in the present state of New Mexico. Miguel Baca, Carmen's grandfather, who just died at 104 while still living on his own 2.5-acre farm near Albuquerque, was known to his neighbors as *el viejito,* "the little old man."

Carmen, who has a face framed by a mass of copper-red ringlets, can trace this side of her family back to Spain, where the family name was Vaca, shortened from the ancestral Cabeza de Vaca (head of a cow). Cristobel, son of Juan de Vaca, arrived in New Mexico in 1600; the name changed to Baca.

In Santa Fe, reading the history of New Mexican families in a genealogy of the Spanish colonial period, I noted the exploits in the year 1681 of one Ignacio Baca, an army captain who at twenty-four was "tall, slim, with an aquiline face, fair complexion, no beard, and wavy red hair." When I told Carmen that I had discovered the genetic explanation for her red hair, she said, "Oh, you've found Nacho. My *abuelito* [grandfather] Miguel always calls him by his nickname." Today there are Bacas in the little towns of Española, Chimayó, Velarde, and Socorro as well as in Santa Fe and Albuquerque, all places accessible from Mexico by the royal road, El Camino Real, now U.S. 25.

In no other state does the food so completely reflect its historical roots. Its original austerity remains today despite modern conveniences, an increase in affluence, and the ever-growing influx of outsiders, from the first Anglo-American settlers to the scientists of Los Alamos, the

New Age types who came seeking a close spiritual relation to the land and sky, and the legions of tourists, artists, and retirees seduced by Santa Fe's unique charm.

The land-based way of life may have given way to a different life-style, but in practically all of the homes I visited they prepared the same food as their parents and grandparents. Most of the foods are seasoned heavily with New Mexico's long, skinny chiles. It is a matter of taste which ones are used—the dried, mature red chile, like the ones braided into *ristras,* or the same variety picked and dried when still green. Perhaps a dish of red chile *colorado* or *chile con carne* with beans is served one day, the next a green chile stew or *pozole,* a hominy stew. The tortillas are usually flour, and a surprisingly large number of women of all ages roll out a goodly supply for any meal—and for after-school snacks with peanut butter and jelly. I was blessed to be able to share some dishes with direct descendants of these first settlers.

Some women, such as Leóna Medina-Tiede, have turned tortilla making into a profession. Formerly a Pan-American Airline flight attendant, Leóna grew up as the eldest of eleven children, in a family that raised its own beans, corn, chiles, and even wheat. After she married and returned to the small remote community of Chimayó, she opened a small tortilla and *tamal* concession, adjoining the famous Santuario de Chimayó Church. Leóna's reputation spread, and she now owns and operates a large tortilla factory specializing in natural, preservative-free products, including flavored tortillas and vegetarian tamales that are distributed throughout the western United States. Even with her growing success you may find Leóna at the take-out window of her tiny restaurant, serving hungry visitors a variety of filled tortillas and burritos to enjoy at tables and counters under the large shade tree facing the Santuario.

Fall is chile time. The air at this time of year is rich with the pungent aroma of roasted chiles. The chiles are now largely the product of consolidated businesses, especially around Hatch in the southern part of the state, but many families still grow their own, bringing the chiles to local roadside stands to roast them in their propane chile roasters. In Santa Fe, Mary Jane Chavez described the way it was when she was growing up, in her great-grandmother's home: "We spent many long hours roasting the green chiles over a hot wood stove. Then we peeled them and strung them up to dry on a clothesline. If it looked like rain, we brought the chiles in, only to hang them up again until they were dry enough to store in an old cloth bag for use during the cold winter and spring."

For many of us, holidays bring a return to traditions. As Christmas approaches, even those who have been popping frozen dinners in the microwave succumb: Cooks are busy steaming tamales, baking spicy mincemeat *empanaditas* and *biscochitos,* those rich aniseed cookies, and frying fritters of chile and shredded meat. During Lent, especially on Ash Wednesday, *panocha,* a long-cooking, caramelized pudding of swollen grains of sprouted wheat, is baked, or a syrup-drenched bread pudding is prepared that is called by the deceptive name of *sopa.* It is not a soup but the New Mexican version of the traditional *capirotada*. Dora Chavez, with many of her forty-five grandchildren and twenty-six great-grandchildren in attendance, will separate dozens of eggs, add garlic and red chiles, and quickly fry up her special *tortas de huevos*, egg fritters that are sometimes flavored with pulverized dried shrimp. From what I saw, more than a few of Dora's grandchildren will make sure New Mexican traditions survive.

Beginnings
Botanas

*Since growing up I have come to realize that the essence of Mexican
hospitality is to socialize with an epic-scale family of relatives and friends.*

—ZARELA MARTÍNEZ

LATE ON A HOT JUNE AFTERNOON we parked beside a large two-story house in Detroit. The tide of the party spilled well-wishers out onto the porch and front lawn. They were celebrating the high school graduation and acceptance to Princeton of Pedro Hernandez, an African Mexican American.

As we made our way through the crowd, we were stopped by an impressively good-looking young man. It was the guest of honor himself. Though we had not met, Pedro greeted us as though we were part of the family, introducing us to the people around us, who in turn made sure we met everyone else. We were taken into the house; each room was packed with a loving hodgepodge of all races and ages. Babies slept on the downstairs beds, toddlers wandered among the grown-ups' legs, needing only to stretch up their arms to be lifted and hugged. It was a wonderful party, with the joy of the occasion reflected in the exuberance of the food.

In Mexico as in Spain, hundreds of tidbits are offered for casual eating. They can be as simple as a crisp wedge of jicama enlivened with a squirt of lime and ground chile, a few marinated carrots, or a quick bite of a taco or tostada. We chose from a continually changing array of *botanas*—foods for instant gratification. There were chile-fired nuts, baskets of fresh-crisped tortilla chips to scoop up guacamole or to dip in salsa, meatballs and turnovers so tiny that they scarcely made a bite. All were savory treats for relaxed sociable eating—to snack on while standing, talking, or moving around, and usually with a drink of some sort in one hand. *Botanos* are not as much a type of food as a way of life—to briefly enjoy something in convivial surroundings and then try a different taste while turning to talk with yet a different friend.

Spicy Nuts and Seeds

Nueces y Pepitas Picantes

ALBUQUERQUE, NEW MEXICO

MAKES 4 CUPS   *When the first settlers came from central Mexico to the northernmost frontier lands, they utilized local ingredients that were frequently part of the local Indians' diet. In New Mexico, pine nuts and the seeds of native squash were used as snacks, and in California even a greater variety of seeds and nuts were available. Nuts and pumpkin seeds are still popular nibbles at parties or for casual snacking, especially when enlivened with chiles and garlic.*

1–2 tablespoons peanut oil

10 cloves garlic, peeled

1 cup raw peanuts, papery husk removed

1 cup pecan halves

1 cup shelled pine nuts (optional)

1 cup hulled green pumpkin seeds

1 teaspoon sea salt, or more

about ¼ teaspoon ground cayenne or ground pequín chile

Preheat the oven to 275 degrees F.

Warm the oil in a heavy skillet and sauté the garlic over low heat about 2 minutes, until it turns yellow. Stir in the nuts and seeds, and mix until well coated with the oil. Add the salt and stir in the cayenne or chile, a pinch at a time, until the mixture has the pungency you want; ¼ teaspoon is usually plenty.

Spread the nuts and seeds evenly on a baking sheet and bake for 20–25 minutes, stirring occasionally.

When the nuts and seeds begin to toast lightly and give off a rich nutty aroma, transfer to a paper bag. Sprinkle with more salt if needed. Serve warm or at room temperature. The mixture will last in a sealed container for several weeks.

PINE NUTS OR PIÑÓNES
(Pinus cembroides edulis)

*M*an and animal alike relish the nutty flavor of the teardrop-shaped seeds that nestle in the small cones of the piñon pine (Pinus cembroides edulis), a small, hardy tree that thrives throughout the dry open slopes of the Southwest and parts of Mexico. As a little girl I used to stay with my grandmother in Colorado Springs, and I remember scavenging for the tiny pine nuts by reaching into the shallow burrows of ground squirrels and helping myself to a handful of their abundant hoard.

While all pine trees have seed cones, fewer than a dozen different species are prized for their edible nuts. The three most common are the North American piñon; the pignolia (Pinus pinea), rich and sweet and grown primarily in Spain, Portugal, North Africa, and Turkey; and the larger Chinese or Korean pine nut (Pinus koreinsis), the one most commonly sold in the United States. They have different characteristics, so when you have the opportunity, try cooking with all of them.

What makes these nuts expensive to buy is the labor involved in the shelling and their tendency, like that of all vegetable products, to easily become rancid. Though pine nuts keep well in the shell, once shelled they should be stored tightly sealed in the freezer.

Tortilla Chips
Totopos

SERVES ABOUT 6   *You can just walk into any grocery store and buy enormous cellophane sacks filled with plain or even flavored tortilla chips, but fresh homemade ones are so much more delicious and a perfect way to use up the remaining corn tortillas taking up space in your refrigerator or freezer.*

Though the chips can be eaten plain, they are perfect for scooping up your favorite salsa, Guacamole (page 274), or Chile con Queso (page 42), or in Nachos (page 35). In New Mexico these crispy corn chips are used to make tortilla "pie": A handful of chips are dropped in a bowl and stirred together with cooked beans, chopped onions, lettuce, and lots of salsa.

16 store-bought corn tortillas (see Note)   sea salt (optional)
corn or peanut oil for frying

Stack the tortillas in piles of 3–4 each. With a sharp knife, cut each pile into 4–6 wedges. Spread the wedges out in a single layer, cover with a kitchen towel so they do not curl up too much, and let them dry for several hours.

Pour the oil to a depth of at least 1 inch and heat to medium-high (375 degrees F.). It should not be smoking but hot enough that when a test piece of tortilla is added, it should crisp quite quickly. Fry a few chips at a time, tossing them with a slotted spatula so they are crispy and just a light golden brown, about 30–45 seconds. Do not let them darken, or they will be bitter.

Drain the chips on absorbent paper and repeat with the remaining pieces. Keep warm in a 250-degree F. oven until all the chips are fried. Salt them, if you want, while still warm.

These tortilla chips are much better when eaten warm. If you can't serve them right away, cool and store in an airtight container, then reheat them in a 250-degree F. oven.

NOTE: If you like tortilla chips and tostadas that are very crispy, buy the thinnest tortillas you can find. Purchase those that are light in color and with no preservatives if possible.

VARIATION: CRISPY TORTILLA STRIPS OR SQUARES   For garnishes and as an ingredient in some soups, cut the store-bought tortillas into ¼- by 1-inch strips or ½-inch squares.

VARIATION: OVEN-CRISPED TORTILLA CHIPS   While not as tasty as fried chips, acceptable ones can be made by spreading the tortilla pieces in a single layer on a baking sheet and baking in a 350-degree F. oven for about 10 minutes. Rick Bayless suggests placing an inverted cooling rack on top to keep the tortillas from curling as they bake.

Nachos
Nachos

SERVES 6 *This recent concoction of Mexican ingredients has been adopted by Mexican Americans throughout the country. Though it's best with fresh-made Tortilla Chips (page 33), Miguel will often use packaged unsalted corn tortilla chips to make the preparation fast and easy.*

1 cup well-fried beans (page 227) or canned
1 14½-ounce bag round corn tortilla chips or one recipe Tortilla Chips (page 33), about 36
4 ounces shredded Monterey jack cheese
3 pickled jalapeño chiles, sliced

For the Toppings (optional)
Guacamole (page 274) or Chunky Fresh Tomato Salsa (page 264)
shredded chicken or beef
tiny cooked shrimp or shredded crab
sour cream
chopped green onions

Preheat the oven to 400 degrees F.

Spread a thin layer of beans on each chip and place on a heatproof platter or baking pan. Sprinkle on the cheese and top with the chiles. Bake in the oven for about 5 minutes, until the cheese is melted. Serve immediately as is or add any of the toppings, alone or in combination.

Jicama with Cucumbers and Melon
Pico de Gallo de Jalisco

SERVES 6 AS A SNACK, 4 AS A SALAD *Translating the name* pico de gallo, *which means rooster beak, is not much help in knowing what it is. The name refers perhaps to the sharp-angled bits of fruit and vegetables or to the mixture's spicy bite. If you are in Texas or northern Mexico and ask for* pico de gallo, *you will be offered a fresh tomato salsa, but in Guadalajara it will be more like this delightfully crunchy, colorful medley of melon, jicama, and cucumbers.*

Pico de Gallo *is usually served as a casual snack with beer or shots of a good-quality tequila. Have a small container with toothpicks nearby for spearing the chunks of jicama, cucumber, and melon, though don't be surprised if most people prefer to use their fingers.*

As a salad, scooped into leaves of endive, this is a refreshing companion to Chicken Breasts in Green Sauce (page 155) and King Salmon Grilled in Cornhusks (page 142).

This recipe was given to me in Seattle by a group of folks from Jalisco who were active in establishing an official Washington–Jalisco sisterhood relationship.

1 small jicama, peeled and cut into ¾-inch cubes
or wedges
2 medium cucumbers, peeled, seeded, and cut
into ¾-inch cubes or wedges
½ cantaloupe, scooped into melon balls or cut
into ¾-inch cubes or wedges, or ½ fresh
pineapple, peeled and cut into ¾-inch cubes or
wedges

4 tablespoons freshly squeezed lime juice
about ½ teaspoon sea salt
1 fresh serrano or jalapeño chile, chopped
ground cayenne or pequín chile, or a milder pure
chile powder

Toss the jicama, cucumbers, and melon with the juice and salt to taste. Stir in the chile, cover, and refrigerate until chilled, stirring occasionally. Drain off any excess juice and arrange the *pico de gallo* in a bowl or on individual plates. Sprinkle with a little of the ground chile, starting with a small amount and adding to taste.

VARIATION: JICAMA STICKS　Peel and slice the jicama into ½-inch-wide strips and marinate with the juice of 2 limes and 2 tablespoons of finely chopped white onion for several hours. When ready to serve, sprinkle with 1 cup of chopped roasted peanuts and ground dried chile.

Tuna-Stuffed Jalapeño Chiles
Chiles Rellenos con Atún
SAN DIEGO, CALIFORNIA • VERACRUZ, MEXICO

SERVES 10 TO 12 AS APPETIZERS OR *BOTANAS* 　*It may seem absurd to use canned tuna in a recipe originally from Mexico's premier seaport, Veracruz. However, Tila Muñoz finds using the canned fish is a convenient shortcut in putting together this mildly explosive party appetizer. The recipe actually comes from her brother, Ricardo, the food expert in the family. He tries to recapture the dishes*

they remember eating while growing up in Veracruz and Tabasco. The minilla, *a mixture of shredded fish, capers, and olives, can be made with almost any freshly poached or leftover cooked fish, and even shrimp or crabmeat.*

Any extra filling can be reheated and served over rice. These stuffed chiles are shown to their best advantage when they are the solo act at either an informal get-together or before a dinner party. If a heartier presentation is wanted, include less fiery snacks, such as Quesadillas with Cheese or Mushroom Filling (page 109) or Guacamole (page 274), and Tortilla Chips (page 33). In the summer, hot-pink watermelon water (page 378) is a refreshing beverage, and a glass of malty Dos Equis XX beer is always welcomed.

24–30 large fresh jalapeño chiles
2 cups mild vinegar
sea salt
½ cup *piloncillo* (page 25), in small chunks, or
   dark brown sugar
¼ cup olive oil
¾ cup finely chopped white onion
3 cloves garlic, minced
1½ pounds (about 4 medium) ripe tomatoes,
   finely chopped

½ cup raisins
½ cup chopped green olives
¼ cup finely chopped large capers
3 6½-ounce cans oil-packed tuna, drained
½ teaspoon dried oregano, preferably Mexican
3 bay leaves
1 tablespoon lemon juice

Carefully slit the chiles down 1 side from the top to the tip and scrape out the seeds and membranes. Place in a pot and cover with cold water, 1 cup of vinegar, and ½ teaspoon of salt. Bring to a boil and drain. Cover again with cold water and the remaining 1 cup of vinegar and ½ teaspoon of salt, bring to a boil, and drain. The third time you add cold water, dissolve the sugar in it, bring to a boil, and simmer about 6 minutes, until tender. Set aside to let cool.

Pour the olive oil into a large skillet over medium-high heat. Sauté the onion until translucent, then add the garlic and cook for about 2 minutes. Stir in the tomatoes, raisins, olives, and capers, and cook for another few minutes. Add the tuna, oregano, and bay leaves. Continue to fry and stir for 8–10 minutes, until the mixture is almost dry and has a wonderful aroma. Add the lemon juice and salt to taste, remove the bay leaves, and set aside at room temperature for 20–30 minutes.

When the tuna mixture is completely cool, fill each chile so it can barely close, still leaving a gap. Arrange attractively on a serving platter. The stuffed chiles can be refrigerated for several hours in advance, brought to room temperature, and then served.

recipe continues

NOTE: Multiple blanchings soften the flesh of the chiles and subdue their heat a bit. Even so, because jalapeño chiles vary so much in degree of hotness, some may still prove a challenge to the taste buds.

Ceviche

Ceviche

AUSTIN, TEXAS

SERVES 6   *Ceviche—which is often spelled* seviche *or* cebiche*—is seafood prepared in a centuries-old method of cooking by contact with the acidic juices of citrus fruit instead of with heat.*

Miguel Ravago sometimes adds sweet bay scallops or shrimp to his seafood mixture. He prepares his ceviche as a cooling appetizer to be shared with friends on a hot day along with a chilled glass of a Mexican beer such as Bohemia or Superior, followed by a plate of Garlic Chicken with Spicy Prune Sauce (page 153) and Green Rice (page 236).

1 pound boneless red snapper, swordfish fillets, or other very fresh fish, cut into ½-inch cubes; shrimp or scallops can be substituted for some of the fish (see Note)

1½ cups freshly squeezed lime juice (about 7 large limes)

2 medium ripe tomatoes, finely diced

1 small red onion, finely diced

3 pickled jalapeño or serrano chiles, finely chopped

½ cup sliced green olives (optional)

3–4 tablespoons olive oil

2 teaspoons lime juice, if needed

about ¾ teaspoon sea salt

½ teaspoon coarsely ground black pepper

½ teaspoon dried oregano, preferably Mexican

1 firm but ripe avocado, peeled, pitted, and cut into ½-inch cubes

For the Garnish

6 Bibb lettuce leaves (optional)

3 tablespoons finely chopped cilantro

large crisp Tortilla Chips (page 33) or store-bought chips

Put the fish and other seafood in a nonmetallic bowl and cover with lime juice. Mix thoroughly, cover tightly with plastic wrap, and refrigerate for 4–5 hours, until the fish is no longer opaque. Drain off any excess lime juice. Ceviche can be refrigerated, after draining, for up to 12 hours, but it tends to become a little chewy after this much time.

About 1 hour before serving, stir in the tomatoes, onion, jalapeños, and olives, if using them. Add enough olive oil to lightly coat all the ingredients. Taste and, if needed, sprinkle on some additional lime juice. Add the salt, pepper, and oregano, and return to the refrigerator until just before serving. Taste again for seasoning and mix in the avocado. Spoon into a large attractive bowl or place on lettuce leaves on individual plates. Sprinkle with cilantro. Serve with the tortilla chips for scooping up the ceviche.

NOTE: If you worry about possible fish parasites, it is recommended that you use seafood that has been commercially frozen for two days, then thawed. The shrimp can be precooked.

Squid in an Orange Vinaigrette
Calamares en Vinagreta de Naranja
SANTA MONICA, CALIFORNIA • MEXICO CITY, MEXICO

SERVES 6   *With an aromatic hint of citrus, tiny rings of quickly cooked squid, combined with green olives, pickled chiles, and golden carrot coins, become an unusual seafood snack. Ricardo Villareal serves this as an appetizer. It can be made into a refreshing salad or, after draining, used as a tostada topping. Together with Pickled Beets (page 283), Tuna-Stuffed Jalapeño Chiles (page 36), and a plate of Crab Turnovers (page 45), these make delicious party eating. Try serving them as a seafood prelude to a festive dinner with mole or before a meal of Chipotle Crab Enchiladas (page 207).*

sea salt
1½ pounds small squid, cleaned and sliced, with
  tentacles (see Notes)
½ small red onion, finely chopped
1 cup fresh orange juice
½ cup fresh lime juice
12 pimiento-stuffed green olives, sliced

3 canned pickled jalapeño chiles, sliced into rings
  (see Notes)
6 marinated carrot slices from the chiles (optional)
2 tablespoons vinegar from the chiles
½ cup extra-virgin olive oil
freshly ground black pepper

In a pan over medium heat, bring 2 cups of salted water to a boil. Add the sliced squid and tentacles, and cook for 1 minute.

Remove the squid from the water, rinse in very cold water, and drain on absorbent paper. Mix the squid in a medium-size bowl with the onion and orange and lime juices. Add the olives, chiles, carrots, and vinegar. Stir in the olive oil and season to taste. Let sit, covered, in the refrigerator for at least 2 hours. The squid can be marinated 1 day in advance.

The squid is most flavorful served cool but not chilled or at room temperature. Arrange in a bowl that everyone can dip into with a fork for some tasty morsels of squid, or spoon the mixture into small individual goblets as a seafood cocktail.

NOTES: When selecting the pickled jalapeño chiles at the store, try to buy those that include brightly colored carrots. The chiles may be variously labeled *chiles en escabeche, chiles en vinagre,* marinated jalapeño peppers, or pickled jalapeños.

Much of the squid sold in the store is already partially cleaned, but if not, it is quite a simple process. Hold the body of the squid in one hand and pull the tentacles away from the body. Cut them apart from the rest of the head, just below the eyes. Set aside the tentacles if they are to be used in the recipe and discard the rest. Pull out the quill in the mantle of the body and discard. Holding the squid in one hand, squeeze out the remainder of the material in the body cavity and rinse thoroughly. If possible, cut or pull off the fins from the body and remove the gray skin. Rinse and dry on absorbent paper. Turn the mantle inside out, rinse, then turn it back again.

VARIATION: SEAFOOD AND VEGETABLE SALAD As a luncheon salad or when served with a bowl of soup for supper, the marinated squid can be combined with cauliflower, fresh tomato, and tiny shrimp. Simmer ¼ pound of cauliflower, cut in small florets, in just enough salted water to cover. Remove when just tender, cool, and fold gently into the squid mixture. Add 1 medium-size chopped tomato and 6 ounces of cooked bay shrimp before serving.

Bacon-Wrapped Shrimp Stuffed with Cheese
Camarones Rellenos
GIG HARBOR, WASHINGTON • OAXACA, MEXICO

SERVES 4 TO 6 AS APPETIZERS *This is probably the recipe I am most often asked for by my Mexican-American friends. I learned to make it on one of my first trips to Veracruz, and it has been a*

favorite ever since. Camarones Rellenos *are usually the beginning focus of any of my casual gatherings, especially those featuring Mexican food. With them I often serve Guacamole (page 274) and Tortilla Chips (page 33), and, for a more extensive seafood array, Tuna-Stuffed Jalapeño Chiles (page 36) and Crab Turnovers (page 45).*

For the Dipping Sauce

1 cup sour cream
2 cloves garlic, minced
1–2 canned chipotle chiles, chopped
about ⅛ teaspoon sea salt

For the Shrimp

16 large raw shrimp, shelled and butterflied, but
  with the tail attached (see Note)

freshly ground black pepper
1 cup grated mozzarella cheese
16 slices lean bacon (half slices can be used if the
  shrimp are small)
¼ cup olive oil

For the Garnish

1 tablespoon chopped parsley

Blend the sour cream, garlic, chiles, and salt in a food processor or blender. Chill in the refrigerator. This is best prepared several hours in advance, covered, and refrigerated.

Dry the shrimp with paper towels. Sprinkle with pepper and stuff with the cheese. Fold the sides of the shrimp together and wrap with a bacon slice, making sure all the cheese is covered so that it doesn't ooze out. Secure the wrapped shrimp with a toothpick if necessary. The shrimp can be prepared in advance and refrigerated, covered, for several hours.

Heat a large, heavy skillet and add as much oil as necessary to keep the shrimp from sticking. Fry the shrimp over medium heat a few at a time, turning frequently, about 10 minutes, until the bacon browns. Remove from the heat and drain on absorbent paper. Keep warm.

Fill a small bowl with the sauce, sprinkle with the parsley, and place in the middle of a serving platter. Arrange the shrimp around the outside and serve right away. If preparing several batches, the shrimp can be only partially fried—for 6–8 minutes—drained, and set aside until time to serve. Then reheat the oil and continue cooking the shrimp.

NOTE: Since most large shrimp are first frozen, then thawed, and deteriorate quickly, I recommend that you always ask to inspect one and give it the sniff test. The shrimp should have the fresh smell of the sea, not of ammonia.

Melted Cheese with Roasted Chiles
Chile con Queso
EL PASO, TEXAS • CHIHUAHUA, MEXICO

SERVES 8 TO 10 AS A DIP OR 4 TO 6 AS A FILLING FOR TORTILLAS *Thick with roasted chiles and onions, this melted cheese dish is a far cry from those gooey processed cheese versions sold in cans in supermarkets or served with nachos in some local taverns. Lucinda Hutson (who herself has published two cookbooks, one on herbs, the other on tequila) got this recipe from her housekeeper, Hermila Contreras. When friends are coming over for a casual gathering, the chiles and melted cheese can be spooned into hot flour tortillas for a substantial snack or, more commonly, scooped up with tortilla chips, rather like a Swiss cheese fondue.*

This is a natural with a Mexican beer such as Negra Modelo and as part of a light meal. A Cactus Salad (page 54) goes well as a companion dish.

2 tablespoons unsalted butter or safflower or
  canola oil

1 cup chopped onions

3 cloves garlic, chopped

2–3 fresh jalapeño chiles, seeded and chopped

16 fresh Anaheim or poblano chiles, roasted
  (page 21), seeded, and chopped

1 (5.33-ounce) can evaporated milk or ¾ cup
  chicken broth

sea salt

½ pound Monterey jack or other melting cheese,
  grated

2 teaspoons chopped fresh oregano, preferably
  Mexican, or other fresh herb

Melt the butter or heat the oil over low heat in a medium-size casserole dish—earthenware is ideal. Add the onions, garlic, and jalapeños, and sauté for 10 minutes. Add the Anaheim chiles and cook another 5 minutes. Stir in the milk, salt to taste, and simmer just until the mixture thickens slightly. The chiles can be prepared in advance to this point. Cool and refrigerate, covered, and reheat before continuing.

Mix in the cheese and oregano over low heat, stirring until the cheese melts and becomes soft and glossy. Serve immediately from the dish or pour into a smaller heated bowl. The cheese must be kept warm. If it will sit out for a long time, transfer it to a chafing dish over low heat.

Savory and Sweet Empanadas— the Dough

Masa de Trigo para Empanadas

GARDEN CITY, MICHIGAN • NUEVO LEÓN, MEXICO

MAKES ABOUT 16–20 EMPANADAS OR 30 *EMPANADITAS*   *Half-moon-shaped* empana-ditas *and their cousins, the larger empanadas, are extraordinarily versatile pastries. The tender crusts hold fillings of savory chopped meats, seafood, or sweet fruits.* Empanaditas *are ideal party fare because they can be assembled in advance, then refrigerated or frozen until baking time, or baked ahead and served at room temperature, or reheated. Best of all, they can be eaten with your fingers. Serve the more substantial empanadas with a salad for a light meal.*

Every Mexican-American cook I met who prepared empanadas was eager to share his or her own special way of making the dough, and hardly any two fillings I tried were alike. We found the easiest dough with which to work was Maria Petra Vasquez's low-fat cream cheese version. Its flaky consistency held up equally well whether it was fried or baked. Any of the fillings can be used with this dough.

6 ounces low-fat cream cheese at room temperature

1 cup (2 sticks) unsalted butter or margarine at room temperature

2 cups unbleached flour

½ teaspoon sea salt

If baking the *empanaditas,* preheat the oven to 375 degrees F.

Mix the cream cheese and butter together until well blended. Add the flour and salt, and mix well. Gently knead the dough, then form into a ball. Wrap with plastic wrap and let the dough sit for 15 minutes in a cool place. The dough can be prepared in advance.

Spiced Pork and Apple Turnovers
Empanaditas de Cerdo
CHIMAYÓ, NEW MEXICO

While the biscochitos baked, she prepared the filling for the empanaditas.
A bowl full of meat, cooked dried apples, a large pinch of salt, cinnamon,
clove, ground coriander seed, a touch of ginger, two cups of thick molasses,
and two handfuls of raisins made the filling. This would cook while she made
the dough. Señora Martina was there to help with the frying and making
of the empanaditas.

—FABIOLA CABEZA DE BACA GILBERT

MAKES ABOUT 30 EMPANADITAS, TO SERVE 10 TO 15 *Little has changed in the nearly fifty years since this description of making empanaditas was written; Nolia Martinez may vary the ingredients a bit, but the end result is virtually the same. Nolia prefers to fry her empanaditas, which she makes small enough so they can be eaten in a single bite, but they can be baked.*

For the Dough
1 recipe Savory and Sweet Empanadas—the
   Dough (page 43)

For the Filling
¾ pound lean pork, ground
1 tablespoon safflower or canola oil
½ cup pine nuts or chopped pecans
1 cup raisins

½ teaspoon ground allspice
¼ teaspoon ginger
2 cups applesauce or cooked pumpkin
¼ cup sherry or sweet wine
sea salt and freshly ground black pepper

For the Glaze
1 egg lightly beaten with 1 teaspoon water (optional)

Preheat the oven to 375 degrees F. to bake the *empanaditas.*

Prepare the dough according to the directions in the recipe.

In a large skillet, fry the pork in the oil over medium-high heat. Drain off any extra grease.

Add the nuts, raisins, allspice, ginger, applesauce, and wine, and continue to cook for 5 minutes. Season well with salt and pepper. If the mixture starts to stick, add a little water. Set aside to cool.

Roll the dough out on a lightly floured surface until it is less than ¼ inch thick. Divide the dough in half and roll again to at least ⅛ inch. Cut into 3-inch circles. Any remaining scraps of dough can be rerolled. Place about 1 teaspoon of filling in the center of each piece of dough. Fold one side over the filling and seal tightly with your fingers. Crimp the edges with the tines of a fork. Brush the tops with the egg wash and place the *empanaditas* on a lightly greased baking sheet. Bake the *empanaditas* for 12 minutes, then check to see if they are browning evenly. If not, rotate the pan and bake for another 4 or 5 minutes.

To fry the *empanaditas:* Omit the egg wash and heat ¾ inch of oil in a skillet until very hot but not smoking. Fry a few *empanaditas* at a time until they turn a crusty golden brown. Drain on absorbent paper.

Crab Turnovers
Empanadas de Jaiba
SAN FRANCISCO, CALIFORNIA • VERACRUZ, MEXICO

MAKES 16–20 EMPANADAS OR ABOUT 30 EMPANADITAS   *Seafood empanadas make delightful picnic treats, and this crab version was a specialty of María Teresa Ramírez when she was living in California. It comes from her mother, Carmen Ramírez Degollado, a well-known cook in Mexico City. The filling used for Tuna-Stuffed Jalapeño Chiles (page 36) is another favorite of ours, and in Chicago, Priscilla Gomez Satkoff stuffs smaller ones with* bacalao *for Christmas and the holy days of Lent.*

For the Dough
1 recipe Savory and Sweet Empanadas—the
   Dough (page 43)

For the Filling
4 tablespoons olive oil
1 white onion, chopped (about ¾ cup)
3 cloves garlic, minced
1½ pounds ripe tomatoes, peeled and chopped
8 pimiento-stuffed green olives, sliced

1 tablespoon chopped flat-leaf parsley
8 capers
1 bay leaf
sea salt and freshly ground black pepper
12 ounces crabmeat
1 fresh jalapeño chile, seeded and chopped

For the Glaze
1 egg lightly beaten with 1 teaspoon water (optional)

Preheat the oven to 375 degrees F.

Heat the oil in a large skillet and sauté the onion and garlic until the onion is soft. Add the tomatoes, olives, parsley, capers, bay leaf, and salt and pepper to taste. Lower the heat and continue cooking about 20 minutes. The mixture should be well seasoned and quite dry.

Stir in the crabmeat and chopped jalapeño, adding a little at a time to taste. Cook 5 minutes more, discard the bay leaf, and let the mixture cool.

Roll the dough out on a lightly floured surface until it is less than ¼ inch thick. Divide the dough in half and roll again—to at least ⅛ inch. Cut into 3-inch or 5-inch circles. Place about 2 teaspoons of the filling in the center of each smaller circle of dough or 3–4 teaspoons in the larger. Fold one side over the filling and seal tightly with your fingers, then crimp the edges with the tines of a fork. Brush the tops with the beaten egg and place the turnovers on a lightly greased baking sheet. Bake for 15–20 minutes, until lightly brown.

California Impressions

Mexico's presence in California is everywhere. With more than 20 percent of the population originally coming from Mexico, California's cuisine, which includes the border foods that most Americans associate with Mexican cooking, has been continually infused with the richness of the diverse regional dishes from all over Mexico—especially from Oaxaca, Michoacán, Chiapas, and Veracruz.

North Fair Oaks is near Atherton, south of San Francisco Bay. In this community close to twelve thousand of the fourteen thousand residents are from Mexico, mostly from just one rural area in the "hot country" of Michoacán.

When I am in North Fair Oaks, I could just as easily be in a small town from that state. I buy *pan dulces,* flaky sweet breads, at Panaderia Michoacán, and a little farther down the street some Michoacán-style coconut ice cream. At Taquería Apatzingán I eat a taco filled with savory *carnitas,* bringing back memories from Michoacán of the most sensational *carnitas* I've ever eaten—chunks of pork, tender on the inside and with a crispy, slightly orange-flavored exterior.

Walking along the sidewalk of the main street of Huntington Park near Los Angeles brought back different kinds of memories for Miguel Ravago. As a teenager he often went there with his sister, Betty, to attend regional meetings of LULAC (League of United Latin American Citizens), an organization that sponsored dances to raise money to teach Mexican children the five hundred basic American words. Today the street is much the same as it was more than thirty years ago. The evening we were there, we drank *horchata,* a refreshing beverage of sweetened ground rice and melon seeds enjoyed in all regions of Mexico and in most Mexican communities in the United States.

In Palm Desert I sat at the kitchen table with Rosa Nava. Her mother was from El Paso, her dad from central Mexico, but they moved to this part of California in 1918. Her experiences mirror the lives of so many Mexican Americans in the 1930s, '40s, and '50s. Rosa's husband, Ramon, was a field manager at the Crane date ranch in Indio. Rosa told how the word would be spread around that workers were needed to prune or pick dates, and hundreds would gather in Sonoran towns along the California-Mexico border. A man in a white straw hat, the *enganchista,* or labor contractor, would select fifty men for one ranch, thirty for another, and they would be driven to various destinations in the Imperial Valley. These *braceros* were paid $1.75 a day, and food was deducted from their wages. Since cooking was not permitted in the housing provided for the workers, Rosa began to serve meals in shifts of fifteen at a time. Her refrain went, "Fifteen in, fifteen minutes to eat, and out you go." The men sat at oilcloth-covered tables; for breakfast they got a bowl of hot oatmeal cereal and two raw eggs, which they sucked, flavored with salt and lime. On Sunday the eggs would be cooked, and they received slices of white bread. The midday meal was a nourishing soup, salsa, and stacks of flour tortillas, and for dessert a sweet pudding; on Sunday always *menudo*. At supper she would set out a big pot of her economy *picadillo*, ground beef simmered with tomatoes and potatoes until it was a thick chunky gravy eaten with rice. Leftovers would be used the next day for tacos. Rosa cooked for the crews for over twenty years; now that she is virtually retired, her enchiladas, *chiles rellenos*, and tamales win her blue ribbons at festivals and lots of hugs from her forty-five great-grandchildren.

Almost everyone who lives in Chula Vista, a pleasant middle-class San Diego suburb just a hop, skip, and jump from Mexico, thinks of Tijuana as a continuation of "their town." Husbands and sons often work in Tijuana, and the women usually do their grocery shopping there, especially for breads such as *bolillos* and *pan dulces* (sweet breads). To them the border hardly exists. Gloria Anaya López's family is typical. Born in Tijuana, they live in Chula Vista, where all five children went to school. Her children work in the United States, but her husband prefers Mexico, where he drives trucks on construction sites. Gloria continues to do the cooking when her grown children drop by the house. Seldom is there a meal with only two or three at the table. And for celebrations, it is still Gloria who oversees the cooking—turkey for Thanksgiving and Christmas, *menudo* for New Year's Day, and dried shrimp *tortas* during Holy Week.

One of the most distinctive aspects of Mexican cooking in California is the unrivaled abundance of ingredients. Even before the advent of the Spanish, the California Indians had a more varied diet than those in the other southwestern territories. With the arrival of the Spanish came plants native to Spain and other Mediterranean countries, including olives, grapes, and artichokes, which flourished in California's rich soil and agreeable climate, and trading ships, able to provide an even wider variety of foodstuffs to enhance their tables. The Spanish landowners—the Californios—were renowned for their numerous fiestas and generous hospitality.

Carlos Andrea Dondero arrived in New York from Italy in the 1850s and sailed to San Francisco through Panama. After crossing the Isthmus by foot and being shipwrecked on the trip north, the seventeen-year-old finally landed in San Diego. Dondero became a frequent guest in the home of Governor Pio Pico, the last Mexican governor of California. In *Go West: Autobiography of Carlos Andrea Dondero, 1842–1939* (Garlic Press, 1992), he wrote, "[It was] nothing for them to invite hundreds of guests. The foods served were hardy and delicious. There were chickens, turkeys, enchiladas, tamales, tender tacos, peppery frijoles, huge platters of *juevos*, scrambled eggs, *chiles rellenos*, chiles fried in olive oil, and a huge platter loaded with joints of barbecued beef. The phrase given by the host when guests arrived, 'my home is your home,' was meant literally, and the abundance of the meals and entertainment offered knew few bounds."

Salads and Seafood Cocktails
Ensaladas y Cocteles de Marisco

*The weekly Saturday morning visit to San Juan market in Mexico City was mouth watering and time consuming. Slim bunches of the most delicate scallions—*cebollitas de cambrai; *delicate little radishes, crisp and nutty; avocados of all shapes and sizes; watercress, cucumbers, and every type of lettuce imaginable. . . . But it was on Sunday mornings that there was a brisk run on the salads already prepared and displayed on large shallow wheels of trays, of* nopalitos *or green or broad beans mainly, elaborately garnished with tomato and onion rings and sprinkled with chopped green coriander.*

—DIANA KENNEDY

IN THE DRY HIGH COUNTRY OF southern Colorado, crispy greens are always a welcome treat. Teresa Vigil will often rinse off a head of iceberg lettuce in icy pump water, shake off some of the water, and sprinkle the lettuce with sugar or spread the leaves with a little mayonnaise. Though on her table and in most other Mexican-American homes, green salads are commonplace, in Mexico lettuce, cabbage, tomatoes, and radishes are more likely to be a condiment for tacos or soups than a separate salad course. More distinctively flavored greens—perhaps spinach or watercress or combinations of different fruits and vegetables—are apt to fill the salad bowl when I am offered a salad. I also have grown accustomed to expect a colorful plate of lightly steamed vegetables such as green beans, chayote, or something more substantial made with meat or seafood. In the United States some of these more traditional Mexican salads are still treasured. The methods and ingredients may have changed a bit, but they retain their Mexican identity.

Gardening has added immensely to the enjoyment and understanding of my own life. Experiencing the inevitable rhythm of the seasons has helped me cope with and accept the unexpected, whether it is a bed of spinach devoured by marauding slugs or the much greater tragedy of a life-crippling accident to one of our children. It is my way of keeping my day-to-day life in perspective. Gardening coaxes me out of doors and into the benign weather of the Pacific Northwest, where some blossom is beckoning every month of the year. A part of many of our meals was still growing, only hours before, in either my garden or in the garden of one of our daughters. Jessica, Amy, and Lisa all share their crops with us, and another daughter, Sara, helps me tend my own patch where in season I grow epazote and other Mexican herbs and an abundance of tomatoes, greens, fruits, and vegetables.

In Mexico, even tiny villages have their markets where locally grown and foraged plants are brought to sell, to be transformed into simple but distinguished dishes. Happily, nowadays many towns and cities in the United States have at least weekly farmers' markets during the summer growing season. For those without the space, time, or inclination to garden, wandering up and down the open-air stalls is a convenient and pleasant way to obtain that same wonderfully fresh produce.

Caesar Salad with Chipotle Chile
Ensalada Cesar con Chile Chipotle
SANTA MONICA, CALIFORNIA • MEXICO CITY, MEXICO

SERVES 4 *The now world-famous Caesar salad was created in Tijuana, Mexico, by an Italian. These days almost every restaurant serves some sort of Caesar salad, and the grocery shelves stock a plenitude of different bottled "Caesar" dressings. It's a long way, though, from the original salad from Tijuana. Ricardo Villareal's version adds a truly Mexican touch—the warm smoky-flavored chipotle chile.*

If there was ever a salad to accompany a steak, it is this bold Caesar salad. Start with Melted Cheese with Roasted Chiles (page 42); add some Cowboy Beans (page 226) and end with Chocolate Rice Pudding (page 354) for a most satisfying meal.

COCINA DE LA FAMILIA

For the Salad

1 head romaine lettuce, leaves separated, or the
 inner leaves from several heads

For the Croutons

2 tablespoons virgin olive oil
2 tablespoons unsalted butter
4–6 cloves garlic, minced
2 thick slices stale or partially dried-out French
 bread, cut into ½-inch cubes

For the Dressing

5 oil-packed anchovy fillets, coarsely chopped
 (optional)

3 cloves garlic, coarsely chopped
¼ cup grated Parmesan cheese
1 tablespoon Dijon mustard
½–1 canned chipotle chile *en adobo* with ½–1 teaspoon *adobo* sauce
1 tablespoon red wine vinegar
sea salt
⅓ cup extra-virgin olive oil
1 tablespoon peanut oil

For the Garnish

1 small chunk Parmesan cheese
freshly ground black pepper

Rinse the lettuce leaves and pat dry. If small enough, leave the lettuce leaves whole; otherwise, tear them into large pieces. Wrap in a towel and refrigerate for several hours to crisp the
lettuce.

Preheat the oven to 275 degrees F.

Warm the oil, butter, and garlic in a large skillet over medium heat. When the butter melts,
add the bread and toss for several minutes.

Spread the bread cubes on a cookie sheet and bake for about 20 minutes, until crisp and
browned. Turn several times so they toast evenly.

Place the anchovies, garlic, cheese, mustard, and ½ of the chipotle chile, vinegar, and salt in
a blender or food processor and process until smooth. Taste and add more chile if you want.
With the motor running, pour the olive and peanut oils into the blender in a fast stream as the
dressing thickens. Transfer to a bowl, taste for seasoning, and add additional salt to taste.
Cover and set aside. This can be refrigerated for up to 3 days, but stir and return to room temperature before using.

When ready to serve, place the lettuce leaves in a salad bowl. Add the croutons and enough
dressing to coat each leaf, and toss. Using a vegetable peeler, shave thin slices of Parmesan
over the top and sprinkle with the pepper. Serve immediately.

VARIATION: CAESAR SALAD WITH GRILLED SHRIMP Marinate 12 large peeled
shrimp for 1 hour in a small amount of the dressing. Grill for about 5 minutes, turning once,
until the shrimp turn pink, then remove from the fire and cool slightly. Use the shrimp to top
the salad.

Watercress Salad with Pine Nuts

Ensalada de Berros

EL PASO, TEXAS

SERVES 4 TO 6 *Watercress, with its sharp peppery tang, is a popular salad green throughout Mexico. Since it is found quite easily year-round in the United States, I've never understood why it is not used more often in this country. Adding pine nuts was the suggestion of Aída Gabilondo, who still remembers family outings as a young girl to gather wild watercress. For texture I've added Belgian endive and mushrooms.*

This elegant salad is a good choice to partner with Minted Lamb Shanks with Thin Pasta (page 187) followed by Eggnog and Raisin Ice Cream (page 355).

For the Dressing
2 tablespoons good-quality sherry vinegar
1 clove garlic, finely minced
sea salt and freshly ground black pepper
4 tablespoons virgin olive oil

For the Salad
2 bunches watercress
3 white Belgian endive

4 ounces fresh white mushrooms, stemmed and sliced (about 1 cup)

For the Garnish
½ cup pine nuts, lightly toasted

Whisk the vinegar, garlic, and salt and pepper to taste in a small bowl. When the salt is dissolved, whisk in the oil. Taste and add more seasoning if necessary.

Tear the leaves of the watercress from the thick stems. Rinse in a colander and pat the leaves dry.

Slice the endive diagonally and discard the core. Toss together in a salad bowl with the watercress and mushrooms. Some pieces will be leafy, others in crunchy circles.

Just before serving, pour enough dressing over the greens to coat them and sprinkle with the pine nuts.

Pepper Slaw
Ensalada de Col y Chiles
SANTA MONICA, CALIFORNIA

SERVES 6   *I love coleslaw. Just hearing the word conjures up memories of potluck picnics in the park. Other kids went for the wobbly gelatin filled with little marshmallows. I headed for the slaw: shredded cabbage with boiled dressing, sweet and sour with mustard, mayonnaise, and sugar, or extra crispy with just oil and vinegar and lots of tiny celery seeds. There was chopped cabbage with sour cream and dill or with speckles of carrots and green peppers. I loved them all.*

Coleslaw is more American than Mexican, though shredded cabbage is used as a topping for tacos, pozole, and menudo. Ricardo Villareal makes this version of my old favorite. This salad is a natural to spark up simple fish or chicken dishes, and it more than holds its own with Tacos of Crispy Pork Bits (page 116). For a change, add some mayonnaise, sour cream, or yogurt, or even cubes of fresh pineapple.

4 cups finely shredded cabbage

⅓ cup olive oil

½ small white onion, finely chopped

1 red bell pepper, seeded and cut into very narrow strips

1 orange or yellow bell pepper, seeded and cut into very narrow strips

1–2 fresh jalapeño chiles, seeded and minced

pinch of dried oregano, preferably Mexican

5 tablespoons red wine vinegar

1 tablespoon sugar

about 1 teaspoon sea salt

Place the cabbage in a large bowl.

Heat the oil in a medium skillet. Add the onion, bell peppers, jalapeños, and oregano, and lightly sauté. Add the vinegar and sugar, and bring just to a simmer. Remove the pan from the heat and let the mixture cool slightly. When barely warm, pour it over the cabbage and toss thoroughly. Sprinkle on the salt.

Let the slaw season for at least 1 hour in the refrigerator, tossing it occasionally.

NOTE: Those who prefer the crunchy texture of raw bell peppers should add them as the mixture is cooling and not sauté them.

Cactus Salad

Ensalada de Nopalitos

TUCSON, ARIZONA • SONORA, MEXICO

SERVES 4 TO 6   *When I was in Tucson, I came across some wonderful local recipes that had been compiled, unedited, from students at Carrillo Intermediate School about fifteen years earlier. It was titled* Festival of Foods: A Carrillo School Project, *and among the numerous recipes with cactus was this one by Delia Figueroa. Although I couldn't locate her to get more information, her instructions were quite complete; we modified it only slightly, primarily reducing the amount of oil. In southern Arizona where Delia went to school, the prickly pear cactus is almost as common as dandelions, and a lot more useful. In the spring the new bright green growth is carefully removed from the ends of the cactus branches and used in a variety of dishes.*

As an attractive simple salad, the crunchy cactus provides a contrasting side dish to Gloria's Red Chicken Enchiladas (page 204), or the same mixture can be used more as a condiment for tacos or scooped up with Tortilla Chips (page 33).

1 pound fresh cactus paddles *(nopales),* cooked (page 55) and diced, or one 15–16-ounce jar cactus pieces, drained and rinsed

½ small white onion, sliced into very thin rings

2 cloves garlic, roasted (page 21) and minced, or ½ teaspoon garlic salt

1 large ripe tomato or 4 plum tomatoes, diced

1 scant teaspoon dried oregano, preferably Mexican

juice of 1 lime or 1 tablespoon garlic-flavored vinegar

2 dried *chiltepín* chiles, crumbled, or 1 teaspoon crushed dried red chile (optional)

3 tablespoons extra-virgin olive oil

sea salt and freshly ground black pepper

4 tablespoons minced cilantro

For the Garnish

4 inner leaves romaine lettuce

4 tablespoons crumbled *queso fresco* (see page 112) or feta cheese

2 radishes, sliced

Toss together the cactus, onion, garlic, tomato, and oregano in a medium bowl. Sprinkle with the lime juice and chiles, and add just enough olive oil to bind the ingredients together. Season to taste. The salad can be prepared in advance and kept cool. If refrigerated, bring to room temperature before serving.

Toss with the cilantro just before serving and scoop onto small leaves of romaine lettuce. Top with the crumbled cheese and radish slices.

VARIATION: CACTUS-STUFFED TOMATOES   Slice the tops off 6 medium-large tomatoes with flat bottoms and scoop out the pulp. Add any solid pieces of the tomato to the cactus mixture. Spoon the cactus salad into the hollow tomatoes and garnish with the cheese.

NOPALES (PRICKLY PEAR CACTUS)
(Opuntia ficus-indica)

*T*he nopal, or prickly pear cactus, is more than just a food source for Mexico, it is a historic symbol of the beginning of the Aztec empire. According to legend, one of the seven tribes of the Chichimecas—barbaric bands of nomadic Indians from the north—was instructed by their tribal god to stop their wandering and settle wherever an eagle was seen perched on a nopal with a snake in its talons. The sighting occurred at Tenochtitlán, one of two small barren islands in the middle of Lake Texcoco, site of the present Mexico City. These people became the Aztecs, and the probable date was A.D. 1325. In the almost two hundred intervening years before Hernán Cortés and his soldiers arrived, the Aztecs conquered almost all of what is now Mexico, and today the nopal is depicted on the Mexican flag.

The nopal is considered the most widely distributed of any cacti. They grow wild or are cultivated in Africa, Asia, Australia, and southern Europe, as well as the Americas, where Mexico is most probably its native home. Both the tender new pads, coming at the end of older jointed oblong pads, and the green or purple-red fruit, called tuna, are edible and are usually available in the United States in the spring and summer. Canned nopales are also available in the ethnic section of most supermarkets, and while not as crisp as the fresh-cooked ones, will work well in most dishes.

To prepare the nopales or nopalitos, as the smaller ones are called, first scrape off any stickers and their eyes with a sharp paring knife or vegetable peeler, then trim off the base and edges. Boil in small pieces for salads, to mix with eggs, or grill whole with a brushing of oil and lime juice.

If you see the sweet tunas in the market, buy them, because they are a special treat. The fruits are superb pureed, used in ices, or as an agua fresca, mixed with cold water and sugar. As the saying goes, "Al nopal sólo lo van a ver cuando hay tunas." Visit the cactus only when it is bearing fruit.

Potato and Vegetable Salad

Ensalada Madrid

CHICAGO, ILLINOIS • MEXICO CITY, MEXICO

SERVES 8 TO 10   *This very Spanish potato salad with its colorful vegetables accompanies Silvia de Santiago's holiday turkey, as it did when she was growing up in Mexico City. In Madrid, where almost every other restaurant is an informal tapas bar serving small earthenware dishes filled with all sorts of "little bites," this salad is one of the popular standbys.*

I like to serve this salad at a buffet featuring a good-quality sliced ham and smoked or roasted turkey. Tuna-Stuffed Jalapeño Chiles (page 36) is a good flavor contrast, as are cups of icy cold Tomato Soup (page 83).

1¼ pounds new potatoes or baby red (about 10 small potatoes)

2 tablespoons extra-virgin olive oil

about ½ teaspoon sea salt

½ teaspoon freshly ground black pepper

2 medium carrots, peeled and diced

2 pounds fresh peas in the shell, shucked (about 2 cups) or one 10-ounce package frozen

¼ cup chopped celery

3 tablespoons finely chopped sweet yellow onion

20 small stuffed Spanish olives, each cut in 4 slices

1 tablespoon capers

2 tablespoons chopped gherkins

1 tablespoon chopped canned pimientos

1 teaspoon celery seeds

1 tablespoon chopped flat-leaf parsley

juice of ½ lime

1 cup mayonnaise

1 clove garlic, crushed or very finely minced

For the Garnish

pimiento strips

sliced stuffed olives

chopped flat-leaf parsley

Place the unskinned potatoes in a medium-size pot or saucepan. Add water to cover and boil about 15 minutes, until they are just tender. Drain and let cool. Peel the potatoes, cut them into ⅓-inch squares, and place them in a large bowl. Drizzle with 1 tablespoon of olive oil and add the salt and pepper.

In another medium-size saucepan, bring salted water to a boil and cook the carrots. After 2 minutes, add the peas and cook another 3 minutes. Drain and cool under cold running water. Pat dry with a towel.

Add the carrots and peas to the potatoes in the bowl. Mix gently with the celery, onion, olives, capers, gherkins, pimientos, celery seeds, and parsley. Taste for seasoning and add more pepper and salt if necessary. Drizzle with the remaining 1 tablespoon of olive oil and sprinkle with the lime juice.

Mix together the mayonnaise and garlic. Spoon over the vegetables and toss gently. Press into an oiled mold (1½-quart capacity), filling the corners gently. Cover and chill until needed. Before serving, work a thin spatula around the edges of the mold, then turn it over onto a serving plate. Decorate the salad with the pimiento strips, olives, and parsley.

VARIATION: POTATO, VEGETABLE, AND TUNA SALAD   For a pleasant summer meal, mix in a drained 3-ounce can of light chunk-style tuna and 2 coarsely chopped hard-boiled eggs.

Jicama, Melon, and Orange Salad
Ensalada de Jicama y Melón con Naranja
TUCSON, ARIZONA

SERVES 8 TO 10   *In the stark and brutally hot desert lands of Arizona, the early settlers encircled any available body of water with lush oases of vegetation. Fig, lime, orange, and pomegranate trees, grapes and grain, seasonal crops of chiles, tomatoes, and sweet melons all thrived under the scorching sun. It is hard to imagine now the effort that this growth required, for today extensive irrigation makes these fruits and vegetables almost commonplace. Yolanda Mesa finds the cooling flesh of cantaloupe a welcome contrast to the jalapeño chiles in this jicama salad. Pieces of orange and tomatoes provide a vibrant color accent.*

This versatile salad will fit alongside most simple meat and chicken dishes. Try it with Roasted Pork Yucatecan-Style (page 178) or in the company of Sautéed Fish Fillets with Garlic (page 140).

1 small jicama (about ¾ pound), peeled and cut into thin matchstick strips
⅓ cup orange juice
2 tablespoons lime juice
½ teaspoon sea salt
3 oranges, peeled and sectioned (see Note)
2 medium ripe tomatoes, cut in small cubes

½ cantaloupe, seeded and cut into small balls or cubes
2 green onions, thinly sliced with some of the green tops
1–2 fresh jalapeño chiles, seeded and finely chopped, or ½ teaspoon dried red chile flakes
1 tablespoon minced fresh cilantro

Place the jicama in a large bowl and toss with the orange and lime juices and salt. Refrigerate for up to 1 hour while preparing the rest of the fruits and vegetables.

With a small sharp knife, remove the membranes from the orange segments and cut each into thirds. Add to the marinated jicama along with the tomatoes, cantaloupe, green onions, and jalapeños. Toss well and taste for seasoning. Mix in the cilantro right before serving. This salad can be made several hours in advance, covered, and refrigerated.

NOTE: To peel and section oranges so that all the white pith or membrane enclosing the segments are removed, it is important to use a very sharp paring knife. Cut a ½-inch-thick slice off the top and bottom of each orange. Slide the edge of the knife under the rind from top to bottom, following the curve of the orange. Repeat until peeled. Put the tip of the blade under the membrane at the edge of one section. Slice down to the center of the orange from top to bottom, separating one side of the section. Turn the blade so that it is facing out and is lined up beside the membrane on the opposite side of the section. Slide the blade from the center out along the membrane, freeing the section. Continue with the other sections.

Christmas Eve Salad
Ensalada de Noche Buena
McMINVILLE, OREGON • MORELOS, MEXICO

SERVES 10 TO 12   *The deep red of beets is about the only constant in the hundreds of versions of this colorful holiday salad. Most family recipes add jicama, apples, oranges, nuts, and scarlet pomegranate seeds; I've also found recipes that call for pineapple, bananas, grapes, radishes, cheese, or shredded coconut. Even the dressings vary, sometimes using mayonnaise, sometimes soured cream. Martha Gonzalez uses a simple vinaigrette in this traditional version, but she adds a splash of fizzy club soda water. Her kids think it's fun to add orange soda pop instead, so then she omits the sugar.*

A platter of this festive salad is perfect when lots of friends and family are gathered. Use as part of a Christmas season buffet with sliced turkey or ham, several kinds of tamales, perhaps Fiesta Tamales (page 295) or Sweetened Bean Tamales (page 304), and cups of hot Christmas Punch (page 382) to drink.

6 small beets, cooked, peeled, and diced

3 crisp apples, peeled and diced

3 oranges, peeled, sectioned, and cut into ½-inch pieces

1 medium-size jicama, peeled and cut into matchstick strips

1 cup shelled roasted unsalted peanuts, coarsely chopped

4 tablespoons sugar

¼ cup rice vinegar or other mild vinegar

2 tablespoons olive oil

sea salt

¾ cup club soda

2 bananas, sliced (optional)

1 cup cubed fresh or canned pineapple (optional)

1 head of iceberg lettuce, thinly sliced

For the Garnish

¼ cup chopped roasted salted peanuts or pine nuts

seeds from 2 pomegranates (see Note)

In a large bowl, mix together the beets, apples, oranges, jicama, and peanuts.

Dissolve the sugar in the vinegar and whisk in the oil. Add salt to taste and pour over the fruit. Add the club soda and with your fingers or a wooden spoon, gently mix everything together. Refrigerate, covered, for 1 hour.

When near time to serve, mix in the bananas and pineapple, if using. The lettuce can either be tossed together with the fruit or used as a bed with the fruit spooned on top.

Garnish with the nuts and pomegranate seeds.

NOTE: The tart ruby red seeds of the pomegranate are prized throughout Mediterranean and Middle Eastern countries, but in the New World it is only in Mexico and the Southern Hemisphere that they are used in any abundance—especially as a garnish. Available in the late summer and fall, they will keep for three or four months if kept dry in the lower part of the refrigerator. When you are ready to use the pomegranates, score the leathery skin in four parts from top to bottom, taking care not to cut into any of the seeds. Break through each cut and bend back the rind, exposing the many seeds, which are easily removed. Extra seeds can be tightly sealed and frozen for later use.

VARIATION: CHRISTMAS SALAD WITH A HONEY-MAYONNAISE DRESSING Combine 4 tablespoons of mayonnaise, 2 tablespoons of honey, the juice and zest of 1 lime, 1 tablespoon of cider vinegar, 1 teaspoon of ground pure chile, 1 minced clove of garlic, and sea salt to taste. Add to the salad instead of the vinaigrette with soda water and mix well.

VARIATION: CHRISTMAS SALAD WITH A SOUR CREAM AND POMEGRANATE DRESSING This colorful salad topping was a specialty of Miguel's grandmother. Put the seeds of 1 pomegranate in a blender with ½ cup of sour cream or yogurt, 4 tablespoons of sugar, and ½ cup of fruit juice. Process until it is a thick puree. Add to the salad as a substitute dressing and mix well.

COLACIÓN

*A*t Christmas time in Mexico there is a special confection that is used to top the Christmas Eve Salad. Made of orange and lime peel, coriander seeds, peanuts, or pine nuts, and with a hard coating of pastel-colored candy, colación *also shows up among the fruits and nuts inside the fanciful papier-mâché piñatas or in little wicker baskets to be passed out during the Christmas season* posadas, *as small processions go from house to house reenacting Joseph and Mary's search for lodgings in Bethlehem. I found a similar small candy used throughout Texas and in a few other Mexican-American communities.*

Vegetable Salad with Pears and Cherries
Ensalada de Corpus Christi
ALLEN PARK, MICHIGAN • QUERÉTARO, MEXICO

SERVES 6 TO 8   *There is an extravagant gamut of colors, shapes, and tastes in this heirloom salad, and just as unusual is its name, which translates as "Body of Christ Salad." Florencio Perea combines various shades and shapes of green vegetables and accents them with golden corn kernels, wine-red cherries, and tiny dicelike squares of ivory pears. Although he oversees the work, smaller hands have the fun of pitting the fresh cherries, a chore that can be made simpler with the use of a little gadget that pops the pits right out.*

I had never heard of this dish before I met Florencio, but I recently found a similar version in a book by Lotte Mendelsohn, Healthy Mexican Regional Cooking *(Front and Center Press, 1995). She comments that in the household of Jose N. Iturriaga, whose recipe she included,* Ensalada de Corpus Christi *was always served with lightly breaded veal cutlets. Iturriaga, a Mexican economist/historian, shared his recipe with Mendelsohn "in the hopes that it will not be lost in the vagrant files of oral history." Happily, it is very much around in Michigan.*

This is just the dish to serve alongside enchiladas or, as suggested by Jose Iturriaga, Breaded Veal Cutlet (page 132), a filling included in the recipe for Mexican sandwiches.

For the Vinaigrette

2 tablespoons fresh lime juice
1 tablespoon mild white vinegar
2 tablespoons finely chopped fresh cilantro
  leaves
1 clove garlic, minced
¼ teaspoon sea salt
freshly ground black pepper
6–8 tablespoons virgin olive oil

For the Salad

2 small zucchini, ends trimmed and cut into ⅓-
  inch slices
kernels from 2 ears of fresh corn or ½ package
  frozen corn (about 1½ cups)

1 pound green beans, ends removed and cut into
  1-inch pieces, or 1 package frozen green beans
½ small white onion, diced
sea salt
2 medium cucumbers, peeled, sliced in half, and
  seeded
2 ripe but still firm avocados
2 pears
½ pound fresh or defrosted frozen Bing cherries,
  pitted and halved
small inner leaves of romaine lettuce (optional)

For the Garnish

2 ounces *queso Cotija* or feta cheese, crumbled

Place the lime juice and vinegar in a bowl with the cilantro, garlic, salt, and pepper. Whisk in 6 tablespoons of olive oil. Taste and adjust for tartness, adding either more lime juice or oil, whichever is needed.

Steam the zucchini and corn for several minutes over boiling water. Do not overcook. Drain, rinse in cold water, and set aside.

In a saucepan, place the green beans and onion in 1 cup of salted water and cook, uncovered, 10–12 minutes, until just tender. Drain in a fine-meshed colander and run cold water over them to stop the cooking. Set aside.

Slice the cucumber halves into ⅓-inch pieces and place in a serving bowl.

When the zucchini, corn, beans, and onion are cool, add to the cucumbers. Toss well.

Peel and cube the avocados and pears, and add to the bowl along with the cherries. Mix lightly with enough vinaigrette to thoroughly moisten the fruit and vegetables. Chill for 1–2 hours before serving, tossing occasionally to distribute the vinaigrette. It can be presented family-style in a large bowl or cupped in a lettuce leaf on individual plates, with the crumbled cheese on top.

recipe continues

NOTE: It is important to use a very mild white vinegar in the vinaigrette, either a rice wine or an even softer pear, pineapple, or champagne vinegar, now sold in some specialty food shops.

Clam and Avocado Cocktail with Tiny Shrimp

Cocktel de Almejas y Aguacate con Camaroncitos

SAN DIEGO, CALIFORNIA • MICHOACÁN, MEXICO

MAKES 2 LARGE SERVINGS OR 4 APPETIZERS   *The people-deserted beaches of Michoacán, where many of Ana Rosa Bautista's family live, are home to the sweet clams that were a part of the original recipe for this dish. Living now in San Diego, she finds it easier to use canned clams. Serve this in tall, clear glasses, perhaps large wineglasses or old-style ice-cream sundae dishes.*

This "cocktail" is a perfect way to begin almost any meal. Delicate foods such as Poblano Chile–Stuffed Crêpes (page 201) or Tequila Shrimp and Pasta (page 147) follow well.

¼ cup ketchup

2 tablespoons lime or lemon juice

¼ teaspoon Worcestershire sauce

¼ teaspoon ground horseradish

Tabasco or other hot chile sauce to taste

1 ripe plum tomato, diced

2 inner stalks of celery, chopped

1 6½-ounce can chopped clams with their juice

2 green onions, finely chopped

1 large firm but ripe avocado

4 ounces tiny shrimp, peeled and cooked

sea salt and freshly ground black pepper

For the Garnish

several small inner leaves of romaine lettuce or celery stalks (optional)

2 teaspoons finely chopped cilantro or flat-leaf parsley

In a bowl mix together the ketchup, juice, Worcestershire sauce, horseradish, and Tabasco. Add the tomato, celery, clams, and green onion, and stir lightly. There should be a lot of liquid in the seafood mixture. Chill in the refrigerator until time to serve.

Cut the avocado in half and discard the seed. Slice the flesh into ½-inch cubes and mix lightly with the other ingredients. Add the shrimp and salt and pepper to taste. Taste for seasoning and add more lime juice or Tabasco if needed.

Place the leaf of romaine or celery to the side in a large chilled cocktail glass. Spoon in the seafood mixture and garnish with the cilantro.

Return-to-Life Seafood Cocktail

Vuelve a la Vida de Juan Felipe

AUSTIN, TEXAS • MALINALCO, MEXICO

SERVES 6 AS AN APPETIZER OR 4 AS A MAIN COURSE *While visiting Miguel Ravago in Austin, Texas, we had dinner with Juan Felipe Chancellor. We ate from a wide selection of Chinese dishes, but the conversation was about the foods of Mexico. Juan Felipe serves this medley of seafood as either an appetizer or a light main course; "return to life" refers to the restorative powers of seafood and chile after a night of heavy drinking. The quantities and varieties of fish can differ as long as you end up with approximately the same amount. What you want is a balance of shapes, flavors, and textures. Try this with small raw oysters or tiny octopi with tentacles.*

For a light summer meal, serve some Quesadillas with Cheese or Mushroom Filling (page 109) alongside the seafood cocktail. If a more filling companion dish is wanted, try the Spanish Potato Omelet (page 335). Have a crisp, dry Fumé Blanc to drink during the meal.

4 ounces uncooked bay scallops

4 ounces crab pieces, precooked and shelled (big, chunky claw meat is best)

4 ounces small squid, precooked, cleaned, and, if needed, sliced into ½-inch rings

4 ounces uncooked skinless sea bass, red snapper, salmon, or tuna, cut into chunks 1 by ½ inch

¾ cup freshly squeezed lime juice

4 ounces small shrimp, precooked and peeled

¾ cup ketchup

1½ teaspoons Worcestershire sauce

juice of 1 orange

1 tablespoon wine vinegar

1 heaping teaspoon dried oregano, preferably Mexican

2 tablespoons olive oil

½ white onion, coarsely chopped

1 large ripe tomato or 3 ripe plum tomatoes, coarsely chopped

½ cup minced cilantro leaves

1 canned chipotle chile *en adobo,* chopped

1 pickled jalapeño chile, chopped

1 cup canned small peas (optional)

½ cup sliced stuffed green olives

sea salt and freshly ground black pepper

For the Garnish

quartered limes

Place the scallops, crab, squid, and fish in a medium-size glass or plastic container. Pour the lime juice over and allow to marinate. Store, covered, in the refrigerator for several hours, tossing it occasionally so that the juice thoroughly saturates the seafood. When ready to use, add the shrimp.

Mix the ketchup, Worcestershire sauce, orange juice, vinegar, oregano, and oil together in a glass bowl large enough to hold all the ingredients. Drain the excess lime juice from the seafood mixture and discard. Gently stir the seafood into the sauce. Add the onion, tomato, cilantro, chipotle chile, jalapeño, peas, and olives. Mix thoroughly and taste before adding salt and pepper.

Heap into icy cold goblets with a piece of lime on the side. The cocktail can be made 1 hour in advance and kept in the refrigerator, covered, until ready to serve, but chilling may dull the flavor a bit.

Shredded Beef Salad

Salpicón de Res
EL PASO, TEXAS

SERVES 6 AS A MAIN COURSE OR 8 TO 10 AS A SIDE DISH OR APPETIZER *A salpicón should be like an abstract painting, with bits of brilliant color and contrasts of textures bespattering the muted background. It's a party dish that's ideal for a summer buffet. Though similar to the cold meat salads I've enjoyed so much in Yucatán, in this version the mustard, added by Virginia Lopez, a fourth-generation Texan, brings a distinctly American taste.*

The wonderfully rich flavor that beef brisket imparts to the broth makes this Virginia's choice of meat. If you want to speed up the process, however, Miguel uses flank or skirt steak braised for an hour or less. And in Texas, as well as in parts of Mexico, the same cuts of deer are often substituted for the beef.

3 pounds lean flat-cut beef brisket
2 white onions, quartered
3 cloves garlic, peeled and roughly chopped
2 bay leaves
8 peppercorns

1 tablespoon dried oregano, preferably Mexican
1 teaspoon sea salt

For the Salad Seasonings
3 heaping teaspoons old-style Dijon mustard
  (with the seeds)

1 firm but ripe avocado

juice of 2 limes

juice of 2 oranges

5 pickled jalapeño chiles, cut into strips, with 2 tablespoons of the vinegar

¾ cup diced white cheddar cheese or Monterey jack

2 teaspoons freshly ground black pepper

½ cup chopped cilantro

sea salt (optional)

For the Garnish

inner leaves from 1 head romaine lettuce

1½ cups fresh farmer's or feta cheese

2 firm but ripe avocados, sliced

8 radishes sliced in rounds

½ cup chopped cilantro

In a large pot filled with enough water to cover the meat, place the meat, onions, garlic, bay leaves, peppercorns, oregano, and 1 teaspoon salt. Bring the water to a boil over high heat, then lower the heat and simmer, uncovered, for about 1½ hours, adding a little more water if needed. When the meat is tender and ready to be shredded, remove the pot from the heat and let the meat cool in its own broth. Save the broth.

When the beef is cool enough to handle, remove any excess fat from it and thoroughly shred the meat with your hands. Put the shredded beef in a large bowl with 1 cup of the broth. Let sit for at least 30 minutes, tossing occasionally, until the liquid is absorbed.

Drain off any remaining broth. Smear the mustard on your hands and rub the meat to coat it. Mash the avocado with a fork and smear it on the meat. Toss with the lime and orange juices, chiles, cheese, pepper, and cilantro. Add salt if necessary.

Arrange a bed of romaine lettuce leaves on a platter. Mound the *salpicón* on it and decorate with the cheese, avocado slices, radishes, and cilantro. Serve at room temperature with hot tortillas.

Texas Impressions

My first impression of Texas is also the very first food memory I have. I was two or maybe three. I was outside under a tree, playing with a shiny spoon. All of a sudden a green jay hopped down from a branch and took my spoon away. I started to cry, and Teresita, the Mexican woman who watched over me, scooped me up and as a pacifier gave me a piece of a flour tortilla smeared with buttery avocado. Even now, when I'm sad, I eat avocados.

Tex-Mex food is what most non–Mexican Americans consider Mexican food, but it is not. It is Rio Grande border food—a blending of Native American ingredients: corn, pinto beans, squash, cactus, and chiles, with the meat and cheese sources introduced by the Spaniard frontiersmen. Soon came the wheat for flour tortillas, rice, and then a few of the traditional Mexican foods, such as the tamales favored by the Tlaxcalan Indians of central Mexico, who as co-conquerors of the Aztecs came north with the Spaniards and colonized the area around Saltillo in northern Mexico and parts of Texas. From these ingredients the early settlers of what is now the American Southwest prepared the spartan dishes of chiles and meat stews, thick, long-simmering soups of dried corn or beans, breakfast eggs with shredded dried meats, and for special occasions, desserts of rice pudding, or *panocha,* made from sprouted wheat. Even today in parts of the Southwest these simple foods continue to have a major place in home cooking. I was blessed to be able to share some dishes with direct descendants of these first settlers.

To me the most distinctive Texas dish is chili. Chili historians galore have long argued over the beginnings of this simple, robust concoction of meat and chiles, but everyone seems to agree that it was the "Chiliqueens" of San Antonio who made it famous. In the mid-1800s these *lavanderas* (laundresses) made chili in their washtubs and sold it in the evenings at stands in the Military Plaza. They had come north with the Mexican army and stayed on to serve the Texas militia. They would have used the little border deer, stray goats, and the almost-wild range cattle for meat, and the native *chiltepín* and marjoram, which still grow wild in southwest Texas, for seasoning. There is also good evidence that cumin brought by colonists from the Canary Islands could have been used in early San Antonio chiles. It soon became an essential flavor in a Texas "bowl of red." In fact, cumin, red chile, and oregano are the most identifiable of Tex-Mex flavors. You most often find chili served in a bowl like a stew with crackers on the side, but quite often I enjoy it as a thick sauce on beans, rice, or enchiladas.

Texas is an immense state: 3,800 miles of boundaries circumscribing 267,338 square miles of plains, deserts, and woodlands, all of which was once a territory of Spain and then of Mexico, though originally only the southern region was settled. Mexican Texas is big, too. In 1840, five years before Texas became a part of the United States, only 10 percent of the total population was Mexican, but now it is almost 23 percent, a higher percentage than in any other state.

In keeping with the grandiose size of Texas, it is fitting that Texas chefs also came up with the ubiquitous Mexican combination plate. Putting different types of dishes on the same plate is virtually unknown in Mexico, with the notable exception being *carne asada a la Tampiqueña,* a 1930s signature dish of a Mexico City restaurant that included a large, thin steak, beans, a saucy enchilada and guacamole but no rice. In Mexican-Texas homes, when I was served both beans and rice on the same plate, it was only with enchiladas, and whenever I discovered this combination in other states, it was invariably from a cook who had previously lived in Texas.

When I was a biology major in college, one of the first things I learned was that "osmosis is the passage of essential life material back and forth through the semipermeable membrane of a cell." That is what I think of when I visit any part of the border between El Paso and Brownsville or their counterparts on the Mexico side, Juarez and Matamoros. Members of the same families work, play, and visit in both places. The foods are virtually identical, though it seems easier to find *barbacoa de cabrito* (barbecued young goat) on the Mexican side and *barbacoa de cabeza* (barbecued beef head) in Texas. Texan Mexicans shop in Mexican markets for a wider assortment of traditional cooking ingredients, and Mexicans come to Texas to check out the supermarket. The land of *la frontera*—the borderland—is neither Mexican nor American but some of each. It has its own fusion music, *tejano,* and its own unofficial language, Spanglish. As Luis Helio Estavillo in Juarez told me, "Our family has a foot on each side of the border."

It was over a breakfast bowl of hominy-studded *menudo* (hominy and tripe soup) in El Paso that I first met Estella Ríos-Lopez, a vivacious young woman thoroughly committed to the long hours needed to make a go of her chosen profession in public relations. The energizing properties of the soup with its chile kick were evidently one of her secrets. Like most El Paso food lovers, Estella likes to drench her food with salt, black pepper, cumin, and oregano, though she has an even greater craving for the intense heat of chile than most Texans I met. "I'd eat Styrofoam if it had a *chile de árbol* sauce on it."

Besides talking about food, Estella related the first account I had ever heard of crypto Jews in Texas, or Ladinos—those Jews who, to escape death during the Spanish Inquisition, ostensibly converted to Christianity. Since it was illegal for known Jews to reside in New Spain, those who did would seek out areas to live, such as the northern territories. One day when Estella was at her Catholic grandmother's, she found hidden in the closet a menorah, the special candelabra lit by Jews all over the world to observe the Sabbath. She later learned that her great-great-grandmother and -father had been Jews in Bilbao, in northern Spain. They had come to Jalisco as Christians. Their family later intermarried with the Indians and, several generations later, moved to Durango, where her grandmother and family even helped build the Catholic church. It was not until she was dying and in the hospital that her grandmother gave evidence of her hidden faith and by gestures tried to summon a rabbi instead of a priest.

I've stayed in frequent touch with Aurora Cabrera Dawson during the five years since we first spent time together in her Oaxaca family home. A talented artist, she now lives with her husband, Don, and young son, Nathan, in a small city north of Dallas. She uses her time decorating furniture on consignment, taking art classes, helping out at Nathan's school . . . and cooking. In Texas, Aurora cooks most of the same foods she grew up with, but in a simpler manner, buying her tortillas already made, and though she cooks beans frequently, if there are none left over in the refrigerator, she is perfectly happy to open a can of black beans. (For Aurora, a purist, the black beans of southern Mexico are the only ones to use.) She has yet, however, to use canned chicken broth for soups or sauces. "I just couldn't do that; it wouldn't taste right." She even grows Oaxacan herbs and brings back the distinct regional chiles from home to ensure that the taste stays the same. When Aurora came to the United States, she quickly gained ten pounds from eating fast foods. "Everything here is so greasy and fatty compared to Oaxaca." These days, she says she just tries "to cook the healthiest and best-tasting foods I can for my family and as easily as possible. That means I take advantage of what I learned in Mexico and use it primarily with the ingredients I can buy here in Texas. They may not be quite the same dishes, but they taste good." Cooking practices will always change as long as there are cooks preparing food under different circumstances. A country's cuisine, like its language, evolves by adaptation and use.

Soups and Meals in a Pot
Sopas, Caldos, Pozoles, y Menudos

Soup has seven virtues: It silences hunger, provokes little thirst, makes one
sleepy, also patient, always pleasant, never angry, and gives a flush
to the face.

—MEXICAN KITCHEN SAYING

I CAN HARDLY IMAGINE A MEXICAN home without soup, whether a long-simmering broth thick with meat and vegetables, chiles, and crispy tortilla strips, or a pot of *pozole* that is full of seemingly everything. For those who are Mexican, eating soup each day is an almost indispensable part of life. What a pity that soup seldom finds a spot on the menus of the Mexican restaurants in the United States, since it is among the great delights of the Mexican-American kitchen.

It was the Spaniards who first brought to Mexico the notion of cooking and serving food in liquid. The Indians quickly adopted these robust soups, substituting their own regional ingredients. Since the chickpeas of Spain's *cocidos* and *caldos,* the traditional Spanish soups, were not found in the New World, they were replaced with dried corn kernels or native beans: red, black, white, yellow, or spotted, and chiles, tomatoes, and local herbs were added. During the long lean years that faced most Mexican families crossing the border to make their homes in the United States, these meals-in-a-pot became an economical way to satisfy daily hunger.

Light soups were originally used as a prelude to elaborate Roman-style banquets held by Mexico's upper classes. These meals, like the manners and customs of the wealthy families who served them, reflected the tastes of Austrian Prince Maximilian and his Belgian wife, Carlotta, the emperor and empress of Mexico, placed on their thrones in late-nineteenth-century

Mexico City by Napoléon III of France. They reigned only three years, but their influence on the cuisine of Mexico was dramatic and permanent.

There are probably as many kinds of soups made today in Mexican-American kitchens as there are Mexican-American cooks. Throughout the United States, the Mexican staples of beans and corn are served up in a surprising number of variations, but potatoes, I found, seem to assume an even stronger role. Around Corpus Christi, Texas, and in Florida, from Miami to the little backwater towns with their concentration of migrant workers, freshly caught fish or other seafood shows up in often intimidating chile-fired soups that offer an incredible way to start the day.

Other soups are also eaten in the morning, the most common being *menudo*. That favorite restorative is undoubtedly the one dish most Mexican Americans identify as their own. Usually served as a breakfast meal, the little squares of tender tripe and the zinging wake-up shock of chiles are usually combined with hominy to make an even more substantial soup that can be enjoyed at any time. I've eaten *menudo* at church breakfasts in Nampa, Idaho, for supper in homes in Sacramento and Chicago, and at lunch in numerous little cafes across the United States. When I asked why it was so universally popular, the answer was "If you like *menudo*, you are a true Mexican," or, "It's ours. Everyone else eats our tacos and salsas, but you won't find *menudo* at Taco Time."

Once it was the struggle for survival that necessitated the daily serving of these nourishing soups, but today it is more a matter of convenience and a love of their familiar flavors. Many young married women working outside the home are relieved to be able to reheat a pot of wonderfully hearty soup to serve for supper, with just rolls or tortillas. Whether or not these modern women have ever been to Mexico, the soups still reflect the traditional way their mothers, grandmothers, and great-grandmothers prepared soup in their kitchens in Mexico.

From clear broth to thick stews, homemade soups harbor the tastes that recapture family remembrances of meals past while nurturing the present generation.

Chicken Stock

Chicken stock is the basis of many of Mexico's soups, and like that of the Chinese, it has a subtle, delicate nature that enhances and does not overpower the other ingredients. Right along with how to make brownies, the young Mexican American usually learns how to create a basic chicken stock. The usual way is to start with a large pot of cold water (using about one quart of water for every pound and a half of chicken), to which ideally are added all those pieces of the chicken that nowadays are seldom eaten—the backs, wing tips, necks, and, of course, any skin. These can be cut off your fryers and frozen until you have three to four pounds of bones—or buy them packaged separately. If you can find a fat stewing hen, splurge and add it to the pot. Besides adding additional flavor, those meatier pieces of the chicken, such as the breasts, thighs, and legs, can be removed after twenty to thirty minutes and saved to use later in the soup or in other dishes. Do remember to put the bones back in the pot after the meat is removed. When the broth just comes to a soft boil, skim off any foam and immediately lower the heat. Once the broth is gently bubbling, the seasonings are added: slices of a small carrot, pieces of white onion, several garlic cloves, whole black peppercorns, a sprig of parsley, and, only at the end, sea salt. As the *dicho,* or saying, goes, *"Ahora es cuando el chile verde le ha de dar sabor al caldo."* (Now is the time for you to season the pot. Or, in a more literal translation: Now is the time for the green chile to give flavor to the broth.) Simmer, only partially covered, for three to four hours, adding more water if necessary to keep the bones covered, then cool, remove the chicken bones, and strain.

If time allows, after the stock is done and cooled, my friend Lupe sets the whole pot in the refrigerator overnight, bones and all. The next day she breaks off the layer of solidified fat and throws it away, puts the pot back on the stove, reheats the stock to boiling, and then strains it. The best way to do this is to line a large sieve or colander with several layers of damp cheesecloth, place it over a large bowl, and carefully ladle or pour the sediment-laden broth through the sieve into the bowl. Lupe uses this aromatic liquid to prepare whatever soup she is planning to make. The stock can be refrigerated for up to five days. If you need to keep it longer, simmer for ten minutes to kill any bacteria, let it cool, and refrigerate up to another five days. It can also be cooled and frozen in one- or two-cup containers or ice cube trays. The frozen cubes can be taken out and stored in freezer bags. The secret to Lupe's clear, flavorful stock is to simmer, skim, and strain.

RICH CHICKEN BROTH   To make the intensely flavored broth used as the foundation flavor in some soups, follow the above recipe, but this time use homemade stock or a good-quality canned unsalted broth instead of water as the base. Add a piece or two of chicken and a quarter of an onion. Simmer until the flavor is as concentrated as you want. You can also add instant chicken-flavor granules. Yes, the taste will be more intense, but remember that both the granules and the canned broth are usually loaded with monosodium glutamate.

IS IT STOCK OR IS IT BROTH?   Although the words *stock* and *broth* often are used interchangeably, *stock* refers to a liquid that has been simmered with lots of bones (or, in the case of some seafood, the shells) and occasionally some meat until all the taste has been extracted to create a flavorful base for soups and other dishes. The bones and meat are discarded. *Broth,* on the other hand, is really just the liquid, water, or stock that meat, chicken, seafood, or vegetables are simmered in until they are cooked and ready to eat. Because of its more common usage, the term *chicken* or *beef broth* will be used throughout this book.

Beef Stock

Writers of cookbooks often take it for granted that everyone who cooks knows how to make a good, rich, beefy stock, but just in case you don't, here is the way a Mexican butcher in Santa Fe said to prepare it. It's hardly any work, although it will have to simmer for quite a while.

Take several pounds of meaty beef bones, preferably marrow bones, and place them in a large stockpot. Cover the bones with three quarts of water and heat to boiling. (For a darker broth, brown the bones in a 400-degree oven, pouring off any melted fat before adding to the pot.) Skim off any foam that comes to the surface. Add an onion, several cloves of garlic, a small carrot, ten to twelve peppercorns, and a bay leaf or two. Lower the heat, cover, and simmer for three to four hours. If the liquid boils down too much, a cup or so of water may have to be added, so that you will end up with 1½ to 2 quarts of stock. Keep tasting, and when the flavor seems just right, add salt, simmer a bit longer, and then remove the pot from the heat. Cool, strain, and refrigerate long enough to let the fat solidify so you can scrape or lift it off. It's now ready to use or to freeze for a later meal.

Carrot Soup

Sopa de Zanohoria

MIAMI, FLORIDA • MEXICO CITY, MEXICO

SERVES 4 TO 6 *When Patricia Varley wants to have a dinner party but is, as usual, short on time, she will start the meal with this modest but colorful soup—one she learned from her grandmother, Eva Aguilar Vehovec. Tiny slivers of carrot sweeten the broth while cumin adds a warming flourish.*

Because of its lightness, this soup can successfully introduce a dinner built around Pork Loin with Poblano Sour Cream Sauce (page 171), Chicken in a Red Sauce of Pumpkin Seed and Dried Corn (page 158), or any of the moles. The Gelatin of Three Milks with an Orange Prune Sauce (page 347) would be a complementary finale.

4 cups Rich Chicken Broth (page 71)
4 medium-size carrots, peeled and coarsely
  shredded
⅛ teaspoon ground cumin (see Note)
sea salt and freshly ground black pepper

For the Garnish

½ cup finely chopped flat-leaf parsley
1 hard-boiled egg, finely chopped (optional)
4 radishes, sliced paper thin (optional)
1 lime, cut into wedges

Bring the chicken broth to a slow boil over medium heat. Add the shredded carrots and cumin, then simmer for 10 minutes or until the carrots are tender. Season to taste.

Serve in heated shallow bowls, garnished with the parsley, egg, or radish slices. The wedges of lime can be squeezed into the soup for extra flavor.

NOTE: It is best to use whole cumin seeds that have been dry-roasted for several minutes in an ungreased small skillet over medium-low heat. Cool and then grind in a spice grinder or mortar and pestle.

Cold Avocado Soup
Sopa Fría de Aguacate de Uruapan
SAN DIEGO, CALIFORNIA • MICHOACÁN, MEXICO

SERVES 4 *During San Diego's long summer days, Ana Bautista usually doesn't feel like cooking when she comes home from the office. One solution is this quickly prepared cold soup, pale green in color and with the rich but delicate flavor of avocados. Ana's affinity for avocados is a natural one. Her father owns one of Michoacán's most productive avocado orchards, which stretches up and down the hillsides outside Uruapan. Her brother, Enrique, processes and packages the avocado pulp for distribution to U.S. chain restaurants, and Ana herself manages his San Diego–based company.*

This soup is a fine opening for a light supper of Tequila Shrimp and Pasta (page 147). For a cold meal, pair it with a large Return-to-Life Seafood Cocktail (page 63). A Vouvray is a surprisingly complementary wine to drink throughout the meal.

3 large firm but ripe avocados, cut in half and
   seeded (see Note)
3 tablespoons lime juice
1½ medium cucumbers, peeled, seeded, and cut
   in chunks
¾ cup sour cream
3 cups defatted chicken broth (page 71), cold or
   at room temperature

½ teaspoon sea salt
splash of Tabasco

For the Garnish
½ cup crumbled corn tortilla chips (optional)
1 large ripe tomato or 2 ripe plum tomatoes,
   diced
coarsely freshly ground black pepper
2 tablespoons chopped chives (optional)

Scoop the avocado flesh into a food processor or blender and puree until smooth. Add the lime juice, cucumbers, and sour cream. Process again. Blend with the chicken broth and season to taste with the salt and Tabasco. Mix thoroughly.

Cover and refrigerate until very cold or put it in the freezer for just a short time, about 10 minutes. When ready to serve, taste again and, if needed, add more salt or lime juice to sharpen the flavor. If using the crumbled tortillas, place them in the bottom of each chilled bowl and pour in the soup. Garnish with the tomatoes and a dusting of pepper and chives.

NOTE: Since avocado pulp has a tendency to discolor when left standing, Ana finds this soup more attractive if made right before serving, using broth that is very cold. Set the bowls in the refrigerator to chill, too.

Cilantro Soup

Sopa de Cilantro

NEW YORK, NEW YORK • MEXICO CITY, MEXICO

SERVES 4   *The day I was talking about food with New York engineer Benito Lerma, I was constantly distracted. The art collection in his apartment is exceptional, but it competes for attention with the superb view of Saint Patrick's Cathedral.*

I'd heard that one reason so many people eat out in Manhattan is that their kitchens are so inadequate. Not here. Benito and his partner often entertain, and Benito usually cooks dishes as distinctive as this cilantro soup. Although not a native plant of Mexico, cilantro (fresh coriander) is probably now that country's most used herb. Luckily, it is found year-round in almost all grocery stores, for there is absolutely no substitute for its pungent flavor. Benito uses chayote to give a thicker texture to this soup, but an equal amount of zucchini would work as well. Another semisoft cheese can be substituted for the queso panela, *named for its flat bread–like shape.*

The subtle flavor of cilantro both cools and complements a dish made with chiles, so it nicely prepares the palate for the explosion of tastes in a main course of Chicken with Spicy Prune Sauce (page 154) or Meatballs in a Chipotle Sauce (page 182).

2 cups peeled and diced chayote

sea salt

3 tablespoons safflower or canola oil

3 store-bought tortillas, cut into strips ¼ by ½ inch

¾ cup minced white onion

1 clove garlic, minced

2 medium ripe tomatoes, peeled and chopped— or one 14-ounce can tomato pieces, drained

3 tightly packed cups chopped cilantro

6 cups Rich Chicken Broth (page 71)

2 fresh jalapeño chiles, halved and seeded

2 tablespoons cornstarch

¼ teaspoon freshly ground white pepper

For the Garnish

8 ounces *queso panela* or Monterey jack cheese, diced

¼ cup Mexican *crema* (page 23) or sour cream thinned with milk

fried tortilla strips

Place the chayote in a small saucepan, cover with water, salt to taste, and cook over medium-high heat about 8–10 minutes, until tender. Drain and set aside.

In a Dutch oven or large heavy-bottomed pan, heat the oil over medium-high heat and fry the tortilla strips until golden brown. Remove from the oil and drain on absorbent paper.

Add the onion and garlic to the same pot and sauté until transparent, about 5 minutes, stirring frequently. Stir in the tomatoes and cook until the mixture is thickened, another 5 minutes.

Blend the cilantro and cooked chayote with 3 cups broth, leaving a little texture. When the tomatoes are cooked, stir the cilantro and chayote into the pot and add the jalapeños. Dissolve the cornstarch with ¼ cup broth, stir into the soup, and pour the remaining broth into the pot. Simmer over medium heat for 15 minutes. Add the white pepper and additional salt if needed.

Before serving, remove the jalapeños. Place the cheese on the bottom of each bowl, ladle on the soup, and top with a teaspoon of *crema* and 3 or 4 tortilla strips.

Soup of Pasta Stars
Sopa de Estrellitas
McMINVILLE, OREGON • MORELOS, MEXICO

SERVES 4   *Tiny star-shaped pasta adorns this simply made soup, or if you are trying to entice children, use pasta in the shape of the letters of the alphabet. Matha Gonzalez's six-year-old son enjoys both.*

Although canned broth can be used, "for the best-tasting soup, always use a rich homemade broth," Matha stresses, "the tomatoes red ripe and the onion white." Yellow onions are seldom used in Mexico: in the United States, since they cost so much less than white ones, they are often substituted—but not in this soup.

Such a homey soup fits in with an equally simple main course, such as Garlic Chicken (page 153). For the same reason, Rum-Spiked Bread Pudding (page 353) is a very good ending to the meal.

4 cups Rich Chicken Broth (page 71) or Beef
  Stock (page 72)
2 medium-size ripe tomatoes or 3 fat plum tomatoes, quartered
¼ large white onion, roughly chopped
1 clove garlic
3 tablespoons safflower or canola oil
4 ounces little star-shaped pasta
sea salt and freshly ground black pepper

For the Garnish
½ cup crumbled *queso añejo* or other dry crumbling cheese
2 tablespoons chopped cilantro
Chunky Fresh Tomato Salsa (page 264) (optional)

Heat the broth over low heat in a medium-size saucepan and keep warm.

Place the tomatoes, onion, and garlic in a blender or food processor with a little broth or water and blend until smooth.

Pour the oil into another medium-size saucepan. Heat over medium-high heat, and when hot, stir in the pasta. Fry until quite brown but not burned. Add the tomato mixture to the pasta and stir. Simmer about 2 minutes, until the pasta starts to soften.

Pour the warm broth over the pasta and simmer for 10–15 minutes, or until soft but not mushy. Season to taste with salt and pepper.

Ladle into heated soup bowls. Sprinkle with the cheese and cilantro. If you want, enliven the soup with a spoonful of Chunky Fresh Tomato Salsa.

Garlic Soup

Caldo de Ajo

SANTA FE, NEW MEXICO

MAKES 4 CUPS   *Most of the garlic soups I've eaten in Mexico and the United States are the traditional Spanish blending of garlic, olive oil, and chunks of dried bread in a light broth or sometimes only in water. An egg is often added to cook in the hot liquid. A spartan dish, yes, but very satisfying. Surprising to me, this soup is virtually unknown in the United States except by those Mexicans with strong blood ties to Spain. These two versions—one with a bit of chile, the other with the refreshing taste of mint—were described to me by a group of Hispanic New Mexicans.*

For a light meal, have this understated soup with the Watercress Salad with Pine Nuts (page 52), toasted French bread, and a glass of very dry sherry or a robust red wine, preferably a Spanish one. Add the Red Snapper Veracruz-Style (page 139) and Ancho Chile Flan (page 364), and you have a very special meal.

2–4 tablespoons olive oil

8 cloves garlic

4 slices French bread, cut ¼ inch thick

4 cups Rich Chicken Broth (page 71) or Beef
    Stock (page 72)

sea salt and freshly ground black pepper

4 eggs

For the Garnish

2 tablespoons thinly sliced green onion

3–4 dried *chiles caribes* (see Note) or other red
    chiles, crumbled

Heat 2 tablespoons of the oil in a Dutch oven or a deep-sided sauté pan. Add the garlic and sauté until pale gold. Remove and set aside. Fry the bread slices in the remaining oil until golden brown on both sides; add more oil if necessary. Set aside on absorbent paper and keep warm.

Slowly add the broth to the pan and add salt and pepper. Place the garlic in a blender with 1 cup of the broth and process briefly. Stir into the rest of the broth. Heat the broth until simmering, cover, and let cook over very low heat for 15–20 minutes. Taste for seasoning.

To poach the eggs: Break each egg separately into a saucer, remove the pan from the heat, and slip the egg into the hot broth. Repeat the process for each egg and then immediately return the pan to the heat. Spoon some of the hot broth over the eggs, cover the pan, and simmer gently until the eggs have poached and are set the way you like them, usually 2–3 minutes.

Place the fried bread in the bottom of each bowl, spoon on an egg for each serving, then ladle in the broth. Garnish with the onion, and serve the chile on the side to be added individually.

NOTE: *Chile caribe* is a New Mexican term, usually used for their crushed dried red chiles. Other types of dried red chiles can be crumbled and substituted, including the generically named "crushed red pepper" sold in the spice section of grocery stores.

VARIATION: MINTY GARLIC SOUP   Sometimes the egg is eliminated and the broth simmered with 3–4 tablespoons of chopped fresh mint, creating a springtime flavor appropriate for the Lenten season. This is especially good when made with tender young garlic freshly dug from the garden after a long winter.

Chicken and Garbanzo Soup
Caldo Tlalpeño
CHICAGO, ILLINOIS • GUANAJUATO, MEXICO

SERVES 6 GENEROUSLY   *This light and spicy soup with the smoky flavor of chipotle chile is a favorite among Mexican Americans with family roots in and around Mexico City. Although it appears to be named for Tlalpan, a Mexico City suburb on the road to Cuernavaca, no one seems to know if that is really where it originated. Our version comes from Pamela Díaz de León, who grew up outside San*

Miguel de Allende and knows that the key to this soup is to use a great broth. During the summer rainy season, wild mushrooms were plentiful in the hills where she lived, and her grandmother enriched her stock with their earthy flavor. In Chicago, Pamela relies on the cultivated mushrooms from the grocery store but tries to include a few of the more exotic varieties often available.

This pairs happily with Quesadillas with Cheese or Mushroom Filling (page 109) for a simple supper.

1 pound chicken breast
2 quarts Rich Chicken Broth (page 71)
2 white onions, 1 cut in half and 1 chopped
6 cloves garlic, peeled
1 teaspoon dried thyme
1 sprig flat-leaf parsley
sea salt
1 tablespoon safflower or canola oil
½ pound mushrooms, sliced
1 cup frozen corn kernels
1 15½-ounce can garbanzo beans, drained and
  rinsed

1 large sprig fresh epazote or 1 teaspoon dried, stems removed (page 223) (optional)
1–2 canned chipotle chiles *en adobo*, chopped, plus 1 teaspoon *adobo* sauce
1 firm but ripe avocado, peeled and diced

For the Garnish
6 radishes, trimmed and thinly sliced
1 large lime, cut into wedges

Place the chicken and broth in a large stockpot or Dutch oven. Add the onion halves, garlic, thyme, parsley, and salt to taste, and bring to a gentle boil. Lower the heat and let everything simmer until the chicken is tender and no pink flesh remains, about 15 minutes.

Remove the chicken from the pot, shred the meat, and set aside. Strain the broth into another container and skim off most of the fat that floats on the surface. If time allows, prepare this in advance so that the broth can be refrigerated and the solidified fat removed.

Reheat the same cooking pot and add the oil. When hot, stir in the chopped onion and mushrooms, and sauté for about 5 minutes. Pour in the broth and add the corn, garbanzo beans, and epazote. Simmer for 15 minutes. Taste and add more salt if necessary.

Just before serving, stir the chipotle chiles and the sauce into the pot and heat briefly.

Divide the shredded chicken and avocado among 6 heated bowls and ladle in the soup. Sprinkle on the radishes and serve immediately with lime wedges on the side.

Summer Garden Soup

Sopa de Milpa

PHOENIX, ARIZONA • SONORA, MEXICO

SERVES 4 TO 6 *Miguel's most vivid food memories are from the years he and his sister lived in Phoenix with their grandmother, Lupe Velasquez. He loved to sit in the kitchen watching her roll out incredibly huge Sonoran-style flour tortillas and listening to her talk about the people she had met at her father's Tucson bakery back when Arizona was still part of Mexico. Those early settlers were true frontiersmen: Indian fighters, stockmen, mule-team drivers, and entrepreneurs out to make their fortunes in this isolated land, and their exploits made for good storytelling. Before long, Miguel was helping with the cooking, and he became especially able at chopping all the colorful vegetables that enriched his grandmother's chicken broth. This vegetable soup can be cooked with some canned or frozen vegetables, but it is at its best when made with those sweet overripe tomatoes of summer's end and the last little squash left in the garden.*

This soup is so colorful that it really doesn't need any garnishes and is so hearty that it is often served as the main dish for supper, with, perhaps, a crunchy torta *(see the chapter "Quick Bites," page 105), with your favorite filling, on the side.*

6 cups Rich Chicken Broth (page 71)

2 chicken breasts, with bone and skin left on

1 white onion

1 bay leaf

6 peppercorns

3 cups chopped zucchini or crookneck squash

2 ripe tomatoes, roasted (page 22), peeled, and roughly chopped, or one 14½-ounce can diced tomatoes, drained

4 fresh poblano or Anaheim chiles, roasted (page 21), peeled, seeded, and chopped

1½ cups fresh or frozen corn kernels

1 teaspoon dried oregano, preferably Mexican

1 teaspoon ground cumin

sea salt and freshly ground black pepper

For the Garnish

2 tablespoons chopped cilantro (optional)

Put the chicken broth in a medium-size soup pot and bring to a low simmer. Add the chicken breasts, onion, bay leaf, and peppercorns, and cook gently, partially covered, for 20–30 minutes, until the chicken is just firm to the touch. Remove the chicken from the broth and, when cool, skin and shred. Set aside.

Strain the broth, skimming off any fat, or, if time allows, refrigerate it a few hours so that the fat will congeal and be more easily removed. Pour the broth back in the pot and add the zucchini, tomatoes, chiles, corn, oregano, cumin, salt, and pepper. Bring to a slow boil, lower the heat, and simmer about 20 minutes, until the vegetables are tender but not mushy. Add the chicken, adjust the seasoning, and serve immediately.

Green Chile and Corn Soup
Sopa de Elote y Rajas
MIAMI, FLORIDA • MEXICO CITY, MEXICO

SERVES 6   *Even during Miami's sultry summer days, Patricia Varley will serve hot soup—especially quick-to-make ones like this one. The green chile strips and kernels of golden corn float on the clear broth, and there is the surprise of creamy avocado and cheese at the bottom of each bowl. When she is in a hurry, Patricia will use canned green chiles but definitely prefers the flavor of freshly roasted poblanos.*

Small bowls of this soup are excellent before casual dishes, such as Crispy Tortilla Flutes Stuffed with Pork and Nuts (page 122) or Tacos of Crispy Pork Bits (page 116), accompanied by Well-Fried Beans (page 227).

2 fresh poblano chiles, roasted (page 21) and
   peeled, or 2 canned green chiles
2 tablespoons unsalted butter
1 white onion, finely chopped
6 cups Rich Chicken Broth (page 71)
16-ounce package frozen corn
¼ teaspoon dried oregano, preferably Mexican
sea salt and freshly ground black pepper

For the Garnish
1 firm but ripe avocado, peeled and cut into ¼-
   inch cubes
2 ounces Monterey jack cheese at room temperature, cut into ¼-inch cubes
Tortilla Chips (page 33)
1 dried ancho chile, toasted (page 21) and crumbled, or dried crushed red chile

Cut the chiles into ⅓-inch strips and set aside.

Melt the butter in a Dutch oven or heavy pot and sauté the onion over medium-low heat until golden and soft. Pour in the chicken broth and bring to a simmer. Add the corn, oregano, and chiles, and cook over medium heat for 3–5 minutes, until the corn is tender. Add salt and pepper to taste.

To serve, put a few cubes of avocado and cheese in the bottom of each bowl. Ladle the soup over the top and serve immediately, garnished with tortilla chips and flakes of dried ancho chile.

Tortilla Soup

Sopa de Tortilla

AUSTIN, TEXAS • MEXICO CITY, MEXICO

SERVES 6 GENEROUSLY   *Although Nushie Chancellor was born in Santa Barbara, California, she was raised in Mexico City. Her father was French, her mother Mexican, and a former seventeenth-century Dominican convent was her home. There in its huge kitchen, with its cazuelas of simmering moles, the family's Oaxacan cook introduced Nushie to the world of cooking. Then there were those many weekends and vacation times when she would stay with her grandmother, Virginia Coutlolenc de Kuhn, in Cuernavaca. Situated in the neighboring state of Morelos, this lovely enclave has for centuries provided a retreat where the more fortunate can escape the hectic life and harsher climate of the capital. For Nushie it meant a time when her grandmother would share her culinary secrets with her.*

Nushie's family recipe for tortilla soup differs from most versions by the inclusion of corn, merging all the familiar flavors and textures of Mexican food into one bowl.

Serve this homey soup as a prelude to a typically Mexican meal. Chicken in a Piquant Tomato Sauce (page 152) would be a good choice, followed by Compote of Mango, Papaya, and Strawberries (page 345) and Aniseed Cookies (page 362).

5 large ripe tomatoes, roasted (page 22), or two 14½-ounce cans tomatoes, drained
1 large white onion, roughly chopped
2 cloves garlic, roughly chopped
6 sprigs cilantro
¼ cup safflower or canola oil
2 quarts Rich Chicken Broth (page 71)
2 cups fresh or frozen corn kernels
sea salt

½ cup Mexican *crema* (page 23) or sour cream thinned with a little milk
1 avocado, peeled and diced
1 cup crumbled fried pork rinds (see Note) (optional)
8 ounces mozzarella cheese, cubed
Crispy Tortilla Strips (page 33) made from 6 corn tortillas

For the Garnish

2 dried pasilla chiles, seeded and deveined
1 tablespoon safflower or canola oil

Blend together the tomatoes, onion, garlic, and cilantro in a blender or food processor. There should still be a little rough texture.

Heat the oil in a heavy skillet over medium-high heat. Add the tomato mixture quickly (it will splatter, so be careful) and stir constantly for 3–4 minutes, until it thickens and turns a darker color.

Put the broth into a soup pot or large saucepan, bring to a boil, and stir in the corn and the tomato mixture.

Add salt to taste, return to a boil, then lower the heat and cover. Simmer for 10 minutes.

Cut the chiles into small squares. Heat the oil in a small skillet and very briefly crisp the chiles. Remove and drain. These can be prepared in advance.

Set the *crema*, avocado, pork rinds, and chiles aside in individual bowls.

When ready to serve, put equal amounts of the cheese cubes and tortilla strips in the bottom of each bowl. Ladle on the hot soup and serve immediately. The topping can be added to taste.

NOTE: *Chicharrones,* the crisp-crackling residue of deep-fried pork rinds, add both taste and texture. And when they are used as a garnish, you are not adding that many calories. Pork rinds can be found in huge, puffy sheets in Mexican neighborhood markets, and for this dish you can use the smaller pieces in cellophane bags that are in the snack section of many grocery stores along with the corn and potato chips.

Tomato Soup
Sopa de Jitomate
TUCSON, ARIZONA

SERVES 6 TO 8   *I'd been looking a long time for a true Mexican tomato soup, one in which the rich mellow flavor of tomato was the main feature and not used primarily as a color accent. I found it, not in Mexico but in Arizona, and in a restaurant, not a home. This is my version of an old family recipe of Carlotta Dunn Flores, one that her mother's aunt, Monica Flin, brought to the El Charro Café in Tucson almost eighty years ago.*

For a rustic, satisfying meal, start with Spiced Pork and Apple Turnovers (page 44), then cups of the hot soup. Have King Salmon Grilled in Cornhusks (page 142), accompanied by Crunchy Cabbage Salsa (page 277). Cajeta Cheesecake (page 366) would be the ideal finish.

2 tablespoons safflower or canola oil
1 clove garlic, finely minced
½ cup finely minced white onion
2 tablespoons flour
3 cups Beef Stock (page 72), heated, or canned
  beef broth
1 28-ounce can tomato puree
about 1 teaspoon sea salt
½–1 teaspoon cayenne pepper

¼ cup sugar (optional)
½ cup frozen corn kernels, partially thawed

For the Garnish
½ cup chopped flat-leaf parsley
Tortilla Chips (page 33) made from 4 corn tortillas or 1 cup roughly crumbled commercially
  made corn tortilla chips

Heat the oil in a large Dutch oven or heavy soup pot over low heat. Add the garlic, onion, and flour, and stir until lightly browned.

Gradually stir in the broth, taking care to break up any lumps. Add 3 cups hot water, turn the heat to medium-high, and bring to a boil before returning to a low heat. Let simmer for 10 minutes.

Add the tomato puree, salt, cayenne, and sugar if using. Allow to simmer for several minutes, then set aside for 10 minutes or so to allow the flavors to blend. Taste and adjust the seasoning.

Reheat and add the corn kernels. Serve in heated bowls, garnished with parsley and crumbled tortilla chips.

VARIATION: GAZPACHO   For a very simple cold soup—virtually a liquid salad—make 6 ice cubes using 1 cup of the tomato soup. Peel, seed, and finely chop 2 cucumbers and finely chop 1 seeded green pepper. Stir them into the remaining soup. Add a splash or two of red wine vinegar and serve in chilled bowls with the iced tomato cubes. Carlotta also uses these ice cubes to intensify the color and flavor of a Bloody Mary.

Cream of Chayote Soup
Crema de Chayote
SACRAMENTO, CALIFORNIA • MICHOACÁN, MEXICO

SERVES 4 GENEROUSLY   *Chayote, which looks something like a fat, pale pear, is one of those vegetables that almost all supermarkets now carry in their produce bins. The flavor is rather similar to a cooked cucumber, if you can imagine it, and the neutral taste is ideal for combining with other ingre-*

dients. Val Hermocillo usually serves this gentle cream soup hot, but summer can become mighty warm in Sacramento, and Val has a quiet shaded patio—an ideal place for enjoying a cup of chilled soup. When she serves it cold, it is served with just the salsa and crema, and she omits the cheese.

To expand on the jalapeño flavor, serve before a main course of Chicken and Vegetables Flavored with Pickled Jalapeño Chiles (page 156).

Aurora Cabrera Dawson of Texas makes a similar soup, using whatever vegetables are on hand: peas, spinach, carrots, or even canned green beans.

1 tablespoon unsalted butter or olive oil
1 small fresh jalapeño chile, seeds removed and finely chopped
½ cup minced white onion
2 cloves garlic, minced
1 pound chayote, peeled and coarsely chopped
3 cups Rich Chicken Broth (page 71)
sea salt and freshly ground black pepper
1 cup half-and-half or milk
2 heaping tablespoons roughly chopped cilantro

4 ounces Muenster or Monterey jack cheese, cubed

For the Garnish
¼ cup Chunky Fresh Tomato Salsa (page 264) (optional)
½ cup Mexican *crema* (page 23) or sour cream thinned with milk
4 small sprigs cilantro

Place the butter or oil in a small skillet and sauté the jalapeño, onion, and garlic gently.

Simmer the chayote in the broth in a large pot, and while it is cooking, add the onion and jalapeño. Cook about 8–10 minutes, until the chayote is tender.

When the chayote is soft but still firm, puree the mixture in a blender or food processor until the texture is as smooth as you want and pour it back into the pot. This may have to be done in 2 batches.

Stir in the salt, pepper, half-and-half, and cilantro. Simmer, uncovered, for 2 minutes. Do not let it boil.

To serve, place a small handful of cheese cubes in the bottom of warmed bowls and ladle in the soup. Spoon on the salsa if using. Add a dollop of Mexican *crema* and a sprig of cilantro, and serve.

Corn and Zucchini Chowder

Crema de Elote y Calabacita

AUSTIN, TEXAS • PUEBLA, MEXICO

SERVES 6 HEFTY BOWLS OR 8 TO 10 SMALL CUPS *Mexicans everywhere love soup made from corn. Sometimes the kernels are simply simmered in chicken broth with other vegetables, but often the soup is enriched with milk, as in this version by Nushie Chancellor's grandmother, Virginia Coutlolenc de Kuhn. This creamy, colorful chowder was so good that it was added to the menu of the Rivoli Restaurant, one of the best in the famous Zona Rosa district in Mexico City.*

This is a substantial soup that can be served along with your favorite tostada or Crispy Chicken Tacos (page 121).

4 cups fresh corn kernels or three 10-ounce packages frozen corn

2 medium white onions, chopped

5 cloves garlic, chopped

4 tablespoons butter (see Note)

4 medium zucchinis

6 large epazote leaves or 1 teaspoon dried epazote, stems removed (page 223)

2 quarts whole milk

sea salt

½ teaspoon freshly ground black pepper

For the Garnish

Crispy Tortilla Strips (page 34) from 5 tortillas

4 fresh poblano or Anaheim chiles, roasted (page 21), peeled, and cut into strips, or two 4-ounce cans peeled green chiles, cut into strips

1 avocado, peeled and cut into wedges for garnish (optional)

Divide the corn in half. In a medium-size skillet, sauté the onions and garlic in the butter until slightly translucent. Add half of the corn, the zucchini, and most of the epazote, reserving a pinch to use later. Stir.

Puree the corn mixture in a blender or food processor until it is velvety smooth. (If parts of the corn kernels are still chunky, mash the blended squash and corn through a fine-meshed sieve, using the back of a spoon to press out all the liquid.) Put it all together in a large pot.

Stir in the remainder of the whole corn kernels, milk, salt, and pepper to taste. Bring to a simmer, then lower the heat. Continue to simmer for 30 minutes. Add the remainder of the epazote during the last 5 minutes.

To serve, place a handful of tortilla strips and a few strips of chile in each warmed bowl. Ladle the hot soup over them and garnish with the rest of the chile strips and the avocado.

NOTE: Butter is important to the taste of this soup, but if for health reasons you must omit it, substitute a good-quality corn oil. Thyme can be substituted for the epazote, but the flavor will be quite different.

VARIATION: CHILLED CORN AND ZUCCHINI SOUP   This chowder is very refreshing when served icy cold. A few leaves of mint instead of the epazote create a very different flavor.

VARIATION: CREAMY POTATO CHOWDER WITH CORN AND GREEN CHILES
Adela Amador substitutes diced potatoes for the zucchini and uses three times as many chiles. She prefers half chicken broth and half light cream or milk for the liquid and tops her chowder with a crumbled white farmer's cheese or feta.

Cheese Soup with Potato Slices
Sopa de Papas y Queso
PHOENIX, ARIZONA • SONORA, MEXICO

SERVES 4 GENEROUSLY   *At one time cattle ranches encompassing hundreds upon hundreds of acres straddled both sides of the Rio Grande. In those days Mexico's boundaries extended far to the north; frontiersmen and their families lived in virtual isolation from one another. Cut off by distance from the more sophisticated life in Mexico City and Guadalajara and constantly faced with the threat of Indian raids, by necessity each ranch became a community unto itself. Rich and filling soups such as this one of Miguel's grandmother, Lupe Velasquez, recall those days when making your own cheese was an ordinary part of a woman's routine. Long after Arizona, Texas, and New Mexico became part of the United States, this tradition of self-sufficiency remains, and in the homes of quite a few of the old Hispanic families that I visited, queso fresco was still made from both goat's and cow's milk. In one home I even found requesón (ricotta) made from the whey left over from cheesemaking—draining in a cheesecloth bag over the bathtub.*

Serve Crispy Chicken Tacos (page 121) with this soup and Little Pickled Carrots (page 282) or Pickled Vegetables with Chiles (page 281). Anna Navarro in Tucson likes to spoon on a green salsa, such as Chile de Árbol Salsa with Tomatillos (page 268), and provides a crusty French bread or rolls. Follow with the Almond Meringue Pudding (page 350) or offer a bowl of fresh fruit.

3–5 tablespoons safflower or canola oil

1 large white onion, diced

4 large russet potatoes, peeled and sliced into ⅓-inch pieces

2 tablespoons flour

sea salt and freshly ground black pepper

1 teaspoon dried oregano, preferably Mexican, or leaves from several fresh sprigs

3 large ripe tomatoes, roasted (page 22) and diced, with their charred skins, or one 13–14-ounce can tomato pieces

4 fresh Anaheim chiles, roasted (page 21), peeled, seeded, and chopped, or 1 7-ounce can mild green chiles, drained and chopped

6 cups Beef Stock (page 72) or canned broth

½ cup half-and-half or evaporated milk (optional)

½ pound longhorn cheddar or Monterey jack cheese, cubed

For the Garnish

1 teaspoon crushed red chiles (optional)

2 ounces longhorn cheddar or Monterey jack cheese, shredded

Heat 4 tablespoons of the oil in a heavy-bottomed saucepan (an iron Dutch oven would be ideal). Sauté the onion over medium heat for about 2 minutes, then add the potato slices and cook another 3 minutes, stirring often. If the potatoes begin to stick, pour in more oil, sprinkle the flour over them, and stir for another 3 minutes so they don't burn. Season well with salt, pepper, and oregano.

Add the tomatoes, chiles, and broth to the potatoes, and simmer, uncovered, for about 30 minutes. The potatoes should be soft but not breaking apart. For a richer soup add the half-and-half or evaporated milk. Taste again for seasoning. The soup may be made in advance and then reheated.

Before serving, divide the cheese among 4 large heated soup bowls. Pour in the hot soup and garnish with the chiles and shredded cheese.

Beef and Vegetable Broth

Caldo de Res

ALBUQUERQUE, NEW MEXICO • MICHOACÁN, MEXICO

SERVES 6 WITH LEFTOVERS   *Soups like this one made by Rosa Gomez show up regularly on most families' tables.*

Chunks of beef cook in a lazy simmer on the back of the stove; the tougher the cut of meat, the longer it stays. When close to done, all sorts of vegetables are dropped in. The result is a rich broth filled with large chunks of carrots, corn on the cob, green beans, and red tomatoes. A potato or two, some zucchini, and wedges of cabbage usually share the pot.

This tomato-enriched version would be more typical of what Rosa cooked in her home in Zamora, Michoacán, than of New Mexican cooking. The vegetables may vary, but they are always in big pieces, and sometimes chicken may replace the beef. Whatever the variation, whenever I find a caldo like this on the menu of a Mexican restaurant, I order it and finish my meal satisfied and eager to return.

The flavors intensify after resting awhile, so try to make this a full day in advance.

In larger portions, served with plenty of hot tortillas, this is a meal in itself. At the most, all that is needed are some Quesadillas with Cheese or Mushroom Filling (page 109).

3 pounds short ribs of beef, cut into 2-inch cubes, with excess fat removed

sea salt and freshly ground black pepper

1½ quarts Beef Stock (page 72) or canned broth

¾ cup chopped white onion

3 cloves garlic, minced

1 bay leaf

6 small red potatoes, cut in half unless very small

3 carrots, peeled and cut into 1-inch rounds

1 large ripe tomato or 2 plum tomatoes, diced, or 1 cup canned tomatoes, drained and diced

½ cup long-grain rice (optional)

3 small ears of corn, shucked and cut into 1-inch rounds

⅓ pound fresh green beans, trimmed and cut in half

2 small zucchini (about 1 pound), cut into 1-inch slices

¼ head of cabbage, cut into 3 small wedges

For the Garnish

6 sprigs of cilantro, chopped

2 limes, cut into wedges

3 fresh jalapeño or serrano chiles, finely minced

Rub the meat with salt and pepper, and let it sit for several minutes, then place in a large pot and cover with broth and about 4 quarts of water, so that the liquid is at least 2 finger joints over the meat. Salt lightly.

Bring to a boil and skim off any foam that collects on the surface. Add the onion, garlic, and bay leaf, then lower the heat, cover, and simmer about 1½ hours, until the meat is just tender. When the meat is done, skim the fat from the surface with a large spoon or put everything in the refrigerator overnight and lift off the congealed fat the next day.

Bring the broth to a simmer and add the potatoes, carrots, tomatoes, and rice. Add more liquid if necessary. Remember that this is meant to be a broth with meat and vegetables, not a stew.

Continue to simmer for 20 minutes. Stir in the corn, beans, zucchini, and cabbage, and cook until all the vegetables are tender. Taste again for seasoning.

Serve in wide bowls with lots of broth and a sprinkling of cilantro. Lime juice and chiles can be added to taste.

Meatball Soup

Sopa de Albóndigas

PHOENIX, ARIZONA • SONORA, MEXICO

SERVES 8 AS A FIRST COURSE OR 6 AS A MAIN COURSE *I found versions of this lusty meatball soup in almost every home I visited during my search for recipes. Once, in California, meatballs were served in a chile-rich bean broth, and several times I discovered that chicken or turkey had replaced the ground beef. This recipe of Miguel's granny is one that he cherishes. When he was little, it was his job to roll the meat into balls, the trick being to make them all the same size and not have any left over at the end.*

As a rule, the Mexican foods eaten in Arizona are made with the milder New Mexican–type chiles or with no chiles at all. Those who crave that searing chile flavor might try chiltepines, *a natural choice because these tiny chiles are the wild form of the* pequín *and thrive in the higher elevations of southern Arizona's Sonoran Desert. These are the chiles that Miguel likes to crumble on top of his meatball soup.*

This recipe makes enough for several light but nourishing meals, with even a better flavor the second day. Enjoy with a good crunchy roll and end the meal with Chocolate Rice Pudding (page 354). A light red wine from Spain, perhaps a Rioja label, is the ideal accompaniment.

For the Broth

1 teaspoon safflower or canola oil

2 tablespoons finely chopped white onion

1 green onion, finely chopped

1 large clove garlic, minced

½ cup chopped ripe tomato

2 quarts Beef Stock (page 72) or Rich Chicken Broth (page 71)

2 carrots, peeled and sliced into ¼-inch rounds

1 whole fresh jalapeño chile

¼ cup uncooked long-grain white rice

¼ teaspoon dried oregano, preferably Mexican

1 8-ounce can tomato sauce

sea salt and freshly ground black pepper

For the Meatballs

1 pound lean ground beef or ½ pound each lean ground pork and beef

¼ medium white onion, finely chopped

1 green onion, finely chopped

½ ripe tomato, chopped

1 large clove garlic, minced

2 heaping tablespoons uncooked long-grain white rice

3 large sprigs of fresh mint, chopped

1 tablespoon flour

1 egg, lightly beaten

½ teaspoon sea salt

½ teaspoon freshly ground black pepper

For the Garnish

6 sprigs of cilantro, chopped

dried chiltepine or pequín chiles crumbled (optional)

Heat the oil in a large stockpot or Dutch oven and sauté the onion, garlic, and tomato over medium-high heat for about 2 minutes.

Pour in the broth and add the carrots, chile, rice, oregano, and tomato sauce. Lightly season with salt and pepper and bring to a boil. Lower the heat and simmer.

Place all the ingredients for the meatballs in a mixing bowl. Mix together with your hands, then shape into bite-size balls (about 1¾ inch). There should be 25 or so when you are done.

When the meatballs are made, carefully place them in the simmering broth. Cook, uncovered, for about 1 hour, until the vegetables are soft and the meatballs are cooked through.

Warm the soup bowls. When ready to serve, remove and discard the chile. Ladle an equal number of meatballs into each bowl and pour the broth and vegetables around them. Sprinkle with cilantro and, if you want to spark it up, the crumbled chiles.

Steak and Potato Stew

Caldillo de Papas

SANTA FE, NEW MEXICO

SERVES 4 TO 6 *In Santa Fe I spent a good part of a day in Dora Chavez's home, surrounded by at least three generations of her family. Ten kids of all ages seem to live with her still, and others just dropped by to give her a hug or get a bite to eat. As she said several times, "It gets lonely here whenever they are not around." Now in her mid-seventies, Dora, having raised fifteen of her own children—and having now forty-five grandchildren and twenty-six great-grandchildren—learned by necessity how to cook frugally, especially during the lean years of the 1930s. Beans and potatoes in one form or another were served at least daily; the family consumed a one-hundred-pound gunny sack of potatoes in a week. When there was money for a bit of meat, a favorite dish was* caldillo de papas, *a thickish potato stew mixed with small cubes of beef.*

Farther north, in a part of the state that gets even colder in winter, Sally Borrego cooks a similar stew, using lean hamburger, for a quick warming supper with her husband.

The big flavors of this one-dish meal need only a refreshing Cactus Salad (page 54) as contrast and lots of hot flour tortillas. The best are those you make yourself (page 125).

2 or more tablespoons safflower or canola oil

½ cup finely chopped white onion

10 cloves garlic, finely chopped

1 teaspoon dried oregano, preferably Mexican

1½ pounds sirloin tip or chuck steak, cut into ½-inch cubes or very coarsely ground (chili grind)

sea salt and freshly ground black pepper

1 tablespoon flour

5 cups Beef Stock (page 72) or canned beef broth

6 canned green chiles, preferably New Mexican, cut into ¼- by 1-inch strips

1½–2 pounds potatoes, peeled and cut into ½- by 1½-inch strips

For the Garnish

3 tablespoons chopped fresh flat-leaf parsley

Warm the oil in a heavy Dutch oven over medium heat. Stir in the onion, garlic, and oregano, and cook until the onion wilts and becomes pale gold.

Raise the heat and add the meat by the handful, stirring and scraping the bottom of the pan occasionally. The meat should cook until all the pink is gone, then add salt and pepper to taste. Add the flour and stir diligently but gently until the flour has absorbed all the moisture. Stir in the broth a bit at a time and simmer, uncovered, for 20–30 minutes, until the meat is tender. (If using ground meat, cook only 15 minutes.) Add more broth if necessary.

Add the chiles and potatoes, and cook, covered, about another 20 minutes, until the potatoes soften and the broth is thickened. Taste again and adjust the seasoning. Freshly ground black pepper seems to pull out even more flavor from the green chiles.

Ladle into heated soup bowls and scatter parsley over the top just before serving.

VARIATION: STEAK AND POTATO STEW WITH TOMATOES   For over twenty years, Rosa Navez cooked a very similar dish several times a week for the migrant date pickers who lived at her boardinghouse in Indio, California. She used cumin instead of the chiles, added a small can of tomato sauce, and called it *picadillo,* like the thick meat mixture usually used to stuff chiles. Rosa serves her *picadillo* with small bowls of salsa, sliced radishes, and a plate of plain rice on the side.

Fran and Leo Duran in El Paso add a 14½-ounce can of diced tomatoes, a bit of cumin, and at least 5 chopped jalapeño chiles to their steak and potato stew. At the end, chopped cilantro is sprinkled on top, to be mixed in when it is eaten.

Lentil and Fruit Soup
Sopa de Lentejas y Fruta
CHICAGO, ILLINOIS • MICHOACÁN, MEXICO

SERVES 6   *Chicago's harsh winters mean soup time for Priscilla Gomez Satkoff, a businesswoman who puts in long, stressful hours before heading home at the end of the day. Tiny orchards of pears, peaches, and apples dotted the high slopes of the mountains in Mexico near where generations of Priscilla's family were raised, and using fruit in dishes like this soup was a tradition passed down to her. The invigorating tang of fruits combines with an earthy, almost meaty-flavored base of lentils to make this a belly-warming, soul-satisfying dish that can be mainly put together a day in advance. This soup is utterly satisfying when eaten with just a big green salad, crusty French bread, and a red table wine such as Beaujolais or a red "jug" wine.*

1 pound lentils

1 large red onion, roasted (page 22) and coarsely chopped

4 large cloves garlic, roasted (page 22) and minced

½ teaspoon dried thyme

2 bay leaves

½ teaspoon ground cinnamon (cassia)

½ teaspoon freshly ground black pepper

4 slices lean bacon

1 tablespoon safflower or canola oil, if needed

1 ripe plantain or firm banana, cubed

1 pound tomatoes, roasted (page 22), peeled, and diced, reserving the juices, or one 14½-ounce can diced tomatoes

sea salt

2 slices peeled fresh pineapple, cubed

1 small fresh pear, peeled and cubed

1 small tart apple, such as Granny Smith or Gravenstein, peeled and cubed

For the Garnish

crisp bacon, crumbled

freshly ground black pepper

Rinse the lentils in cold water, drain, and place in a large pot. Add enough water to cover by 2 inches. Add the onion, garlic, thyme, bay leaves, cinnamon, and pepper. Bring to a boil, cover, lower the heat, and simmer gently until quite tender but not mushy, from 40 minutes up to 2 hours, depending on the type of lentils and their age. Add more hot water when necessary.

While the lentils are cooking, place the bacon slices in a cold skillet over medium heat and lightly fry until brown and crisp, turning several times. Remove, saving the leftover grease in the pan, drain on absorbent paper, and crumble.

Reheat the bacon grease, adding oil if necessary, and quickly fry the plantain cubes until browned. Remove with a slotted spatula and drain on absorbent paper, then set aside.

When the lentils are just tender, add the tomatoes and salt lightly. Simmer 20 more minutes.

Add the plantain, pineapple, pear, and apple pieces. Simmer 10 more minutes, or until all the fruit is soft.

Ladle out approximately one third of the soup and put it in a blender or food processor. Pulse until thoroughly mashed together, then stir the blended mixture back into the pot. Simmer just until the soup is reheated. Taste, then add more salt if necessary.

Serve in large heated bowls with a topping of the crumbled bacon and a few more grinds of pepper.

Black Bean Soup
Sopa de Frijol Negro
DENTON, TEXAS • OAXACA, MEXICO

SERVES 6 AS A MAIN COURSE OR 8 IN SMALLER CUPS *Aurora Dawson's busy schedule as a mother and designer of Mexican furniture doesn't give her much time to cook the large meals
that her mother and grandmother cooked when she lived at home with her family in Oaxaca. However,
she does evoke their lingering tastes whenever she recreates this simple soup made from black beans. This
is an ideal dish to start one evening, refrigerate, and then reheat the next day for supper. The recipe can
be doubled or even tripled and served for a buffet. Black bean soup can be made completely vegetarian by
substituting vegetable broth for the chicken broth.*

*If there is any soup left over, you can blend it the next day and eat it cold with a dollop of Mexican
crema (page 23) or sour cream. It is a hearty soup and could be a main dish served by itself, but try pairing it with Crab Salad Tostadas (page 114). A light- to medium-bodied zinfandel will complement your
meal.*

12 ounces black beans
1 tablespoon safflower or canola oil
¾ cup finely chopped onion
½ cup finely chopped celery
6 cloves garlic, minced
2 quarts Rich Chicken Broth (page 71)
1 teaspoon minced cilantro
1 large sprig of fresh epazote or 2 tablespoons
  dried, with twigs removed (page 223) (optional)
¼ teaspoon ground cayenne pepper or ground
  chiles de árbol
sea salt

For the Garnish (use 1 or more)

1 cup diced Monterey jack cheese, or crumbled
  queso fresco (page 112)
5 tablespoons finely chopped white onion
2 tablespoons minced cilantro
strips from 4 oven-toasted or crisp-fried Corn
  Tortillas (page 108)

Thoroughly wash the beans and pick through for rocks and other debris. When clean, put
the beans in a large pot big enough to hold 4 quarts of liquid. Add 8 cups of water and remove
any beans that float to the top. Bring to a boil and simmer for 2 minutes. Remove from the
heat and let stand 1 hour. Drain the beans into a colander.

Add the oil to the same pot and, when hot, sauté the onion, celery, and garlic until tender.
Add the drained beans, broth, cilantro, epazote, and ground cayenne. Bring to a boil, lower

the heat, partially cover, and simmer for 1–2 hours, until the beans are very tender. More water or broth may have to be added to keep the beans submerged. Add salt to taste.

Ladle the soup into warmed bowls and top with 1 or more of the garnishes.

A USEFUL HERB
TO KNOW ABOUT . . .

*H*oja santa *or* hierba santa *in Veracruz,* acuyo *in Tabasco, and* momo *in Chiapas all refer to the same large, semi-woody herb* Piper auritum. *It grows in large clumps not only in southern Mexico but also in the United States. I've seen it thriving along riverbanks in Texas, and every year in Washington State I plant a new root stock in a whiskey barrel on the patio, and every year it grows just large enough for me to harvest enough leaves to season one or two dishes. Peer closely at the underside of an* acuyo *leaf, and tiny pearl-like globules become apparent. These oil sacks, when crushed, release the distinct aroma that characterizes this plant.*

The heart-shaped leaves of this plant are big enough to wrap completely around a piece of fish, imparting its musty anisy taste throughout the flesh. Its flavor is also used to enhance certain pork and chicken dishes.

Plants can be ordered from It's About Thyme (see Product Sources, page 391), and should grow well in any warm climate.

Red Snapper Soup
Sopa de Huachinango
SAN DIEGO, CALIFORNIA • TABASCO, MEXICO

SERVES 6 TO 8 *In Mexico seafood soups are much more common than in the United States, especially in those states washed by the Gulf of Mexico. This soup, made by Ricardo Muñoz, has large chunks of a firm-fleshed fish floating in a tomato-tinted broth. With just the fish, it is sophisticated* *enough for a dinner party, but the addition of carrots and potatoes turns it into a heartier fishermen's stew, just as it is made on board the local fishing boats using freshly caught fish.*

Eat with a good crunchy bread and perhaps a bottle of a medium-dry white wine or a pitcher of Sangria (page 380).

This fish soup suffers if canned tomatoes are used instead of the ripe fresh ones; the seeds and skins give a needed consistency and flavor to the broth. Also, Ricardo does not like to cut back on the amount of olive oil used in the recipe as, again, it is important to the flavor.

In Tabasco, where the recipe for this soup originated, it would be faintly perfumed with an aromatic large-leafed herb, called acuyo *in that area but more commonly known as* hoja santa *throughout the humid regions of southern Mexico where it grows (see sidebar). When Ricardo was living in San Diego and could not find* acuyo, *he doubled the amount of cilantro that he usually used in the broth. A different flavor, but still very good.*

3 large ripe tomatoes or 6 plum tomatoes, cut in
   wedges
¼ teaspoon freshly ground black pepper
pinch of allspice
6 cloves garlic, peeled
1 medium white onion, cut in wedges
2 corn tortillas
½ cup olive oil
1 pound fish bones, with head if possible
2 bunches cilantro, stems included
2 bay leaves
¼ teaspoon dried oregano, preferably Mexican

1 teaspoon sea salt
3 small new potatoes, peeled and diced (optional)
1 medium carrot, peeled and diced (optional)
1½ pounds thick red snapper steaks, cut into 2-
   to 3-inch chunks

For the Garnish

4 limes, quartered
1 dried pasilla chile, toasted (page 22) and crumbled, or 2 tablespoons other crushed dried red chile (optional)

Place the tomatoes, pepper, allspice, garlic, onion, and tortillas in a food processor or blender. Add ½ cup of water and process until smooth.

Heat the oil in a medium-size saucepan or skillet until it just starts to smoke. Pour in the tomato sauce, let it sizzle for several minutes, then turn the heat to low and simmer, covered, about 30 minutes. Stir occasionally.

While the sauce is cooking, place the fish bones in a large pot with 2 quarts of water. Add the cilantro, bay leaves, oregano, and salt. Boil over medium-high heat for 20 minutes. Remove from the heat, strain, return the fish broth to the pot, and reheat. Stir in the blended tomato sauce and the potatoes and carrots, if using, and cook over medium-low heat about 10 minutes, or until the added vegetables are tender. This can be made in advance to this stage and kept warm.

About 5 minutes before serving, gently lower the fish chunks into the barely bubbling soup, adjust the seasoning, and simmer until the fish turns white on both sides. Allow 5 minutes per ½ inch of thickness.

Carefully ladle the fish and the soup into heated individual serving bowls or serve from the pot or tureen at the table.

Serve with the limes on the side. A squeeze of lime juice into the soup accentuates the flavor. The crushed chile should be available in a small bowl for each person to add as wanted.

"LAS MAÑANITAS"

These are the early mornings in which King David sang.
Today, because it is your birthday, we sing them to you.

The day you were born, so were all the flowers,
And at your baptismal pool, the mockingbirds sang.

Awaken, my dear, awaken. Watch the morning sun rise.
The birds are singing, and the moon is gone.

*I*n the United States the silence of dawn is not always broken on a birthday morning by the sounds of guitar and violin and voices singing the lyrics of "Las Mañanitas"—the traditional birthday song of Mexico—but the occasion of a birthday is still a time for a fiesta in the home. And a fiesta means a celebration with favorite foods as well as family, friends, and music. Of course, hamburgers or pizza may also be served now, but for families from many parts of Mexico, the wonderful aromas coming from the kitchen will likely be those of the rich hominy soup called pozole, an Indian word meaning foam, which refers to the way the dried corn flowers open when cooking.

Hominy and Pork Soup

Pozole

McMINVILLE, OREGON • SINALOA, MEXICO

SERVES 4 *"The poorer we were, the more Mexican we ate."* Now those foods that once were dishes of necessity are considered by Maria McRitchie's daughters-in-law as exotic. Maria, a recently retired medical-social worker, lives in a quiet Oregon town set among oak-covered hills. Here in the heart of the Willamette Valley wine country, the surrounding vineyards provide employment for many families of Mexican heritage who live in the valley. Maria's husband, a Scotsman, is the winemaker and general manager of nearby Flynn Wineries. This version of Maria's pozole still recalls the flavors of central Mexico but requires less work than some traditional recipes.

Pozole, a thick hominy stew, is eaten in one form or other throughout Mexico. One is green with herbs and tomatillos, another red with dried chiles, and the simplest of all is plain and white. Essential to all versions are the various toppings, which are added *al gusto* (to taste) depending on the type of pozole and family preferences. It may be shredded cabbage, sliced radishes, dried oregano, chopped onion, chunks of avocado, chile, or even crisp-fried pork rinds, and always a good squirt of lime juice to finish it off.

Serve with warm tortillas. Have a dish of Pickled Vegetables with Chiles (page 281) on the table to munch on and a bottle of Mexican lager beer to drink.

2 tablespoons safflower or canola oil

1 pound pork shoulder or butt, excess fat removed, cut into bite-size pieces

1 medium white onion, chopped

2 cloves garlic

1 15-ounce can white hominy, drained

4 cups Rich Chicken Broth (page 71)

sea salt

For the Garnish

2 limes, cut into quarters

½ cup white chopped onion

2 tablespoons dried oregano, preferably Mexican

1 or more tablespoons crumbled or ground pure chile, such as New Mexican or guajillo chile

12 radishes, thinly sliced

¼ small head cabbage, finely shredded

Warm the oil in a Dutch oven or heavy-bottomed pot. Add the pork, onion, and garlic and fry over medium-high heat. When the pork is slightly crispy, about 25 minutes, add the hominy and broth. Season to taste, bring the soup to a very slow boil, and then simmer, partially covered, for 30 minutes.

recipe continues

To serve, fill large heated bowls with the soup and put the various condiments in smaller bowls, letting the diners create their own meals.

VARIATION: RED HOMINY AND PORK SOUP For a *pozole* red-rich with chiles, Mexican Americans with ties to Jalisco and Michoacán may add 1 tablespoon of ground chiles while the soup is simmering. They may use a combination of ancho and guajillo chiles, if available. Olivia Dominguez in Chicago uses the rather nutty-flavored cascabel to add the heat and color to her *pozole*.

VARIATION: HOMINY AND CHICKEN SOUP For a lighter soup, Virginia Ariemma of Florida substitutes 1 chicken breast for the pork, which she simmers for 15–20 minutes in the broth before shredding. Instead of garlic, a stalk of chopped celery is sautéed with the onion, and ¾ cup of canned tomato pieces is added for quite a different flavor.

POZOLE . . . OR POSOLE, BOTH JUST ANOTHER NAME FOR HOMINY

rom the humble corn plant comes the foundation of all Mexican cooking. It is used, of course, as a vegetable, but we know it best when it is made into masa *(dough) for tortillas and tamales.*

Another very useful form is a pozole. *When the dried field corn is boiled with* cal *(calcium hydroxide), dissolving the tough hull, instead of grinding it into* masa *the kernels are simmered until tender, then added to the earthy soups of the same name or to* menudo.

Almost everyone I talked to seems to buy the already prepared pozole *that is found either freshly made or frozen. I was introduced to an excellent prepared dried* pozole *packaged by Peter Casados (see Product Sources, page 392). Canned white (not yellow) hominy is a shortcut, usually offered apologetically because while it may look the same, it lacks the distinct smell and firmer texture.*

Hominy and Tripe Soup
Menudo
DENVER, COLORADO

SERVES 4 TO 6   *Until a year or so ago, I was not really a fan of* menudo—*tiny bits of tender tripe in a richly seasoned broth. But then I had never eaten it in combination with hominy, the way I found it everywhere in the United States. I tried it cautiously in Detroit, with enjoyment in El Paso, and by the time I got to New Mexico, I was a true connoisseur of the dish.*

I did not get to meet Gina Vigil, who lives in Denver, but her mother, Teresa Vigil, with whom I spent time in the San Luis Valley farther south in Colorado, told me about Gina's exceptional menudo—*so good that, evidently, on Sundays after mass the whole neighborhood "just happens" to drop by to visit and stays to eat. This is our version of her* menudo *recipe, which includes the small chunks of beef that Adela Amador, farther south in New Mexico, likes to add.*

Have lots of steaming hot Flour Tortillas (page 125) or toasted slices of French bread, both with plenty of butter, to serve on the side. If you are serving the pozole *for supper, Egg Nog and Raisin Ice Cream (page 355) would add a pleasant contrast.*

½ pound honeycomb tripe, precleaned
2 teaspoons cider vinegar
½ pound beef chuck (fat and connecting membranes removed), cut into 1-inch pieces (optional)
2 pig's feet, each split into 2 pieces
about ½ teaspoon sea salt
1 pound prepared dried or frozen *pozole* or one 28-ounce can white hominy, drained and rinsed
1 white onion, chopped
2 cloves garlic, chopped

2 teaspoons dried oregano, preferably Mexican
2 dried pequín chiles (optional)
2 tablespoons pure chile powder, preferably New Mexican, or ½ cup red chile paste

For the Garnish
½ cup chopped green onions
2 limes or lemons, quartered
2 tablespoons dried oregano, preferably Mexican
2 tablespoons ground pequín chiles
½ cup minced cilantro leaves

Trim off any excess fat from the tripe and thoroughly wash in several changes of salted water. Cut the tripe in ½-inch squares, place in a large stockpot, and cover with cold water. Add the vinegar, bring to a slow boil, and simmer for 5–10 minutes. Drain in a colander, rinse with warm water, and return to the pot.

Add the beef and pig's feet to the pot and cover with 2 quarts of water. Salt to taste. If using prepared dried or frozen *pozole,* put it in at this time. Bring to a boil over medium-high heat and skim off any foam that comes to the surface. Lower the heat and let the pot simmer for several minutes, then add the onion, garlic, oregano, pequíns, and chile powder.

Regulate the heat so that the bubbles in the broth just break the surface. Cover and simmer for 2 hours. Add the canned *pozole* if using. If more water is needed, add it along with additional herbs and spices to taste. Continue cooking for another 30–60 minutes, until the tripe and beef are both tender.

Remove the pig's feet from the broth and skim away any excess fat from the surface. When the feet are cool enough to handle, cut off any meaty parts and return them to the pot, discarding the bone and cartilage.

Place the green onions, limes, oregano, ground chile, and cilantro in small bowls on the table. The *menudo* should be served in individual large, deep bowls with lots of hot tortillas. The diners can add condiments to their own liking. The *menudo* is very good reheated the next day, with any congealed fat first removed.

Arizona Impressions

Desert country. Heat. Harsh, unforgiving land. Rock, sand, forests of giant saguaros and organ pipe cacti, thickets of mesquite, everywhere spiny cholla, barrel cactus, the omnipresent prickly pear, and scorpions, rattlesnakes, and toxic toads. Springs and streams are few, and when the summer rains come, they are accompanied by lightning and violent thunder showers. Here in the Sonoran Desert, south of the meandering Gila River, is where most of the 16 percent of Arizona population who trace their descent to the Spanish or to the Mexican Indians have settled. This is the northern part of the land called the Pimería Alta by the Jesuit missionary and cartographer Eusebio Francisco Kino, the famous "padre on horseback." Though intersected in 1854 by an international boundary, it shares one historical and cultural heritage and is also linked environmentally with the southern portion in Mexico.

In 1691 when Father Kino was invited north to visit the Pima Indians in the small village of Tumacacori, the Indians lived frugally on the squash, beans, and corn they raised and shared, acorns they gathered from the mountain slopes, and a little meat from game, rodents, and snakes. He was able to provide seeds and livestock. Seven years later, according to the priest, there were "fields of wheat and herds of cattle, sheep, and goats." Though by 1843 the few Indians who still lived at the old Tumacacori mission, by now deserted, had mainly abandoned the communal fields, today it is the preponderance of cream and cheese, sun-dried beef, *carne seca,* and the gigantic paper-thin tortillas made from wheat flour that characterize the Mexican cooking in southern Arizona, just as it does across the border in Sonora.

Even the marauding Apaches made flour tortillas. The grandfather of Carmen Villa Prezelski used to relate how once, when out in the desert, he was surrounded by Apaches who first took away his tobacco pouch and then brought him to their village to share a meal. The meats were all wrapped in flour tortillas, shaded gray by the dirt-covered hands of the women who were patting them out. He ate them with such apparent gusto that he must have made friends, for after having a smoke he was allowed to leave.

Several times I was asked to watch the preparation of *carne seca,* which in its pounded and shredded form is *machaca.* Hands wielded a knife so sharp that it sliced a tough slab of beef, back and forth with the grain, turning skillfully right before it reached the end and doubling back. When finished, there was one long, thin, continuous sheet of meat ready to be rubbed with lime juice, garlic, and maybe a little black pepper, ground chile, and salt, and hung or spread out under Arizona's broiling sun until it was as dry and as tough as leather. It keeps forever and is used, pounded and shredded, then stewed, as a filling for tacos, *flautas,* or *burros,* or scrambled with eggs. Some cooks, especially in restaurants, now skip the drying process entirely and merely stew and then shred the meat, still calling it *machaca*. Although it can provide a tasty meal, it will not have the taste and texture of the original.

By the late 1800s the Salt River irrigation project had provided the water needed to transform the arid landscape, and Roosevelt Dam, opened in 1911, assured a continuous supply. Today citrus fruit, melons, dates, and pecans flourish in the year-round heat and attract an increasing number of willing workers from Sonora.

Unlike Texas, where more is always best, the true Sonoran-style cooking is restrained in the use of chiles and unadulterated with other spices; even herbs are seldom used. The tiny, fiery wild *chiltepin* are used with moderation.

This is also the region of the green corn tamale. Made with fresh corn ground with cheese, fluffed with lard, and laced with fresh green chiles before being wrapped in green corn husks and steamed, it can be incredibly good. One afternoon my husband and I sat around the kitchen table in Adela Bacahui's Tucson home and watched while she and her teenage daughter made a batch for us. While the tamales were steaming, Adela's husband, Ramon, a master tile setter, came home and joined us. Friends and relatives dropped by, but while we were sampling the first of the tamales, Ramon, off and on, talked about his earlier life.

My mom was Mexican, and I was born in Sonora, coming to the United States as a baby. My dad was an Apache from New Mexico, and I was the second oldest of his thirty-nine kids. Since he was the only male left in the Bacahui family, I guess he felt as if he should do something to keep the name going. There are now over a hundred of us Bacahuis—a name taken from the word for both a little flower that survives in the crevices of the rocks on our reservation and "running water." The women in our family prefer the flower meaning; the men don't want to be any sort of flower, so for us it is "running water."

Unlike in New Mexico, whose early Mexican and Spanish settlers had several centuries of virtual isolation before becoming part of the United States, Arizona early on was a mixture of races: black mule-team drivers from Mexico, Chinese who came with the railroad and learned to speak Spanish, and of course the Anglo-American frontiersmen and those who followed after. I met many, like Ramon, who had forefathers—or -mothers—who were originally from the local tribes of the area. Even today, southern Arizona is a polyglot culture, although English and Spanish are the primary languages—and Sonoran-style Mexican food dominates.

Quick Bites
Antojitos y Tortas

TORTILLAS LIKE AFRICA

When Isaac and me squeezed dough over a mixing bowl,
When we dusted the cutting board with flour,
When we spanked and palmed our balls of dough,
When we said, "Here goes,"
And began rolling out tortillas,
We giggled because ours came out not round, like Mama's,
But in the shapes of faraway lands.

Here was Africa, here was Colombia and Greenland.
Here was Italy, the boot country,
And here was Mexico, our homeland to the south.

Here was Chile, thin as a tie.
Here was France, square as a hat.
Here was Australia, with patches of jumping kangaroos.

We rolled out our tortillas on the board
And laughed when we threw them on the comal,
These tortillas that were not round as a pocked moon,
But the twist and stretch of the earth taking shape.

So we made our first batch of tortillas, laughing.
So we wrapped them in a dish towel.
So we buttered and rolled two each
And sat on the front porch—
Butter ran down our arms and our faces shone.

I asked Isaac, "How's yours?"
He cleared his throat and opened his tortilla.
He said, "¡Bueno! Greenland tastes like México."

—GARY SOTO

THINK ABOUT THE "FAST FOOD" OF Italy, England, or the United States, and what usually comes to mind are pizzas, fish and chips, and hamburgers. For Mexican Americans it means grabbing a taco, a tostada, or perhaps a burrito. All are fast and quick to eat, even though not necessarily quick to prepare. And if made of good-quality ingredients, they are very satisfying eating indeed.

Almost as popular as these snacks made of *masa* (mixture of ground corn and water) is that Mexican sandwich, the *torta*. On Manhattan's West Thirty-ninth Street Mario made us a memorable sandwich similar to the *cemitas* he had eaten in Puebla as a child—crusty round rolls slit in two, then layered with fried potatoes, smoky chipotle chiles, slices of avocado, shredded cabbage, and thick sour cream. To get just the right remembered taste he even added one pungent leaf of *pápalo*, an herb he grows in his large garden in upstate New York. A ham and cheese sandwich may sound quite ordinary, but not when squished together in a thick roll and embellished with well-fried beans, sliced onion, tomato, chiles, and avocado. It's those surprising extra flavors that make *tortas* so magnificently different.

Antojitos—cravings or "little whims"—is the right word for Mexican snack food. Mexico is a country of people who are comfortable standing while eating. In towns of any size there are always street vendors selling quick bites of home cooking to passersby. You may find a thick patty of crisp *masa* filled with well-fried beans and salsa, tacos filled with a wonderfully rich stew of shredded chicken, or a quesadilla, the folded tortilla enclosing a wedge of melted cheese and the contrasting flavor of pungent herbs. The one thing all these *antojitos* have in common is that they include some sort of a tortilla made of ground corn or wheat that allows all but the more embellished enchiladas or burritos to be eaten directly from the hand.

Nothing translated more quickly and easily to Mexican-American communities than the food, sold on the sidewalk or from small neighborhood cafes. The offerings—grilled meat, stewed tripe, shredded chicken, fried pigskin softened in a red or green sauce, roasted lamb, spicy sausage, tongue, barbecued pieces of meat and brains from beef heads, a rustic, highly seasoned lamb stew, or succulent pieces of crispy pork—seldom changed whether I was in Pueblo, Colorado; Detroit, Michigan; or North Fair Oaks, south of San Francisco. In Texas and Oregon tacos *al pastor* was added to the list; they are made by roasting pork vertically on a spit next to a small flame. In Huntington Park outside of Los Angeles you can get tacos filled with *machaca,* dried shredded beef; with *picadillo,* a minced meat stew with potatoes, carrots, and raisins simmered in a deep-red sauce of guajillo chiles; with *tinga,* shredded beef, braised with chipotle chiles, as well as almost any other filling.

Along the border states of Texas, Arizona, and New Mexico, floppy flour tortillas are the wrappings, and the fillings are much less varied. The simplest ones are burritos filled with well-fried beans and maybe a little onion, cheese, and salsa. My favorites were those with *chile con carne,* or, as it is called in New Mexico, *carne con chile.* Like most tacos, they can be eaten out of hand. I tried many burritos, though, where I needed a plate and a fork, especially with the larger *burros* that were crammed with the ultimate amount of meat, rice, beans, chopped lettuce, guacamole, sour cream, and salsa, and often served enchilada-style with a chile sauce over all.

It was in the Southwest that I mainly encountered crispy-fried tacos, which had little resemblance to the famous supermarket taco shells. And as a grand variation on the theme, Arizona cooks crisped up their filled flour *burros* and created chimichangas.

I sampled all of these and a multitude of other *masa* snacks, and seldom could I settle for just one, whether around a kitchen table or in a little cafe, at a taco stand or a neighborhood restaurant. As Ray Aguilera explained to me one cold morning in Pueblo, Colorado, when we went out to get a late breakfast at his favorite spot, "This is home cooking; the women are just cooking for a larger family and are able to offer more choices. I was born here, but so many men when they first come to the United States are without their families, and places like this are the closest they can be to the familiar flavors of Mexico."

Corn Tortillas
Tortillas de Maíz

MAKES 14 TO 16   *Flour tortillas may be the foundation of Mexican border cooking, but for the majority of Mexican Americans there is no tortilla unless it is made of ground corn. Coming from Oaxaca as a ten-year-old, Susy Torres never realized until the first time she landed at the airport in Los Angeles that there was even such a thing as a flour tortilla.*

Store-bought, factory-made tortillas, especially if quite fresh from a tortilleria (tortilla factory), are usually best to use in enchiladas and in any dish where the tortilla is fried or cooked. Most cooks even use them for soft tacos. They can be reheated and used to accompany your meal, but this is a time when home-made tortillas are a special treat. There is no excuse not to make these occasionally. Fresh-ground masa, *the dough used to make corn tortillas, is now available in any community with a sizable Mexican population. Fresh* masa *usually comes in five- or ten-pound plastic bags; use what you need and form the rest into smaller portions and freeze. (Note that tortillas made from frozen* masa *will be chewier.) Otherwise,* masa harina, *or corn flour (not cornmeal), is carried in virtually all grocery stores and can be made into dough by adding water. The brand that Quaker puts out is quite good.*

The only other item you need is a tortilla press. This is made of metal and has two flat plates hinged at one side so that the top plate can be lifted and lowered to flatten a small ball of masa. *It's much easier than pressing by hand and, once you get the hang of it, quite a lot of fun. Presses are available in both specialty food stores and Mexican markets. Sometimes when I have a small informal party, I have the guests gather around and make their share of the tortillas.*

Though they taste best freshly made, room-temperature tortillas may be reheated by wrapping them in foil, 5 or 6 to a package, and placing them in a 275-degree F. oven for 5–10 minutes. Or for just a few, I usually heat my griddle again and reheat for several seconds on each side. Tortillas can be frozen, if sealed air-tight, defrosted, and then reheated. Some cooks I know use the microwave to reheat frozen tortillas, but I haven't been too satisfied with the results.

1½ pounds freshly prepared tortilla *masa* or
  2 cups *masa harina* for tortillas

If you are using prepared *masa*, put it in a large mixing bowl. If it is a little dry and crumbly, work in a small amount of water at a time and mix until soft but not sticky. Cover with plastic wrap. If using *masa harina*, pour in 1¼ cups of warm water all at once and mix together with your hands. Knead briefly. The dough should be as soft as possible but not sticky. Cover with plastic wrap.

Let the *masa* rest about 15 minutes. Set out the tortilla press and 2 pieces of heavy plastic, such as from freezer bags. Place one of the sheets of plastic on the bottom of the tortilla press.

Check the consistency of the *masa,* sprinkling in a bit more water if needed, then roll into about 15 equal-size balls. Cover with plastic wrap.

Heat a large griddle, *comal,* or cast-iron skillet over medium heat.

Open the tortilla press and put a ball of *masa* on one sheet of the plastic. Cover with the other and gently press down the top plate of the press.

Open the press and carefully peel off the top sheet of plastic. Lifting up the bottom piece of plastic, flip the tortilla onto the upper part of one hand and remove the remaining piece of plastic.

Slowly slide the tortilla off your hand—don't flip it—onto the hot griddle and cook for a mental count of 20. The underside should just be freckled. Flip the tortilla over with a spatula or your fingers and cook for another 30 seconds, then back again to the first side for a few more seconds. The total process should not take more than 1½ minutes.

Ideally, the tortillas will puff up, but it isn't necessary unless you plan to open and stuff them. In that case, it helps to press the tortilla down gently with a towel after the last turn.

Stack the tortillas on top of each other as they are made. Cover with a towel or large napkin to keep them warm. If not ready to serve, they can be kept, wrapped in the towel and foil, in a warm, not hot, oven.

Serve them warm in a basket, still wrapped, making certain that they are covered completely after each one is taken to be eaten.

Quesadillas with Cheese or Mushroom Filling
Quesadillas
McMINVILLE, OREGON • MORELOS, MEXICO

MAKES ABOUT 12   *Take a homemade tortilla, fold it over a bit of cheese and a leaf of that pungent herb epazote, and grill, and you will have made the traditional quesadilla. Although quesadilla refers to the cheese filling, many other combinations of ingredients find their way inside. When she can find them, Martha Ruiz Gonzalez, who grew up in Cuernavaca, likes to use Oregon's wild mushrooms* or a filling of chorizo (page 170) and fried potatoes. But almost any taco stuffing, including seafood, can be used.

Quesadillas are perfect to offer with drinks or to serve with a soup or fish cocktail for a light meal. Try the mushroom-filled quesadilla with *Summer Garden Soup* (page 80), or a cheese-filled quesadilla with *Black Bean Soup* (page 95).

If you don't have a tortilla press, use Martha's technique: She presses the golf-ball-size pieces of dough between two flat plates covered with plastic cut out of a storage bag.

If you want smaller quesadillas to serve as party appetizers, use the bottom of a washed tuna fish can. Make 1-inch balls and flatten a bit with your hands. Put a ball on a sheet of plastic and cover with another piece. Press down with the can, forming a 3-inch circle. Remove the plastic and continue the process; you should have about 24 small quesadillas. Fill each one with 1 heaping teaspoon of filling.

2 cups fresh *masa* or 1¾ cups *masa harina* for tortillas mixed with 1 cup plus about 2 tablespoons
 warm water (page 108)
safflower or canola oil for grilling or frying

For the Cheese Filling

2 cups grated Muenster or Monterey jack cheese
12 or more leaves fresh epazote (see page 223)
 (optional)
1 canned green chile, cut into strips (optional)

Divide the dough into balls, 1 to 1½ inches in diameter depending on the size of the quesadilla wanted. Always keep *masa* covered with a damp towel so that it doesn't dry out. Cover the balls with plastic wrap.

If using a tortilla press, place a ball of *masa* between 2 sheets of plastic cut from a plastic bag and flatten the dough to make a thick 4- to 5-inch tortilla. Remove the top piece of plastic and place 1 tablespoon of the grated cheese on half of the tortilla but near the edge. Add the optional *epazote* or chile. Turn the other side of the tortilla over the filling and press the edges together. Cover with plastic wrap and continue making the rest of the quesadillas.

Heat an oiled *comal*, griddle, or cast-iron skillet and grill each side of the quesadillas for about 5 minutes. The dough will be crusty and flecked with brown. Try to serve immediately, but they can be kept warm in an oven on very low heat until all are cooked.

For the Mushroom Filling

1 pound mushrooms, preferably boletos or
 morels
1 tablespoon safflower or canola oil
2 cloves garlic, finely minced

1 fresh serrano chile, finely chopped, or canned
 chipotle chile, chopped
2 tablespoons chopped epazote leaves (page 223)
 (optional)
½ teaspoon freshly ground black pepper
sea salt

Wipe the mushrooms with a paper towel or dry cloth to remove any dirt or debris. Cut off any part of the stem that is dried and stringy. Chop the mushrooms into ½-inch pieces.

Heat the oil over medium-high heat in a medium skillet and lightly sauté the mushrooms, garlic, and chile for about 5 minutes. Mix in the epazote, pepper, and salt to taste, lower the heat, and continue to cook until the mushrooms are tender. Set aside to cool before using as a filling.

When ready, spoon onto the tortillas and fold. Cook on a griddle or fry on a skillet until crusty and speckled with brown.

QUICK QUESADILLAS MADE WITH STORE-BOUGHT TORTILLAS

*N*othing can be easier to fix than grilling store-bought tortillas (corn or flour) that are stuffed with cheese alone or combined with slivers of meat, chiles, onions, or salsa. Rub oil over the bottom of a heavy skillet or griddle and warm it over medium heat. When hot, lay in the corn or a small flour tortilla, heat it quickly on that side, and flip it. Add cheese, grated or in strips, and any other toppings, and fold the tortilla in half. As the cheese begins to melt and the tortilla to brown, flip it over several more times until it is crispy on both sides.

VARIATION: CRISPY QUESADILLAS   Quesadillas can also be quick-fried in a heavy skillet with 1 inch of hot oil. They should cook until they are lightly browned, about 2 minutes on each side. Drain on absorbent paper and keep in a warm oven until all are cooked.

MEXICAN CHEESES

*U*nlike typical Mexican-American restaurant food, which is invariably smothered with melted cheese, most Mexican cooks use cheese mainly as a garnish. The major exceptions are in the popular quesadillas and its use in the dairy-rich northern part of Mexico, where cheese soups and queso fundido (melted cheese dip) are a part of the regional cuisine.

continued

In obtaining the ingredients for Mexican cooking, good authentic cheese is my greatest challenge, and in many cases I opt for using a substitute.

Three basic types of cheese are used in Mexican cooking: melting cheeses, fresh cheese to be crumbled, and aged cheese to be crumbled or grated. The most famous Mexican melting cheeses are made in northern Mexico: the pale-colored, slightly tangy asadero *and the flavorful, almost white* queso Chihuahua. *Both can occasionally be found in good cheese stores or at some larger Mexican markets, but you can also use a good-quality Monterey jack cheese or the very special Sonoma jack or, in a pinch, the somewhat blander domestic Muenster.*

Queso fresco *is a soft, slightly salty fresh cow's milk cheese that is used, crumbled or sliced, in or on almost anything that will benefit from its acidic tang. Although no fresh cheeses are allowed to be shipped into the United States from Mexico, several U.S. companies are producing quality fresh cheeses, with California's Cacique* Queso Ranchero *and Chicago's Supreme brand seemingly the most widely available. I use a feta or a solid farmer's cheese in certain dishes if I don't have a* queso fresco *on hand.*

A queso fresco *that has been aged,* queso añejo *is a cheese with a definite tangy taste and very dry texture. It is usually grated, then sprinkled on top of* antojitos (masa *snacks), enchiladas, and similar dishes. I'm very fond of this cheese, having first become acquainted with it during visits to Michoacán, where a version,* queso Cotija, *was originally made in the small town of Cotija. I keep trying to find a good imported* añejo *in the United States but so far have not suceeded, although there are some satisfactory local brands. I'll keep trying, but in the meanwhile, I use a pecorino romano from Italy.*

Chicken Tostadas with Green Sauce

Tostadas de Pollo con Salsa Verde

AUSTIN, TEXAS

SERVES 4   *What do acclaimed chefs who happen to be Mexican cook at home? Most often for David Garrido, the executive chef at a pair of Austin restaurants, it will be simple* antojitos (masa *snacks) like this chicken tostada with its vivid sauce of chiles and tomatillos—full of flavor and so fast to prepare.*

Chicken Tostaditas (small tostados) are a natural companion to soups, especially smooth and rich ones such as Cream of Chayote Soup (page 84) and Corn and Zucchini Chowder (page 86). For a larger casual gathering, set out several different kinds of tostadas and have a pot of hearty pozole (see page 100) as a main course, followed by Almond Meringue Pudding (page 350).

¾ cup corn oil

4 store-bought corn tortillas, 4–6 inches in diameter

4 tablespoons olive oil

1 white onion, thinly sliced

1 fresh serrano or jalapeño chile, seeded and finely chopped

sea salt

juice of 1 lemon

1 6-ounce skinless chicken breast, cut in ¼- by 1½-inch strips

For the Sauce

6 tomatillos, husked and quartered

2 fresh poblano or Anaheim chiles, roasted (page 21), seeded, and roughly chopped

1–2 fresh serrano or jalapeño chiles, roasted (page 21) and seeded

1 garlic clove, sliced

¼ cup white wine, preferably sweet

½ cup cilantro leaves

about 1½ teaspoons sea salt

For the Garnish

½ cup crumbled *queso fresco*, feta, or farmer's cheese

4 sprigs cilantro

Preheat the oven to 325 degrees F.

In a medium-size skillet, heat the oil at medium-high temperature and fry the tortillas for 20 seconds, until crisp. Remove from the oil and place on absorbent paper to drain any excess oil.

In a small skillet or sauté pan over medium heat, cook the onion in 1 tablespoon of olive oil about 12 minutes, stirring frequently, until brown and translucent. Add the serrano chile and ½ teaspoon of salt and cook 3 more minutes. Stir in the lemon juice, boil briefly, and set aside on a plate.

Add the remainder of the olive oil and the chicken strips to the skillet. Cook for 5–6 minutes, until cooked through. Remove from the pan and set aside.

For the sauce, add the tomatillos, chiles, and garlic to the skillet and cook for 3 minutes. Stir in the wine and simmer until the liquid is reduced. Puree the mixture in a blender until smooth. Strain and set aside.

To assemble the tostadas, divide the onion mixture and the chicken among the 4 tortillas. Add 1 tablespoon of sauce. Sprinkle with *queso fresco*, place in the oven, and heat for 3 minutes. Remove, drizzle on more sauce, and garnish with a cilantro sprig.

Crab Salad Tostadas
Tostadas de Cangrejo
SANTA MONICA, CALIFORNIA • MEXICO CITY, MEXICO

SERVES 6   *One of the most enthusiastic and creative cooks I met during the last few years was Ana Lorena Zermeño, who at that time was managing Lula's Restaurant in Santa Monica, California. She loves to make various* antojitos, *or snacks, for her own parties, and this crab-topped tostada, brightened with olives and capers, is a favorite of her guests.*

For a simple supper, serve the tostadas only with a soup; Tomato Soup (page 83) or, in the summer, Cold Avocado Soup (page 74) would be a good choice. Drink a crisp white sauvignon blanc with your meal, and I confess I like to indulge in Cajeta Cheesecake (page 366) for dessert.

½ pound crabmeat, shredded (see Note)
4 ripe Italian plum tomatoes, finely chopped
½ white onion, finely chopped
2 pickled jalapeño chiles, chopped
2 tablespoons capers, chopped if large
3 tablespoons chopped green olives
¼ cup olive oil
juice of 1 lime
sea salt and freshly ground black pepper

For the Tostadas
6 6-inch corn tortillas
¾ cup corn oil
1 avocado, sliced in half and seeded
⅛ teaspoon lime juice
sea salt
about 2 cups shredded iceberg lettuce

For the Garnish
3 green olives, sliced, or flat-leaf parsley leaves
   (optional)

In a medium-size skillet, heat the oil at medium-high heat and fry the tortillas for 20 seconds, until crisp. Remove from the oil and place on absorbent paper to drain.

Lightly toss the crabmeat together with the tomatoes, onion, jalapeños, capers, and olives. Sprinkle with the olive oil and lime juice, and season to taste with salt and pepper. Toss the mixture well and chill, covered, in the refrigerator for at least 30 minutes.

When ready to serve, mash the avocado pulp with the lime juice and a sprinkle of salt. Coat each tostada with this avocado paste. Add a layer of lettuce and top with the crab salad.

Decorate with the slices of olive or parsley. Serve immediately or the tostadas will become too soggy to hold the topping.

NOTE: With such a small amount of crabmeat needed, this is not the place to skimp and use surimi, a substitute for crab made of pollack or hake.

Tacos of Charcoal-Grilled Beef
Tacos al Carbon
SAN DIEGO, CALIFORNIA • SONORA, MEXICO

MAKES 8 HEFTY TACOS   *The provenance of these simple grilled beef tacos is the vast cattle ranches of those northern Mexican states that once encompassed Texas, but in the last twenty years their fame has spread. Taquerias serving thin sheets of skirt steak grilled over charcoal are plentiful throughout Mexico, and the similar fajitas show up in all sorts of U.S. restaurants. These have become so popular that menus boast fajitas of chicken and even shellfish—definitely a misnomer because the word fajitas refers only to a certain flat cut of beef that is the diaphragm muscle. Similar in appearance to flank steak or London broil, it can also be cooked in a similar manner.*

Steven Ravago, who shared this recipe with me, uses the first cut of the round—the most tender part. Many say the flavor is best if real mesquite charcoal is used or mesquite wood chips are added to the ordinary briquettes, but since this trend is depleting the borderlands of this erosion-preventing plant, I suggest using the mesquite beans that are available in some stores—or do without altogether. The steaks can be broiled in the oven, but that intriguing smoky flavor will be absent.

These tacos are very good with just the grilled beef and Chile de Árbol Salsa with Tomatillos (page 268) or with the Chunky Fresh Tomato Salsa (page 264). Serve with Griddle-Fried Onions and Chiles (page 253) and bowls of Cowboy Beans (page 226). To drink, set out pitchers of Hibiscus Flower Water (page 379), Sangria (page 380), and in the summer cold Mexican beer and Fruit Shakes (page 378) made with watermelon and water.

2 pounds top round steak

2 cloves garlic

½ teaspoon sea salt

½ teaspoon ground cumin

½ teaspoon crushed dried oregano, preferably
 Mexican

½ cup red wine

3 tablespoons safflower or canola oil

juice of 1 lemon or 2 limes

½ teaspoon freshly ground black pepper

½ teaspoon sugar

flour tortillas, warmed

ingredients continue

For the Garnish

2 cups salsa of choice

2 cups Guacamole (page 274) (optional)

1 white onion, finely chopped (optional)

1 cup chopped radishes (optional)

2 limes, quartered

Trim the fat from the meat, then pound it slightly to tenderize it. Chop the garlic and mash with the salt. Combine the garlic paste, cumin, oregano, wine, oil, lemon or lime juice, pepper, and sugar in a glass or stainless-steel bowl. Add the meat to the marinade, turning several times so it is thoroughly coated. Cover and refrigerate, turning occasionally, for about 6 hours. When almost ready to cook, remove the meat from the marinade and set both aside. Bring the meat to room temperature if possible.

Light a charcoal fire and let it burn until the coals are evenly white and quite hot.

Grill the meat until cooked as you like it *(al gusto)*, usually 2–3 minutes per side, depending on the thickness of the meat and the heat of the fire. Set the steak on a cutting board, brush on the remaining marinade, and let the meat stand, covered with aluminum foil, a minute or so to reabsorb the juices.

When ready to serve, cut the meat across the grain at a slight angle into thin slices and heap on a heated platter with a pile of hot tortillas close by. Have everyone fix their own tacos. Pile some of the meat on a tortilla, add salsa and other condiments, wrap it up, and start eating.

Tacos of Crispy Pork Bits
Carnitas
SACRAMENTO, CALIFORNIA • MICHOACÁN, MEXICO

SERVES 6 TO 8 WITH SEVERAL APIECE Carnitas, *literally "little meats," are one of the splendid specialties of central Mexico, especially the state of Michoacán. Large pieces of pork are boiled in seasoned oil until tender on the inside and with a crispy exterior. They are then usually shredded, daubed with salsa, and crammed into a freshly made tortilla. It is a dish that gives strength to weary spirits. These tasty nuggets of pork can also be used in burritos and enchiladas.*

Not being a big meat eater, I am always perplexed that I succumb so easily to the tantalizing taste of carnitas—*a taste that owes much to its wicked fat content. Val Hermocillo, whose mother was from Morelia, Michoacán, devised a way to cook the pork, maximizing that flavor—not the fat. The meat is first boiled in water, then browned in the oven with orange juice and Dr Pepper.*

4 pounds boneless pork shoulder, butt or meaty
    country-style ribs
2 white onions, quartered
6 cloves garlic
2 teaspoons dried oregano, preferably Mexican
2–3 canned whole pickled jalapeño chiles
sea salt
¾ cup Dr Pepper or Coca-Cola
¾ cup orange juice

zest or peel of ½ orange, cut in narrow 1-inch-
    long strips
freshly ground black pepper

For the Tacos

store-bought corn or flour tortillas, warmed
Guacamole (page 274)
1 or more salsas of choice

Trim off much of the excess fat from the outside of the meat but leave the thin inner strips. Cut into irregular chunks approximately 1½ inches square.

Place the meat in a wide, heavy pot, such as a Dutch oven or cast-iron skillet, with a lid. Cover with water by ½ inch—no more. Bring to a boil over medium-high heat and skim off any foam that may rise to the surface. Add the onions, garlic, oregano, chiles, and salt to taste. When the water begins to boil again, lower the heat and simmer, partially covered, about 1 hour, until the meat is almost tender. A bit more water might be needed if the pork is still tough. Stir occasionally. If there is liquid remaining in the pan when the meat is ready, turn up the heat and boil until it is all evaporated, but watch the meat so that it doesn't scorch.

Preheat the oven to 450 degrees F. Remove the chiles from the pot. Add the soda pop, orange juice, zest, pepper, and any needed additional salt, and mix well with the pork. If the meat is not in a single layer, it should be put into a flatter pan so that it can brown evenly. Bake, uncovered, about 30–40 minutes, until the meat is crispy and glazed with the syrup. The meat will have to be stirred often because the sugar in the soda and orange juice will burn easily.

Drain off any accumulated melted fat and put the *carnitas* in a serving dish. Scoop the *carnitas* up with the tortillas, add some chunky *guacamole,* and fold into the tacos with lots of salsa. Chunky Fresh Tomato Salsa (page 264), *Chile de Árbol* Salsa with Tomatillos (page 268), or any other salsa will provide a lift. Well-Fried Beans (page 227) and Mexican Red Rice (page 235) are a traditional combination to be served alongside.

Fish Tacos Ensenada-Style

Tacos de Pescado Estilo Ensenada

SAN DIEGO, CALIFORNIA • BAJA CALIFORNIA NORTE, MEXICO

MAKES 10, ENOUGH FOR 3 OR 4 HUNGRY EATERS *The key to Steven Ravago's fish tacos is their simplicity. With their crisp exterior and moist flesh, the fried fish are delicious.*

If you are on a strict diet, the fish can be grilled or broiled. Marinate lightly with lime juice, oil, and garlic. The flesh, though flavorful, tends to be a little drier. The tacos are served with small bowls of different condiments so that everyone can create a meal to their own liking.

Tacos like this are usually served as a single-course meal at the little taco stands up and down the Pacific Coast between Los Angeles and Ensenada in Baja California Norte. Hungry eaters may also order a Return-to-Life Seafood Cocktail (page 63), and all can be washed down with a very cold Mexican lager beer such as Superior or Bohemia. For a nonfish accompaniment, Corn and Zucchini Chowder (page 86) would be my choice to complete the menu.

For the Condiments

½ red onion

¼ cup fresh lime juice

1 cup shredded cabbage

1 cup Chunky Fresh Tomato Salsa (page 264)

½ cup chopped cilantro leaves

1 cup Mexican *crema* (page 23) or sour cream
thinned with milk

1 cup Guacamole (page 274) (optional)

3 limes, quartered

1 cup all-purpose flour

about ½ teaspoon sea salt

½ teaspoon freshly ground black pepper

⅔ cups milk or beer at room temperature

safflower or canola oil for deep frying

1 pound red snapper fillets or any firm-fleshed
white fish, cut into large bite-size pieces

10 store-bought corn tortillas

Cut the onion in half vertically and thinly slice into half-moon-shaped pieces. Place in a strainer and pour boiling water over them. Drain and set aside in a small bowl with the lime juice, stirring from time to time. Add salt before serving.

Put the marinated onions, shredded cabbage, salsa, cilantro, *crema*, guacamole, and quartered limes in small bowls to be served at the table.

Mix the flour with the salt and pepper to taste in a mixing bowl and gradually add the milk or beer, mixing until it is the consistency of pancake batter. Let the batter rest for 10 minutes.

Pour the oil in a deep, heavy skillet at least 1 inch deep (or use a deep fryer if you have one) and heat until the oil is very hot—375 degrees F. (see Note). Depending on the stove, it may take 6–8 minutes. Dredge the fish fillet pieces, 1 at a time, in the batter. Carefully lay them in the hot oil and fry to a pale golden brown. Drain on absorbent paper. Cooked pieces can be arranged on a serving platter and kept warm in a 200-degree F. oven for 5–10 minutes.

While frying the fish, heat the corn tortillas on an ungreased griddle, then place them in a clean cloth-lined basket and keep warm in the oven.

When the fish are ready, set everything out, assemble the tacos, and start eating.

NOTE: Don't shy away from deep-fried fish because you think it is bound to be greasy. The trick is to use a good-quality vegetable oil that is hot enough so that it cooks the fish but doesn't penetrate the batter. Heat the oil to 375 degrees F., if possible, using a cooking thermometer to monitor the heat. If you don't have one, drop a small piece of bread into the oil. The oil should foam before the bread turns light brown, which will be in 20 seconds if the oil is hot enough. Since you may have to fry the fish in batches, make sure that the oil maintains an even temperature. It helps if with every piece of fish you take from the oil, you add another slice.

Cascabel Chile–Sauced Tacos
Tacos de San Luis Potosí
SANTA MONICA, CALIFORNIA • SAN LUIS POTOSÍ, MEXICO

SERVES 8 AS AN APPETIZER   *Tacos are one of those superb combinations of a tortilla wrapped around a filling with some sort of salsa that lends itself to infinite variations. This version of Ana Lorena Zermeño's is similar to those sold by the ubiquitous food vendors of San Luis Potosí in the central region of Mexico. Like an enchilada, the tortillas are first dipped in a sauce of chiles and then quick-fried before being plumped with cheese. Tiny cubes of sweet carrots and potatoes mingled with a generous amount of spicy chorizo (Mexican sausage) top the tacos, making this definitely a dish to eat with a fork.*

For a simple meal, partner these tacos with the Jicama, Melon, and Orange Salad (page 57) or make them a part of an informal buffet with one or more other kinds of tacos. Cactus Salad (page 54) and Well-Fried Beans (page 227), followed by Chocolate Rice Pudding (page 354) would be good complements to the meal. A rich dark Negra Modelo beer goes down well with this hearty meal.

For the Sauce

2 tablespoons safflower or canola oil

4 ounces dried cascabel chile (about 20), seeded and deveined

1 small white onion

2 cloves garlic

1 bay leaf

sea salt

For the Tacos

1 pound Mexican chorizo (page 170), crumbled

1 cup plus 1 tablespoon safflower or canola oil for frying

2 medium-size new potatoes, cooked and cut into small cubes

4 carrots, peeled, cooked, and cut into small cubes

12 store-bought corn tortillas

2 cups grated Monterey jack cheese

2 cups shredded lettuce

Warm the oil in a medium-size skillet and fry the chiles for 2 minutes over medium heat, stirring constantly to avoid burning. Drain and cool slightly.

Put the chiles in a blender or food processor with the onion, garlic, bay leaf, salt, and 1½ cups of water. Blend until smooth.

In a medium-size skillet, sauté the chorizo in 1 tablespoon of oil over medium heat until well cooked. Stir in the potatoes and carrots, and fry until they begin to brown. Remove with a slotted spoon and keep warm. Discard all but 1 tablespoon of the oil. Strain the sauce into the hot oil, stir, and let it thicken for 3–4 minutes. Everything can be made to this point and re-heated before continuing making the tacos.

In another medium-size skillet, heat 1 cup of oil over medium heat. Dip the tortillas in the chile sauce, then immediately fry in the hot oil for about 10 seconds on each side. The tortillas should still be soft. As each tortilla is fried, place it on a plate, spoon some cheese in the center, and roll it to form a taco.

Arrange a bed of the shredded lettuce on a platter. Place the tacos on the lettuce and cover with the vegetables and chorizo. Serve immediately.

NOTE: If not using your own homemade chorizo (see page 170), make certain that you buy it freshly made from your butcher: most plastic-wrapped commercial brands are filled with mainly chopped pork fat and acrid-tasting chile powder. If the chorizo is eliminated altogether, this becomes an exceptionally delicious vegetarian dish.

Crispy Chicken Tacos
Tacos Dorados de Pollo
PHOENIX, ARIZONA

SERVES 4 TO 6 AS A MAIN COURSE *"Just like eating crunchy chicken salad" is the way Miguel describes the traditional Arizona tacos of his aunt, Linda Mendivil. I found similar ones in California around San Diego, and in Texas they were usually filled with various versions of picadillo, a mixture of coarse ground or shredded meat textured with nuts, raisins, or potatoes. They all use corn tortillas that are first softened in hot oil and then folded over and stuffed before the final quick frying. It is not much more difficult than using the packaged taco shells—and much better.*

Serve bowls of different salsas. Chunky Fresh Tomato Salsa (page 264) is the traditional favorite, but Chipotle Salsa with Radishes and Two Kinds of Tomatoes (page 270) provides a much different flavor. Some Avocado Salsa (page 276) and thick Mexican crema (page 23) or sour cream are always welcome. Well-Fried Beans (page 227) or perhaps a bowl of Corn and Zucchini Chowder (page 86) is all that is needed to complete a light but satisfying supper.

For the Filling

1–2 tablespoons safflower or canola oil

1 medium white onion, cut in half vertically and thinly sliced

4 fresh serrano or jalapeño chiles, seeded and minced

3½ pounds whole chicken or 1½ pounds chicken breasts, poached and shredded (see Note)

sea salt and freshly ground black pepper

1 cup canned tomato pieces with some juice

For the Tacos

oil for frying

12 store-bought corn tortillas

2 cups shredded lettuce or cabbage

1 cup grated Monterey jack cheese

1 cup grated longhorn cheese

1 ripe tomato, finely chopped

Heat the oil in a large skillet over medium-high heat. Add the onion and chiles, and cook, stirring often, about 2 minutes. Stir in the chicken and salt and pepper to taste. Add the tomatoes and simmer until the liquid is reduced, about 10 minutes. Taste for seasoning and add more salt and pepper if necessary. Set aside and keep warm.

Heat at least ½ inch of oil in another heavy skillet over medium-low heat. Using tongs, quickly pass 1 tortilla at a time through the oil, just long enough for it to become limp. Drain on absorbent paper. Fill each tortilla with about 3 tablespoons of the chicken mixture, fold over into a half-moon, and secure with a toothpick.

recipe continues

Add more oil to the skillet if necessary and turn up the heat to medium-high (the oil should be 350 degrees F.). Fry each taco about 30 seconds on each side and drain on absorbent paper.

Remove the toothpicks and fill with the chopped tomato, cheese, and lettuce, or let the diners stuff their own.

NOTE: The shredded remains of a Thanksgiving turkey can be used instead of the poached chicken breasts.

Crispy Tortilla Flutes Stuffed with Pork and Nuts
Flautas de Picadillo
McMINVILLE, OREGON • MORELOS, MEXICO

MAKES 12 TO SERVE 2–3 PER PERSON   *These crunchy "flutes" made of stuffed and fried, tightly rolled tortillas are regional favorites of little restaurants close to both sides of the border. These are a favorite of Martha Gonzalez's young son and his friends. Although Martha never ate flautas when she was growing up in central Mexico, she learned to prepare them later when she lived in Arizona. As a filling she uses the all-purpose stuffing,* picadillo, *from Morelos, a mixture of well-seasoned shredded meat and nuts. Well-Fried Beans (page 227) are a natural accompaniment, as is a glass of cold beer.*

2 tablespoons safflower or canola oil, plus extra
  for frying
1 small white onion, finely chopped
2 fresh jalapeño chiles, seeded and chopped
½ pound lean pork, coarsely ground
4 medium ripe tomatoes, chopped
½ teaspoon dried oregano, preferably Mexican

¼ cup finely chopped pecans
about ½ teaspoon sea salt
8 corn tortillas (see Notes)

For the Accompaniments
Guacamole (page 274)
Tomatillos and Green Chile Salsa (page 265)

Heat 2 tablespoons of oil in a heavy skillet over medium heat. Add the onion and chiles, and sauté for a few minutes, until softened. Add the pork and fry until it just begins to become crispy. Stir in the tomatoes, oregano, pecans, and salt to taste. Continue to simmer another 5 minutes or so, until most of the liquid has evaporated.

Lay a tortilla in a heavy hot skillet and warm, first on one side and then the other, until heated through and just soft.

Fill each tortilla with about 3 tablespoons of *picadillo* and roll it up tightly. Secure with a wooden toothpick. Repeat the process to make the rest of the *flautas*. They can be filled up to 1 hour ahead of time.

Heat at least ¾ inch of oil in a heavy, deep skillet over medium-high heat. Working in batches, fry the tacos, turning them once until they are almost crisp. Lift the tacos out of the oil with tongs and lean them so that they drain on absorbent paper.

Serve immediately with Guacamole and a salsa such as the Tomatillos and Green Chile Salsa (page 265). Crumbled *queso fresco* (see page 112) and chopped cilantro are other good toppings. It's your choice whether to eat them directly with your hands, dipping them into the guacamole and salsa, or to cover them with the toppings and present them more formally on a bed of lettuce, and eat with a fork.

NOTES: Often store-bought corn tortillas are quite dry and will crack if softened in a dry skillet. It is best to pass the tortillas through hot oil, just enough so they relax and become limp. Drain on absorbent paper and then proceed to make the *flautas*.

To make the larger size *flautas* so popular in the United States, either use the biggest corn tortilla you can find or take two of the smaller ones and overlap them so the edge of one is in the center of the other. Fill and roll them both as if they were one tortilla.

Sopes with Chicken
Sopes con Pollo
NAMPA, IDAHO • JALISCO, MEXICO

MAKES ABOUT 15, TO SERVE 4 TO 6   *Lupe Quezada and her husband, Ausencio, grew up in a little town north of Guadalajara, near the state of Zacatecas, which has a climate and terrain not all that different from where they now live in Idaho. Though they both work weekdays, Ausencio always finds the time to do what he likes best, to sing. He is in great demand at weddings and* quinceañeras, *those special fiestas for young girls who are celebrating their fifteenth birthday. They also both share the cooking, but it is usually Lupe who prepares the day-to-day meals. A plate of* sopes—*small, fat masa tortillas like a boat with crunchy pinched-up edges—is often placed on the table filled with all sorts of good things, including leftovers from yesterday's dinner.*

There are hundreds of versions of these little boats made from corn masa *and quickly fried and topped with various ingredients. Cooks from every region in Mexico make them in different sizes and shapes and call them by different names, but they are all basically the same.*

Hot, crispy sopes *are a perfect way to start a small festive Mexican dinner. Or pass several kinds during a large party, alongside Crab Salad Tostadas (page 114). For a light supper, pair with a hearty soup such as Green Chile and Corn Soup (page 81).*

For the Filling

1 tablespoon safflower or canola oil
½ cup chopped white onion
1 clove garlic, chopped
1 large ripe tomato, roasted (page 22) and
  chopped, or ½ cup chopped canned tomatoes,
  drained
2 whole chicken breasts, poached and shredded
  (see Note)
sea salt and freshly ground black pepper

For the Sopes

2 cups *masa harina* (page 108)
2 tablespoons flour

1 teaspoon baking powder
¾ teaspoon sea salt
1 cup plus 2 tablespoons hot water
peanut or safflower oil for frying

For the Toppings

2 cups Chunky Fresh Tomato Salsa (page 264) or
  Chile de Árbol Salsa with Tomatillos (page 268)
1 cup crumbled Mexican *queso fresco* or feta
  cheese
1 cup Mexican *crema* (page 23) or sour cream
  thinned with milk (optional)
1 cup shredded lettuce or cabbage (optional)

Warm the oil in a medium-size skillet and sauté the onion and garlic until softened. Add the tomato and continue to cook for several minutes. Remove from the heat and stir in the shredded chicken. Season to taste with salt and pepper. Set aside until the *sopes* are made. This recipe may be prepared well in advance to this point.

Mix the *masa harina* in a bowl with the flour, baking powder, and salt. Stir in the water a little at a time. All of the water may not be needed to form a soft dough. Knead with your fingers until everything is well combined.

In the palms of your hands roll the *masa* into 1¼-inch balls, about the size of Ping-Pong balls. Make 14–16 balls. Cover with plastic wrap.

Put one of the *masa* balls on a piece of wax paper or on top of a plastic storage bag. Flatten it with your hand to make a patty ¼ inch thick and 2½ inches in diameter. Cover it with plastic wrap while you make the remaining *sopes*.

COCINA DE LA FAMILIA

Coat a griddle or large, heavy skillet with a few drops of oil and warm over medium heat.

When the griddle is quite hot, flip the *sope* onto one hand. Remove the paper or plastic and lay the tartlet directly on the surface of the griddle. You can cook 3 or 4 at a time. Let them brown lightly on the bottom, about 1 minute, then turn and brown the other side. They should be turned only once. The *sopes* will puff a bit; the dough inside will still be soft. Remove them from the heat.

While the *sopes* are still warm, pinch up the edges with your fingers to form a ¼-inch rim around the outside. When they cool, cover with plastic wrap until ready to proceed with the final frying and filling. The *sopes* can be made in advance to this point and stored, covered, on a flat pan in the refrigerator up to 1 day.

About 50 minutes before serving, reheat and set out the selected toppings.

Heat ½ inch of oil over medium-high heat. The oil needs to be very hot but not smoking. Add several *sopes* at a time to the oil and fry about 30 seconds on each side, until golden brown. They should be crispy but still moist on the inside. Drain on absorbent paper and keep warm in the oven while completing the rest.

Spoon in a bit of salsa and fill with the shredded chicken mixture or other type of filling and top with more salsa, crumbled cheese, or *crema*. Some also like to add a few shreds of lettuce or cabbage. The *sopes* should be served immediately because they do not hold their crispy texture very long.

NOTE: Don't limit yourself to the chicken filling. Combine anything that appeals to you or that you have on hand. Lupe likes to use a layer of Well-Fried Beans (page 227) and Mexican Chorizo (page 170) and, for one of my favorite suppers, with Mexican-Style Scrambled Eggs (page 332) on top. Any of the fillings for tacos and quesadillas can be used, and any salsas or toppings.

Flour Tortillas
Tortillas de Harina
SANTA FE, NEW MEXICO

8 TORTILLAS 11–12 INCHES IN DIAMETER OR 12 TORTILLAS 7–9 INCHES IN DIAMETER   *Forty-eight years ago Dora Chavez's husband made her a board and a special stubby rolling pin with no handles for making her large, pliant flour tortillas. For most of the half-century that* *they and their large family have lived in this home, Dora has rolled out stacks of tortillas twice a day. I could find no better practitioner to show me the secrets behind making the lightest and tastiest tortillas possible. To get an idea of the quantity she turns out, compare the three handfuls of lard that Dora uses each time she mixes the dough with the four tablespoons we use.*

Flour tortillas are definitely better when freshly made, especially when using as a bread. Just tear off a piece and scoop up any zesty thing on your plate that needs transporting to your mouth. Flour tortillas are especially handy when eating New Mexican Red Chile with Meat (page 174). They are also a treat with butter, and many of the people I spoke with in the border states had vivid memories of coming home from school and eating hot flour tortillas with peanut butter and jelly. Maybe not traditional, but it tastes good, so who cares.

2 cups unbleached white flour
1 teaspoon double-acting baking powder
1 teaspoon sea salt

4 tablespoons lard (page 291) or vegetable shortening

Mix the flour, baking powder, and salt together in a large bowl. Add the lard in small pieces and rub it together with the flour between your fingers until it is like coarse meal.

Pour in ½ cup of hot water and quickly work it into the flour and lard, adding more water, 1 teaspoonful at a time, if necessary to dampen all the flour.

Turn the dough out on a lightly floured surface and knead for at least 5 minutes. (Dora explained to me, "Knead it until the dough farts.")

Depending on the size of tortillas needed, roll into 8 to 12 balls, cover with plastic wrap, and let sit for 30 minutes.

Heat an ungreased griddle or large, heavy skillet over medium heat.

Place a ball on a lightly floured board and pat it down. The dough will be springy. Roll the rolling pin back and forth from the center out, rotating the dough every few strokes. If it is too sticky, sprinkle a bit more flour on the surface. Continue rolling until a tortilla the size you need is formed. It should be quite thin.

Cook the tortilla for 30 seconds to 1 minute on each side, until it is puffed and barely flecked with brown. (Dora says, "You are not making crackers; you want them limp.") If the tortilla doesn't puff when it's flipped over, push down on it with a towel and it should balloon up.

As the tortillas are cooked, wrap them in a heavy towel to keep them "warm and lazy." If they are not to be eaten right away, wrap the towel and the tortillas in aluminum foil and keep warm in a 200-degree F. oven.

If making the tortillas earlier in the day, let them cool, seal in a plastic bag, and refrigerate. Reheat a stack of 6 or so at a time, wrapped in foil, in a 300-degree F. oven for 20 minutes.

Cheese Crisps
Tostada Grande con Queso
TUCSON, ARIZONA

SERVES 4 OR MORE *Kids love this fun, fast, pizzalike creation that seems to have developed in Arizona during the last thirty or so years but is now found farther afield. The crisps are usually made with the very large, very thin Sonoran-style flour tortillas but can be easily adapted to a smaller size. Make these hearty snacks for impromptu, informal gatherings, offering them plain or with a variety of toppings.*

Cheese Crisps take only a short time to make, but they lose their appeal if not eaten right away, so cook only one or two at a time.

Although many find that more is better, I like to serve my Cheese Crisps with just a scoop of Guacamole (page 274) in the center and keep a shaker of chile flakes nearby so I can add a fiery touch between bites. For a casual meal, follow with a bowl of Hominy and Pork Soup (page 99).

2 thin 12-inch or larger flour tortillas, or 4 thin 7–8-inch flour tortillas, store-bought

1 cup grated longhorn cheddar cheese

1 cup grated Monterey jack cheese

Optional Toppings (1 or more)

4 small plum tomatoes, chopped

½ cup chopped green onions

¼ cup minced fresh cilantro

2 fresh, long green chiles, roasted (page 21), peeled, seeded, and chopped, or 1 pickled jalapeño chile, chopped

¼ pound Mexican Chorizo (page 170), cooked

4 slices lean bacon, fried and crumbled

1 firm but ripe avocado, peeled, seeded, and cubed

20 black olives, sliced or chopped

1 cup Mexican *crema* (page 23) or sour cream thinned with milk

salsa of choice

Heat the oven to 375 degrees F.

Place the tortillas directly on the oven rack and bake about 3–4 minutes, until they start to puff up and become crispy. Remove from the oven, sprinkle with the cheese, and return to the oven until the cheese melts, another 4–5 minutes. Remove from the oven and place on a large plate or round tray. A large cake dish on a pedestal is a convenient way to serve a big tostada and creates a dramatic presentation.

recipe continues

Spoon the selected toppings on the melted cheese or place in separate bowls and have everyone create individual Mexican-style pizzas. Serve immediately, with everyone breaking off bite-size pieces. This may be easier if the tostada is first scored in pie-shaped triangles before the toppings are added.

Three-Days-in-the-Making Beef Burritos

Burritos de Carne

CHICAGO, ILLINOIS • CHIHUAHUA, MEXICO

FILLS 8 BURRITOS OR 10 TACOS *When Maria Antonia Garcia Tasson was in the ministry in Texas, a friend gave her this recipe. The rich, robust flavors of the beef take three days to develop, but the result is this favorite burrito or taco filling of Toni and her husband.*

Pepper Slaw (page 53) is a natural companion for the burritos, along with Well-Fried Beans (page 227). And Toni likes the Japonés Chile Salsa with Garlic (page 269) for a complementary flavor. The Pineapple Cake with Ginger Icing (page 369) and a cup of Sweet Spiced Coffee (page 385) follow nicely after this homey meal.

The First Day

¼ cup chile powder
6 cloves garlic, chopped
5 tablespoons lime juice, strained
3 tablespoons olive oil
1 teaspoon sea salt
¼ teaspoon ground cumin
2½ pounds sirloin or round steak, trimmed of fat
  and cut into 1-inch cubes

The Second Day

1 28-ounce can crushed tomatoes
2 cups Beef Stock (page 72) or canned beef broth
1 12-ounce bottle dark beer
1 teaspoon dried oregano, preferably Mexican

The Third Day

3 tablespoons safflower or canola oil

¾ cup chopped white onion

3–6 fresh jalapeño chiles, chopped

10 ounces frozen corn kernels

1 cup sliced stuffed green olives

sea salt and freshly ground black pepper

For the Burritos

Guacamole (page 274) (optional)

Salsa of choice (optional)

1 tomato, chopped

¼ head of lettuce, thinly sliced

1 cup Mexican *crema* (see page 23) or sour cream thinned with milk (optional)

8 Flour Tortillas (page 125) or store-bought tortillas, 7–8 inches in diameter

On the first day, mix the chile powder, garlic, lime juice, oil, salt, and cumin together in a small bowl. Place the pieces of beef in a shallow glass baking pan and cover with the chile mixture. Seal tightly and refrigerate overnight, stirring it a few times if you can.

On the second day, preheat the oven to 350 degrees F. Combine the cubed beef in a large Dutch oven with the tomatoes, broth, and beer. Stir in the oregano and adjust the seasonings. Bring to a boil over high heat, then cover, place in the oven, and bake for 45 minutes. Uncover and bake an additional 45 minutes. Cool. Remove the beef from the broth and shred. Place in a large bowl, pour the liquid over the meat, and refrigerate overnight.

On the third day, about 1 hour before serving, pour the oil into a large skillet and heat over medium-high heat. Add the onion and chiles, and cook about 5 minutes, until the onions are transparent.

Pour the cooked beef mixture into the skillet, lower the heat so that the liquid maintains a simmer, and cook about 20 minutes, until the sauce thickens.

Add the frozen corn, olives, and salt and pepper to taste, and continue to cook for several minutes, until the corn is tender.

Set out all the condiments: the guacamole, salsa, tomato, lettuce, and *crema*—and plenty of hot flour tortillas. Spoon the beef filling on the tortillas and some lettuce and tomato. Add your choice of guacamole, salsa, or *crema*—or layer on all of them—and roll up, folding in both ends so the burritos can be eaten in hand. They also can be served just rolled, without tucking in the ends, on a plate, with the condiments spooned over the top. Any leftovers can be refrigerated and will be equally good reheated 1 or 2 days later.

Chimichangas

Chivichangas

TUMACACORI, ARIZONA

MAKES 6   *As anyone who eats at fast-food Mexican restaurants knows, a chimichanga is just a fried burrito. What isn't known is why a chimichanga is called a chimichanga, or in Spanish, chivichanga. Lots of theories but no facts.*

I've never been a fan of chimichangas, but in Arizona, where they are a culinary phenomenon, I finally found myself enjoying them, especially when they are homemade. The extra-thin flour tortillas, usually filled with a Sonoran-style machaca, or shredded beef, come out toasty brown; and the whole package is covered with a wonderfully thick red chile gravy or sauce.

Heading south through the lonesome emptiness from Tucson to the border town of Nogales, you pass near the abandoned Mission San Jose de Tumacacori, once a Pima Indian village.

On the other side of the old road there is a small museum depicting olden ranching days and a hustling family business, Santa Cruz Chile and Spice Co. It puts out some of the best chile products I've ever come across, including the robust pure chile powders I like to use in this rich chimichangas sauce.

This is a filling dish by itself, but for hungry folks a bowl of Beef and Vegetable Broth (page 89) makes a good start, or serve them both together.

For the Meat Filling

2 pounds boneless beef stew meat such as beef
  brisket
2 tablespoons safflower or canola oil
1½ cups Beef Stock (page 72) or canned beef
  broth or water with beef bouillon cube
2 cloves garlic, minced
1 medium white onion, sliced
1 bay leaf
⅛ teaspoon freshly ground black pepper
¼ teaspoon garlic powder
sea salt

For the Sauce

2 tablespoons safflower or canola oil
4 cloves garlic, minced
2 tablespoons all-purpose flour
⅓ cup ground mild or medium hot red chiles,
  preferably New Mexican
2 cups tomato juice diluted with 2 cups water
1 teaspoon dried oregano leaves, preferably Mexican
sea salt

For the Chimichangas

6 thin 10- to 12-inch flour tortillas at room temperature
½ cup diced fresh long green chiles, roasted (page 21), peeled, and chopped, or canned
safflower or canola oil for frying
½ head iceberg lettuce, shredded

For the Toppings

2 cups Guacamole (page 274) or sliced avocado
1 cup Mexican *crema* (page 23) or sour cream thinned with milk
2 ripe tomatoes, diced
8 green onions, finely chopped, or 1 small white onion, sliced
1 cup grated Monterey jack or longhorn cheese (optional)

Trim most of the fat off the beef. Heat a Dutch oven over medium heat, add oil, and brown the meat on all sides. Pour off any excess oil and add the beef stock, garlic, onion, bay leaf, and pepper. Bring the liquid to a slow boil, lower the heat, and skim off any foam that rises to the surface. Cover the pot and simmer until the meat is very tender, about 2 hours. Uncover, turn up the heat, and continue to cook for 5–10 minutes, reducing the liquid, but make sure the meat doesn't burn.

While the meat is simmering, prepare the sauce. Heat the oil in a large, heavy skillet over medium heat. Add the garlic and sauté for a few seconds. Sprinkle in the flour and cook, stirring, until it begins to brown. Remove the skillet from the heat and stir the chile into the flour. Slowly add the tomato juice and water, a little at a time, stirring well with a fork to eliminate any lumps. Add the oregano and salt to taste, then put the skillet back on the burner. Lower the heat to just keep the sauce at a simmer. Cook, stirring often, 15–20 minutes, until the sauce is quite thick. Serve hot. Or the chile sauce can be stored in the refrigerator for up to 5 days and reheated before using.

Remove the cooked beef, reserving the broth. When cool enough to handle, shred the meat with your fingers and set aside. Sprinkle with pepper, garlic powder, and salt, and toss to mix well. The meat can be cooked ahead to this point and refrigerated for several days. Add a little broth and reheat before using.

Heat the tortillas in a heavy skillet or on a griddle without oil until softened. Wrap in a towel to keep warm; or while still wrapped, they can be heated in a microwave, turning once.

Spoon equal amounts of the shredded beef into the center of each tortilla and top with the chiles. Fold over the 2 sides, then roll up into a fat package. Hold together with toothpicks.

Heat at least 2 inches of oil in a large, heavy skillet or Dutch oven, or use a deep fryer. When the oil is 350–375 degrees F., fry each chimichanga about 2 minutes per side, until it is crispy and a light golden brown. Using a slotted spatula, remove it from the hot oil and drain on absorbent paper. Keep warm, though they should be eaten as quickly as possible. Put on individual plates and let each person top his own chimichanga with the heated sauce and other toppings. Alternatively, the chimichangas can be arranged on a bed of shredded lettuce with a dollop of *crema* and garnishes of tomatoes, green onions, guacamole or avocado, and grated cheese. Serve the warm chile sauce on the side.

VARIATION: CHIMICHANGA HANDROLL   For an easier chimichanga to eat, mix 1 cup of the sauce or ¼ cup of chopped pickled jalapeños together with the meat, then spread it on the tortilla. Chop 2 avocados and layer over the meat. Sprinkle on some grated cheese, then wrap and fry the chimichangas. Between bites, the crispy creation can be dunked into a mixture of mashed avocados and sour cream.

Mexican Sandwiches with Breaded Veal Cutlet
Tortas con Filete de Ternera Milanesa
NEW YORK, NEW YORK • PUEBLA, MEXICO

MAKES 2   Tortas *are sold on virtually every city street in the Hispanic areas of the United States as well as throughout Mexico. Thin slices of breaded veal are one of the many fillings that Mario Ramirez likes to fix, but roast pork, ham, and chicken are just as compatible. Virtually anything goes, but the sandwiches almost always start with a layer of well-fried beans and include chiles and avocado. The rest of the ingredients can vary, but there is always something soft and something crispy.*

A refreshing Licuado (page 378) made with cantaloupe, strawberries, and orange juice is an ideal drink with this hefty sandwich.

1 veal cutlet (about 8 ounces), cut ½ inch thick
1 cup milk
flour
sea salt and freshly ground black pepper
1 egg, lightly beaten
1 cup fine dry bread or cracker crumbs
¼ cup peanut or olive oil
juice of 1 lime

1 cup Well-Fried Beans (page 227)
2 *bolillos, teleras,* or large crusty rolls (see Note), split horizontally
½ cup Poor Man's Butter (page 276) or Guacamole (page 274)
1–2 canned chipotle chiles *en adobo,* finely chopped, or pickled jalapeño chiles, sliced
½ cup shredded cabbage or lettuce

2 slices Monterey jack cheese or 2 ounces *queso*
  fresco or feta cheese, crumbled (optional)
½ ripe tomato, sliced (optional)

¼ cup sour cream or mayonnaise
¼ cup sliced radishes (optional)

Before cooking the veal, trim off any fat from the edges of the meat and lay the meat between 2 sheets of wax paper or plastic wrap. Using a broad, heavy object such as a rolling pin, pound it thin and flat. Soak in the milk for 30 minutes to 1 hour. Cut in half.

Using 3 flat bowls, place flour, well seasoned with salt and pepper, in the first; the egg in the second; and the crumbs in the third. Quickly dip the meat on both sides, first in the flour, then in the beaten egg, and finally in the crumbs.

Heat the oil in a large, heavy skillet. When it is bubbling hot but not smoking, sauté the cutlets over medium-high heat for 3–4 minutes on each side. Lower the heat if the meat is browning too fast. Turn the cutlets carefully so that the breading doesn't pull away.

Remove the cutlets from the heat and squirt with a little lime juice. Keep warm.

Spread the well-fried beans on half a roll. On the other half spread the guacamole. Build the sandwich in layers on top of the beans, adding the chiles, cabbage or lettuce, cheese, tomato, sour cream or mayonnaise, and radishes. Place the avocado-spread roll on the top and press down.

The *tortas* are usually served at room temperature, or they can be wrapped in aluminum foil and heated in a 325-degree F. oven for 10–15 minutes. With a sharp knife, slice the *torta* in half to make it into a more manageable size, and set out lots of napkins.

NOTE: The Mexican version is usually made of a flatter version of the *Bolillos* (page 310) called a *telera,* but any crusty French roll can be used. I have found the *telera,* however, in Mexican bakeries in both Chicago and Los Angeles. For parties, long baguettes can be split, filled, and sliced into individual serving portions.

Illinois Impressions

The Chicago I remembered from the 1940s and '50s was one of the most ethnically and culturally diverse of American cities. As a young girl I had been to Polish, Greek, and German neighborhoods. I remember my dad taking me to a Lucia Day parade and then to his favorite Italian restaurant on Taylor Street. Being of Irish descent himself, my father had many Irish friends in Chicago's South Side. When we went every morning early to the huge produce loading docks where my dad's business partner had his office, my young ears were spellbound by the confusing cacophony of what sounded like a hundred different languages. When I returned to Chicago to gather recipes for this book, the only changes I noticed were in the size and location of the ethnic neighborhoods.

I was surprised to learn that more Mexican Americans live in Illinois than in any state except California and Texas, and that Chicago is the third largest Mexican city in the United States. The first Mexican immigrants to Illinois were those like Lázaro Alvarado, who left his home in Guanajuato in search of a better life. He found work on the railroad in Illinois in 1897, and five generations and one hundred years later, his many descendants call this region home. Bennie Rosas's father arrived in Illinois about 1917. At that time Mexicans fleeing the revolution could cross the border freely. Congress had passed laws restricting European immigration, and the onset of World War I had produced a shortage of skilled and semiskilled labor. Mexican workers were in great demand, especially in the Midwest's industrial heartland. For the first time Mexican Americans came in large numbers to parts of the United States that had never been part of Mexico. They flocked to the automobile factories of Detroit, the steel mills of Gary, Indiana, and above all to Chicago.

These men built the railroads and worked in the steel mills and meat-packing houses, and on the surrounding farms. Bennie's dad was recruited to work for the railroad and sent by train to Illinois. Bennie was born in the boxcar where the railroad company housed them (living there until he joined the army and was sent to fight in Korea). During the Depression, all this changed. At least one-third of Chicago's Mexican population was forced to return to Mexico—even those who were born in Illinois and were now American citizens. Those who stayed lost their jobs and were deprived of social services. Even though those families came from different parts of Mexico, they became as one community in those sections of the city where they lived and worked, sharing what they had with one another. Catholic churches were opened on the south and west sides of Chicago and became their spiritual centers, just as beans and tortillas nourished their bodies.

But another war came. Again Mexican laborers were needed, and many of the new workers and their families remained in the United States after the war.

Something happened to the familiar dishes of Mexico this far north. They had to change. Beans, corn, and rice were still available, and, when they could afford it, meat and chicken could be purchased. It was the special seasonings—the regional chiles and herbs—that were missing, and through several generations of cooks, the Mexican food prepared in Chicago homes began to taste and look the same regardless of where in Mexico the family was from originally.

Now it's easy to find a wide assortment of these ingredients. The venerable Maxwell Street Sunday Market, which moved a few blocks over to Canal Street, is more Mexican than ever with a big assortment of fresh and dried chiles, tropical fruits, including the small key limes, and, in season, *verdolagas, quelites,* and other wild greens. For many Mexican-American cooks it has been a learning experience to use these. As Mona Garcia told me, "I'd never even seen a tomatillo and finally realized it was what my mother had called a *tomate verde.* Luckily, I had a neighbor who grew up in Mexico and explained to me that you shouldn't try to eat them raw but should cook them in sauces. I've even had to buy Mexican cookbooks written by Anglos to learn how to make a real *mole.*"

The Pilsen neighborhood on Chicago's south side has long been the "port of entry" for Mexico's immigrants, although first it was the Irish and then different central and eastern European groups that settled here and gave the neighborhood its name. The ornate buildings that still stand are testimony to the Czech, Polish, and Lithuanian architects of the last century, but today the storefront signs are in Spanish, and ice-cream vendors on the street corners in summer proclaim, *"¡Ah, qué calor hace! Pero aquí 'sta la nieve tan dulce para resfrescarse. Muy rica."* Oh, how hot it is! But here you have sweet ice cream with which to refresh yourself. Very delicious.

Olivia Dominguez's dad left Guanajuato fifty years ago, going first to Texas to work in the onion fields. "We were lonely there, nobody was in the streets, so we came to Pilsen. Here we have our church and can talk to all our friends on the sidewalk when we go shopping. Over ninety families from Mexico live right on our street, mostly from Michoacán, Guerrero, and a few from Jalisco. We all worked together to encourage the school board to build Benito Juarez High School here in our neighborhood so that our children could go to school together and not be bused to other districts." Even the Mexicans' love of bright, startling colors was apparent amid the stolid central European buildings. Geometric shapes painted yellow, purple, orange, and green decorate the five-foot fence enclosing her yard, and a gaily painted purple bench is on her stoop. Though Pilsen still has the highest density of Mexicans in Chicago, a great number of the families have moved to nearby Little Village or farther out to the more affluent suburbs.

We sipped wine and nibbled bread and cheese with Josepha Danenberger and her mother, María Concannon, in Chicago's northwest suburb of Parkridge. Maria, who was from Mexico City, married an Irishman, and when they came here in 1963, Josepha recalled that all her school friends thought they ate "really weird food—*pozole* made with a half a pig's head in the pot—and when we roasted our *poblanos,* the potent fumes really covered the neighborhood."

In a reverse family migration, Pamela Díaz de León's mother was from Chicago. While at Vassar College she attended summer school in San Miguel Allende and fell in love with a young farmer from Celaya, Guanajuato. They married in Boston but returned to Guanajuato and bought a farm; soon, however, Pamela's father was killed in a car crash. Her mother returned to the United States, leaving Pamela to be raised by her father's family. Spanish became Pamela's first language, and she grew up eating traditional Mexican food, although her grandmother would occasionally make pizza for her and her brother.

After Pamela graduated from college, she was one of twelve chosen to play basketball for Mexico at the Pan-American games in Cuba, but since it would mean giving up her U.S. citizenship, she declined. At the age of twenty-three she went to Chicago to live with her other grandfather in his high-rise apartment on Lake Michigan. She continued to go back and forth between the two countries for several years, working in both and learning new skills. Being able to find in Chicago virtually all the same ingredients she used when cooking with her aunt, Yolanda, and her grandmother in Mexico, whenever she finds time to cook she makes those same soups, enchiladas, and desserts she learned from them.

Mexican families have settled throughout Illinois and in the adjacent states during the past century, some remaining in primarily Hispanic neighborhoods, others becoming part of the mainstream culture. Wherever they live, Mexican Americans continue to come together on holidays. Each year on the Saturday closest to September 16, the date that marks Mexico's political separation from Spain, a large parade is held in downtown Chicago and in Little Village. On religious holidays thousands of worshipers attend mass and return to their homes for the traditional meals associated with each celebration.

Main Dishes
Fish, Poultry, Meat, and Lighter Fare
Platillos Principales

*And daily a man, the steward, set out for the ruler [his food]—two thousand
kinds of various foods; white tamales bound up on top; chili-red tamales; the
main meal of rolled-up tortillas and a great many things: his sauces—with
turkey, quail, venison, rabbit, jackrabbit, pocket gopher, crayfish, topotli fish,
tlaca fish; then every kind of sweet fruits.*

—FRAY BERNARDINO DE SAHAGÚN

Florentine Codex: *General History of the Things of New Spain,*

Book 8—Kings and Lords. School of American Research,

Santa Fe, 1954. Retranslated from the Aztec by Michael Coe.

THROUGH THE CENTURIES IT HAS ALWAYS been the sauces that dominated the main part of
any Mexican meal. The cooked meat, poultry, and even the fish are cloaked with sauce. If
there are leftover tortillas, they are dipped in a spicy sauce and rolled or folded around a bit of
something for enchiladas or are torn up, crisped, and cooked in a sauce making a homey dish
of *chilaquiles. Mole*—literally, mixture— is a quintessential example of a Mexican sauce marrying the indigenous ingredients of Mexico into a sauce of the nuts, seeds, and spices brought
by the Spaniards and adding the flavor and texture of chicken, beef, or pork. A few of these,
especially the well-known *mole poblano,* even contain a shading of chocolate to enrich the taste.
And there are the offshoots, *moles* swimming with vegetables or even with fruit, and the *pipianes* with their sauce thickened with ground pumpkin seeds. All the dishes still are represented
in the United States, although to save time the cooks often take the more convenient prepre-
pared *moles* sauces found on most supermarket shelves and add their own special ingredients.

Looking back, I doubt if I was ever served anything unadorned during my travels. I even enjoyed meals of Kentucky fried chicken smothered with a tasty homemade enchilada sauce and
hamburgers with fresh salsa—fast food made personal. Ready-made fresh or dried pastas are
another satisfying convenience food that many Mexican-American cooks have readily adopted

for quick suppers. With the addition of a few fresh shrimp or a handful of ground meat—and, of course, a compatible sauce—a perfect light meal is ready.

Another fact about the main dishes in a Mexican meal is that really anything goes. It primarily depends on the time of day, what ingredients are available, and how hungry you are. A big bowl of *menudo* or *pozole* is just as apt to be served alone for breakfast as for supper. Sometimes a pasta dish will be the forerunner to the main course; sometimes it is the main course. Tacos, tamales, or enchiladas can be quick snacks or the whole meal, and even a cheese-stuffed zucchini—with a sauce, of course—makes a satisfying central focus.

Fish

Sea Bass Baked in a Spicy Red Sauce
Robalo en Salsa Roja
SACRAMENTO, CALIFORNIA • MICHOACÁN, MEXICO

SERVES 2 TO 3   *Valerie Hawkins-Hermocillo's husband, Jose, loves Chilean sea bass, or corbinas, when Val bakes it smothered in a chile-enriched tomato sauce. Its firm flesh stands up well to oven cooking, and the mild, slightly sweet-tasting flesh readily melds with the flavors of the sauce, creating a very healthy and savory dish.*

I like to nestle a scoop of Mexican Red Rice (page 235) next to the fish so that it can mix with the flavorful tomato sauce, but Val prefers well-fried black beans and serves plenty of warm tortillas. For a simple menu serve the fish with Corn Cooked in the Husk (page 243) and the Pepper Slaw (page 53), or a Jicama with Cucumbers and Melon (page 35) served as a salad. Try an Italian Pinot Grigio with the fish or a pitcher of Sangria (page 380).

2 thick fillets of sea bass, 2 inches thick (about
  1½ pounds)
1 teaspoon safflower or canola oil
juice of 2 limes or 1 lemon

sea salt
1 teaspoon coarsely ground black pepper
¼ teaspoon ground cumin

COCINA DE LA FAMILIA

4 fresh serrano chiles or 3 jalapeño chiles, roasted
   (page 21) and peeled (see Note)

3 ripe medium tomatoes, roasted (page 22), or
   one 28-ounce can diced tomatoes

2 cloves garlic with papery husk on, roasted
   (page 22) and peeled

sea salt

sprigs of parsley or cilantro

1 lime, quartered

½ firm but ripe avocado, sliced

Preheat the oven to 375 degrees F.

Place the fish fillets in a lightly oiled baking dish. Sprinkle with lime juice, salt, pepper, and cumin. Let stand while you prepare the sauce.

Place the chiles, tomatoes, and garlic in a food processor and pulse a few times until roughly chopped. Add salt to taste and mix again. There should be a rough texture to the sauce. Taste and add more salt if needed.

Pour the sauce over the fish and bake, uncovered, about 25 minutes, until it flakes. Arrange the sea bass on individual plates and spoon on any remaining sauce. Garnish with the parsley and put the wedges of lime and avocado slices on the side. Serve immediately.

NOTE: On the East Coast, Geraldo Reyes, who has an addiction to the fierce heat of the habanero chile, uses one seeded, finely chopped, and roasted habanero instead of serrano chiles. Other firm-fleshed types of fish can be substituted for the sea bass. But always remember this Basque saying when cooking any fish, "Fish and guests go bad after two days and must be tossed out."

Red Snapper Veracruz-Style
Huachinango a la Veracruzana
SANTA MONICA, CALIFORNIA • VERACRUZ, MEXICO

SERVES 4   *This recipe for the classic Veracruz style of cooking fish has been in Ana Lorena Zermeño's family for ages. It is much simpler than any version I've made before, though it still shows the Spanish influence of olives and pimientos.*

Although the more easily found jalapeño chiles in vinegar, usually labeled en escabeche, *can be used to flavor this dish, the blond or light yellow güero is available in many supermarkets and Hispanic grocery stores and provides a color contrast. Güero refers to any light-colored chile, so the intensity of heat will depend on the variety of chile used.*

Though in Mexico this would usually be served with rice, Ana and her family prefer it with a scoop of mashed potatoes or little steamed new potatoes. With this festive dish, start with Tuna-Stuffed Jalapeño Chiles (page 36) or Bacon-Wrapped Shrimp Stuffed with Cheese (page 40). Creamy Coffee Liqueur Gelatin (page 346) provides a sweet ending.

1 tablespoon olive oil

½ large white onion, finely chopped

3 cloves garlic, chopped

2 tablespoons chopped flat-leaf parsley

1 red bell pepper, roasted as for chiles (page 21), seeded, and cut into ¼- by 1-inch strips, or one 2-ounce jar pimiento strips, drained

3 ripe tomatoes, roasted (page 22) and chopped, or one 28-ounce can tomato pieces with ¼ cup of the juice

sea salt and freshly ground pepper

½ cup pitted and roughly chopped green olives

2 canned *güero* chiles *en escabeche* or jalapeño chiles *en escabeche,* sliced into rings

1 tablespoon vinegar from the chiles

4 red snapper fillets, each 4–5 ounces and about ½ inch thick

For the Garnish

1 tablespoon large capers

sprigs of fresh flat-leaf parsley

Warm the oil in a large skillet and sauté the onions, garlic, parsley, and bell pepper over medium heat for about 5 minutes.

Add the tomatoes, lower the heat, and simmer for 5 minutes. Season to taste with salt and pepper. Add the olives, *güero* chiles, and vinegar, and continue to simmer 10 more minutes.

Once the tomato sauce is cooked, put the snapper fillets carefully into the skillet and blanket them with the sauce. Let them poach gently for 7–10 minutes, basting them frequently but carefully so they don't break apart. Serve smothered with the sauce and topped with capers and parsley.

Sautéed Fish Fillets with Garlic
Pescado al Mojo de Ajo
DETROIT, MICHIGAN • GUERRERO, MEXICO

SERVES 4   *The winters in Detroit are harsh, so Florencio Perea, a retired butcher, spends his winters in Acapulco, where he and his wife indulge themselves with both sunshine and fish so fresh that it still carries the aroma of the sea. One of the simplest ways to prepare it at home is, luckily, one of his favorites—fillets of red snapper briefly marinated in lime juice and garlic, and then quick-fried with even more garlic.*

Mexican Red Rice (page 235) is a natural accompaniment, as is Crunchy Cabbage Salsa (page 277). A Mexican beer such as Dos Equis XX goes down well, or if you prefer a wine, try Chilean Caliterra sauvignon blanc.

4 cloves garlic, finely minced

3 tablespoons lime juice

4 fillets of red snapper or rockfish, about 8
  ounces each and ½ inch thick

sea salt and freshly ground black pepper

½ cup flour

⅛ teaspoon ground cayenne (optional)

2 tablespoons olive oil

For the Sauce

2 tablespoons unsalted butter

8 cloves garlic, thinly sliced

1 teaspoon lime juice

3 tablespoons chopped flat-leaf parsley

Using a mortar and pestle, puree the garlic with the lime juice.

Lay the fish fillets in a glass dish, rub the garlic and lime juice paste over both sides of the fillets, and sprinkle with salt and pepper. Cover with plastic wrap and refrigerate about 20 minutes.

On a plate, mix the flour with more salt and pepper, and, if a spicy undertone is wanted, the cayenne. Put the fish on absorbent paper and pat dry. Dredge the fillets with the seasoned flour, shaking off any excess.

Heat the oil in a large skillet over medium-high heat, and when it is hot, put the fish in to fry, turning once when the flesh becomes opaque and starts to crisp—about 3 minutes per side, depending on the thickness of the fish. They should be flaky when gently broken with a fork. If needed, season again with salt and pepper. With a spatula, remove the fish to a hot platter or individual plates and keep warm.

Melt the butter over medium heat in a small skillet or saucepan. Add the garlic and let it fry slowly about 3 minutes, until golden brown. Add the lime juice and parsley to the pan, swirl around, and pour the mixture over the fish and serve immediately.

King Salmon Grilled in Cornhusks

Tamal de Salmón Adobado

SEATTLE, WASHINGTON • MICHOACÁN, MEXICO

MAKES 6 PACKETS, ENOUGH FOR 4 TO 6 *Lupe Ortiz Peach was born in Michoacán; the name means region of fishes. There, street vendors used to grill packets of tiny fish called* charales *that were first rubbed in* adobo, *a pungent chile paste, and wrapped in dry cornhusks like tamales. When she was still a small girl, Lupe moved with her family to Seattle, Washington, a state very like the one where she was born. Several times when she has visited me in the summer, we have substituted finger-sized pieces of freshly caught king salmon for the* charales, *creating this wonderfully rustic dish. Other species of fish can be used, but king salmon's dominant flavor is a good foil for the fearsomely strong sauce.*

In lieu of grilling, these salmon packets can be broiled in the oven or cooked on a griddle, but they seem to taste better cooked and eaten outdoors. Guacamole (page 274) and Crunchy Cabbage Salsa (page 277) are good additions, and lots of warm Corn Tortillas (page 108) are a necessity. I also usually serve Corn Cooked in the Husk (page 243). For a beverage, try the Cucumber Cooler (page 380) or pour from a pitcher of sangria (page 380).

18 large dried cornhusks, ideally at least 5 inches across at the biggest end

For the Adobo

3 dried ancho chiles, roasted (page 21), and seeds and veins removed

2 dried guajillo chiles, roasted (page 21), and seeds and veins removed

5 cloves garlic, unpeeled and roasted (page 22)

2 tablespoons mild white vinegar

2 tablespoons fresh orange juice

2 tablespoons fresh grapefruit juice

½ teaspoon dried oregano, preferably Mexican

½ teaspoon dried thyme

¼ teaspoon ground cinnamon (cassia)

¼ teaspoon freshly ground black pepper

pinch of ground clove

For the Fish

1½ pounds king, Atlantic, or sockeye salmon fillets, skinned, boned, and cut into 2- by ¾-inch strips

sea salt

For the Garnish

½ cup chopped white onion

2 lemons, quartered

Chunky Fresh Tomato Salsa (page 264)

Several hours before needed, place the cornhusks in a big bowl and submerge in very hot water, soaking until pliable. It helps to weight them down with a heavy pan.

Place the chiles in a small bowl, cover with boiling water, and let sit until soft, about 15 minutes.

Drain the chiles, tear into smaller pieces, and put into a blender or food processor. Peel the garlic and add to the blender with the vinegar, orange and grapefruit juices, oregano, thyme, cinnamon, pepper, and clove. Blend to a thick paste by pulsing on and off, and scraping down. A tad bit more juice can be added, but keep it to a minimum.

Rub ½ cup of the *adobo* paste on the salmon strips. Put the fish in a plastic bag or other container, close tightly, and marinate for 2 hours or more in the refrigerator. Set the rest of the paste aside.

When ready to make the salmon packets, drain the cornhusks and pat them dry. Select the 12 largest, or if there are not enough big ones, overlap 2 smaller ones. From the extra husks, tear off 24 strips ¼ inch wide, tying 2 together to make 12 long ones.

Remove the salmon from the refrigerator, salt lightly to taste, and divide the fish into 6 portions.

The next step sounds difficult, but it's really quite easy. Smear 1 spoonful of the remaining *adobo* on the middle of the wide end of the husk. Lay several portions of the fish in a layer over the *adobo*. Fold the sides up around the fish, tucking one under the other. Fold the narrow end of the husk over the filled portion and turn onto the wide end of another husk with the open end toward the center. Wrap the sides up around the packet, overlapping them, and fold the narrow end over the filled part. Use 2 of the strips to encircle the husks, tying them about 1 inch in from each end and around the narrow width of the packet. Repeat with the remaining fish and husks, and then wrap each of them in heavy aluminum foil. The salmon packets can be prepared to this point and then refrigerated.

About 15 minutes before serving, place the fish packets on a grill over medium-hot coals. Cook for 5–7 minutes on each side. Carefully open 1 package and test for doneness.

When ready, remove the aluminum foil, and have your guests unwrap their own salmon packet. Serve small bowls with the chopped white onion, lemon wedges, and fresh salsa.

Crispy Catfish Served with a Tomato Sauce

Bagre Rebozado en Salsa

ALLEN PARK, MICHIGAN • QUERÉTARO, MEXICO

SERVES 4 *Querétaro, where Florencio Perea spent his childhood, is mineral-rich high country pocketed with valleys. While still a teenager he worked as a jeweler's helper creating rings, earrings, and necklaces from the gold, silver, and luminous opals of the region. Not much fresh seafood ever found its way inland as far as Querétaro, but the wispy-whiskered river catfish were not too hard to catch. Florencio, now a retired butcher, finds the sweetly flavored farm-raised fillets of catfish at the supermarket and fries them up for an occasional fish dinner. The crisp, light crust seals in the natural clean taste of the fish and its seasonings. For a less traditional presentation, with fewer calories, the catfish can be baked.*

Wild Greens with Pinto Beans (page 240) make a contrasting accompaniment in taste, texture, and appearance. Any leftover catfish can be used as a tasty taco filling.

1½ pounds boneless and skinned catfish fillets
sea salt
½ teaspoon freshly ground black pepper
½ teaspoon dried oregano, preferably Mexican
4 tablespoons fresh grapefruit juice
3 tablespoons fresh lime juice
2 tablespoons fresh orange juice
1 teaspoon finely grated grapefruit peel

For the Sauce

1 tablespoon safflower or canola oil
½ white onion, chopped
3 cloves garlic, minced
1 fresh jalapeño chile, chopped

2 large ripe tomatoes, diced and chopped, or one
    14½-ounce can tomato pieces
sea salt and freshly ground black pepper

For the Batter

1 cup buttermilk
½ cup flour
½ cup *masa harina* (page 108) or cornmeal
sea salt and freshly ground black pepper
pinch of cayenne pepper
oil for frying, preferably peanut or safflower oil

For the Garnish

3 tablespoons chopped flat-leaf parsley or
    cilantro

Place the fish in a single layer in a flat glass dish. Sprinkle with salt, pepper, and oregano. Mix the grapefruit, lime, and orange juices together along with the grapefruit peel and pour over the fish. Cover and refrigerate about 1 hour.

To make the sauce, heat the oil in a heavy medium-size skillet. Add the onion, garlic, and chile, and fry until the onion is golden. Stir in the tomatoes and salt and pepper to taste, and cook about 10 minutes, until thickened. Keep warm until ready to use.

Pour the buttermilk in a shallow pan or bowl big enough to fit the fish fillets.

Mix the flour, *masa harina*, salt, pepper, and cayenne together in a pie tin or a plate with a lip. Pat the fish dry, then dip each piece into the buttermilk and dredge it in the flour mixture, shaking to remove any excess.

Pour the oil into a heavy skillet to the depth of ½ inch and heat to 350 degrees F. over medium-high heat. It should be very hot but not smoking.

Place the fish fillets in the hot oil until a light golden crust forms, about 2 minutes a side. The oil must always be hot enough to sizzle when the fish makes contact. Remove the catfish from the skillet and place on absorbent paper to drain off any excess oil.

Place the fish on a plate and drizzle the tomato sauce over the top. Sprinkle with parsley and serve.

VARIATION: BAKED CATFISH   Place the marinated fish in a lightly oiled shallow baking dish. Sprinkle with 1 teaspoon of chile powder, salt, and freshly ground black pepper, and bake at 425 degrees F. for about 20 minutes. Pour the tomato sauce over the fish and continue to cook about another 5 minutes, until the fish is firm. Sprinkle with chopped parsley and serve.

Prawns with Chipotle Sauce
Camarones a la Diabla
GIG HARBOR, WASHINGTON • OAXACA, MEXICO

SERVES 4   *Sweet but hellishly hot, this distinctive shrimp dish comes with wonderful memories for me. It was in the isolated coastal fishing village of Puerto Angel in the southernmost part of Oaxaca, Mexico, that Gerarda Torres, years ago, gave me my first Mexican cooking lesson. With sand beneath my feet in their two-room, palm-thatched home and beach restaurant, Gerarda showed me how to make camarones a la diabla on a small two-burner propane stove, soothing the fire of the chiles with a splash of Coca-Cola. It quickly became one of my favorite dishes. Through the next decade three of her girls, Norma, Licha, and Susy, came to live in our home in Washington, and I am now the "other mother" to Susy. Our family returns often to Puerto Angel, an idyllic spot to relax: a protected crescent-shaped bay with warm waters to swim in, soft white sand for stretching out and snoozing on, and all the seafood* you can eat. There are tiny red clams with just a squirt of lime, huge lobsters lathered with melted butter, fish caught less than an hour before and quickly grilled with garlic, and, of course, my camarones a la diabla, which I eat every day I'm there.

In Oregon, Martha Ruiz Gonzalez prepares her shrimp in a very similar manner, only moderating the chile fire with a bit of tomato sauce and using white wine instead of cola for the liquid.

It is messy to eat, but if you don't mind getting your fingers covered with sauce, leave the shrimp in their shell with just the heads removed. The shrimp stays very moist, and, even more important, there is an excuse to lick the rich sauce off your fingers. Along Mexico's west coast, Pepsi-Cola or Coca-Cola is often used for sweetener because sugar absorbs so much moisture from the air that it becomes caked. The cola flavor combines surprisingly well with the smoky chipotle chiles to create a luscious sauce for the shrimp. This is not a dish for the fainthearted, so add the chiles one at a time to taste.

Serve with White Rice with Plantains (page 234) on the side or in the center of a molded ring of the rice. I like to drink the malty Dos Equis XX with my shrimp.

1 pound large raw shrimp or prawns	2–3 canned chipotle chiles *en adobo* with a little
sea salt and freshly ground black pepper	sauce
3 tablespoons olive oil	⅛ teaspoon dried oregano, preferably Mexican,
5 large cloves garlic, thinly sliced	or 2 tablespoons chopped fresh oregano
1 cup canned tomato sauce	½ cup white wine, Coca-Cola, or Pepsi-Cola

Unless cooking the shrimp in the shell, remove all but the tail segment and butterfly by cutting them partway through with a small, sharp knife. Sprinkle the shrimp with salt and pepper.

Heat the oil in a heavy skillet and sauté the garlic over medium heat until golden. Remove and put in a blender or food processor. Put the shrimp into the skillet and cook briefly until the outside just turns pink and the meat is white. Remove and set aside. Put the tomato sauce, 1 or 2 of the chipotle chiles, and the oregano in the blender or food processor with the garlic and process briefly. Taste and add another chile if more fire is needed. Pour into the skillet and simmer for 4–5 minutes. Add the wine or cola, taste for seasoning, and adjust if necessary. Add the shrimp and cook 1 more minute.

Tequila Shrimp and Pasta

Camarones y Pasta con Tequila

SAN DIEGO, CALIFORNIA

SERVES 6 AS AN APPETIZER OR 4 FOR DINNER   *Since Steven Ravago's family has been in the United States for generations, it is the frequent trips to Mexico while growing up that have inspired him in his cooking. "I remember eating* carnitas *as a child, under a big tent, somewhere in Mexico. I remember eating incredibly wonderful roasted chicken with crunchy, buttered* bollillos. *It was times like these that made me realize that Mexico has the best food in the world. I want to cook it all." This festive shrimp dish uses pasta to capture the big, strong flavors of the ancho chile and tequila sauce.*

The light, delicate Cilantro Soup (page 75) is a good introduction to this shrimp and pasta dish, and don't be afraid to expand on the tequila flavor by serving a fine-quality tequila blanco such as El Tesoro or Herradura blanco during the meal. If you prefer a wine, a flowery, slightly spicy gewürztraminer, especially Washington's Covey Run, Celilo label, is a good choice if you can find it.

For the Chile Paste

3 large dried ancho chiles, stemmed, seeded, and
  broken into small pieces
1 tablespoon rice vinegar
3 cloves garlic
½ teaspoon dried oregano, preferably Mexican
¼ teaspoon sea salt

For the Shrimp

3 tablespoons butter or olive oil
½ pound raw shrimp, peeled, tails left intact

¼ cup plus 1 teaspoon 100 percent blue agave
  tequila
1½ cups heavy cream
sea salt and freshly ground pepper

For the Pasta

½ pound penne or other stubby tubular- or shell-
  shaped pasta

For the Garnish

¼ cup minced fresh cilantro

Place the chiles in a small bowl, cover with boiling water, and let them soak for 30 minutes. Drain. Transfer the chiles to a blender and add the vinegar, garlic, oregano, and salt. Blend until smooth and set aside. It should make about 4 tablespoons of paste.

Put a large pot of water on to boil.

Melt the butter in a large, heavy skillet over medium heat. Add the shrimp and sauté about 3 minutes, until just pink. Remove the skillet from the heat. Add the tequila and ignite with a wooden match. Be careful to stand back because the flame will be quite spectacular. Return to the heat and cook, stirring with caution, until the flames subside. Transfer the shrimp to a bowl using a slotted spoon and cover with foil to keep warm. Boil the remaining tequila in the pan for 1 minute, until reduced. Lower the heat and add the cream to the skillet. Simmer about 5 minutes, until it is reduced to a sauce consistency.

Add the chile paste and stir until smooth. Season with salt and pepper, then return the shrimp to the sauce.

As you start cooking the sauce, add the pasta to the boiling water and cook until just tender or to your own liking. No salt should be necessary in the water because the sauce is well seasoned.

Drain and transfer to a large heated bowl. Pour the sauce over the pasta and toss so that it is thoroughly coated. Sprinkle with cilantro and serve.

ABOUT BACALAO

*T*he name bacalao *is thought to be derived from the name of the island of Bacalieu near Newfoundland, but other experts say it comes from the Gaelic word* bachall, *which is a pole on which the cod was once dried.*

History records dried cod as being eaten as long ago as the ninth century, but it was the sea faring Basques from northern Spain in the sixteenth century who began fishing the huge shoals of cod they found while pursuing whales in the icy waters between Norway and Newfoundland, then preserving them in salt. During the next four hundred years this salted cod was an important nutritional and economic factor throughout Europe, but for these intrepid Basques it was much more. The fishermen from the region encircling the Bay of Biscay are superb cooks, with exclusive male-only cooking and eating societies. Even with all the fresh fish available, it is the dry salted cod that provides them with the basis of their favorite specialties—the supreme one being bacalao a la Vizcaína. *This dish made an early transition into Mexican cuisine: As could be expected, salt cod was one of the staples aboard the many sailing ships of the Spanish conquistadors, and the Basques were among the crews. In its new home, Mexico, the cod was enlivened with the indigenous chiles and tomatoes that the creative cooks quickly utilized in the dish that today is as much a part of Mexico's Christmas holiday meals as turkey is at Thanksgiving in the United States.*

continued

Today's cod comes primarily from the waters between Iceland and the east coast of Canada; unfortunately, it is sold mainly in closed wooden boxes or wax paper cartons that prevent you from seeing what you are buying. Until recently it wasn't difficult to find hook-and-line-caught fish that was brine-packed and dried in the open air; now most of the fish you get has been caught in nets and prepared in factories with the use of artificial heat and chemicals. It may be more uniform in quality, but that quality is lower. Look for the lightly salted, brine-packed, and sometimes even sun-dried cod from Nova Scotia or Norway, or the unpackaged traditional slabs of thick, ivory-white center cuts. Buy it when you find it, and you can save this delicacy (up to three months) until you are ready to prepare a truly memorable feast.

Salt Cod with Raisins and Macadamia Nuts

Bacalao con Pasas y Nueces de Macadamia

SAN DIEGO, CALIFORNIA • MEXICO CITY, MEXICO

SERVES 6 OR MORE   *As exceptional as the fresh seafood dishes of Mexico are, dried and salted shrimp and fish are traditionally eaten during the major holidays. Dozens of dishes using baby-finger-size dried shrimp and ground shrimp are served during Lent, and there are few Mexican families that do not serve the festive* bacalao a la Vizcaína *for either their Christmas or New Year's Eve meal.*

This version of Mexico's most traditional Christmas dish was shared with me by Ana Rosa Bautista, a very talented businesswoman originally from Mexico City.

When you first see that hard-as-a-board slab of dry cod with which this dish is made, it is impossible to imagine the gastronomic miracle that can be created. The salting process turns a bland piece of fish into something much greater.

Bacalao is usually served only with Crusty Bread Rolls (page 310), or other hard French-type rolls, but a leafy salad with some spinach or bitter greens is a good addition. Leftovers make wonderful fillings for tortas *(page 132), using the same hard rolls, slices of avocados, tomato, and, if your palate can take it, some sliced jalapeño chiles. Since this is such a festive dish, I like to serve a bubbly semi-dry champagne or, for something more sedate, a dry Riesling, and then end the meal with Ancho Chile Flan (page 364).*

The secret of transforming a piece of hard, dry fish into a masterpiece is in the soaking process to remove the salt. Back in the "good old days," you would simply wrap the dried fish in a net, put it in a fast-running stream around 6 o'clock one evening, pull it out at noon the next day, and start the cooking. Ana Rosa puts her salt cod in a pot with very cold water and refrigerates it from sixteen to twenty-four hours, changing the water every six hours or so. The only way to really know when the salt crystals have been replaced by liquid is by tasting. If it soaks too long, it will lose its special taste and texture, but if it soaks for too short a time, it will still be salty. For the last soaking period I always substitute cold milk. I can't say that it makes a difference, but it was the way I was first taught when I lived in Spain, so that's the way I do it. Totally close your eyes to any directions on a package that suggests you simmer the fish instead of soaking it to remove the salt, and always start this dish three or four days in advance.

2 pounds salt cod, soaked for at least 12 hours
3 tablespoons olive oil, preferably a good-quality
  Spanish oil
½ white onion, finely chopped
6 cloves garlic, minced
6 tablespoons finely chopped flat-leaf parsley
12 medium ripe tomatoes, peeled and diced, or 6
  cups peeled and diced canned tomatoes

3 bay leaves
½ cup raisins
¾ cup coarsely chopped macadamia nuts
36 small green pimiento-stuffed olives
3 tablespoons capers (optional)

Place the soaked and desalted cod in a pot of fresh cold water and *very* slowly bring the water to a simmer, about 30 minutes. Drain and break the fish into 1½-inch pieces and set aside.

Heat the oil in a large skillet or Dutch oven and sauté the onion just until it softens. Add the garlic and parsley, and continue to cook for a few more minutes. Turn up the heat, add the tomatoes and bay leaves, and cook about 5 minutes, stirring often so that the sauce does not stick to the pan. The mixture should become somewhat thicker and reduced in volume.

Shred the cod and stir it into the tomato mixture. Add the raisins and macadamia nuts, and continue to cook over low heat for another 15–20 minutes, until the mixture is almost dry. Stir in the olives and the capers, if using, and simmer until the flavors are well blended.

The last step is the simplest and the one that makes *bacalao* perfect for a holiday meal. Cover the dish and set it aside in the refrigerator for 6–12 hours. It will be dramatically better when it is reheated (adding a little water, if needed) and served at a later time; the distinct flavors of both the fish and the sauce are intensified.

Poultry

Drunken Chicken
Pollo Borracho
LOS ANGELES, CALIFORNIA • OAXACA, MEXICO

SERVES 4 *One evening while eating dinner at a Los Angeles Oaxacan restaurant with Aurelia Lopez Momo and her fifteen-year-old daughter, Josephine, they started describing how to inebriate the chicken for this dish. It was so wonderful to watch their faces as they relived inhaling the fragrance of frying onions and garlic, and the heady odor of the beer and chiles, that I became hungry all over again. The Lopezes typically buy a whole chicken and cut it into serving-size portions, saving the neck, back, and wing tips to make a rich soup broth. Just a mixture of thighs and breasts works well, though, and if you're concerned about calories, remove the skin after cooking.*

Accompany the chicken with Seasoned White Rice (page 233) or Green Rice (page 236) and a good sturdy bread in order to sop up all the sauce. And what would be more natural than to continue drinking the same beer?

2 tablespoons safflower or canola oil

2½–3 pounds chicken thighs and breasts

1 white onion, thinly sliced

3 garlic cloves, chopped

4 ripe plum tomatoes or one 14½-ounce can diced tomatoes

1 cup beer, preferably Dos Equis XX or an amber ale

2 sprigs fresh oregano, chopped, or 1 tablespoon dried oregano, preferably Mexican

2–3 pickled jalapeño chiles, sliced

2 tablespoons vinegar from the chiles

about ½ teaspoon sea salt

½ teaspoon freshly ground black pepper

For the Garnish
3 tablespoons minced cilantro

1 firm but ripe avocado, peeled and sliced

Choose a good-sized skillet with a lid or a big Dutch oven large enough to hold all the chicken. Warm the oil over medium-high heat and sauté the chicken pieces about 20 minutes, until golden. This may have to be done in several batches. As the pieces brown, remove them from the pan and set aside.

Add the onion to the still hot oil and cook until quite soft and brown. Add the garlic and tomatoes, and cook for 10 minutes, scraping the bottom of the pan and stirring occasionally.

Return the chicken to the pan, lower the heat to medium, and add the beer, oregano, jalapeños, their vinegar, salt, and pepper. (This dish seems to benefit from an abundance of black pepper.) Stir once and cover. Simmer for 20–30 minutes, until the chicken is tender and cooked through completely. The dish can be cooked in advance and reheated, covered, in a 300-degree F. oven until warmed throughout, about 20 minutes.

Serve on a wide platter or on individual plates, preferably with a lip to contain the sauce. Sprinkle cilantro on top and add slices of avocado on the side.

Chicken in a Piquant Tomato Sauce
Pollo en Salsa Chichimeca
SANTA MONICA, CALIFORNIA • HIDALGO, MEXICO

SERVES 4 TO 5   *How this unusual chicken dish, a favorite of Ricardo Villareal, became named after an ancient tribe of nomadic Indians is unclear. I can only conjecture that it is because the sauce includes flavors derived from different regions of Mexico, ingredients that would not commonly be cooked together, such as the olives and capers from Veracruz and chocolate from Oaxaca and Tabasco. Ricardo was born in Hidalgo, a rugged state directly north of Mexico City, an area where the Chichimeca Indians are thought to have occasionally wandered. In a seemingly chaotic fashion, both dried and pickled chiles are added to intensify the flavor of the chicken, and then milk and wine are used to mellow it out. Miguel has modified the cooking method a bit, but the ingredients remain the same.*

Serve this dish with Seasoned White Rice (page 233) and either hot Corn Tortillas (page 108) or Crusty Bread Rolls (page 310) or other crunchy French rolls. For dessert I like to serve Mexican Eggnog Gelatin (page 349).

For the Sauce

¾ pound ripe tomatoes, chopped, or 1 cup
  canned tomato pieces, drained
1 clove garlic, coarsely chopped
½ medium white onion, coarsely chopped
1 large dried ancho, California, or New Mexican
  dried red chile, seeded, deveined, and broken
  into smaller pieces
about 2 slices bread, toasted and broken up to
  make 1 cup
½ ounce Mexican chocolate, coarsely chopped
¾ cup white wine

For the Chicken

2 teaspoons safflower or canola oil
3–3½ pounds chicken pieces
1 cup milk
1 medium white onion, thinly sliced
about 2 ripe medium tomatoes or 4 plum tomatoes, coarsely chopped, or 1 cup canned tomato
  pieces, drained
18 pitted green olives
4 whole pickled serrano or jalapeño chiles
2 tablespoons vinegar from the chiles
2 teaspoons capers
sea salt and freshly ground black pepper

Put the tomatoes for the sauce in a blender or food processor with the garlic, onion, ancho chile, bread, chocolate, and white wine, and blend thoroughly.

Warm the oil in a large skillet and fry the chicken over medium-high heat about 20 minutes, until golden brown. Remove the chicken from the pan to a plate and lower the heat. Add the blended ingredients and cook over medium heat for 3–4 minutes, stirring often.

Meanwhile, warm the milk over low heat and slowly stir into the sauce. If the temperature is too high, the milk may curdle. Add the onion slices and tomato pieces, then stir in the olives, chiles, vinegar, and capers. Salt and pepper to taste. Return the chicken to the pan, cover, and cook about 45 minutes, until tender.

Garlic Chicken
Pollo al Ajillo
VICTORIA, BRITISH COLUMBIA, CANADA • MEXICO CITY, MEXICO

SERVES 4   *Garlic chicken is a dish that is in the repertoire of almost any cook with a Spanish heritage. This easy version of a recipe from Maria Elena C. Lorens cooks beautifully in an earthenware dish and can be served directly from the pot. It's best to keep the skin on while cooking, both for appearance and to keep the chicken moist. Most of the fat melts off during the first baking. If you're in a hurry and* *calories are of little concern, the chicken can first be browned in oil in a heavy skillet, then put into a baking dish with the garlic sauce for final baking.*

Serve with Mexican Red Rice (page 235) or small new potatoes to sop up the garlic sauce. Scalloped Chayote and Corn (page 244) is a good side dish. The recipe can easily be doubled or tripled and served as part of a buffet.

1 whole chicken (2½–3 pounds), cut into small serving pieces (thighs cut in half, breasts in 4 pieces), or selected parts	⅓ cup olive oil
	⅓ cup lime juice
	12 cloves garlic, cut into small chunks or slices
sea salt and freshly ground black pepper to taste	3 tablespoons brandy (optional)

Preheat the oven to 375 degrees F. Rinse and pat the chicken pieces dry. Remove any of the big globules of fat and sprinkle with salt and a good dose of pepper. Arrange, skin side up, in 1 layer in a shallow baking dish. Place in the oven and brown on both sides about 25 minutes each, basting from time to time with the melted fat.

In a blender, mix the oil, lime juice, and garlic. Process until the mixture turns white and is thoroughly blended. Set aside.

When the chicken is golden brown, remove the baking dish from the oven and drain off as much of the fat as possible. Turn the chicken skin side up and pour the garlic sauce over the chicken pieces, coating thoroughly.

If using brandy, sprinkle it over the chicken, stand back, and light the liquid with a wooden match. Stir until the flames subside. Bake the chicken around 20 minutes, until thoroughly cooked, basting occasionally.

Chicken with Spicy Prune Sauce

Pollo en Salsa de Ciruela Pasa

LOS ANGELES, CALIFORNIA • OAXACA, MEXICO

SERVES 4 *An amazing synergism takes place in the flavorings for this chicken dish: prunes, raisins, Coke, and chipotle chiles. Aurelia Lopez Momo's recipe dates back to 1943, when Coca-Cola first showed up in Oaxaca. What surprised me was how extraordinarily good this combination was when blended with the dried fruits. The sweetness of the cola drink goes a long way in diminishing the heat of the*

chiles. Aurelia fries the chicken in a quarter pound of butter plus oil; we've reduced the amount of fat considerably. For a richer sauce, you may want to substitute some butter for part of the oil.

Serve with Seasoned White Rice (page 233). A glass of a medium-bodied zinfandel complements the rich smoky-sweet sauce. Green Beans, Onions, and Tomatoes Bound with Egg (page 242) or another colorful vegetable make a contrasting side dish.

¼ cup safflower or canola oil
2 pounds chicken thighs
about 1 teaspoon sea salt
1 large white onion, thinly sliced
1 cup roughly chopped pitted prunes

1 cup raisins
2–3 canned chipotle chiles en adobo, roughly chopped
2 cans Coca-Cola or Pepsi-Cola

Heat the oil in a large, heavy skillet with a lid. Add the chicken pieces and brown on all sides, about 10 minutes. Season to taste with salt. Remove the chicken, add the onion, and sauté until the slices become limp. Pour off any excess oil. Return the chicken to the skillet, lower the heat, and cook gently for another 5 minutes.

While the chicken is cooking, put the prunes, raisins, and chipotle chiles in a blender with some of the cola. Blend until smooth. Continue to blend in the remaining cola.

Pour the prune sauce over the chicken, stir, and simmer over medium-low heat, covered, about 30 minutes, until the chicken is well done and the sauce thickened. Taste for seasoning and add more salt if necessary.

Remove the chicken to a hot platter and pour the sauce over the chicken.

Chicken Breasts in Green Sauce
Pechugas de Pollo en Salsa Verde
BROOKLYN, NEW YORK • OAXACA, MEXICO

SERVES 4   The pleasantly tart taste of tomatillos combines with the warmth of chiles to create a simple and satisfying sauce for chicken, a flavor combination that often comes together in kitchens where the cooks are originally from central or southern Mexico. Geraldo Reyes usually sautés the pieces of chicken until golden, but I like to substitute poached chicken breasts. If you use poached chicken, reduce the oil by half to cook the tomatillo sauce and add the chicken five minutes before serving.

This should be paired with Seasoned White Rice (page 233) and perhaps a salad of sliced avocados and tomatoes. The Red Radish Relish (page 280) served as a small salad is also a good choice. In Mexico I'd drink beer with this tart, tangy dish, but at home it would be a glass of sauvignon blanc.

For the Sauce

8 fresh tomatillos, husked and rinsed

¼ medium white onion

2 unpeeled cloves garlic

3 fresh serrano chiles, stemmed, quartered, and
  seeded

1 dried *chile de árbol,* toasted (page 22), seeded,
  and crumbled (optional)

⅓ cup plus extra chicken broth

For the Chicken

2 tablespoons safflower or canola oil

4 pieces boneless chicken breasts

sea salt and freshly ground black pepper

Heat a small, heavy skillet over medium-high heat, using no oil. Toast the tomatillos, onion, and garlic, and toss them around as they start to blister and turn black in spots. Don't worry if the pan smokes a bit.

When the flesh of the tomatillos softens, put them in a blender or food processor. Peel the garlic and add it, along with the serrano chiles, *chile de árbol,* onion, and chicken broth. Blend until smooth.

In a large skillet, warm the oil over medium-high heat and sauté the chicken until it is golden on each side. Turn the heat to low and add the tomatillo sauce. Add salt and pepper to taste. Let simmer, covered, for about 30 minutes, adding more broth if necessary.

Chicken and Vegetables Flavored with Pickled Jalapeño Chiles

Pollo con Chiles Jalapeños en Escabeche y Legumbres

McMINVILLE, OREGON • SAN LUIS POTOSI, MEXICO

SERVES 4   *This recipe combining chicken thighs with pickled jalapeño chiles, carrots, and potatoes is very similar to the classic* fiambre *of San Luis Potosí, Mexico—an extravagant ensemble of cold meats and vegetables in a vinaigrette sauce. In the version that Martha Gonzalez learned from her*

mother-in-law, who is also from San Luis Potosí, the dish is much simplified and served hot. Serve hot with Crusty Bread Rolls (page 310) or French rolls. I like to serve Chocolate Rice Pudding (page 354) for dessert.

4 cloves garlic, minced

1 teaspoon freshly ground pepper

sea salt

3 pounds chicken thighs

3 tablespoons safflower or canola oil

2 pounds new potatoes, sliced, or left whole if quite small

about 16 baby carrots, or 4 medium carrots, peeled and sliced into 1½-inch pieces

¼ cup white onion, chopped

1 tablespoon flour

5 pickled jalapeño or *güero* chiles, cut into strips

4 tablespoons vinegar from the chiles

½ cup sliced green olives (optional)

½ teaspoon dried oregano, preferably Mexican

freshly ground black pepper

Mix the garlic, pepper, and ½ teaspoon of salt together with just enough water to make a thick paste. Rub the garlic mixture on all sides of each piece of chicken and place in a shallow glass dish. Let it marinate for about 1 hour.

Heat the oil in a Dutch oven over medium-high heat. Pat the chicken dry with paper towels and add to the hot oil. Fry until golden brown on all sides. Remove the chicken and set aside.

Meanwhile, place the potatoes and carrots in a saucepan of boiling water. Add 1 teaspoon of the salt and cook for about 10 minutes. They should be cooked through and tender but not soft. Drain the vegetables and set aside.

Remove all but 1 tablespoon of the oil remaining. Add the onion and sauté until softened. Stir in the flour and cook a few seconds until it thickens. Gradually stir in 1 cup of water, the chiles, and vinegar. Return the chicken to the pot. Add the cooked potatoes, carrots, and onion. Add the olives, if using, and the oregano. Add pepper to taste and more salt if needed.

Chicken in a Red Sauce
of Pumpkin Seed and Dried Corn
Pollo en Pipián Rojo
TOPPENISH, WASHINGTON • CHIHUAHUA, MEXICO

SERVES 6   *In New Mexico Tasty Recipes by Cleofas M. Jaramillo (published by Santa Fe's Seton Press in 1942), Jaramillo instructs us to "grind together a handful of roasted white corn and two red chiles from which the seeds and veins have been scraped. Grind into a fine powder, dissolve in a cup of water, and cook until it thickens. Fry quail or spring chicken and add to this gravy. Cover and simmer until meat is tender. Add salt."*

Ester Diaz was raised in Kansas and New Mexico, but when she described to me her family pipián, it was almost identical to Jaramillo's recipe of fifty years ago. I can only surmise that since Ester's parents were originally from Chihuahua, a border state with New Mexico, this pipián shares a common heritage. It is a mild dish, the ancho chiles imparting a deep rich resonance to the nutty taste of the pumpkin seeds, while the corn lends a distinctive rustic flavor. Pipián is an excellent company dish, for both the chicken and sauce can be prepared in advance and combined and reheated right before serving.

Serve with Seasoned White Rice (page 233) and lots of hot Corn Tortillas (page 108). A small bowl of Cilantro Soup (page 75) is a good choice to start the meal, and the Compote of Mango, Papaya, and Strawberries (page 345) is a natural ending. A zinfandel, maybe a Napa Ridge or a Souverain, would stand up well to the earthy sweetness of the dish.

2½–3 pounds chicken, cut into serving pieces
   (thighs and breasts)
1 white onion, quartered
2 large cloves garlic
4 cups Chicken Stock (page 70) or canned
   chicken broth
sea salt

For the Sauce
1½ cups raw, unsalted pumpkin seeds
½ cup dried corn
2 dried ancho chiles or dried California or New
   Mexican red chiles, roasted (page 21), deveined,
   and seeds removed
1 large clove garlic, peeled and coarsely chopped
1 tablespoon safflower or canola oil
sea salt and freshly ground black pepper
½ teaspoon cumin (optional)

Place the chicken, onion, and garlic in a stockpot with the stock and enough water to cover, about 1 cup. Salt to taste. Bring to a boil, skim off any foam, and lower the heat. Simmer the chicken about 15 minutes, until it is tender. Remove the chicken pieces and set aside. Strain the broth and, if made in advance, refrigerate so that the fat congeals and can be more easily removed.

Toast the seeds and corn in a heavy skillet over medium heat, turning constantly until light brown. Set aside to cool.

Soak the chiles in boiling water about 10 minutes, until the water cools and the chiles are softened. Drain and tear the chiles into pieces and place in a blender. Add garlic and 1½ cups of broth, and blend until smooth.

Finely grind the seeds and corn in a spice grinder. Mix with 3 cups of chicken broth. Or, if you have a strong blender, mix the seeds and corn with 1 cup of chicken broth and thoroughly grind to a paste, then add the remaining cups of broth.

Heat the oil in a Dutch oven over medium-high heat. Pour in the chile mixture and let it reduce for 1 minute or so. Add the pumpkin seed and corn mixture, stir well, and bring to a simmer. Continue cooking over low heat about 10–15 minutes, until the *pipián* begins to thicken. The sauce should be the consistency of thick cream, so if it becomes too thick, add more broth.

Season to taste with salt, pepper, and cumin. Add the chicken pieces and cook until the chicken is heated through.

Arrange the chicken pieces on a platter or individual plates and pour the sauce on top and around the chicken.

NOTE: You can use the hulled green pumpkin seeds found in health food or specialty food stores. The dried corn can also be purchased in most health food stores, or if you live in or around New Mexico, the dried and roasted corn kernels called *chicos* may be used.

Tangled Vermicelli and Chicken
Sopa Seca de Fideos y Pollo
SACRAMENTO, CALIFORNIA • TAMAULIPAS, MEXICO

SERVES 4   *The entwined coils of delicate vermicelli, a pasta now found in most supermarkets, are the favored noodles used by Mexicans, just as they are in Spain. In Mexico a dish like this or rice would usually be served as a separate course—a "dry soup"—before the entree. With today's emphasis on lighter eating, cooks such as Bettie Lee Taylor sometimes serve this dish as a main course when they want a casual meal that can be completed in less than an hour, accompanied by a salad, hard rolls or*

Crusty Bread Rolls (page 310), and a light red wine. Garlic Soup (page 77) is a flavorful and light beginning to the meal.

Bettie Lee's mother was from the Mexican border town of Reynosa, her father from Alabama. She grew up with both parents cooking the foods they knew best, so it was not unusual to have beans and rice alongside southern-style corn bread. Bettie Lee remembers living in a one-room house in Sullivan City, Texas, that they had in exchange for plowing two acres of land and growing corn for the owner. There they ran the ice station and post office, and in the little grocery store they sold the chicken and eggs they raised. Her mom's tamales were a favorite of the roughnecks working in the nearby oil fields. This was not an easy life. To get milk you milked the cow, and to put meat on the table you went hunting for rabbit, pheasant, or white-wing doves. Today, putting a meal together is a lot simpler. A hint: Once the chicken is ready, have all the ingredients measured and close at hand. You'll need to add them in quick succession.

one 1-pound whole chicken breast
4 cups Chicken Stock (page 70) or canned
   chicken broth
2 tablespoons safflower or canola oil
1 small white onion, chopped
½ pound vermicelli coils (about 5 nests)
2 cloves garlic, minced
1 large ripe tomato or 1 cup canned tomatoes,
   chopped
1 cup young peas, fresh or frozen

½ teaspoon cumin
about ½ teaspoon sea salt
freshly ground black pepper

For the Garnish

2 tablespoons roughly chopped fresh cilantro
   leaves
½ cup crumbled *queso fresco* (page 112), farmer's,
   or feta cheese

Simmer the chicken breast in the stock for approximately 10–15 minutes, until it is just cooked through. Remove from the pan, reserving the broth. When cool, remove the skin and bone, shred, and set aside.

Heat the oil in a Dutch oven or other large covered pot, over medium heat. Add the onions and cook until soft, then add the noodle nests, breaking each nest into 3 parts. Stir the tangle of noodle strands continually until toasted a golden brown. (A chopstick works well for this.) Do not let the noodles burn. Stir in the garlic. After a minute add the chicken, tomatoes, peas, cumin, salt, and pepper to taste. Pour in the broth. Mix thoroughly and bring to a boil. Lower the heat and simmer for 8–10 minutes, until most of the broth is absorbed.

Sprinkle on the cilantro and crumbled cheese, and serve at once.

Braised Chicken with Rice and Vegetables

Arroz con Pollo

BROOKLYN, NEW YORK • OAXACA, MEXICO

SERVES 6 TO 8   *Braised chicken combines with rice, soft and moist from a flavorful tomato broth, to provide those of Spanish heritage one of their most popular meals in a pot. I found it, in one form or another, in virtually every Mexican-American community I visited—from the basic New Mexico version flavored with just a taste of onion and garlic and colored yellow with wild safflower to an elaborate presentation with red and green bell peppers. It is very much like the paella-type arroz con pollo I loved in Spain, except that there a short-grain rice would be used.*

Rice with chicken dishes are comfort food—filling but light, and usually somewhat bland but tasty. Food that children enjoy as much as everyone else. In Geraldo Reyes's version, small cubes of potato are added, but some cooks add chickpeas as well, creating an even more substantial meal. Instead of simmering all the vegetables in the tomato puree, the green peas and chunks of bright red tomatoes are stirred in at the last moment for a fresher taste. To cut down on calories, Minerva Diaz poaches and shreds chicken breasts and thighs before adding them to the tomato rice mixture.

This is a substantial one-pot supper, needing only a simple salad alongside and perhaps some fruit for dessert. You could serve Ceviche (page 38) as a light starter. A glass of California zinfandel or a chardonnay will make the meal more festive.

For the Chicken

4 tablespoons olive oil
2½–3 pounds chicken, cut into small serving
   pieces (see Note)
4 cloves garlic, minced
juice of 1 large lime
sea salt
¼ teaspoon freshly ground black pepper

For the Rice

one 14½-ounce can tomato pieces, drained
1 small white onion, roughly chopped
6 cloves garlic

2 tablespoons safflower or canola oil
1½ cups long-grain rice
½ teaspoon dried oregano, preferably Mexican
sea salt
freshly ground black pepper
2 cups Chicken Stock (page 70) or canned
   chicken broth
½ pound red potatoes, peeled and diced
1 cup frozen peas
1 large ripe tomato, chopped

For the Garnish

¼ cup chopped flat-leaf parsley

Drizzle a little oil over the chicken and rub to coat each piece. Mash the garlic with the lime juice and 1 teaspoon of salt. Spoon the mixture over the chicken. Sprinkle each side lightly with pepper. Cover and refrigerate in a glass or plastic container for several hours or more, turning at least once. When ready to cook, pat the chicken dry and set it out at room temperature for another 30 minutes.

Heat the remaining oil in a large Dutch oven or a heavy skillet, or a large casserole dish with a lid. Sauté the chicken over medium-high heat about 20 minutes, until golden on all sides. Sprinkle with additional salt and pepper to taste. If the pan isn't large enough, the chicken may have to be cooked in batches. Transfer the pieces to a warm pan lined with absorbent paper. Any bits of skin or meat stuck to the bottom of the pan should be scraped up but left to flavor the rice. The chicken can be sautéed several hours in advance of completing the dish.

While the chicken is frying, put the tomatoes, onion, and garlic in a blender or food processor and puree until smooth.

Add the oil to the pan. Stir in the rice, coating well with the oil, and cook over medium heat until the grains begin to turn a golden tan. Stir in the tomato puree and oregano, add salt and pepper to taste, and let the mixture sizzle for several minutes. Pour in the chicken broth and taste for seasoning. (This dish benefits from an abundance of black pepper.) Add the potatoes and chicken pieces, pushing them down into the rice. When the broth begins to boil, lower the heat, cover the pot tightly, and simmer gently about 20 minutes, until the broth has been absorbed.

While the rice is cooking, slightly defrost the frozen peas. Remove the rice from the stove, add the peas and chopped tomato, and toss together with the rice using a fork. Cover and let sit another 4–5 minutes.

Sprinkle with the chopped parsley and serve from the pot, or the rice can be spooned onto a serving platter and the chicken and parsley set on top.

NOTE: The chicken should be marinated at least 2 hours in advance of cooking.

VARIATION: SAVORY CHICKEN BRAISED WITH RICE Several cooks I met in Florida added 1 teaspoon of cumin to the tomato puree and stirred into the rice a 4-ounce can of chopped drained mild green chiles and 2 ounces of drained chopped pimientos instead of the peas and potatoes.

Rabbit Stew with Lentils and Mushrooms

Guisado de Conejo con Lentejas y Hongos

BERKELEY, CALIFORNIA

SERVES 4 TO 6 *In the Southwest, Idaho, and Colorado, I found many people still hunting rabbit; usually it was so they could have pan-fried rabbit with chile-flavored gravy or they made chorizo from the tougher jackrabbit. Rabbit stew, especially with lentils and a reckless variety of vegetables, was another favorite, with the entire meal being cooked in one pot. This is a variation on a recipe given to me by Irma Aguilar. I added the mushrooms after several Colorado cooks told me they used the wild ones they gathered themselves. It is a dish most appreciated during the bleak months of winter: Its sturdy flavors serve to warm the body.*

This is a wonderful buffet dish for casual entertaining. Watercress Salad with Pine Nuts (page 52) is a good partner, especially with a flattering wine like Riesling. Use the same wine in the stew.

For the Rabbit

3–4 pounds rabbit (legs and thighs)
3 cloves garlic, minced
1 cup dry white wine
sea salt and freshly ground black pepper

For the Vegetables

3 thick slices bacon, chopped into ½-inch pieces
½ pound fresh mushrooms, sliced
2 medium white onions, minced
2 cups chopped celery
4 cloves garlic, minced
4 medium ripe tomatoes, chopped, or two 14½-ounce cans tomato pieces

1 teaspoon dry oregano, preferably Mexican
1 bay leaf
½ teaspoon ground allspice
1 tablespoon dried chile flakes
1½ cups quick-cooking lentils
4 cups Chicken Stock (page 70) or canned chicken broth
sea salt
2 medium potatoes, peeled and cut into ½-inch cubes

For the Garnish

3 tablespoons chopped flat-leaf parsley

Wipe the rabbit with a damp cloth and discard any fat. Rub the pieces with half of the garlic, then marinate them in the wine and remaining garlic for at least 1 hour; overnight is even better. When ready to start cooking, remove the rabbit, pat dry, and sprinkle with salt and pepper. Reserve the wine marinade.

Fry the bacon in a large Dutch oven over medium-low heat until crisp. Set aside to drain on absorbent paper, saving 2 tablespoons of the melted fat to sauté the rabbit.

Add the rabbit to the pot and sauté until golden brown on all sides. Remove the rabbit pieces and set aside. Sauté the mushrooms briefly and set aside with the rabbit. Add the onions and celery to the pot, stir in the garlic, and cook several more minutes. Add the wine marinade and cook for another minute. Add the bacon, tomatoes, oregano, bay leaf, allspice, and chile flakes, and stir to mix thoroughly. Continue to cook until the tomatoes are soft and thoroughly incorporated.

Rinse the lentils, drain, and add to the tomato mixture along with the broth. Season well. Arrange the rabbit pieces on top of the lentils and pour on any accumulated juices from the rabbit. Cover, lower the heat, and cook for about 15 minutes.

Stir in the potatoes and mushrooms, and taste again for seasoning. Cook for another 20 minutes, until the potatoes are tender. Turn the rabbit and stir so that nothing sticks or scorches.

Serve in the pot with a sprinkling of parsley. Or remove the rabbit pieces, put the lentils in an earthenware or other serving dish, arrange the rabbit on top, and sprinkle with parsley.

CINNAMON OR CASSIA?

*N*ot just a flavoring for dessert, cinnamon is used in many of Mexico's treasured fiesta foods—especially in the moles. Finding the delicately fragrant, slightly sweet true cinnamon bark that is sold in Mexico's markets is much more difficult in the United States, and Mexican Americans usually adjust to using cassia, the similar but much more aggressively aromatic bark sold in U.S. grocery stores as ground cinnamon or cinnamon sticks, the rolled bark. It's not. Cassia is a wonderful spice, but it has a stronger taste than the true cinnamon. For the recipes in this book, if you are substituting cassia for cinnamon, use a lesser amount. Though both are made from the bark of an evergreen laurel, the real stuff is from Sri Lanka (Ceylon). Cassia is from southern China, Indonesia, and Burma. Cinnamon bark is quite fragile and flaky, and easily ground, while the bark of cassia is very woody. What I find ironic is that the true cinnamon, which is used in most of the world, is evidently shipped first to the United States and then resold to Mexican markets. Luckily, most specialty food stores and ethnic markets also have it on hand, or it can easily be brought back from a vacation trip to Mexico.

Turkey Breast in Red Mole

Mole Rojo de Guajolote

HOMESTEAD, FLORIDA • MICHOACÁN, MEXICO

SERVES 6 TO 8 *The most voluptuous of Mexico's fiesta dishes, the traditional red mole is a tapestry of intricately interwoven flavors. Each state has its own regional version, but you can be sure it will include several kinds of dried chiles, a wide spectrum of herbs, spices, nuts, and seeds, and, often, even fruits and a hint of chocolate. Mole (from the Nahuatl word for sauce) will most likely be served to cloak a piece of turkey, chicken, or meat, but like the elegant covering it is, the mole itself is the star.*

I met with Candelaria Resendez as she was taking a break from her work at Brooks Tropical Fruit Company, outside of Homestead, Florida. She is from Morelia, Michoacán, a city I know and love, and we found we had much in common, including that we both had seven children and we both loved to cook. This is her very special mole that she makes for weddings and other fiestas, although we reduced the quantity in half.

Serve with Seasoned White Rice (page 233) and hot Corn Tortillas (page 108). The hint of chocolate in Negra Modelo, a creamy dark beer, makes it just the drink with this rich mole. Try Cinnamon Ice Cream with Iced Coffee (page 358) for dessert. If you prefer wine, have an Australian shiraz or a merlot. Hopefully there will be some leftovers, for a torta (page 132) made with a mole of turkey or chicken is just as much a treat as the turkey sandwich everyone looks forward to after Thanksgiving. Simply slice the roll in half, spoon on the shredded turkey and thick sauce, top with avocado slices, squish the roll together, and eat.

For the Turkey

3–4 pounds turkey or chicken breasts, cut into
    serving pieces

1 white onion, cut into pieces or quarters

4 cloves garlic

5 sprigs flat-leaf parsley

about 1 teaspoon sea salt

For the Mole Sauce

4 dried mulato chiles, toasted (page 22), seeded,
    and deveined

4 dried ancho chiles, toasted (page 22), seeded,
    and deveined

4 dried guajillo chiles, toasted (page 22), seeded,
    and deveined

¼–⅓ cup safflower or canola oil

1 cup hulled raw pumpkin seeds

¼ cup shelled unskinned and unsalted peanuts

8 unskinned almonds

¼ cup raisins

1 thick slice dry French bread or roll, or 6–8
    crackers

ingredients continue

3 cloves garlic

½ ripe plantain, peeled and cut into ½-inch cubes

2 teaspoons dried oregano, preferably Mexican

¼ teaspoon freshly ground black pepper

¾ teaspoon ground cinnamon (cassia)

1 bay leaf

1 ounce Mexican chocolate, roughly chopped

sea salt

Place the turkey pieces in a large pan with the onion, garlic, and parsley. Add cold water to cover and salt to taste. Bring to a boil over medium-high heat, then lower the heat to maintain a simmer. Cook about 15 minutes, until the turkey is just tender. It should still be under-cooked. Skim off any foam as it comes to the surface. Remove the turkey and strain the broth. There should be at least 6 cups of broth. This can be made ahead to this point and stored, cov-ered, in the refrigerator. Before using the broth, remove the layer of solidified fat.

Place the chiles in a bowl, cover with very hot water, and let them soak for 30 minutes.

Heat 1 tablespoon of the oil in a small skillet and fry the pumpkin seeds. Stir over medium heat until they begin to snap and pop. Keep a lid handy to cover them if they jump too much; shake the pan so they do not brown or burn. Spoon into a blender jar.

Add more oil, if necessary, to the skillet. Add the peanuts and almonds, and fry until golden. Put the nuts in the blender jar, add 1 cup of broth, and blend thoroughly. Add more oil to the skillet if needed and fry the raisins, bread, garlic, and plantain cubes separately. (The plantain may need up to 5 minutes of frying to turn a rich golden color.) Add each to the blender jar with a little more broth and blend until it is the consistency of a rough paste.

Heat 2 tablespoons of oil in a Dutch oven or large, heavy pot over medium-high heat and add the blended mixture. Lower the heat and sprinkle in the oregano, pepper, and cinnamon. Add the bay leaf and stir often as the mixture bubbles and spurts. Cook for about 5 minutes.

While the nut and seed mixture is cooking, drain the chiles, reserving the soaking liquid. Tear the chiles into pieces a few at a time, place into the blender jar (it doesn't have to be rinsed out) with about 1 cup or more of the soaking liquid. Blend until smooth. Add them to the cooking mixture and stir well for several minutes. Continue until all the chiles have been added.

Add the chocolate and stir until it has melted into the *mole*. Scrape the bottom of the pan as you stir. Add the remainder of the broth and cook about 2 minutes more. (The dish improves in flavor if made ahead to this point and then allowed to set for up to several days.) Add the turkey and continue cooking for about 15 minutes. Salt to taste. The sauce will be brick red in color and the consistency of thick cream.

Remove the turkey to a serving platter or individual plates and spoon the *mole* over the top, letting it puddle around the turkey.

Holiday Stuffed Turkey

Pavo Relleno para Días de Fiesta

CHICAGO, ILLINOIS • MEXICO CITY, MEXICO

SERVES 10 TO 12, WITH LEFTOVERS FOR TACOS AND ENCHILADAS   *Mexican families and friends love to come together for holidays, and adding Thanksgiving to the calendar as a fiesta is just another excuse for a celebration. On this day, Día de Acción de Gracias, Silvia de Santiago serves this splendidly glazed turkey and zesty sauce with mashed potatoes, ending the meal with a bread pudding and, as a tribute to her new home, apple pie. Silvia works every day as a waitress in a Mexican restaurant and still cooks mainly Mexican food at home, making the dishes that her mother taught her. Her father, who was a well-known guitar maker from Paracho, a small village in Michoacán, traveled often to the United States. When Silvia was in high school, she went with him to stay for a year with an aunt in Chicago and decided this city was where she wanted to live when she grew up. Eight years later she returned, and Chicago has been her home ever since.*

Even if it is not Christmas, Ponche de Navidad (Christmas Punch, page 382) will set the festive tone for the meal to follow, served with a collection of different kinds of tiny empanaditas (turnovers) (pages 43–45, and 363) to nibble on. After the blessing, the turkey is carved and the table or sideboard is loaded with dishes, some brought by other members of the family and guests. Mashed potatoes are always part of the meal, but usually someone brings Stuffed Sweet Potatoes (page 251). A colorful salad such as Vegetable Salad with Pears and Cherries (page 60) or Christmas Eve Salad (page 58) and a version of Potato and Vegetable Salad (page 56) are usually served, and often (surprisingly to me) Mexican Pasta (page 191). In case that is not enough, in some homes a sliced ham is set out and a dessert such as Pineapple Cake with Ginger Icing (page 369) follows, as well as the traditional bread pudding (Rum-Spiked Bread Pudding, page 353). To carry on the fruity flavor of the punch, I suggest a Gamay beaujolais during the meal.

For the Stuffing

2–3 tablespoons safflower or canola oil

½ small white onion, roughly chopped

1 clove garlic, minced

6 ounces prosciutto or other thinly sliced ham, diced into ½-inch pieces

4 ounces extra-lean ground beef

4 ounces ground pork shoulder

4 ounces fresh mushrooms, sliced

2 large ripe tomatoes, roughly chopped, or one 14½-ounce can peeled and diced tomatoes

8 ounces stuffed green olives, sliced

8 ounces dried prunes, pitted and roughly chopped

ingredients continue

½ cup pine nuts

½ cup red wine

¼ cup finely chopped flat-leaf parsley

½ teaspoon dried oregano, preferably Mexican

about 1 tablespoon sea salt

1½ teaspoons freshly ground black pepper

For the Turkey

one 10–12 pound turkey, preferably field-raised
  (see Note)

½ lemon

1 teaspoon ground cinnamon (cassia) (see sidebar, page 164)

unsalted butter or safflower oil

salt and freshly ground black pepper

2 cups red wine

1 teaspoon dried oregano, preferably Mexican

For the Giblet Sauce

heart, gizzard, liver, and neck of turkey (or you
  may prefer to discard the liver)

3 cups Chicken Stock (page 70) or canned
  chicken broth or enough water to cover giblets

⅓ cup red wine

about 1 teaspoon sea salt

1 white onion studded with 3 cloves

1 carrot, peeled

4 peppercorns

2 sprigs flat-leaf parsley

1 bay leaf

Make the stuffing first. Heat about 2 tablespoons of the oil in a large cast-iron skillet over medium-high heat. Add the onion and garlic, and cook until the onion is just wilted. Stir in the ham, beef, pork, and mushrooms, and cook until lightly browned. Add more oil only if needed.

Stir in the tomatoes, olives, prunes, and pine nuts. Add the red wine, parsley, and oregano, and continue to cook about 5 minutes, until well seasoned and the liquid has evaporated. If the mixture is still soupy, turn up the heat for a few minutes, then remove the pan from the heat and pour off any remaining oil. Add salt and pepper to taste. Set aside and let cool before stuffing the turkey. The mixture can be made in advance and refrigerated, but it should be brought to room temperature before using.

Preheat the oven to 350 degrees F. Remove the neck and giblets from the bird and reserve for the sauce. Rinse the turkey inside and out and dry thoroughly. Rub the cavity with the cut side of a lemon and sprinkle lightly with the cinnamon.

Fill the neck and body cavity lightly with the cooled stuffing. Truss the turkey, closing the 2 openings and tying down the wings and legs. Massage the skin with butter or oil and sprinkle well with salt and pepper to taste. Place the turkey, breast side up, on an oiled rack set in a large, shallow roasting pan.

Roast the turkey for 2½–3 hours, about 15–20 minutes per pound, depending on the oven. The most reliable guide as to when the turkey is done is a meat thermometer inserted in the thickest part of the thigh. The bird is ready to be taken from the oven when it reaches 165–170 degrees F. Baste frequently with the pan juices, and when the breast turns nice and brown, pour on the red wine mixed with 1 cup of warm water and the oregano. Continue to baste. If the turkey is becoming too brown, cover loosely with a large piece of aluminum foil. Do not overcook.

Transfer the turkey to a carving board or plate, tent with foil and a towel, and allow to rest 15 minutes before carving.

While the turkey is roasting, place all the ingredients for the giblet sauce in a large saucepan and bring to a simmer. Skim the surface occasionally to remove any foam. Cover the pan and cook over low heat for 1 hour, adding more liquid if necessary. When the broth has been reduced to about 2 cups, strain, reserving the neck and giblets. (If you like, shred the meat from the neck and finely chop the giblets, and return to the broth.) The sauce can be prepared ahead and refrigerated for up to three days.

Remove any excess fat from the roasting pan. Pour in 1 cup of the broth and deglaze over low heat, scraping to loosen bits of the caramelized turkey drippings. Pour the brown liquid into a saucepan, add the rest of the broth and the turkey giblets, and reduce over low heat for several minutes. Taste and adjust for seasoning, and keep warm until ready to serve.

Remove the stuffing from the turkey and place in the center of a large hot platter. Carve the turkey and arrange around the stuffing. The giblet sauce can be poured over both, or serve it on the side to be added individually.

NOTE: For smaller groups, a turkey breast can be used, putting the stuffing in the trough between the two sides and trussing it together with string. Reduce the cooking time according to the weight.

Meat

Mexican Chorizo
Chorizo
PUEBLO, COLORADO • GUANAJUATO, MEXICO

MAKES 2 POUNDS *Mexicans love their chorizo. Though the spicy sausage is traditionally cured, stuffed into casings, and hung to mellow the flavors, I found most Mexican-American cooks, including Rose Aguilera, are now making and storing it in bulk. It's a lot less work and tastes almost as good. With a batch of her chorizo always in the freezer, Rose can easily transform beans or eggs into a dish for a fiesta. Add to Chilaquiles in a Tomatillo and Green Chile Sauce (page 215), Skillet Potatoes with Green Chiles and Onions (page 254), and even Mexican Pasta (page 191).*

Jesse Berain taught me an excellent way to prepare chorizo. He fries the chorizo until it is well browned and almost dry. Then he adds two cups of well-fried beans, mashes it all together with a potato masher, and continues to cook for another five minutes.

1½ pounds pork shoulder, coarsely ground

½ pound pork fat, coarsely ground

3 large cloves garlic, minced

3–4 tablespoons pure red chile powder, preferably ancho or New Mexican (see Note)

1 tablespoon dried oregano, preferably Mexican

1½ teaspoons sea salt

½ teaspoon freshly ground black pepper

½ teaspoon ground cumin

⅛ teaspoon ground cloves

4–5 tablespoons red wine or cider vinegar

Put the pork, fat, and garlic into a large glass or enamel bowl and toss it with your fingers or a fork until crumbled and well mixed.

Sprinkle the chile, oregano, salt, pepper, cumin, and cloves over the meat and work them in well with your hands. Splash on the vinegar a little at a time and mix again, but do not let the mixture become gummy. Sauté a spoonful in a small skillet and taste for flavor. Add more seasoning if necessary.

Cover tightly in plastic wrap and store in the refrigerator to cure for at least 1 day, preferably several more. The chorizo will keep for up to a week in the refrigerator, but it can be easily divided into smaller batches and frozen for 2–3 months.

Before cooking, squeeze out any excess vinegar, then fry over very low heat.

NOTE: It is important to use pure ground dried chiles such as New Mexico or ancho chile in the chorizo. If you can't find it in a Hispanic market or your supermarket, grind your own (page 19). Rose's recipe calls for equal amounts of ground pork and ground beef; I've used all pork. If you want more heat, just chop in a fresh serrano chile while the sausage fries.

Pork Loin
with Poblano Sour Cream Sauce
Lomo de Cerdo en Crema de Chile Poblano
NORTHBROOK, ILLINOIS • MEXICO CITY, MEXICO

SERVES 8   *Everyone loves a party, and this is definitely a party dish. Elaine González cloaks slices of tender pork in a rich sauce that is dark green with the blended flesh of poblano chiles, then finishes it with crema and a sprinkle of cheese.*

For dessert, try something special such as Creamy Coffee Liquor Gelatin (page 346) with small Cinnamon Sugar Cookies (page 359) on the side. I like to match this special dish with a full-flavored Australian shirz—a wonderfully spicy, textured red wine, or a Cecchi Sangiovese from Italy.

4–6 tablespoons safflower or canola oil

3 pounds boneless pork loin roast

sea salt and freshly ground black pepper

1 small white onion, quartered

2 garlic cloves

4 fresh poblano chiles, roasted (page 21) and
 seeded

2–3 tablespoons chopped cilantro

2 tablespoons unsalted butter

2 cups Mexican *crema* (page 23) or sour cream
 thinned with milk

3 ounces *queso cotija* or feta cheese, crumbled, or
 Parmesan cheese, grated

Heat 2–3 tablespoons of the oil in a Dutch oven or large, heavy pot. Add the pork and sprinkle with salt and pepper to taste. Brown on all sides over medium-high heat. Add the onion and garlic after several minutes. When the meat is brown, add 2 cups of water and cook, covered, about 1½ hours, until the meat is tender. This can be made in advance and refrigerated.

Degrease the pork broth as much as possible. Preheat the oven to 350 degrees F. Put the broth in a blender with the chiles. Add the cilantro, along with the onion and garlic from the broth, and puree until smooth.

recipe continues

Melt the butter and the remaining oil in a large skillet over medium-low heat. Add the chile mixture and sauté, stirring constantly, for about 3 minutes after the butter and oil begin to sizzle. Add 1 cup of the *crema* and salt and pepper to taste, and cook for a few more minutes.

Place several tablespoons of the sauce on the bottom of an oiled baking dish, about 15 by 10 inches. Slice the pork loin into ¼-inch-thick slices and arrange them on top of the sauce. Pour the remaining sauce over the meat and sprinkle with the cheese.

Dot with the rest of the *crema* and bake, uncovered, until the top is lightly browned. It can be served directly from the baking dish or on individual plates accompanied by Seasoned White Rice (page 233).

VARIATION: CHICKEN BREASTS WITH POBLANO SOUR CREAM SAUCE   Boneless chicken breasts can be substituted for the pork. Sauté the chicken until lightly browned and shorten the simmering time to about 15 minutes.

Pork and Purslane Stew
Verdolagas a la Mexicana con Puerco
ALLEN PARK, MICHIGAN • QUERÉTARO, MEXICO

SERVES 3 TO 4   *You are lucky indeed if you have succulent purslane growing in your yard. Don't think of it as a weed but rather as a very special green. When lightly steamed, it has a wonderful fresh flavor that is prized by Mexican cooks. Once in a while during April and May I've also found purslane at farmer's markets. Just keep on the lookout for it. Tell the vendors who sell other greens that you want some, and it will eventually show up. Former butcher Florencio Perea uses meaty pork ribs in this recipe.*

Serve this stew with a stack of hot tortillas, Seasoned White Rice (page 233), Well-Fried Beans (page 227), and perhaps Pepper Slaw (page 53) on the side. Rum-Spiked Bread Pudding (page 353) is a compatible ending.

2 tablespoons safflower or canola oil

2 pounds country-style spare ribs, cut into 2-inch pieces

½ white onion, finely chopped

2 fresh jalapeño chiles, seeded and diced

2 cloves garlic, finely chopped

sea salt

3 medium very ripe tomatoes, diced, or one 14½-ounce can diced tomatoes

½ teaspoon dried oregano, preferably Mexican

1 pound purslane leaves and young shoots or spinach

Heat the oil in a heavy pan. Add the pork and fry over medium-high heat for 8–10 minutes, turning it to make sure it browns on all sides. Add the onion, chiles, and garlic, and continue to cook until the onion is golden brown. Sprinkle with salt to taste. Add the tomatoes and oregano. Lower the heat, cover, and cook about 35 minutes, until very tender. Add water if necessary, scraping the sides and bottom of the pan.

Wash the purslane thoroughly and chop coarsely, using all but the very big stems. Steam the greens in a medium-size saucepan with just a few drops of water about 5–10 minutes, until dark green and very tender. Drain and add to the pork, stir, and taste for seasoning.

VARIATION: BACON AND PURSLANE QUICK FRY Josie Freyte, in a recipe from *Real Comida!* (Colorado Springs: The League of United Latin American Citizens, 1991), substitutes bacon for the ribs and dried chile seeds or caribe (page 263) for the jalapeño, and eliminates the 35-minute cooking time for the meat and tomatoes.

Green Chile with Pork and Potatoes

Chile Verde con Puerco y Papas

PALO ALTO, CALIFORNIA • MICHOACÁN, MEXICO

SERVES 6 TO 8 *Pilar Baca Barnard combines small bits of pork with tiny potatoes and cooks them in a tangy sauce of chiles and tomatillos in a manner traditional to Michoacán, her family home. Pilar, who has lived in Palo Alto for many years, is the older sister of Carmen, my working companion on all my trips to Mexico.*

Even though potatoes are already in this dish, it is still traditional to serve it with plain boiled rice—a combination that is very good indeed. Add a simple green salad and a bottle of Italian chianti. Small glasses of Eggnog and Raisin Ice Cream (page 355) add a special ending to this homey meal.

20 medium tomatillos, husks removed and rinsed

3–4 fresh serrano chiles, stems removed

2 cloves garlic

2 tablespoons safflower or canola oil

2 pounds pork butt or shoulder, including a little
    fat, cut into ½- 1½-inch cubes

sea salt

12–15 small red potatoes

⅓ cup coarsely chopped cilantro

Place the tomatillos, chiles, and garlic in a medium-size saucepan. Cover with about 3 cups of water and bring to a boil over medium heat. Simmer for 10–15 minutes, until the tomatillos are soft. Drain but reserve the liquid.

Place the tomatillos, garlic, and chiles in a blender or food processor and blend well with ¼ cup of the tomatillo liquid.

Warm the oil in a Dutch oven or heavy pan and brown the meat over medium heat until golden and crispy. Pour the blended ingredients over the meat. Add salt to taste and 2 cups of the remaining tomatillo liquid. Cover and simmer about 30–45 minutes, until the pork is slightly tender. Add the potatoes and continue to cook for another 20 minutes. This can be made to this point, covered, and refrigerated overnight.

About 15 minutes before serving, add the cilantro to the simmering meat, taste, and adjust the seasoning.

Red Chile with Meat
Carne con Chile Colorado
NEW MEXICO

SERVES 6 TO 8 *This tangy meat stew is the forerunner of today's popular chili con carne. In 1939, Cleofas M. Jaramillo wrote, "Boil pork meat until tender, drain and cut in small pieces and place in a saucepan. Add the meat stock strained and 1 tablespoon red chile powder dissolved in a little water, or better, a cup of caribe chile. Season with garlic, oregano, and salt, simmer until thickened." Simple, yes. Tasty, very. My interpretation is a little more detailed and very like the many platefuls I consumed while in the upper Rio Grande Valley in New Mexico and Colorado. The main disagreement I found among cooks was whether to simmer the meat first, then brown it, or, as I prefer, to sear it first, then add the liquid. A few cooks intensified the heat level by including the stinging bite of cumin, the pungent caribe chile, or the even hotter pequín.*

While no beans are cooked with the meat, they are usually served on the side or added at the end. Potatoes, rice, or even noodles provide an alternative companion dish. Warm Flour Tortillas (page 125), a salad, and the cool bitter taste of beer complete the meal.

12 dried mild red chiles, preferably New Mexican, or ½ cup mild red chile powder

2 tablespoons safflower or canola oil

2 pounds round steak or pork shoulder, cut into ¼-inch cubes

1 tablespoon flour

4 cloves garlic, minced

about 1 teaspoon sea salt

1 teaspoon freshly ground black pepper

1 tablespoon dried oregano, preferably Mexican

1 teaspoon caribe chile (page 263) or dried red chile flakes (optional)

1 teaspoon ground cumin (optional)

2–3 cups Beef Stock (page 72), canned beef broth, or water

For the Garnish

1 medium white onion, finely chopped

Split the dried chiles and remove the stems, seeds, and veins. Put the chiles in a heavy ungreased skillet over low heat and roast for about 4 minutes, turning them often and pressing down with a spatula. They should change color, form a few blisters, and give off a wonderful aroma. Do not let them burn. Remove from the heat and, when cool, process thoroughly in a spice or coffee grinder. The ground chile can be stored in a small tightly sealed jar or plastic bag for some time.

In a Dutch oven or a large cast-iron skillet with a lid, warm the oil over medium-high heat. Add the meat, sprinkle in the flour, and brown the meat on all sides. Add the garlic, salt, and pepper, and cook briefly. Stir in part of the ground chiles, oregano, and additional chiles or cumin if using. Taste as you add to determine pungency and depth of flavor. Add more if needed.

Pour in the liquid, turn the heat to low, cover, and simmer for 1½–2 hours, stirring occasionally, until the meat is tender. Some broth should still remain. The dish can be made in advance and refrigerated, then reheated. Serve in a wide bowl topped with chopped onion.

BARBACOA

*I*n the past when I thought of barbecuing, it was always of a backyard grill of steak, chicken, or hamburgers—ingredients quickly cooked over an open flame. Mexican barbacoa is a slow, slow process; the meat is wrapped, buried, and baked in the ground for hours. A barbacoa is seldom prepared for just one family. Like the Hawaiian luau, it is an efficient way to serve a large number of hungry guests. Smaller portions of meat slowly baked in the oven or on a covered outdoor grill are much more practical for home cooks to prepare, and though it is not as dramatic as lifting your dinner from a smoldering pit, the results are still quite extraordinary.

If you ask for barbacoa along the Texas-Mexico border, it will probably be the very special cabeza de vaca en barbacoa—meat taken from a pit-roasted whole beef head. It may be a Texas specialty, but it was in Idaho that I first learned the intricacies of the process. I met Joe Torres and his wife, Olivia, when I sat next to him at a church breakfast in Nampa, Idaho. In most communities in Mexico there are a few designated masters of the local style of barbecuing, the ones who prepare the meat for the local fiestas. Joe was such a master. He had just dug a deep hole in his backyard and lined it with brick. The head (or heads) is skinned. The head may be rubbed with garlic and oil; Joe's is usually unseasoned. He wraps the head entirely in white toilet paper, then puts it in several layers of wet potato sacks. In Mexico or Texas he'd have placed huge spears of maguey (century plant) or even cactus pads on top of the coals for their extra moisture and flavor.

The head, in a metal pan, is placed over the coals. More coals are heaped around, the hole is sealed air tight with a plywood or metal cover, and dirt is shoveled over the top. Some people (not Joe) build another fire on top of the pit for additional heat. After seven to ten hours, the head is lifted from the pit and all the edible parts are cut off; one head yields about ten pounds of meat. The tender, smoky meat is eaten as tacos, wrapped in steaming flour tortillas, and fired with salsa. A special meal indeed.

New Mexican cooks like to prepare young goat (cabrito) or baby lamb for special occasions.

continued

Nolia Martínez's favorite is goat. Her secret for subduing the stronger goat flavor is to rub the kid with garlic and ground ginger. She includes the seasoning in the meat drippings for an intriguingly flavored gravy.

The much-esteemed cochinita *or* pollo pibil, *the pit-roasted pork or chicken of Yucatán, is still prepared on special occasions by the Yucatecan cooks I met in the United States. Now it is cooked in the oven, not a pit, and the unique* recado *seasonings come from a package, but it still has the essential flavors of the country they left behind.*

Achiote
Bixa orellana

MAKES ABOUT ¼ CUP   *The first time I saw an annatto tree, dotted all over with large pink blossoms, I knew only that it was one of the most strikingly beautiful trees I had ever seen. Later I identified the tree in a botanical garden in Hawaii; the flowers were replaced by prickly red pods that protect the numerous hard seeds that make this tree so important. While the ground seeds do impart a gently flowery taste to foods, it is their ability to imbue a deep orange tint to whatever they touch that gives the achiote seed its commercial value. The Maya and Carib Indian warriors used it to paint their bodies; during World War II it was the secret ingredient that turned oleo margarine into an almost acceptable substitute for butter; and it is still used to color some cheeses. In many tropical countries, especially the Philippines, Jamaica, Central and South America, and the three states of Mexico that make up the Yucatán Peninsula, it is used as an essential ingredient in many dishes.*

Because the seeds are so very hard, it is easiest to use a spice grinder to make a paste from them.

Achiote Seasoning Paste
2 tablespoons *achiote* seeds
1 teaspoon black peppercorns
1 teaspoon dried oregano, preferably Mexican
1 teaspoon cumin seeds
12 whole allspice

Mix the spices together and grind, a little at a time, in a high-speed spice grinder until thoroughly pulverized. They may have to be ground several times. Mix into a paste with several tablespoons of water. If not using right away, wrap tightly and store in the refrigerator.

Roast Pork Yucatecan-Style

Cochinita Pibil

LYNNWOOD, WASHINGTON, AND MIAMI, FLORIDA • YUCATÁN, MEXICO

FILLING FOR ENOUGH TACOS FOR 8 TO 10 HUNGRY EATERS *For some reason I had not expected to find many cooks from Yucatán in the United States. It was a very happy surprise when I met quite a number, because the Yucatecan cuisine is distinctive, dynamic, and seldom found outside the isolated peninsula that juts out into the waters between the Caribbean and the Gulf of Mexico.*

Today, most Yucatecans cook the traditional roasted pig, cochinita pibil, *in a stove oven instead of stone-lined pits. The first time I was in Yucatán, I was determined to find the real thing. My quest led me to the village of Tixkokob, where I met Silvio Campos. Like his father before him, Silvio still prepares the pork in the same fashion as his ancestors. Quickly and reverently he slaughters a young pig. After cleaning it, he spreads the meat with his own* recado, *a mixture of bitter orange juice, herbs, and achiote paste. He then wraps the meat in freshly cut banana leaves, places it into a deep pit filled with white-hot coals, covers it with earth, and allows it to steam overnight. The next day when the pit is opened and the meat brought forth, the aromas and tastes combine into one of the most memorable meals anyone has ever experienced.*

This recipe, which combines the techniques of Martha Garcia de Kaye of Miami and Ernesto Pino, who lives north of Seattle, nearly duplicates the dish I've eaten many times in Tixkokob. Black beans are a natural and almost essential anytime cochinita pibil *is served. The tortillas can be spread with very smooth well-fried black beans and layered with shredded pork and Red Onion Garnish (page 284) for a traditional Yucatecan taco. If you want, add fresh salsa such as Chunky Fresh Tomato Salsa (page 264) or, in keeping with the foods of the region, Crunchy Cabbage Salsa (page 277). Equally good, I think, is serving a bowl of black Soupy Pot Beans (page 224) on the side.*

5–6 pounds pork loin or shoulder

½ cup bitter orange juice (see Notes) or 2 tablespoons fresh orange juice

2 tablespoons fresh grapefruit juice, and 4 tablespoons fresh lime juice

2 tablespoons *achiote* paste (see Notes)

5 cloves garlic, minced

sea salt

8 banana leaves (see Notes; if frozen, defrost before using)

3 tablespoons safflower or canola oil

1 medium white onion, sliced

4 fresh *güero* chiles, such as banana or other yellow chiles, roasted (page 21), seeded, and cut in
  strips (optional)
1 cup Red Onion Garnish (page 284)

Puncture the meat on all sides with the point of a sharp knife and place it in a large glass or
other noncorrosive bowl or pan.

Mix together the juices, *achiote* paste, and garlic and 1½ teaspoons of salt. Pour all but 2 tablespoons of the mixture over the pork, rubbing it in well so that the surface is saturated. For
best results, cover and refrigerate at least 1 day in advance. The meat should be no less than 6
hours in the marinade. Cover the remaining juice mixture and store in the refrigerator.

When ready to cook the meat, preheat the oven to 350 degrees F.

Divide the banana leaves into 2 parts, removing the thick rib down the center. Cut into manageable lengths, about 18 inches long. Tear off about a dozen ½- by 18-inch strips to use as
ties. Lay out half of the banana leaves, shiny side up, and rub with oil. Put the pork in the center of the leaves (the meat may have to be cut in smaller pieces to fit the pan). Place a layer of
onion slices and sprinkle with the remaining marinade. Cover with more banana leaves, folding the edges together to seal. Tie the package of pork with the banana leaf strips.

Place the meat in a large Dutch oven, pour 1 cup of water around the meat, and cover
tightly. Or place in a foil-lined baking pan, add the water, and seal with another layer of foil
on top. Bake for 3–4 hours, until the meat is so tender that it is almost falling apart or is easily
broken up with a fork. (Meat that has been cut into smaller pieces will require less cooking
time.)

Carefully remove the leaf- or foil-wrapped pork from the pot to a large baking pan or platter. Unwrap and discard the onion and the banana leaves or foil covering. Pour any juices remaining in the pot into a small bowl and skim off as much fat as possible.

Slice or shred the meat when it is cool enough to touch and put it into a medium-size serving dish. Sprinkle with a pinch of salt and moisten with a drizzle of the meat juices. Decorate
the plate with the sliced chiles and red onion garnish (page 284).

NOTES: Bitter orange is grown in the Southwest. *Achiote* paste is available in many Hispanic markets, but if only the seeds are available, it is quite easy to make your own (page 177).

Banana leaves are in the freezer cases of both Asian and Hispanic groceries, and occasionally as fresh produce. The pork is used as a succulent filling to roll in soft, hot Corn Tortillas
(page 108).

Green Mole with Pork and Vegetables

Mole Verde Oaxaqueño

WAPATO, WASHINGTON • OAXACA, MEXICO

SERVES 6 *I met Alejandra Jimenez and her husband, Raymundo, in eastern Washington, where Raymundo was planting and tending several large fields of chiles. They both like to cook, recreating the tastes they enjoyed when they lived near Pinotepa Nacional, close to Oaxaca's sultry coast. They even brought seeds with them to grow special herbs, such as* hierba santa *and epazote.*

Every part of Mexico has its own version of green mole—some made with chicken, some thickened with ground pumpkin seeds, and some with little masa dumplings resting in the bright green sauce. I was delighted to find this herb-fragrant mole that Alejandra textures with both white and green beans as well as chunks of chayote. It is Mexican soul food.

This mole is a substantial dish and needs only rice and hot Corn Tortillas (page 108) to accompany it. Start the meal with Quesadillas (page 109) or Sopes with Chicken (page 123) and perhaps Squid in an Orange Vinaigrette (page 39). Because the greens quickly lose their fresh taste, this dish, unlike other moles, does not improve in flavor the next day.

For the Pork

3 pounds pork shoulder cut into 1½-inch pieces

1 medium white onion, cut in half

2 large cloves garlic

2 tablespoons sea salt

For the Mole

1 small chayote, peeled and cut in long strips ½ inch thick

1 cup fresh or frozen cut green beans

½ pound fresh tomatillos, cooked (page 266) and drained, or one 13-ounce can tomatillos, drained

3 large romaine lettuce leaves, torn into pieces

1 cup chopped flat-leaf parsley

1 cup chopped cilantro

1 medium white onion, chopped

4 fresh serrano or jalapeño chiles, chopped

2 cloves garlic, chopped

1 tablespoon dried oregano, preferably Mexican

2 sprigs fresh epazote or 1 teaspoon dried leaves, twigs removed (page 223) (optional)

sea salt and freshly ground black pepper

pinch of ground clove

½ teaspoon brown sugar (optional)

2 tablespoons safflower or canola oil

2 tablespoons *masa harina* (page 108)

2 cups cooked white or navy beans (page 224) or canned beans, drained

For the Garnish

sprigs of cilantro

Place the meat in a stockpot and add the onion, garlic, and salt. Cover with water and bring to a boil over medium-high heat. Lower the heat and simmer about 45 minutes, until tender. Do not overcook. Let the meat cool in the broth, then set both aside. The meat may be cooked in advance and refrigerated; the congealed fat should be removed.

Set the chayote and green beans on a steamer rack in a saucepan over boiling water. Cover and cook 10–15 minutes, until barely tender. Sprinkle with salt to taste and set aside. The vegetables may be cooked in advance and refrigerated.

Place the tomatillos, lettuce, parsley, cilantro, onion, chiles, garlic, oregano, and epazote into a blender or food processor with 1 cup of the broth and puree. Add 1 more cup of broth if needed. Add salt and pepper to taste and the ground clove. Taste, and if the sauce is too acidic, add a pinch or more of brown sugar.

Heat the oil in a large, heavy pot or Dutch oven and carefully add the tomatillo mixture. It will sizzle and spit in the hot oil. Stir in the *masa harina* and cook over medium-high heat for about 5 minutes, stirring occasionally. Lower the heat, add the pork, and cook another 10 minutes. Add more broth if needed. In the last 5 minutes, stir in the beans, chayote, and green beans. Taste for seasoning and add more salt or pepper if necessary. Serve in deep plates, garnished with cilantro.

Beef Mole Colima-Style with Pineapple
Mole Colimeño
MIAMI, FLORIDA • COLIMA, MEXICO

SERVES 4 TO 6 *Dishes that combine meat and fruit are common in Mexico, and this red mole draws its depth of flavor from the pasilla chile combined with cinnamon and pineapple. I do not recommend substituting another chile.*

Maria Guadalupe Lugo and her mother, Julia Moran, also make this dish with pork or chicken and omit the pineapple for an even more basic mole.

As with most moles, it is best to serve this on deep plates with a lip. Accompany it with Seasoned White Rice (page 233) and lots of Corn Tortillas (page 108). A fine tequila reposado such as Cuervo Tradicional or Herradura is an ideal drinking partner with the mole.

2½–3 pounds boneless beef brisket, cut into 2-
  inch serving pieces
1 small white onion, chopped
3 cloves garlic
about 2 teaspoons sea salt

For the Mole
6 dried pasilla chiles, toasted (page 22) and
  seeded
1 French-style roll, cut in 3 pieces, or 3 slices
  French bread, ½ inch thick

one 1-inch true cinnamon stick or 1 teaspoon
  ground cinnamon (cassia)
2 tablespoons safflower or canola oil
1 tablespoon flour
2 cloves garlic, chopped
⅛ teaspoon sugar
½ pound fresh pineapple, peeled, cored, and
  cubed
¼ teaspoon freshly ground black pepper
about ½ teaspoon sea salt

Place the beef in a large pot with the onion and garlic. Cover with water and add salt to taste. Bring to a simmer over medium heat and cook about 1½ hours, until the meat is tender. Remove the meat and reserve the broth. The meat can be cooked well in advance and then added to the *mole*.

Soak the chiles in a bowl with very hot water for about 15 minutes. After 10 minutes, add the bread so it can soak, too.

Put the chiles, bread, and cinnamon in a blender or food processor with ½ to 1 cup of the soaking water and puree until smooth.

Heat the oil in a large skillet or Dutch oven. When hot but not smoking, stir in the flour and garlic, and cook for 1 minute. Add the chile mixture and sugar, and let bubble for 1–2 minutes. Pour in 1 cup of the beef broth and add the meat and pineapple. Add the pepper and salt. Simmer over medium-low heat for about 15 minutes. The *mole* should be thick enough to lightly coat the back of a spoon.

Meatballs in Chipotle Sauce
Albóndigas en Chipotle
PENBROKE PINES, FLORIDA • MEXICO CITY, MEXICO

MAKES 12–15 DINNER-SIZE MEATBALLS OR ABOUT 30 SMALLER MEATBALLS, SERVING 8 TO 10 AS AN APPETIZER *Meatballs in one form or another—tiny meatballs in broth, bite-size ones as party appetizers, and, to my delight, glorious plump balls of ground meat in some sort of enriching sauce—were served to me more often than any other meat or chicken dish.*

The night I had dinner with Veronica Litton, she served these large meatballs smothered in a rich red sauce redolent with garlic and the smoky overtones of chipotle chile. They were the perfect choice for a busy hostess like Veronica, who also is a wine merchant in Coral Gables, because they can be made in advance and reheated at dinnertime.

Serve with small new potatoes or Mexican Red Rice (page 235). Carrot Soup (page 73) makes a light colorful beginning to the meal, and try the Raspberry Bombe (page 357) for dessert. Veronica would serve a full-flavored Torres Gran Coronas black label wine with the albóndigas.

For the Sauce

1 pound ripe tomatoes, coarsely chopped, or one
   14½-ounce can tomato pieces
2 cloves garlic, minced
½ teaspoon dried oregano, preferably Mexican
1–2 canned chipotle chiles *en adobo*
1 cup Beef Stock (page 72) or canned beef broth
about ½ teaspoon sea salt
1 tablespoon olive oil

For the Meatballs

1 pound lean ground beef
¼ pound lean ground pork
1 clove garlic, minced
1 tablespoon chopped parsley, preferably flat-leaf
about 1 teaspoon sea salt
freshly ground black pepper
½ cup bread crumbs
1 egg
2 tablespoons milk, or as needed
2 hard-boiled eggs, finely chopped

Place the tomatoes, garlic, oregano, 1 chile, broth, and salt in a blender or food processor and blend until smooth. Taste, and add the other chile or more salt if needed.

Heat the oil in a large heatproof casserole dish or Dutch oven over medium-high heat. When the oil is very hot but not smoking, pour in the tomato sauce and cook for 5 minutes. Lower the heat and let simmer for another 5 minutes. The color will change from a raw red to a rich deep-orange brick. This sauce can be made in advance and reheated.

Place the ground beef and pork in a bowl and add the garlic, parsley, salt, and pepper to taste. Mix well with a fork or your hands. Stir in the bread crumbs and the raw egg, and toss until thoroughly mixed. If necessary, add a little milk to dampen the bread crumbs.

Put about 1 heaping tablespoon of meat in the palm of one hand and flatten it. Add a large pinch of chopped egg in the middle, cover with the rest of the meat, and squeeze together firmly so that none of the egg shows. The meatballs are usually made 2 inches in diameter for dinner, but make them bite-size if they are to be used as appetizers.

Bring the sauce to a slow boil over medium heat. Taste again for salt. Drop each meatball in as it is prepared, cover the pot, and let the meatballs simmer over low heat for 20–30 minutes depending on their size. Stir occasionally to make sure they are cooked evenly because the sauce will just barely cover the meatballs. If they start to stick, add a bit more broth or water. They should be thoroughly cooked but still fluffy.

VARIATION: SPICY GROUND CHICKEN BALLS IN A TOMATILLO SAUCE   In Texas, Aurora Dawson makes her sauce using fresh or canned tomatillos instead of tomatoes, adding ½ cup of chopped white onion and eliminating the oregano and chipotle chile. For the meatballs she uses 1½ pounds of ground chicken or turkey breast; 2 tablespoons of uncooked medium-grain white rice or oatmeal; 3 sprigs of fresh mint, chopped; 1 egg; ½ of a canned chipotle chile, chopped; salt and pepper. The process is the same as with the meatballs in chipotle sauce, but the sauce may need a bit more liquid.

Fiesta Meatloaf
Pastel de Carne
DENTON, TEXAS • OAXACA, MEXICO

SERVES 8   *Meatloaf may not be a traditional Mexican dish, but this one, abundantly interspersed with colorful vegetables, is a favorite of Aurora Cabrera Dawson and her family. I prefer using both ground pork and ground beef; however, this can be prepared with only beef. Texan that he is, her husband likes to drench the slices of meat with an even more incendiary* habanera *sauce.*

For a very special family meal, start with Tomato Soup (page 83), and with Fiesta Meatloaf, serve mashed potatoes or Stuffed Sweet Potatoes (page 251), and Pepper Slaw (page 53).

1 tablespoon safflower or canola oil

1 medium white onion, finely chopped

½ red bell pepper, cored, seeded, and finely chopped

2 cloves garlic, minced

2 pounds ground beef chuck with some fat

½ pound ground pork

1 bunch well-washed spinach leaves, chopped

1 medium carrot, coarsely grated

1 cup canned black beans, drained

1 medium ripe tomato or 3 plum tomatoes, chopped

1 small zucchini, coarsely grated (optional)

½ cup oatmeal

2 eggs

½ cup evaporated milk or half-and-half

1 canned chipotle chile, minced, or 1 tablespoon canned chipotle sauce or bottled chipotle salsa

1 teaspoon sea salt

½ teaspoon freshly ground black pepper

½ teaspoon oregano, preferably Mexican

Preheat the oven to 350 degrees F.

Warm the oil in a medium-size skillet. Add the onion, bell pepper, and garlic. Cook over medium-low heat about 5 minutes, until all the vegetables are softened. Transfer the mixture to a large bowl and let cool.

Crumble in the ground beef and pork, and mix together with a fork or your fingers. Add the spinach, carrot, black beans, tomato, zucchini, if using, oatmeal, eggs, and milk. Mix thoroughly with your hands. Season with the chipotle, salt, pepper, and oregano, and mix together again until everything is well incorporated.

Pack the mixture into a 9- by 5- by 3-inch loaf pan. Bake for 1 hour, or until the meatloaf is cooked through.

Remove the pan from the oven and pour off most of the fat. Let the meatloaf rest for 10 minutes, then slice and serve.

Mexican Beef Chow Mein
Morisqueta con Carne y Verduras
TOPPENISH, WASHINGTON

SERVES 4 TO 6 *Ester Diaz was one of the first people I interviewed when I began my research for this book. She lives in Toppenish, a small agricultural town in eastern Washington. The street she lives on is protectively canopied by huge trees, white fences surround the houses, and the air is full of the scent of roses after a rain. Ester's story was in stark contrast to her serene surroundings:*

> *I was only two when my family moved from Texas to Kansas, where my papa went to work in the salt mines. Everyone was supposed to work, so when I was old enough, I tried to sew the sacks to hold the salt, but I was so nervous I was put to work helping to make the salt blocks for the cattle. I got married very young and had my first child at fifteen. My husband became a powder man in the mines, but after his brother, Tony, was crushed in an explosion, we left and brought our three boys here to Toppenish. I've lived here now for fifty years.*

Ester learned this dish from her mother, and it is now the favorite meal of her children and grandchildren.

Nothing is needed to accompany this dish because it already has almost everything—except a salsa. Try the Six Chiles Salsa (page 272) or the Chile de Árbol Salsa with Tomatillos (page 268).

For the Rice

1 cup long-grain white rice
¼ teaspoon sea salt

For the Meat Toppings

1½ pounds top round steak (London Broil),
 sliced diagonally in ⅛-inch narrow strips
2–3 tablespoons safflower or canola oil
sea salt and freshly ground black pepper
2 cloves garlic, finely chopped
3 fresh jalapeño chiles, sliced in rounds

For the Vegetable Toppings

½ head of green cabbage, cut in ¾-inch wedges
1 white onion, cut in half vertically, then thinly
 chopped
2 tablespoons safflower or canola oil
3 ripe plum tomatoes, cut in half vertically, then
 thickly sliced
sea salt and freshly ground black pepper

For the Egg Toppings

4 eggs
3 green onions with 2 inches of tops, sliced
sea salt and freshly ground black pepper
2 tablespoons unsalted butter

Bring 2 cups of salted water to a boil in a medium-size saucepan and stir in the rice, keeping the water at a boil. Turn the heat to very low, cover, and simmer for 15 minutes. Without opening the pot, remove it from the heat and let it sit another 10–15 minutes. Fluff up the rice with a fork and cover until ready to use.

Pat the meat dry. Heat 2 tablespoons of the oil in a large, heavy skillet or wok over medium-high heat. Sear the steak pieces, adding salt and pepper to taste after it is browned. This will take only 1–2 minutes. Lower the heat, cover, and cook for about 10 minutes, stirring frequently. Add the garlic and chiles, and sauté for another 5 minutes. Add more oil if necessary.

In a medium-size skillet or wok, sauté the cabbage and onion in the oil over medium-high heat about 5 minutes, until turning brown but still crispy. Add the tomato slices and salt and pepper to taste, and cook for several more minutes.

Beat the eggs slightly in a bowl with 2 tablespoons of water and the green onions, salt, and pepper to taste.

When the meat is tender, the vegetables are cooked, and you are ready to eat, melt the butter in a medium-size skillet over low heat and add the eggs, stirring gently until they set.

To serve, place a large spoon of rice on a plate, then the cabbage, meat, and eggs on the top and sides.

Minted Lamb Shanks with Thin Pasta

Chambarete de Cordero con Fideos y Menta

SANTA FE, NEW MEXICO

SERVES 4   *Maria Ysabel Mondragón has been in the restaurant business for a long time. When her husband, Robert, was lieutenant governor of New Mexico, Bell was on the go with him, but since his death she has kept busy running LaBell's Carry-Out, specializing in all kinds of burritos. Bell's father was from Spain, so it seems natural that a dish combining the fine noodlelike pasta fideos and lamb is one of her favorite dishes to cook at home. Shepherds from Spain, especially the Basques, came many generations ago through Mexico to the United States, settling in Idaho, Nevada, and New Mexico. They were strong, silent, and patient men with a deep attachment to religion and tradition—all qualities needed to survive in the remote and harsh sagebrush-covered lands where they tended their sheep—although they did love to eat and knew how to party.*

The lamb shanks finish their cooking with the fideos, which absorb the concentrated flavor of the aromatic herbs and orange in the braising liquid.

In keeping with the Spanish provenance of this lamb dish, begin the meal with the flavorful Garlic Soup (page 77) or, in warmer weather, gazpacho (page 84). Add Watercress Salad with Pine Nuts (page 52) and, for a surprise ending, Ancho Chile Flan (page 364).

For the Meat

⅛–¼ teaspoon ground cumin

¼ teaspoon sea salt

¼ teaspoon freshly ground black pepper

4 whole meaty lamb shanks, cut by your butcher into 2-inch-thick pieces (about 3½–4 pounds) (see Notes)

3 tablespoons olive oil

2 cups Chicken Stock (page 71), canned chicken broth, or water

½ cup red or white dry wine

2 cloves garlic, minced

1 sprig fresh rosemary or 1 teaspoon dried rosemary

2 bay leaves

zest or peel from 1 large orange, colored part only, finely minced

3 sprigs fresh mint

For the Pasta

2 tablespoons safflower or canola oil

¾ cup chopped white onion

8 ounces vermicelli coils (*fideos*), about 5 coils

sea salt and freshly ground black pepper

For the Garnish

leaves from 1 sprig of mint

Mix the cumin, salt, and pepper together on a small plate and rub all over the surface of the lamb shanks.

Warm the oil in a deep, heavy skillet or Dutch oven over medium-high heat and brown the lamb on all sides for 10–12 minutes. Add the broth, wine, garlic, rosemary, bay leaves, and orange peel. Bring to a low boil, turn the heat to low, cover, and simmer for 1½–2 hours until the shanks are very tender. Remove the lamb from the cooking liquid and set aside. The lamb can be cooked in advance to this stage and refrigerated, along with the broth.

When the fat on the broth congeals, it should be removed and discarded. Otherwise, degrease the broth as thoroughly as possible. There should be 2½ cups of broth, so add more liquid if needed.

Preheat the oven to 400 degrees F. Reheat the degreased broth and add the fresh mint. Let it simmer for 5 minutes, then remove the mint and bay leaves.

To prepare the pasta: In a heavy skillet or paella pan, heat the oil over medium heat and stir in the onion. Break each coil of vermicelli into 3 parts and stir into the onion, tossing constantly until the pasta is covered with oil and begins to toast evenly. Do not let it burn. A chopstick works well for this. Pour the hot broth over the noodles and cook for 3 minutes, uncovered, stirring occasionally. Lower the heat and continue to simmer until the noodles are no longer soupy and only a little of the broth remains. Salt and pepper to taste.

Press the lamb shanks into the noodles, transfer to the oven, and bake for 10 minutes, or until all the liquid is absorbed and the noodles are crusty around the sides of the pan.

Serve directly from the pan or place on a large platter and garnish with mint leaves.

NOTES: Since lamb shanks tend to be quite fatty, we strongly recommend that you start this dish a day ahead; the meat and broth can then be refrigerated and the solidified fat removed.

If a softer noodle dish with more moisture is preferred, omit the final baking and put the heated lamb shanks on top of the simmering noodles.

Tongue in Tomato Sauce

Lengua en Jitomate

SANTA MONICA, CALIFORNIA • MEXICO CITY, MEXICO

SERVES 4 TO 6, WITH LEFTOVERS   *Ana Lorena Zermeño's braised beef tongue makes splendid eating and is very easy to prepare. Don't be at all reluctant to serve this dish at a dinner party, even though you may think no one will want to try it. Fresh tongue is quite perishable, so it should be cooked as soon as possible after you buy it.*

Accompany with Seasoned White Rice (page 233), Wild Greens with Pinto Beans (page 240), and Crusty Bread Rolls (page 310) or French rolls. Pickled Vegetables with Chiles (page 281) provides a crunchy contrast. In Tucson, Carmen Villa Prezelski cuts any leftover tongue and marinated chiles into thin slices and layers them between pieces of rye bread in a hearty sandwich.

one 3- to 4-pound fresh beef tongue
2 white onions
4 cloves garlic
4 bay leaves
6 whole black peppercorns
sea salt

For the Sauce
2 teaspoons olive oil
1 white onion, finely sliced
1 small red pepper, seeded and cut into ½-inch
  squares

5 medium-size firm ripe tomatoes, finely sliced,
  or two 14½-ounce cans tomato pieces, drained
3 whole canned *güero* or yellow chiles
½ cup sliced green olives
½ teaspoon dried oregano, preferably Mexican
3 tablespoons chopped flat-leaf parsley
sea salt and white pepper

For the Garnish
2 tablespoons chopped flat-leaf parsley

Place the tongue in a large pot with enough cold water to cover. Bring the water to a boil and skim off any foam that comes to the surface. Add the onions, garlic, bay leaves, peppercorns, and salt. Lower the heat, cover, and simmer for 2½ hours over medium heat, or until the tongue is very tender. Remove from the broth and plunge it into cold water to help loosen the skin. Trim off the root end, peel off the skin, and cut in slices ¼ inch thick. Reserve the stock, straining out the seasonings.

To prepare the sauce: Heat the oil in a large skillet or Dutch oven. Add the onion and red pepper, and brown lightly. Add a layer of tongue, then the tomatoes, chiles, and olives. Sprinkle with the oregano, parsley, and salt and pepper to taste. Add ½ cup of the stock. The tongue can be prepared in advance to this point. When cool, cover with plastic wrap and refrigerate until it is time to resume cooking.

Cover the skillet and cook the tongue over low heat for about 45 minutes, moving it about occasionally. Taste the broth for seasoning and add more salt and pepper if necessary. To serve, place the tongue slices on a platter and sprinkle with chopped parsley.

Lighter Fare

Harvest Vegetable and Pork Casserole
Guiso Veraniego con Puerco
AUSTIN, TEXAS

MAKES 4 LARGE SERVINGS *This simple one-pot meal, a delicious hodgepodge of whatever is most plentiful, is best made with vegetables fresh from the garden or farmer's market. The amounts do not have to be exact, and the herbs and vegetables can vary. Just try to have a variety of colors and textures. Mercedes Ramos uses golden corn and zucchini, but baby carrots and green beans work just as well. Traditionally, the vegetables are cooked until very, very soft. Now they are more often left a bit crunchy but still tender. The meat can be eliminated altogether, or scraps of leftover pork can be tossed in for flavor.*

With hot Flour Tortillas (page 125) to scoop up the meat and vegetables and a bowl of soupy Cowboy Beans (page 226), this makes a fine supper. Either a bright and fruity California chardonnay or a Dos Equis XX beer provides a refreshing drink.

2 tablespoons safflower or canola oil

2 pounds boneless pork shoulder or Boston butt, cut into ½-inch pieces, or pork chops, trimmed of fat and cut into small cubes

sea salt

½ teaspoon freshly ground black pepper

1 small white onion, finely chopped

2 cloves garlic, minced

1–2 fresh serrano or jalapeño chiles, seeded and chopped (optional)

3 medium-size ripe tomatoes, chopped, or one 14½-ounce can diced tomatoes

1 teaspoon fresh oregano, chopped, or ½ teaspoon dried oregano, preferably Mexican

1 cup fresh or frozen corn kernels

2 medium zucchini or other summer squash, diced in ½-inch pieces

For the Garnish

¼ cup Mexican *crema* (page 23) or sour cream thinned with milk (optional)

4 sprigs mint or cilantro, chopped

Heat the oil in a heavy casserole or Dutch oven over medium-high heat. Stir in the pork and brown on all sides, turning frequently, about 15 minutes. Sprinkle salt and pepper on the meat to taste.

Add the onion, garlic, and chile to the pot. Toss about 5 minutes, until coated and softened. Stir in the tomatoes and oregano, lower the heat, cover, and simmer for 30 minutes, until the pork is tender. The dish can be made in advance up to this stage and reheated before adding the vegetables.

Add the corn and zucchini, and continue cooking for another 10–15 minutes. Taste for seasoning and add more salt or pepper if necessary; the vegetables seem to need a good amount of salt to bring out their flavor.

When ready to serve, add a drizzle of *crema* and sprinkle with chopped mint or cilantro.

Mexican Pasta
Pasta Mexicana
OXNARD, CALIFORNIA • MICHOACÁN, MEXICO

SERVES 4   *You might think you were in the wrong place if you went into a Mexican restaurant in the United States and were offered pasta. It is, though, a very Mexican dish. During those restless years following the conquest, everything that was considered good in the way of food came from Spain, France, or Italy, including the tradition of serving rice or pasta as a separate first course or* sopa seca *(dried soup). As a busy working mother, Maria Romero often creates a filling main dish by combining meat, chiles, and tomatoes with spaghetti.*

Mexican Pasta can be accompanied by a green salad or Caesar Salad with Chipotle Chile (page 50). Serve Crusty Bread Rolls (page 310) or French bread on the side. A zinfandel wine stands up to the strong flavors of this meal.

two 14½-ounce cans tomatoes, diced

⅓ white onion, coarsely chopped

2 garlic cloves, coarsely chopped

2 fresh serrano or jalapeño chiles, chopped

1½ teaspoons dried oregano, preferably Mexican

⅛ teaspoon ground cumin

sea salt

2 tablespoons safflower or canola oil

½ pound lean ground beef or pork

12 ounces spaghetti or other dry pasta

For the Garnish

grated *queso añejo* or romano cheese

¼ cup chopped cilantro

Place the tomatoes, onion, garlic, and chiles in a food processor or blender. Process until smooth, then mix in the oregano, cumin, and salt to taste.

In a medium-size skillet or saucepan, warm 1 tablespoon oil, and when quite hot but not smoking, add the blended mixture and cook 10–15 minutes over medium heat.

Warm the remaining tablespoon of oil in a medium-size skillet and cook the ground beef about 10 minutes over medium heat. Drain off any excess oil, add the beef to the sauce, simmer 2–3 minutes, and keep warm.

Cook the pasta in a large pot of boiling salted water for about 8 minutes, until just tender. Drain and pour the cooked meat sauce over the hot pasta. Serve in a large bowl or on individual plates, topped with the cheese and cilantro.

Vermicelli with Chipotle Chile

Sopa Seca de Fideos

TOPPENISH, WASHINGTON

SERVES 4   *The pastas most popular in Mexico and with the Mexican-American community throughout the United States are* fideos, *or coils of thin vermicelli. In Texas, potatoes and ground beef seasoned with cumin were added; in Oregon, garlic, olive oil, and clams. This chile-enriched pasta dish, similar to one made by Ester Diaz, was the most typical. I've substituted the smoky overtones of chipotle chile for the fresh jalapeño in her recipe, but either version makes a very enjoyable supper dish.*

This makes an easy and inexpensive meal with just a tossed green salad and, perhaps, a glass of sauvignon blanc or, if you prefer, an oaky Spanish red wine.

3 tablespoons safflower or canola oil

1 medium white onion, finely chopped

2 cloves garlic, minced

8 ounces vermicelli (*fideos*) or angel hair pasta

4 ripe plum tomatoes, coarsely chopped, or 1 cup canned tomato pieces with puree

1 canned chipotle chile *en adobo,* chopped

2 cups Chicken Stock (page 70) or canned chicken broth

sea salt

1½ cups cubed Monterey jack cheese

For the Garnish

¼ cup chopped cilantro

Preheat the oven to 325 degrees F.

In a medium-size casserole dish, preferably earthenware, heat the oil over medium-high heat. Stir in the onion and garlic, and cook until they soften. Add the *fideos,* breaking each coil into 3 parts. Stir and toss constantly until the pasta is covered with oil and begins to toast evenly. A chopstick works well for this. Stir in the tomatoes and chipotle chile, and mix well. Let the tomatoes cook several minutes before adding the broth. Add salt to taste. Stir once, and when the broth starts to boil, lower the heat and let simmer until it is almost gone and the noodles are just done.

Remove the dish from the heat and add the cheese. Reheat in the oven for 4–5 minutes so that the cheese can melt. Mix gently. Serve hot, sprinkled with cilantro.

Cheese-Stuffed Green Chiles in Spiced Tomato Broth

Chiles Rellenos

CHICAGO, ILLINOIS • MICHOACÁN, MEXICO

SERVES 4 TO 6, DEPENDING ON THE SIZE OF THE CHILES *As a child growing up in Michoacán, Sylvia de Santiago usually ate these plump stuffed chiles on Ash Wednesday, the day beginning the forty days of fasting in preparation for Easter. Now it's more apt to be that she just hungers for them.*

Seasoned White Rice (page 233) or Mexican Red Rice (page 235) and Watercress Salad with Pine Nuts (page 52) complement the chiles, accompanied by a glass of fruity merlot. I like to end this meal with the Gelatin of Three Milks with an Orange Prune Sauce (page 347).

For the Sauce

one 28-ounce can tomato pieces with juice
½ medium white onion, roughly chopped
2 cloves garlic, roughly chopped
1 cup tomato juice
1 teaspoon safflower or canola oil
dash of ground cinnamon (cassia)
dash of ground cloves
½ teaspoon dried oregano, preferably Mexican
⅛ teaspoon freshly ground black pepper
sea salt

For the Chiles

6 fresh poblano or 8 Anaheim chiles, roasted (page
  21) peeled, and seeded, with the stem intact

12 ounces Monterey jack or other mild melting
  cheese, grated
½ cup flour, well seasoned with sea salt and
  freshly ground black pepper

For the Batter

4 eggs, separated, at room temperature
½ teaspoon sea salt
peanut or safflower oil for frying

For the Garnish

6–8 tiny sprigs flat-leaf parsley
½ cup crumbled *queso Cotija* or feta cheese

In a blender or food processor, puree the tomatoes, onion, and garlic with some of the tomato juice.

In a heavy saucepan or skillet, warm the oil over medium-high heat. Pour in the tomato mixture and stir constantly as it sizzles. Lower the heat to medium and stir in the rest of the tomato juice, cinnamon, cloves, oregano, pepper, and salt to taste. Simmer for about 5 minutes, until the broth is well seasoned and slightly thickened. This may be made a day in advance and reheated.

Make a slit down the side of each chile, just long enough to remove the seeds and veins. Keep the stem end intact. This is easiest done under warm running water, but some of the flavor is lost. Drain the chiles on absorbent paper until completely dry. Cover and set aside. This can be done a day in advance.

Lightly squeeze the cheese into long narrow sticks, a little smaller than the chiles, and stuff them inside. After making sure the outside of the chile is completely dry, roll them in the seasoned flour. The chiles can be stuffed and floured up to 2 hours before cooking.

Lightly beat the egg yolks together in a small bowl. Beat the egg whites and salt in a medium-size bowl until they hold stiff peaks. Fold the egg yolks gently into the egg whites until well blended.

Pour ½ inch of oil into a large skillet and heat over medium heat until the oil is hot but not smoking. Holding the chiles by their stems, dip them into the egg batter and lay them carefully in the skillet, 1 or 2 at a time. Fry until golden on the bottom, then turn and fry the other side. Drain on absorbent paper and continue until all the chiles are cooked.

Reheat the broth in an attractive casserole dish and add the chiles, or put the chiles on individual plates and spoon the tomato broth over the top. Garnish with the parsley and crumbled cheese, and serve immediately.

NOTES: More likely than not, Anaheim chiles are used for stuffing along the border states, but the poblano chiles are preferred by those Mexican Americans with ties to Central Mexico. The chiles can be filled instead with the *picadillo* used for Stuffed Chiles with Walnut Sauce (page 195), cooked with the batter or not, as preferred, but always swimming in the red spiced tomato broth. They may also be stuffed with well-seasoned well-fried beans and, after frying, served with a topping of Mexican *crema* (page 23).

Stuffed Chiles with Walnut Sauce
Chiles en Nogada
EL PASO, TEXAS • PUEBLA, MEXICO

SERVES 6   Chiles en Nogada *is a study in contrasts: red, green, and white; hot and cold; piquant and sweet; crunchy and smooth. Because of the seasonal nature of the ingredients, this dish can be made properly only in the late summer and autumn. And there is no doubt that it takes a lot of time to make, but it is as beautiful to look at as it is wonderful to eat. This festive dish, resplendent with the colors of the Mexican flag, is still traditionally served on September 16, in honor of Mexico's Independence Day, though it is popular anytime in the early fall when the walnuts are fresh and the pomegranates abundant. In Southwestern gardens, the burnished red fruit can be picked directly from the small trees. Our walnut sauce is similar to one of Aída Gabilondo's, who, along with several other Texas cooks, gave us the idea to use cream cheese.*

It is a perfect party dish, for it is easily done in stages one or two days in advance. The chiles are stuffed and heated at the last minute.

Chiles en Nogada is such a spectacular dish that it should be the focal point of a special meal. Start with Cilantro Soup (page 75) and end with a flan. I usually would not drink a chardonnay with richly complex Mexican food. A friend whose wine judgment I trust, however, recommended a Kendall-Jackson Grand Reserve chardonnay, and it does intensify the rich spice of the chile and the sweetness of the walnut cream sauce.

For the Meat

2 pounds beef brisket or other stew meat or 1 pound beef and 1 pound pork butt

1 small white onion, quartered

2 cloves garlic

about 1 tablespoon sea salt

For the Picadillo

4 tablespoons safflower or canola oil

⅓ cup chopped white onion

3 cloves garlic, minced

½ teaspoon ground cinnamon (cassia) (see sidebar, page 164)

¼ teaspoon freshly ground black pepper

⅛ teaspoon ground cloves

3 heaping tablespoons raisins

2 tablespoons chopped walnuts or pecans

2 tablespoons chopped candied *acitrón* or candied pineapple (see Note)

1 fresh pear, peeled and chopped

1 apple, peeled and chopped

3 large, ripe tomatoes roasted, peeled (page 22), and chopped, or one 28-ounce can chopped tomatoes, with juice

sea salt

For the Chiles

6 fresh poblano chiles, roasted (page 21), peeled, and seeded, leaving the stem intact

For the Walnut Sauce

1 cup fresh walnuts

6 ounces cream cheese at room temperature (not fat free)

1½ cups Mexican *crema* (page 23) or 1¼ cups sour cream thinned with milk

about ½ teaspoon sea salt

1 tablespoon sugar (optional)

⅛ teaspoon ground cinnamon (cassia) (see sidebar, page 164) (optional)

¼ cup dry sherry (optional)

For the Garnish

1 tablespoon chopped flat-leaf parsley or cilantro leaves

½ cup pomegranate seeds

Cut the meat into large chunks, removing any excess fat. Place the meat into a large Dutch oven with the onion, garlic, and salt. Cover with cold water and bring to a boil over medium-high heat. Skim off any foam that collects on the surface. Lower the heat and allow the water to simmer about 45 minutes, until the meat is just tender. Take the pot off the stove and let the meat cool in the broth. Remove the pieces of meat and finely shred them. (If making stuffed chiles with a tomato sauce rather than the walnut sauce, save the broth.)

Warm the oil in a large, heavy skillet and sauté the onion and garlic over medium heat until they turn a pale gold. Stir in the shredded meat and cook for 5 minutes. Add the cinnamon, pepper, and cloves, then stir in the raisins, the 2 tablespoons chopped walnuts, and the candied *acitrón*. Add the chopped pear and apple, and mix well. Add the tomatoes and salt to taste, and continue cooking over medium-high heat until most of the moisture has evaporated. Stir often so that the mixture doesn't stick. Let cool, cover, and set aside. The *picadillo* may be made 1 day in advance.

Make a slit down the side of each chile, just long enough to remove the seeds and veins. Keep the stem end intact. This is easiest done under warm running water. Drain the chiles on absorbent paper until completely dry. Cover and set aside. The chiles may be prepared 1 day in advance.

At least 3 hours in advance, place the 1 cup walnuts in a small pan of boiling water. Remove from the heat and let them sit for 5 minutes. Drain the nuts and, when cool, rub off as much of the dark skin as possible. Chop in small pieces.

Place the nuts, cream cheese, *crema,* and salt in a blender and puree thoroughly. Stir in the optional sugar, cinnamon, and sherry, if using, until thoroughly combined. Chill for several hours.

Preheat the oven to 250 degrees F. When ready to serve, reheat the meat filling and stuff the chiles until plump and just barely closed. Put the filled chiles, covered, to warm in the oven. After they are thoroughly heated, place on a serving platter or individual plates, cover with the chilled walnut sauce, and sprinkle with the parsley and pomegranate seeds.

NOTE: *Acitrón* is crystallized biznaga cactus and comes in bars a little smaller than a cube of butter. I have found it in the United States only in heavily Mexican-populated areas such as Chicago and Los Angeles, but when you go to Mexico, you can buy some at any large city candy store, including at the Mexico City airport. If you can't find it, candied pineapple is an acceptable substitute, but *don't* use citron, a preserved citrus fruit that has a decidedly different taste and texture and is best kept for your seasonal fruitcake.

Unstuffed Stuffed Chiles
Chiles Rellenos de Fiesta
ESPAÑOLA, NEW MEXICO

MAKES ABOUT 3 DOZEN, ENOUGH FOR 2 OR 3 APPETIZERS APIECE FOR 12 TO 20 GUESTS *All over northern New Mexico in both homes and restaurants—if we were served chiles rellenos, we were invariably given green chile fritters instead of the stuffed chiles we expected. According to Sally Borrego and others we spoke to, the reason is that the local chile—the famed chile chimayó—is too small to stuff, so they mix the chile with the filling instead of filling the chiles. Decid-*

edly different—but still very good. The fritters are usually served with a tomato sauce or even a sweet raisin sauce spooned over the top.

Sally usually makes at least double this recipe and freezes the fritters to use for Christmas and New Year buffets, heating them in a microwave.

Vegetable Salad with Pears and Cherries (page 60) and Jicama with Cucumbers and Melon (page 35) are colorful accompanying dishes, and I like to serve a plate of Pumpkin Turnovers (page 363).

For the Filling

1 pound pork shoulder, cut into large pieces
1 pound beef chuck or sirloin tip, cut into large pieces
sea salt
10 fresh long green New Mexico or Anaheim chiles, roasted (page 21), peeled, and chopped
¾ pound longhorn cheese, grated
2 large ripe tomatoes, diced
1 tablespoon safflower or canola oil
1 medium white onion, finely chopped
3 cloves garlic, minced, or ½ teaspoon garlic powder
1 teaspoon dried oregano, preferably Mexican
¼ cup flour

For the Sauce (optional)

1½ pounds tomatoes, roasted (page 22), or one 28-ounce can tomato pieces, drained
½ white onion, roughly chopped
2 cloves garlic, roughly chopped
1 teaspoon safflower or canola oil
pinch of oregano, preferably Mexican
sea salt

For the Batter

4 eggs, separated, at room temperature
½ teaspoon sea salt

For Frying

peanut or safflower oil

Place the meat in a large, heavy pan with salted cold water to cover. Bring to a boil, lower the heat, and simmer about 1½ hours, until tender. Leave the meat in the broth to cool.

When the meat is cool, shred it and mix together in a large bowl with the chiles, cheese, and tomatoes.

While the meat is cooling, warm the oil in a skillet and sauté the onion and garlic over medium-high heat until they are lightly colored. Drain off the oil and add the onion and garlic to the meat mixture. Add oregano and more salt to taste, and toss it all well with your hands.

While the meat is cooling, prepare the tomato sauce if using. In a blender or food processor, puree the tomatoes, onion, and garlic. In a medium-size skillet, fry the sauce in the oil for 2–3 minutes. Lower the heat, add the oregano and salt to taste, and simmer for 10 minutes. This may be prepared ahead, then reheated.

Flour your hands and form the meat and chile mixture into 1- by 2-inch oblong rolls, rather like a fat thumb. Roll or sprinkle lightly with flour, shaking off any excess.

Separate the eggs, putting the egg whites into a mixing bowl with the salt. Beat with a mixer or egg beater until soft peaks form. Break up the egg yolks gently a little at a time and fold into the egg whites until well mixed.

Pour ½ inch of oil into a large, heavy skillet and heat over medium-high heat to 375 degrees F.—until a piece of bread dropped in will begin to crackle, not burn.

Dip the meat-chile rolls gently into the beaten eggs, turning to coat all sides. With a slotted spoon place them in the hot oil and fry quickly. They should be puffy and rather crisp. Fry only a few at a time so the oil doesn't cool off. Drain on absorbent paper and keep warm until all are done. Place the fritters on a warm platter and serve with the tomato sauce.

Forest Mushroom Crêpes
Crepas de Hongos Silvestres
VICTORIA, BRITISH COLUMBIA, CANADA • MEXICO CITY, MEXICO

MAKES ABOUT 12 CRÊPES, 6 INCHES ACROSS *Since 1864 when Napoleon III of France installed the Austrian prince Maximilian as emperor of Mexico, the more sophisticated Mexican cooks have incorporated French and other European techniques into their cooking styles. Crêpes are a favorite, stuffed with such distinctive Mexican ingredients as squash blossoms and the exotic corn fungus cuitlacoche. These crêpes, flecked with cilantro, are quite unusual, and our filling, based on a recipe taken from Maria Elena C. Lorens's book* Mexican Cuisine, *uses either wild mushrooms or any similar cultivated ones now found in many markets. Shiitake, morel, or oyster mushrooms are all excellent, and several types can be mixed together.*

This makes an elegant light supper with just a glass of chardonnay and a green salad. For dessert, serve Creamy Coffee Liqueur Gelatin (page 346).

For the Crêpes

1¼ cups all-purpose flour
3 large eggs, lightly beaten
⅔ cup milk
⅔ cup beer or water
2 tablespoons unsalted butter, melted and cooled
2 tablespoons finely chopped cilantro (optional)
½ teaspoon sea salt
melted unsalted butter or safflower or canola oil
　for cooking

For the Filling

4 tablespoons unsalted butter
1 cup finely chopped white onion
5 cloves garlic, minced
2 fresh serrano chiles, minced
2 pounds fresh shiitake or other mushrooms,
　wiped and sliced in 1-inch-long strips
1 cup minced cilantro
sea salt and freshly ground black pepper

For the Sauce

2 teaspoons unsalted butter
1 clove garlic, minced
2 tablespoons flour
2 cups milk (3 tablespoons dry sherry can be sub-
　stituted for 3 tablespoons of the milk)
1 cup sour cream (low-fat sour cream can be
　used but not nonfat)
sea salt and freshly ground black pepper
1 cup grated Monterey jack cheese

For the Garnish

½ cup chopped cilantro

Place the flour, eggs, milk, beer or water, melted butter, cilantro, and salt in a food processor or blender and mix until smooth. Or place in a bowl and use an electric hand mixer. Add
additional liquid if needed; the batter must be very thin. Cover the bowl with plastic wrap and
let it sit at room temperature for 30 minutes to 1 hour so the batter becomes supple; the crêpes
will be light in texture when cooked.

Over medium-high heat, warm an 8- or 9-inch omelet or crêpe pan that has sloping sides,
preferably nonstick. When moderately hot, brush with a little melted butter or oil. It should
just sizzle, not burn. (If it is smoking, wipe the pan and start again.)

Uncover the batter, beat again, and if it is too thick, add a little more liquid. With a ladle or
large spoon that holds about 3 tablespoons of batter, scoop up the batter and quickly pour
into the middle of the pan. Remove the pan from the heat and quickly tilt it so that the batter
swirls around the sides to form a round, thin crêpe. Return the pan to the heat and cook about
1 minute, until the bottom of the crêpe is slightly brown. Little bubbles will come to the surface, and the crêpe can slide around in the pan when sharply jerked. To turn the crêpe over,
first loosen the edges by shaking the pan and then jerk the pan so the crêpe flips over. This
takes practice, so you may have to help it along with a spatula.

Lightly brown the second side for less than 1 minute, then invert the pan over a large plate.
This will be the inside part of the crêpe. Continue the routine, stacking the crêpes, until all the

batter is used up. They are now ready for filling, or they can be made in advance and stacked with wax paper or foil between them. Or they can be frozen. To thaw, heat them, covered, in a 300-degree F. oven.

Don't discard any leftover or imperfect crêpes. They can be reheated and spread with butter or wrapped around a small hunk of cheese and eaten as a snack.

Preheat the oven to 350 degrees F.

To prepare the filling, melt the butter in a heavy, medium-size saucepan over medium-low heat. Add the onion, garlic, and chiles, and sauté until the onion is transparent. Stir in the mushrooms, increase the heat, and continue cooking until any liquid from the mushrooms has been absorbed. Remove from the heat, add the cilantro and salt and pepper to taste, and set aside. This filling can be made several hours in advance.

To prepare the sauce, melt the butter in a separate saucepan, add the garlic, and lightly sauté. Blend in the flour and add the milk and sour cream. Season well with salt and pepper. Bring to a boil, lower the heat, and simmer for 3–4 minutes, stirring constantly, until the sauce thickens. Mix ½ cup of the sauce into the mushroom mixture.

Spoon the mushroom mixture onto each crêpe and roll into a taco shape. Place the filled crêpes in a single layer in a greased ovenproof dish just big enough to hold all the crêpes. Spoon the sauce over the top.

Sprinkle with the cheese and bake for 8–10 minutes, or until the cheese is melted. Remove from the oven and garnish with the cilantro. Serve immediately.

Poblano Chile–Stuffed Crêpes
Crepas con Rajas de Poblanos
NORTHBROOK, ILLINOIS • MEXICO CITY, MEXICO

SERVES 4, WITH 3 CRÊPES PER PERSON *Elaine González's crêpes marry the earthy flavor of roasted poblano chiles with Chihuahua cheese.*

An ideal partner for these crêpes would be Watercress Salad with Pine Nuts (page 52) and a light fruity California chardonnay to drink. For a fuller menu, start the meal with a Clam and Avocado Cocktail with Tiny Shrimp (page 62).

12 premade crêpes (pages 199–200)

For the Filling

6 fresh poblano chiles, roasted (page 21) and
   seeded
2 tablespoons safflower or canola oil
1 medium white onion, chopped
sea salt and freshly ground black pepper
½ cup grated Chihuahua cheese or a mild white
   cheddar or Monterey jack (see Note)

For the Sauce

2½ cups milk
8 tablespoons (1 stick) unsalted butter
4 tablespoons flour
dash of nutmeg
sea salt and freshly ground black pepper
¼ cup grated Chihuahua cheese or a mild white
   cheddar or Monterey jack or Parmesan (see
   Note)

Prepare the crêpes in advance and preheat the oven to 350 degrees F.

Cut the chiles into narrow strips. Warm the oil in a large skillet over medium heat and add the onion. Cook until it is soft and transparent. Stir in the chiles and season with salt and pepper to taste. Lower the heat and cook together for several minutes. Set the skillet aside and stir in the cheese.

To prepare the sauce, scald the milk in a medium-size saucepan. Set aside.

Melt the butter over medium-low heat in a heavy saucepan. Stir in the flour and cook, stirring constantly, for about 2 minutes. Add the hot milk gradually, continuing to stir, and cook until the mixture begins to simmer. Season with nutmeg, salt, and pepper to taste, and cook briefly over low heat. Remove the sauce from the heat and whisk until smooth. If the sauce is too thick, add ⅓ cup of hot milk and mix well.

Cover the bottom of a 15- by 10-inch baking dish with some of the sauce. Lay out the crêpes with their palest side up and fill each one by putting about 2 tablespoons of the poblano chile strips just below the center of each crêpe. Roll the crêpe up tightly like a sausage and place in the baking dish, seam side down. Cover the filled crêpes with sauce. Sprinkle with cheese and bake for about 10 minutes. Serve immediately.

NOTE: The large yellow wheels of cheese made by the Mennonite communities in Chihuahua are becoming quite scarce even in Mexico, but there are several imitations. Avoid those made in the United States and instead substitute another good melting cheese. I recommend mild white cheddar or Monterey jack. If you prefer not to have melted cheese as a topping, use a coarsely grated Parmesan.

Cheese Fritters with Chile and Fruit Sauce

Tortitas de Queso

NEW YORK, NEW YORK • PUEBLA, MEXICO

SERVES 4 *Of all the food discoveries my husband Fredric and I made while sampling old favorites and new dishes across the country, this lush, big-flavored version of the sometimes spartan Lenten egg fritter is one that we both especially treasure. I can still see my husband's face the first time Apolonio Mariano Ramirez set the plate in front of him. His response was the silence of great appreciation.*

Sopes with Chicken (page 123) can be put on the table at the same time or, more typically, served first. The sweet flavor of chilled sliced melon is a perfect contrast.

For the Sauce

4 ounces dried guajillo chiles (about 10), toasted (page 22) and seeds removed

1½ pounds fresh tomatillos, husked, rinsed, and roughly chopped

2 cloves garlic, roughly chopped

⅛ teaspoon ground clove

⅛ teaspoon ground cumin

¼ teaspoon sea salt

1 tablespoon safflower or canola oil

1 pound firm red or yellow plums, pitted and cut in wedges, sliced (about 2 cups fruit) (see Note)

For the Fritters

6 eggs at room temperature, separated

1 pound *queso cotija, queso añejo,* or feta cheese, grated or crumbled

peanut oil for frying

For the Garnish

minced green onion tops

crumbled *queso cotija, queso añejo,* or feta cheese

Soak the chiles in hot water about 10 minutes, until softened, and drain. Place the chiles, tomatillos, garlic, clove, cumin, salt, and 1 cup of water into a blender or food processor and blend well.

Heat the oil in a large skillet over medium-high heat until very hot but not smoking. Add the blended chile mixture and cook about 10 minutes, until thick. Stir frequently. The sauce can be made in advance to this point, covered, and refrigerated for up to 2 days.

Reheat the sauce in the large skillet, add the plums and cook another 5 minutes on low heat. Set aside and keep warm. Add more liquid if necessary.

Thoroughly mix the egg yolks in a small bowl. Beat the egg whites in a larger bowl until they form soft peaks. Gently fold in the egg yolks and cheese.

recipe continues

In an electric frying pan or large skillet, heat about ¾ inch of oil starting on medium-high heat, 380 degrees F. The oil should be hot enough to sputter when a small piece of bread is dropped in, but not quite smoking.

Fry the fritters in small batches, making sure the oil doesn't cool down between batches. Using a large serving spoon, scoop up a spoonful of the egg mixture and carefully slide it into the hot oil. The fritters should be about 3 inches in diameter. After they begin to brown, it helps to form them by pressing the sides together with 2 spoons or spatulas. Cook 1–2 minutes on each side. When golden brown on each side, remove with a slotted spoon and drain on absorbent paper.

Add the fritters to the sauce and let sit for several minutes. Lift the fritters with a slotted spatula and place on dinner plates. Just as they are to be brought to the table, spoon more of the warm chile sauce with the fruit over the top. Sprinkle with green onions and crumbled cheese.

NOTE: Our host somehow had found tiny yellow Mexican *ciruelas,* or plums. We make do with the larger Japanese plums, which, with their pleasant blend of acid and sugar, seem to come quite close in taste. I expect the flavor of the venerable greengage plum would be quite similar.

Gloria's Red Chicken Enchiladas
Enchiladas Coloradas de Pollo, de Gloria
CHULA VISTA, CALIFORNIA • BAJA CALIFORNIA NORTE, MEXICO

MAKES 12, OR 2 OR 3 PER PERSON   *Back when I was first thinking of writing this book, I had heard about Gloria's Chicken Enchiladas from a friend of mine in Mexico City who had gone to school in San Diego. Of course I had to track them down, a search that ended at the home of Gloria Anaya Lopez's daughter in Chula Vista. That night I watched while Gloria went through the time-consuming double-dipping, filling, and rolling procedure that makes these traditional street-style enchiladas so messy to make—and so special to eat. So special that Miguel and I, and everyone who has sampled them, always refer to them as just Gloria's enchiladas.*

Both Miguel and I find this a good wake-up dish and like to serve it for late-morning Sunday brunches.

COCINA DE LA FAMILIA

Gloria's enchiladas can be a colorful one-dish meal, but well-fried beans are a classic accompaniment. A large green salad or the Jicama, Melon, and Orange Salad (page 57) will provide a crispy contrast. If it is a hot day, set out bottles of a Mexican beer, such as the dark Negra Modelo or a pitcher of iced tea. Other times, I like cold milk.

For the Chicken

Chicken Stock (page 70), canned chicken broth,
   or water to cover (about 6 cups)
3 pounds chicken thighs and breasts
6 cloves garlic, peeled and slightly bruised with
   the flat side of a knife
½ medium white onion, sliced
about 1 teaspoon sea salt

For the Chile Sauce

12 dried red chiles, either New Mexican or California
6 dried pasilla chiles
½ white onion
3 cloves garlic
2 level tablespoons flour
2 teaspoons safflower or canola oil
1 8-ounce can tomato sauce

1 teaspoon dried oregano, preferably Mexican
sea salt and freshly ground black pepper

For the Tomato Sauce

2 tablespoons safflower or canola oil
¼ cup chopped white onion
2 cloves garlic, minced
2 8-ounce cans tomato sauce

For the Enchiladas

12 store-bought corn tortillas (see Note)
½ cup safflower or canola oil for frying

For the Toppings

¼ cup crumbled *queso añejo* or feta cheese
12 radishes, thinly sliced
1 cup thick Mexican *crema* (page 23) or sour
   cream thinned with milk (optional)

Bring the broth or water to a boil in a large (6-quart) pot. Add the chicken thighs, garlic, onion and salt. Bring to a simmer, keeping the heat low so the liquid barely bubbles. Skim off any gray foam that appears. Poach for about 10 minutes, add the breasts, and skim again. Continue to simmer for another 10 minutes. Take the pot off the heat and allow the chicken to cool in the broth. Remove the chicken and shred the meat, discarding the skin and bones. (These can be put back in the broth and simmered a bit more—about 45 minutes—the broth strained, and frozen for future use.) Reserve a cup of the broth for the sauce. The chicken may be cooked ahead, covered, and refrigerated until ready to make the enchiladas.

To prepare the chile sauce: Stem and remove the seeds and veins from the chiles. Put the chiles, onion, and garlic in a medium-size pot of boiling water. Drop a spoon or something else rather heavy into the water to keep the chiles submerged. Turn off the heat and let the chiles soak until they are tender, about 15 minutes, depending on the age of the chiles.

When the chiles are softened, add a third of them to a blender along with the onion and garlic. Add some of the remaining chicken broth so that the mixture doesn't clog the blender. Blend until satiny smooth. If needed, strain through a medium-size sieve. Repeat until all the chiles, onion, and garlic are blended.

In a heavy skillet or Dutch oven, sprinkle on a light layer of flour and lightly toast it to a golden color over medium heat. Pour in the oil and stir well.

Add the strained chile puree all at once. Stir and scrape constantly over low heat until thick and mellow. Do not allow the mixture to stick and burn. Mix in the canned tomato sauce and add the oregano, and salt, and pepper to taste. Set aside. The sauce can be made ahead and kept in the refrigerator with the chicken.

To prepare the tomato sauce: In another skillet, heat the oil over medium heat and cook the onions and garlic until soft. Add tomato sauce and cook 8–10 minutes, until thoroughly blended. The sauce can be made several hours in advance and set aside. Stir in the shredded chicken and continue to cook for 3–5 minutes. Season to taste.

To assemble the enchiladas: Preheat the oven to 325 degrees F. Have ready a heated serving dish, approximately 13 by 9 by 2 inches, that will just hold 1 layer of rolled and filled tortillas.

Heat the oil in a skillet over medium-high heat and reheat the chile sauce over low heat in another skillet. Immerse each tortilla in the hot oil for about 30 seconds, then, using tongs or 2 spatulas, turn it over and heat the other side. Tortillas should be soft, not crispy. Drain off any excess oil on absorbent paper and continue with the remaining tortillas. Dip the softened tortillas in the warmed red chile sauce and lay them on a plate. Spread a heaping tablespoon of the chicken down the center of each tortilla and roll up. Spoon a thin layer of the chile sauce on the bottom of the serving dish and arrange the enchiladas, seam side down, and crowding together in one layer. When all have been filled and rolled, spoon a bit more chile sauce over them and bake for 5 minutes. Remove the dish of enchiladas from the oven and spoon on the rest of the chile sauce. Garnish with the cheese, radishes, and thick Mexican *crema*.

NOTE: In order that the tortillas do not absorb a lot of oil and become soggy, it is impor-tant that they *not* be freshly made.

Chipotle Crab Enchiladas

Enchiladas de Jaiba en Chiles Chipotles

AUSTIN, TEXAS

SERVES 4 WITH 2 ENCHILADAS EACH *As a child during the Depression, I lived up and down the Gulf Coast between Corpus Christi, Texas, and Brownsville, which is right on the Mexican border where the Rio Bravo del Norte (the Rio Grande) enters the Gulf of Mexico. I have memories of my dad carrying a bucket of squiggling greenish crabs back to some auto court where we stayed, and cooking them in a galvanized washtub of boiling water. I know I must have eaten crabmeat enchiladas, but they were never prepared in a creamy chipotle sauce like these of Miquel Ravago's. For a festive meal I like to garnish this dish with colorful flowers made of green onions and a few jalapeño chiles, both green and red, if I can find them.*

Crab enchiladas go particularly well with a starter of Jicama with Cucumbers and Melon (page 35) or a salad of crisp lettuce and garden-fresh sliced tomatoes. It is an especially good dish to serve for a festive brunch, and in summer add the Vegetable Salad with Pears and Cherries (page 60) with its deep red fresh cherries. To continue with the fresh fruit flavors, end the meal with Raspberry Bombé (page 357).

For the Filling

2 cups thick Mexican *crema* (page 23) or sour cream thinned with milk

¼ cup milk

sea salt

4 tablespoons unsalted butter

2 tablespoons safflower or canola oil

1 large clove garlic, minced

½ cup green onion tops, chopped (save the white parts for the garnish)

1 pound crabmeat, in big chunks

2 canned chipotle chiles *en adobo*, sliced into narrow strips

freshly ground black pepper

For the Enchiladas

¼–½ cup safflower or canola oil for frying

8 store-bought corn tortillas, about 6 inches in diameter

½ cup grated Monterey jack cheese

For the Garnish

3 tablespoons minced cilantro

12 plump green onions

8 fresh green and red jalapeño chiles for making chile "flowers" (optional) (see Note)

Heat the oven to 350 degrees F.

Stir together the *crema* and milk in a small mixing bowl. Lightly salt and set aside.

In a medium-size saucepan or deep skillet, melt the butter with the oil over medium heat. Add the garlic and green onion tops, and cook for about 2 minutes, until the onions are softened.

Add the crabmeat, chile strips, and 1 cup of the thinned *crema,* reserving the rest to use as topping. Lower the heat and continue cooking for 5–8 minutes, stirring occasionally. Add pepper to taste. This can be made to this point in advance and reheated before proceeding.

Near the stove, have ready a layer of absorbent paper and an oiled ovenproof dish. All the rolled tortillas should fit snugly in a single layer. It is helpful to have both tongs and a slotted spatula to use while frying the tortillas.

Warm about 2 tablespoons of the oil in a medium-size skillet over medium heat and press each tortilla into the hot oil with the spatula, until it just softens—only several seconds. Turn it over and fry for even a shorter time on the other side. Remove the tortilla and drain on absorbent paper. Continue frying the remaining tortillas, adding more oil if needed.

Place an equal portion of filling across the center of each tortilla. Roll them up and put them side by side in the baking dish. Pour the remaining thinned cream over the top and sprinkle with the grated cheese.

Cover with aluminum foil and bake for 15 minutes, or until thoroughly heated. Serve immediately, sprinkled with cilantro and garnished with green onions or flowers made from the green onions and chiles.

NOTE: If you are making the vegetable flower garnish, start several hours in advance. Use small, sharp scissors to cut through the pointed end of a chile and then cut down each of the four sides to about ½ inch from the stem end. Scrape out the seeds and continue cutting each of the larger chile sections to form thin, pointed petals. Make as many chile garnishes as needed and drop into a small bowl of cold water. Store in the refrigerator until they open out.

The onion flowers are made in a similar manner. Cut off the roots and all but ½ inch of the green tops, saving them to use in the crab sauce. Peel off 1 layer of onion skin, and using a small sharp knife, make V-shaped cuts around the middle of the onion. Be sure the knife cuts through to the center. Separate the "petals" by gently pulling the two sides of the onion apart and put to open in cold water.

Red-Chile Chicken Enchiladas with Carrots and Potatoes

Enchiladas Mineras

MIAMI, FLORIDA • GUANAJUATO, MEXICO

SERVES 4 TO 6 *This recipe for "miner's enchiladas" was passed to Virginia Ariemma from her mother. The state of Guanajuato, where it originated, once produced most of the silver in the world. Many Spanish and criollos became fabulously wealthy but at the expense of the Indians forced to work under the most horrible conditions imaginable.*

Enchiladas were the main food of these miners and their families. Tortillas were made savory by dipping them in an uncooked chile sauce before being fried. Carrots and potatoes were a cheap nutritious addition. Almost identical enchiladas are still cooked over small metal charcoal-burning stoves around Guanajuato's famous vaulted Mercado Hidalgo. Often chicken pieces will also be dipped in the sauce, fried, and served on the side with the vegetables.

I think enchiladas like these are the finest street food in Mexico. If made with chicken, nothing else is needed except a green salad or, if feeding a group of hungry folk, add Well-Fried Beans (page 227). Chunky Fresh Tomato Salsa (page 264) will add a brilliant contrast. This is a beer drinker's delight, although Sangria (page 380) is also a good choice for a beverage.

For the Sauce

6 dried guajillo chiles, toasted (page 22) and
  seeded
¼ cup mild vinegar
½ white onion, roasted (page 22)
3 cloves garlic, roasted (page 22)
about ½ teaspoon sea salt
⅛ teaspoon ground cumin

For the Enchiladas

1 pound carrots, peeled and cut into ½-inch
  pieces
1 pound red potatoes, peeled and cut into ½-inch
  pieces

sea salt
½ cup safflower or canola oil
12 Corn Tortillas (page 108) or store-bought
1 whole chicken breast, poached (page 70) and
  shredded

For the Garnish

2 cups shredded lettuce or cabbage
1 cup Mexican *crema* (page 23) or sour cream
  thinned with milk
½ cup crumbled *queso fresco* (page 112) or feta
  cheese

Place the chiles in a bowl and pour in 3 cups of boiling water. Add the vinegar and let the chiles soften for 20 minutes. Place the onion, garlic, salt, cumin, and 1 cup of the soaking liquid in a blender or food processor with the chiles. Puree until smooth and put in a shallow pan or bowl.

Simmer the carrots and potatoes in enough salted water to cover. When tender, about 10 minutes, drain and set aside.

Heat the oil in a skillet over medium heat. Dip a tortilla into the chile sauce, coating both sides, then slide into the hot oil. Cook for 10–15 seconds, then use a slotted spatula to flip to the other side for a few seconds. Quickly remove from the oil, draining off as much as possible. Loosely bend the tortillas in half, making *dobladas*. Fill with the shredded chicken and keep them warm in a 200-degree F. oven.

Pour a little more oil into the skillet if needed and add the potatoes and carrots along with 2 tablespoons sauce. Fry for several minutes.

Divide the shredded lettuce among the individual plates. Place 2 or 3 folded enchiladas on each bed of lettuce and scatter the vegetable cubes over the top. Drizzle on the *crema* and top with the crumbled cheese. Serve immediately.

VARIATION: MINER'S ENCHILADAS WITH RED CHILE–DRENCHED CHICKEN
Take 3 to 3½ pounds of your favorite chicken parts and poach (page 70). Dip the tortillas in the red chile sauce. Fold, but leave them unfilled. Before frying the carrots and potatoes, rub the sauce over all the chicken and brown the pieces in the oil. After 5 minutes, add the vegetables and 2 tablespoons of sauce, and continue to cook another 5 minutes, or until all are nicely browned.

Green Enchiladas with Spinach and Tofu
Enchiladas Verdes a la "Pingüi"
DETROIT, MICHIGAN

SERVES 4 TO 6 *In these quite atypical enchiladas, Maria Elena Rodriguez substitutes fresh bean curd and spinach for the usual chicken or meat fillings. "Pingüi," as her father calls her (from pingüica, a little berry that grows in the highlands of central Mexico; the name is used to describe a very small person), grew up in a family of good cooks and loves to eat the often calorific dishes of Mexico. Out of necessity she's devising a healthier approach but one that still maintains the intense flavors she loves so well.*

Because the tortillas are not softened in hot oil before being dipped in the sauce, they sometimes break instead of bend. To keep this from occurring, we steam them and, after they are filled, fold them instead of rolling them up.

This is very good served with small cups of Black Bean Soup (page 95) or with Black Beans with Pork (page 231) served on the side. Try Red Radish Relish (page 280) as a colorful side dish.

3 cups Basic Green Tomatillo Sauce for Enchiladas (page 212)

2 fresh poblano chiles or long green chiles, roasted (page 21) and seeded

¼–½ cup defatted canned chicken broth, if necessary

1 pound Chinese-style tofu, well-drained and sliced in ⅛-inch slices

1 medium red onion, sliced into paper-thin rings

16 store-bought corn tortillas, 7 inches in diameter

2 pounds fresh spinach

sea salt

1 pound fresh mushrooms, sliced (about 2 cups)

12 ounces low-fat Monterey jack cheese, shredded

1 cup yogurt, thinned with 2 tablespoons skim milk

¼ cup cilantro leaves

Prepare the Basic Tomatillo Sauce, adding the poblano chiles to be blended with the sauce. Some chicken broth may be needed if the sauce is too thick. Pour into a saucepan and warm over low heat while you prepare the rest of the ingredients. This may be prepared in advance and reheated.

Arrange the tofu in a single layer on a pan and brush or dribble on 1 cup of the tomatillo sauce so that the flavors will permeate the tofu. If possible, let it sit at least 30 minutes before using.

Put the onion rings in a bowl, cover with warm water, and let them soak.

Fill the bottom of a steamer with ½ inch of water. (If you don't have a perforated rack such as that used for tamales or Chinese cooking, you can place a screw ring from a Mason jar in the bottom of a pan and balance a small heatproof plate on top.) Bring the water to a boil. Wrap the tortillas in a thick towel and lay them on the rack in the steamer. Cover and steam for 1 minute. Remove the pan from the heat and let the tortillas sit for 10 minutes, still covered.

Wash the fresh spinach thoroughly and put in a saucepan with only the water clinging to the leaves. Sprinkle with salt and cook over low heat until the leaves are just wilted. Drain, coarsely chop, and mix with the mushrooms.

Preheat the oven to 350 degrees F. Set out a large, flat baking dish and coat lightly with oil or a nonfat spray. Coat the bottom of the dish with about ½ cup of the tomatillo sauce. If necessary, thin the sauce with more chicken broth to make it pourable.

Uncover the tortillas, dip each one into the hot tomatillo sauce, and slide onto a plate.

Quickly fill each tortilla with the spinach-mushroom mixture and tofu, and a sprinkling of cheese. Bend in half and set inside the casserole dish, slightly overlapping. When all the tortillas are filled, cover with the remaining cheese and bake for about 15–20 minutes.

Put 3 or 4 enchiladas on each plate. Drizzle with the diluted yogurt and garnish with the drained red onion rings and cilantro.

Basic Green Tomatillo Sauce for Enchiladas

Salsa Verde para Enchiladas

SAN DIEGO, CALIFORNIA

MAKES ENOUGH FOR 12 ENCHILADAS   *The quantities of the ingredients used in this recipe of Steven Ravago's can be halved or doubled, according to how much sauce is needed. This versatile sauce also can be used on tacos, fish, pork, and chicken dishes as well as enchiladas, and it freezes well, though it may have to be reblended with a cup or so of broth or water.*

2 pounds tomatillos, husked and rinsed

2 large white onions, coarsely chopped

5 cloves garlic, peeled

5–6 fresh serrano or jalapeño chiles, stemmed and seeded

3 tablespoons safflower or canola oil

1¼ teaspoons sea salt

¾ cup chopped fresh cilantro

Preheat the oven to 450 degrees F.

Place the tomatillos, onions, garlic, chiles, and oil in a roasting pan. Sprinkle with salt, and toss to coat all the ingredients with the oil. Roast in the oven for about 45 minutes. When the tomatillos are soft and the onions and garlic are browned, remove the pan from the oven and let cool.

Transfer to a blender and puree to a coarse consistency. Add ⅓ cup of water and the cilantro, blend, and taste. Add more salt if desired. Pour into a saucepan and keep warm while you prepare the enchiladas.

Flat Enchiladas Sonoran-Style
Enchiladas Chatas Sonorenses
TUCSON, ARIZONA • SONORA, MEXICO

ENOUGH FOR 12 ENCHILADAS *These fat, flat enchiladas typical of Sonora, Mexico, were served to us throughout southern Arizona, a conspicuous culinary reminder that we were in a part of that sunbaked landscape which makes up the Sonoran Desert and stretches for hundreds of miles south into Mexico. These are not typical enchiladas but little fat* masa *cakes—covered in a mild but tasty chile sauce. All the toppings are pyramided on top. This version is from Carmen Villa Prezelski. Carmen had to learn to cook from a distance because her mother, Matilde, would never let any of her eight children into the kitchen. At ninety, Matilde is still cooking three meals a day for two of her grown children, and the others live close enough to come and eat with her once or twice a week.*

Serve these with Mexican Red Rice (page 235), maybe with beans alongside, and a refreshing drink of Cucumber Cooler (page 380). For a special treat at breakfast or brunch, put a poached or fried egg on each enchilada after adding the sauce and spoon on more of the sauce.

Carmen and her mother will only make these enchiladas with fresh corn masa, *not with* masa harina, *which to Carmen "always feels rough in the back of my throat."*

The Arizona Red Chile Paste needed to make the sauce should be prepared in advance or a sauce can be ordered from Santa Cruz Chile and Spice Company (see Product Sources, page 392). A family of cattle ranchers south of Tucson, Arizona, in Tumacacori, has been making this chile paste since 1943 from just-picked mature New Mexico chiles. It is now extensively used by Mexican-American cooks all over Arizona.

For the Sauce
2 tablespoons safflower or canola oil

3 cloves garlic, finely minced

2 tablespoons all-purpose flour

2 cups homemade Arizona Red Chile Paste (page 215) or mild red chili sauce without tomatoes

2–3 cups hot Beef Stock (page 72), canned beef broth, or water

ingredients continue

---

1 teaspoon oregano, preferably Mexican
sea salt

For the Enchiladas

1 pound fresh *masa* or prepared from *masa harina*
   (page 292)
2 eggs, beaten
½ cup grated Colby or longhorn cheese
1 teaspoon baking powder
1 teaspoon sea salt
peanut or safflower oil for frying

For the Toppings

1 bunch green onions, chopped
1 cup grated Colby or longhorn cheese or a combination with Monterey jack
½ cup sliced green or black olives (optional)
½ head iceberg lettuce, shredded
1 ounce mild vinegar
1 teaspoon dried oregano, preferably Mexican

Warm the oil in a heavy saucepan or skillet over medium heat, add the garlic, and cook until softened but not brown. Sprinkle in the flour and stir to make a thick roux. Gradually add
the chile paste or sauce and 1 cup of the broth, a little at a time. Bring to a simmer for 15–20
minutes. If using the homemade paste, add another cup or so of liquid, because this Arizona-
style sauce should be quite thin for enchiladas. Add the oregano and salt to taste. Keep warm.
Or make in advance and reheat. It keeps for 4–5 days when refrigerated and retains its texture
and flavor when frozen and thawed.

Preheat the oven to 200 degrees F. or lower, to heat the plates and keep the enchiladas
warm.

In a large bowl, loosen the *masa* with your fingers and work in the eggs, cheese, baking powder, and salt. Shape into balls about 2 inches in diameter. Pat the balls into ¼-inch-thick and
3–4-inch-round patties. If the *masa* is too sticky, put the balls between sheets of wax paper and
then flatten them.

Heat 1–2 inches of oil in a medium-size skillet, and when quite hot but not smoking, carefully submerge the *masa* patty into the oil, using a slotted spatula. Fry each patty until golden
brown and slightly crispy on each side. Remove, drain on absorbent paper, and keep warm in
the oven. (The patties can be cooked in only a slightly oiled skillet, but the texture may be a bit
drier.)

When ready to serve, pass the *masa* patties through the heated sauce for just a few seconds.
Put 2 patties on heated plates and spoon on the additional sauce. Top with the green onions,
cheese, and olives. Toss the lettuce, vinegar, and oregano together in a bowl and serve on the
side of the enchiladas.

Arizona Red Chile Paste
Pasta de Chile Colorado
TUMACACORI, ARIZONA

MAKES 1 QUART

10 dried red chiles, preferably New Mexican varieties or ancho chiles

1 quart water

2 cloves garlic

1 tablespoon safflower or canola oil

½ teaspoon dried oregano, preferably Mexican

1 teaspoon sea salt

Remove the seeds and membranes from the chiles and tear into pieces. Lightly toast the chile pieces on a griddle or a dry cast-iron skillet. The chiles should just begin to change color and blister.

Bring the water to a boil in a large saucepan. Add the chiles and garlic. Remove the pan from the heat and let sit for 20–30 minutes. When the chiles are softened, remove them with a slotted spoon, along with the garlic, reserving the water.

Puree the chiles and garlic in a blender or food processor. Gradually add all the chile water. The mixture should be very smooth and may have to be pureed in several batches.

Heat the oil over medium heat in a medium-size saucepan. Add the chile mixture. oregano, and salt and simmer for 15 minutes. Cool and store in a refrigerator or freezer until ready to use.

Chilaquiles in a Tomatillo and Green Chile Sauce
Chilaquiles en Salsa Verde
SAN DIEGO, CALIFORNIA • MEXICO CITY, MEXICO

SERVES 4 AS A MAIN COURSE, 6 AS AN ACCOMPANIMENT TO OTHER DISHES

Irma Aguilar, like most Mexican cooks I know, recycles leftover corn tortillas, no matter how stiff they may be, into this simple, homey dish. It is such a standard fare in most of Mexico that I was totally taken aback to find chilaquiles *virtually unknown in New Mexico and southern Colorado. There they make a similar dish with scrambled eggs called* migas, *which is popular in all the Southwest border states.*

A glass of juice and a plate of chilaquiles *makes a pleasant supper or breakfast. Try topping each portion with a fried egg and a dollop more salsa; as a brunch dish, it is especially satisfying when combined with chorizo. For supper, Irma may add chunks of cooked chicken. To accompany the* chilaquiles, *serve a pitcher of Fruit Shakes (page 378) and add Poached Eggs in Chile-Tomato Broth (page 331). Ester Diaz in Toppenish, Washington, wraps her* chilaquiles *in tortillas—just like "two clouds coming together."*

1 pound fresh tomatillos, husked and rinsed, or one 13-ounce can, drained

1–2 cups Chicken Stock (page 70) or canned chicken broth

2–3 fresh serrano or jalapeño chiles, roughly chopped

½ white onion, roughly chopped

2 cloves garlic, roughly chopped

sea salt

peanut or safflower oil for frying

12 store-bought corn tortillas (page 108), preferably at least 1 day old, torn or cut into pieces about ¾ by 2 inches

4 tablespoons roughly chopped fresh cilantro leaves

For the Toppings

1 cup Mexican *crema* (page 23) or sour cream thinned with milk

½–1 cup crumbled *queso fresco* or feta cheese

2 thin slices white onion, broken into rings

1 firm but ripe avocado, pitted, peeled, and cut into thin wedges

6–10 thinly sliced radishes

If using fresh tomatillos, simmer them for about 10 minutes in a small pan of boiling salted water. Drain and put the tomatillos in a blender or food processor.

Add ½ cup of broth, 2 chiles, onion, garlic, and salt, and blend well but leave some texture. Add another ½ cup of broth. Taste for "hotness" and add another chile if necessary.

Heat oil in a skillet over medium-high heat, and when quite hot but not smoking, pour all the sauce in at once and stir vigorously. Taste for salt and continue cooking over lower heat until thick and darkened in color. Add more broth if needed and simmer for about 10–15 minutes. The sauce can be made in advance and reheated before using.

While the sauce is cooking, pour ¼ inch of oil into a large skillet. When it is very hot, add a handful or so of tortilla strips and fry quickly until crisp and golden. You will need to watch carefully that they do not burn. Stir constantly for about 2 minutes. Drain on absorbent paper and repeat until all the tortillas are fried. The tortilla strips can be cooked in advance.

Right before serving, add the cilantro to the sauce, carefully stir in the tortilla strips, and simmer for several minutes. More chicken broth can be added if needed. Taste for salt.

To serve, scoop onto a warm dish, spoon on *crema,* and scatter the cheese on top. Serve with onion rings, avocado slices, and radishes.

VARIATION: AZTEC PIE Rose María Trevino's *chilaquiles* are turned into a popular casserole dish. To reduce the fat content somewhat, she cuts thick corn tortillas into small wedges and bakes them in a single layer for about 12 minutes at 350 degrees F. and substitutes 1½ cups of low-fat sour cream and 1½ cups of shredded low-fat Monterey jack cheese. Poach and shred 2 pounds of chicken breasts. Layer half of the tortillas in the bottom of an ovenproof casserole. Top with half the chicken and season with salt and pepper. Drizzle on half of the sauce and cream, and sprinkle with half of the cheese. Repeat with the remaining ingredients, then bake, uncovered, about 20 minutes at 350 degrees F. until the top is lightly browned and bubbly. Garnish and serve.

Colorado Impressions

Colorado is the state where I was born, but I lived there only the two or three months a year when I stayed with my grandmother in Colorado Springs.

It was the first day of spring when I returned this last time, and the countryside was winter-tired. Magpies held on to bent-over remains of last year's cornstalks as windstorms came along with the spring. It was cold and too early in the season for any but a slight greening tinge from the awakening buds of the cottonwoods. The smoky-blue mountains to the north were dusted with snow, and my once familiar landmark of Pike's Peak seemed small and insignificant compared to Washington's Mount Rainier, the mountain I can see from my kitchen window as I write this book.

A few Spanish explorers and priests had made occasional forays into what is now Colorado, but fear of the Indians, mainly Utes, kept the settlers farther south around Santa Fe for more than two hundred years. It took two centuries to go one hundred miles.

As more and more French and Americans ventured west, the Spanish began to buffer Santa Fe and surrounding settlements by granting large tracts of land to those willing to encourage settlement on the territory's northernmost frontier—a practice that continued even after Mexico had won its independence. The Sangre de Cristo Grant, for example, encompassed over one million acres and included much of the largest valley in the United States. This is where San Luis, perhaps the oldest community in Colorado, was built.

Although only 30 percent of the population of San Luis is now Spanish, they are an integral part of the community. In 1863 the owner of the Sangre de Cristo grant gave the settlers in each of the isolated towns in the valley the exclusive rights to the water and the trees on the encircling hills to provide firewood and lumber as well as land for pasturing their sheep and cattle. San Luis's *vega,* or common pasture, which is still in use today by the families of these early settlers, is larger than the more famous Boston Common.

These are families that have lived for generations in much the same manner as their parents. Some of the older people still combine the archaic and sixteenth- and seventeenth-century common words of rural Spain with a potpourri of French, Indian, and English words. If at all possible, the different generations from around the area always get together for Sunday dinner. San Luis women obey some ancient law which says that anyone who comes in at any time of the day or night gets fed. I know I did.

On one such Sunday at Daisy Ortega's house on Main Street, I watched her cook on the same wood-burning stove she'd had for almost sixty years, though an electric stove to be used in hot weather is in the kitchen. We talked while we ate, and I learned about *chicos,* dried sweet corn kernels that are cooked like beans ("Never put ham with your *chicos;* it will ruin them"); how to combine *chicos* with the wonderful round *bolitas,* a locally grown bean; and to make *galletas,* a crunchy biscuit served with lots of butter and a cup of coffee. I learned about the sprouted wheat pudding *panocha,* which is cooked just for Holy Week, and how to make an especially good *chile verde.*

Everyone knew where to find Ernesto Valdez, the man to see if you wanted *bolitas:* "Just go with the wind until you see the willows. That's where his driveway is." We met Ernesto and bought several pounds of the round beans. He sent us along to his brother-in-law, Prudencio Chacon, who raises sheep and has a three-legged sheep dog. He also grows corn for the *chicos* he steams in his *horno,* the traditional adobe outdoor oven, and hangs to dry before breaking off the kernels and storing them to be cooked during the winter. Prudencio likes to keep a pot of *chicos* and *bolitas* simmering on the wood stove so that there is always something ready to eat.

Mary Ann Tafoya is a teacher who lives in the far north part of the valley in Del Norte. This is potato country: *chile verde* with potatoes, potato pie, fried potatoes, alone or with turnips. Although Mary Ann is a young woman, she still lives and cooks guided by the traditional values she learned from her grandmother: "Use common sense and don't waste any of the good food that God provides." When they butchered, all parts of the animal were used. A special favorite she mentioned that I remembered eating as a child, from the Basque sheepherders in Jordan Valley, Oregon, were *buñates,* the thin milk gut of lamb that is wrapped in a veil of caul fat, salted, and fried. And for Mary Ann, as the other families in the valley, elk and deer provide as much of the meat as sheep and cattle, venison being especially prized to use in empanadas.

Traveling out of the San Luis Valley and into the rest of Colorado that had never even been part of Mexico was a curious experience, for here at last I had very Mexican food. As Ray Aguilera in Pueblo told me, "We are not like the Valley. Our roots are in Mexico, not New Mexico or Spain." Ray's grandfather left Chihuahua in the early 1900s, bringing his oldest son, Ted, with him.

"My uncle Ted produced whiskey for the local Mafia," Aguilera said. "He aged his whiskey by giving it two volts of electricity, and he added a spoonful of caramel for color. My uncle Pancho went to the University of Colorado and became a teacher. Uncle Tim opened a drugstore, and my dad became a pharmacist and joined him. They did okay, selling mainly to the Mexicans in the neighborhood. Back then almost everybody else around here was Italian or Slovenian. I was ashamed of the lunch we brought to school, so I used to eat my *burrito* still wrapped in foil, hoping the other kids would think it was a sandwich." His mother, Rose, broke in, "Now everyone else makes money selling the food we've always eaten."

About the same time that Ray's grandfather moved to Colorado, many other Mexicans came but traveled farther north, near Denver, to work in the sugar beet fields. Before long they were the main labor source, and instead of returning south every year, the farm owners encouraged them to settle in the area. Today there is a large Mexican-American community in this part of Colorado.

The Depression brought economic misery and new problems to the Mexican Americans living in the rural communities of southern Colorado and in the Denver barrios, with many of the farmworkers losing their longtime jobs to Anglos now willing to take lower paying jobs. I especially remember the story I heard from Maria Martinez, who died recently in her late seventies:

> *I grew up in a town of dust and despair. The sickly sweet odor of sugar beet pulp permeated our lives as well as the dirt road outside the bad-weather-colored house where we lived. On the dirt road in front, the trucks went back and forth from the fields to the refinery, always dripping that thick liquid smell.*
>
> *During those Depression days in Colorado there wasn't much food for anyone, especially the Mexicans. We were lucky, since we had our family, a place to live, and a belief that if we trusted in God and worked hard, we could solve our own problems. I remember giving thanks to President Roosevelt for the sack of dried beans that my uncle sometimes brought home, so I guess we didn't do it all ourselves.*
>
> *My grandmother always told me stories when we were cooking—how she used to make tacos for her husband to take down into the mines near where they lived in Guanajuato. She told how papa, when he was still very young and handsome, had fought in the Revolution and how mama went right along with him, and when the shooting would stop, she'd make a fire and would cook tortillas on the very same* comal *that we still used.*

Comfortable Companions
Beans, Lentils, Rice, and Vegetables
Comidas Adicionales: Frijoles, Lentejas, Arroz, y Legumbres

A meal is not a meal in México unless beans are served in some form or other.
Generally they are served just before dessert, and the favorite way is refried.

—ELENA ZELAYETA,
Elena's Famous Mexican and Spanish Recipes, San Francisco, Calif.:
self-published, 1944

THERE IS SIMPLY NO OTHER INGREDIENT as essential as the humble bean in the diet of the Mexican people. Chiles add the fun, but beans provide the fundamental nourishment needed to survive. Ninety-three-year-old Eva Celaya de Garcia cannot recall a day without eating beans or rice, a diet that obviously agrees with her. She may not understand the biochemistry that makes beans combined with rice or a bit of meat or cheese such a complete protein, but she and millions of other Mexicans know they are an economical way to feed a large family and, just as important, they taste good.

Daisy Ortega, in San Luis, Colorado, made it clear to me that "beans should taste like beans" and that their flavor doesn't need to be dominated by seasonings or meat. This was a common refrain, especially in such areas as Colorado and New Mexico where high-quality beans are locally grown, including the unusual varieties of mottled purple and white Anasazi and the rounder cream-colored *bolitas.* These and other heirloom beans may be ordered from Elizabeth Berry in New Mexico (see Product Sources, page 392).

Compared to beans, rice is a newcomer to Mexican cuisine, arriving about four hundred years ago. The Mexicans use the longer-grain variety from Asia and Africa and cook their rice in the Spanish style: like a pilaf, sautéing the rice before adding a strong broth as a cooking liquid. With a change in homelands came a change in the way Mexican Americans served rice. In Mexico there is seldom a normal meal that doesn't include a *sopa seca,* or "dry soup," between the regular soup and the main course. Sometimes it is a vegetable pudding or a plate of pasta, but more often it is the classic Mexican rice—tomato red flecked with bits of onion and chiles. This tradition seems to have disappeared on its way north, for I found rice always served alongside a main dish. It also turned up much more often on the same plate as well-fried beans, something that one rarely encounters in Mexico except along the border.

The rice in Mexico is usually sold in bulk and needs to be well washed. Through habit, most of the Mexican-American cooks with whom I cooked still use this process, which also seems to produce a softer cooked rice. Most U.S. rice is enriched with iron, niacin, and thiamin, which will be lost if it is prewashed, so we've adapted the rice recipes with this in mind, using regular milled medium- to long-grain white rice, not parboiled rice which requires both more liquid and also a longer cooking time.

Mexican cooking uses an abundance of vegetables not served in an isolated cluster on the dinner plate but as an integral part of another dish. It is often even the main dish itself. There are exceptions: Squash and green beans are sautéed with onion and garlic, then gently cooked with a bit of tomato. Spinach and especially delicious wild greens like purslane and lamb's-quarters are favored in almost all parts of the United States where they grow—which is about everywhere.

We collected numerous recipes for stuffing vegetables, evidence that cooks had decided the enjoyment of tasting a riot of flavors in each bite was worth the extra effort required to prepare the dish. In the Southwest, particularly, panfried potatoes and even turnips are a mainstay, but they are combined with a gravy, chile sauce, or cheese. Even boiled or roasted corn is gloriously embellished with cream and ground chile.

EPAZOTE, THE POOR MAN'S HERB FROM MEXICO

Epazote may be only a tenacious weed, but for Mexican cooks it is a treasure to be diligently sought out. A close kin to spinach, beets, Swiss chard, or lamb's-quarters, epazote has the melodic scientific species name of Chenopodium ambrosioides. *It also has such a potent, pungent taste and aroma that it is said a strong brew of epazote will deter ants, rid the body of intestinal parasites, and reduce flatulence. Whether this reputation is deserved or not, epazote's unique flavor is irreplaceable and unforgettable in black beans or tucked on top of the oozing melted cheese in quesadillas. The herb's assertive bite is welcomed in soups or sautéed dishes with squash, corn, and tomatoes, and I particularly like its flavor in pork* moles *and stews. Epazote should be added at the end of the cooking process and used quite sparingly, for the flavor is intense.*

Although epazote does not grow in the more arid northern parts of Mexico and the southwest United States, it flourishes in wet, warm soil and has naturalized itself in a surprising number of places in the United States. I found it in Detroit backyards and along the river walk in San Antonio, and I usually have vigorous plants growing in my garden in Washington.

Epazote is much, much better fresh, but for beans it may be bought dried in small cellophane packages at most Latino markets, but unfortunately there are usually more twigs and stems than leaves. It is much better to grow your own, and seeds are available from many mail order catalogs and plant stores. I order mine from J. L. Hudson, Seedsman (see Product Sources, page 391), a seed company devoted to many unusual plants growing in tropical or mountainous regions of Mexico. Fresh plants are increasingly available everywhere in the better nurseries or can be ordered from It's About Thyme (see Product Sources).

Throughout the growing season I pluck off leaves to use in my cooking. At the end of the summer I pot up several of the smaller healthy plants, pinch off the center branch to keep the plant bushy, and bring them indoors where they survive in my sunniest window the rest of the year. I leave a few plants growing in my garden because occasionally they will reseed for me or, if the weather is mild, will survive the winter. The rest of the plants I cut off at the base and hang upside down in bunches in a dark, cool space until they are dry. I save the tiny seeds to plant in the spring, and store the leaves in tightly sealed pint jars in a dark cupboard.

Soupy Pot Beans
Frijoles de la Olla
MIAMI, FLORIDA • MEXICO CITY, MEXICO

SERVES 8 TO 10   *Hardly a family I visited didn't cook a pot of beans at least once a week, though only a few women still utilize the classic clay ollas to prepare their beans. While many just use big metal soup pots, Patricia Varley, like many of the other young Mexican-American women I met around the country, usually cooks her beans in a pressure cooker. When she was nineteen, her brother, exasperated by her culinary ignorance, signed her up for cooking classes in Mexico City. She kept making excuses not to go, but he finally prevailed and Patricia acquired the basic skills that serve her so well now. The day Patricia and I had lunch she had to go home and make sixty* tortas *filled with* frijoles *for a party.*

In spite of the advice in most cookbooks, few of the Mexican-American cooks I spoke with ever soaked their beans. It doesn't make them tender; that is best done by using beans that are as fresh as possible. However, I'm told soaking may *reduce gas-causing sugars. If this is a concern, after bringing the beans and water to a boil, remove the pot from the heat, cover, and let stand for two to three hours. Drain off the water, which contains these sugars, and replace with the same amount of cold water. Continue the cooking process, reducing the time that the beans simmer by ten to twenty minutes.*

This may seem like a whole lot of beans, but remember that these slow-simmered beans will be used as the base for any dish calling for beans, including Well-Fried Beans (page 227), and are wonderful served as is before Chimichangas (page 130) or other rustic foods.

These beans are usually eaten unadorned, but can be garnished with crumbled queso añejo *or a dry white cheese such as feta. Patricia puts whole fried* chiles de árbol *or* quajillos *chiles on a side dish to eat with the beans, and others use chopped fresh or pickled green jalapeños or a salsa. Add hot Corn or Flour Tortillas (pages 108 and 125) and a green salad for a simple but satisfying supper.*

Years ago when I first started visiting Mexico on a regular basis, Fredric and I went to comida *in the home of old friends of his—a retired Supreme Court judge and his wife who lived in the center of colonial Morelia. It was a very formal meal, very elegant. Judge Alfredo Gálvez Bravo spoke little English. I spoke little Spanish. The food, which Amelia had prepared herself, was exceptional course after course. Just when I could truly eat no more, small earthenware bowls were served, brimming with soupy beans and a few chunks of white cheese. It was then I learned that in order for no guest ever to go away hungry from a Mexican table, this sustaining bowl of beans is always offered at the end of the meal.*

1 pound dried beans, pinto, pink, black (about 3 scant cups)

1 white onion, ½ in a chunk, the rest finely chopped

1–2 tablespoons safflower or canola oil, lard, or bacon drippings

about 1½ teaspoons sea salt

2 sprigs epazote if cooking black beans (page 223) (optional)

3 cloves garlic, minced

For the Garnish

½ cup crumbled *queso fresco* (see page 112), farmer's cheese, or feta

Wash the beans thoroughly, removing any small rocks or other foreign materials. Put them in a large, heavy pot (an earthenware *olla,* if possible) and cover with 2 quarts of cold water, which should allow "2 knuckles' worth" of water above the level of the beans.

Bring the water to a boil, then lower the heat to a gentle simmer. Add the half piece of onion and a tiny dribble of oil, and continue simmering until the beans just begin to become tender, usually in 1 hour. Add salt to taste, and if cooking black beans, put in the epazote. Cook 30–45 more minutes. The total time will depend on how fresh the beans are. The beans should be stirred from time to time, and add boiling water whenever it is less than "one knuckles' worth" over the beans. They should be rather soupy.

Warm the remainder of the oil over medium heat in a skillet and sauté the garlic and chopped onion until nicely brown but not burned. Add the onion and garlic to the beans and continue cooking until the beans are very soft and plump.

These can be eaten immediately, along with the broth, or cooled completely and then covered and stored in the refrigerator. The earthy flavor seems to intensify when reheated the next day, and the beans will keep, covered and refrigerated, for at least 4 days.

Serve the broth and beans in bowls. Garnish with the crumbled cheese.

VARIATION: QUICK PRESSURE-COOKED BEANS   Put 2 cups of beans, half of the onion, cut in chunks, and a few drops of oil in a 4-quart pressure cooker with 4 cups of water. Seal and cook for 30 minutes. After the pressure is released, remove the lid, add ½–1 cup more water, the sautéed garlic, onion, salt, and optional epazote. Continue cooking until tender, another 15–20 minutes.

Cowboy Beans
Frijoles Charros
MIAMI, FLORIDA • JALISCO, MEXICO

SERVES 4 TO 6 WITH LARGE BOWLFULS   *Adorned with silver buckles and spurs, elegant clothes, and the classic flat-brimmed sombrero,* charros, *the renowned horsemen of Jalisco, are an extravagant version of the working cowboy. To make their namesake dish, Patricia Varley's aunt takes a simple pot of beans and dresses them up like the* charros *with lots of extras. These beans are an ideal complement to grilled meats.*

Use bacon instead of chorizo unless you have a local butcher who makes his own or you do it yourself (page 170). If you buy those prepackaged commercial brands, you will have done a disservice to your beans.

1 tablespoon safflower or canola oil

6 ounces Mexican chorizo, removed from any casings, or 8 thick slices of bacon, cut into ½-inch pieces

½ white onion, finely chopped

2 medium ripe tomatoes, chopped, or one 14½-ounce can diced tomatoes, drained

6 cups Soupy Pot Beans, with broth (page 224)

5 whole dried *chiles de árbol* or 2 fresh serrano or jalapeño chiles, seeded and sliced

sea salt

For the Garnish
½ cup chopped cilantro

Heat the oil in a heavy skillet and fry the chorizo over medium-low heat until cooked through, breaking it up into small pieces with a fork. If using bacon, omit the oil, and after it is crispy, pour off all but 1 tablespoon of the melted fat. Remove the chorizo or bacon and drain on absorbent paper. Add the onion and, if using the fresh chiles, add them to the hot oil and fry until soft and light yellow. Add the tomatoes, stir, and cook about 3 minutes until the flavors are well mingled.

Put the beans in an earthenware pot or enameled cast-iron casserole dish. Add the meat mixture and dried red chiles. Salt to taste. Cook, uncovered, for 20–30 minutes, adding more water if necessary.

Ladle into heated bowls and sprinkle on the cilantro.

VARIATION: DRUNKEN BEANS (*FRIJOLES BORRACHOS*)   Around McAllen and other southern Texas towns, cooks often add 1 cup of Mexican beer to the pot—a method perfected in nearby Monterrey, the brewery capital of Mexico. The alcohol content disappears, leaving behind its flavor.

Well-Fried Beans
Frijoles Refritos
SEATTLE, WASHINGTON • MICHOACÁN, MEXICO

Sometimes I think I am a good cook because of my nose [said Lupe Ortiz Peach, from Uruapan, Mexico]. If you have ever let the water boil out of a pot of beans and had them burn, you will remember that dark smell forever in your mind. But I also hear my grandmother, Heracia, telling me not to waste anything from the land, so I still do just what she told me and cut an onion into four parts, boil it a bit in water, and then add it all to the burned beans, and most of the bad taste goes away. I've finally learned it is much better to be attentive in the first place and just not let the beans burn.

SERVES 4 TO 6   *My friend was just a small girl when she left her home in the verdant "hot country" of Michoacán and went with her family to the Northwest. Her story is typical of many Mexican Americans now scattered across the United States.*

My husband is from a Scandinavian background, and our three kids have grown up mainly on typical fast foods. Hamburgers and pizza are what they want and usually get. They don't even like spicy foods.

They do, however, like Lupe's well-fried beans, which, when short of time, can be made from well-rinsed canned beans, with water in place of the extra bean broth. In Spanish, re means "well," not "again," so plan to fry them only once, not twice.

These beans are a tasty complement to Crispy Catfish Served with a Tomato Sauce (page 144) or Red Chile with Meat (page 174). Or use them as a dip with Tortilla Chips (page 33).

3 tablespoons bacon grease, flavorful lard, or safflower or canola oil

½ white onion, finely chopped

3 cloves garlic, minced

3–4 cups cooked beans with broth, any variety;
canned beans can be used

sea salt if needed

1 teaspoon ground red chile (optional)

For the Garnish

3 ounces crumbled *queso fresco, queso añejo,* or feta
cheese

18 Tortilla Chips (page 33)

Melt the fat or heat the oil in a large, heavy skillet over medium heat. Add the onion and fry about 5 minutes, until soft and golden, stirring frequently. Add the garlic and cook another several minutes.

Raise the heat under the skillet and add the beans and broth, 1 cup at a time, smashing them down with a potato masher or the back of a big wooden spoon. (In Mexico a special wooden bean masher is used. They are easy to find on any vacation trip to Mexico.) It should take about 10 minutes for the beans to reach a smooth but still quite moist texture. Taste and add salt or chile if needed.

The beans can be served immediately with crumbled or grated cheese sprinkled on top or set aside and kept warm in a double boiler. A little more liquid may have to be used. The crisp tortilla pieces can be stuck into the beans, both as a decoration and as a way to scoop them up.

VARIATION: ROLLED BEANS   Victor Nelson-Cisneros, associate dean at Colorado College, likes his *frijoles refritos* well mashed. When they start to draw away from the edges of the skillet, shake the pan and tip the solidified mass of beans over on itself, rather like an omelet. Slide the bean roll onto a platter to serve. Garnish with crumbled cheese and tortilla chips, and surround with lettuce or cabbage leaves and, for color contrast, radishes with a few small green leaves left on.

Pureed Beans with Cheese and Ancho Chiles
Frijoles Maneados
AUSTIN, TEXAS • SONORA, MEXICO

SERVES 8 TO 10   *In this dish, popular in the dairy-rich state of Sonora where Miguel's grandmother was born, the humble bean is transformed into a voluptuous velvety puree, with a subtle taste of ancho chiles to add a provocative tingle to the palate. Frijoles Maneados are my husband's favorite comfort food, but it is so rich that we save it for very special occasions. Home-rendered lard or lard purchased freshly made from your butcher adds a marvelous flavor, although a good-quality oil can be used.*

Frijoles Maneados is an ideal addition to any meal featuring tacos or burritos, but it is especially good alongside Three-Days-in-the-Making Beef Burritos (page 128).

1 pound pinto beans (about 2 cups)

6 green onions, chopped

1 cup plus 1 tablespoon flavorful pork lard or safflower or canola oil

about 2 teaspoons sea salt

1 medium white onion, quartered

2 cups whole milk

sea salt

2 dried ancho chiles, toasted (page 22), seeded, and cut into thin strips

6 ounces mozzarella or Monterey jack cheese, coarsely shredded

For the Garnish

2 tablespoons chopped flat-leaf parsley

Rinse the beans well, put them in a large pot, and cover with enough water to come 1 inch above the beans. Add the green onions and 1 tablespoon of lard. Bring to a boil and simmer, covered, about 45 minutes, until they begin to soften. Add the salt and continue cooking until the beans become quite mushy. Add more water if necessary to maintain a broth. Set aside to cool.

Heat the remaining 1 cup of lard in a large skillet, preferably cast iron, over medium-high heat and fry the onion for additional flavor. When dark brown, remove and discard.

In a food processor or blender, coarsely puree the cooled beans and some of the broth in batches. Add a portion of the milk to each batch. Set aside the remaining bean broth.

Add the beans carefully to the hot onion-flavored lard, since they will sputter. Taste and add salt if necessary. Simmer gently over medium-high heat for about 10 minutes, stirring occasionally so that the mixture does not stick and burn.

recipe continues

Preheat the oven to 260 degrees F. Spoon the beans into an attractive casserole dish—earthenware is ideal—and gently fold the chile strips and half of the cheese into the bean mixture. If the mixture seems quite dry, stir in some more bean broth. The beans should have body but be moist. Bake, uncovered, for 15 minutes. Sprinkle the rest of the cheese on top and bake another 5–10 minutes, until the cheese melts and begins to brown. Serve immediately, garnished with the parsley.

Pinto Beans with Cactus and Chiles
Frijoles Quebrados con Rajas y Nopales
BROOKLYN, NEW YORK • OAXACA, MEXICO

SERVES 6 TO 8   *This unusual combination of flavors from Huajuapan de León, a small town in the high country of Oaxaca, made the transition to Brooklyn, New York, with Geraldo Reyes in a simplified version. The Mixtec Indians who inhabit the part of Oaxaca where Gerardo grew up use a local type of bean as the base for this substantial dish and, of course, the fresh nopales (cactus paddles) are cultivated throughout the area. Geraldo, who came to the United States as a farmworker in Oregon in 1986, was working as a dishwasher in a New York restaurant when he met Peter Kump, who ran one of the leading cooking schools in the country. Geraldo's enthusiasm impressed Kump, and soon he found himself at the James Beard House prepping food for visiting chefs. Today, Geraldo is a sous-chef in an Italian restaurant on Staten Island, but at home he still cooks the foods he ate as a child.*

These beans with their little pieces of cactus are a versatile side dish. Miguel likes to serve them alongside Tacos of Crispy Pork Bits (page 116), and they also partner well with grilled meats. Serve them as a vegetarian main course with a tossed green salad or Pepper Slaw (page 53).

1 tablespoon safflower or canola oil
½ white onion, chopped
2 fresh jalapeño chiles, seeded and cut in strips
5 cups cooked pinto beans with 1 cup bean broth or water (page 224)
1½ cups canned chopped cactus paddles, drained and rinsed

1 whole head of garlic, outer papery covering removed
2 teaspoons chopped fresh epazote (page 223) or 1 teaspoon dried oregano, preferably Mexican
sea salt and freshly ground black pepper

In a medium saucepan or casserole dish, heat the oil and fry the onion and jalapeños over medium heat. When they are softened, add the beans and broth along with the cactus paddles, garlic, epazote, and salt and pepper to taste. Cook for 30 minutes over medium heat. This dish can be prepared in advance and reheated. Remove the garlic before serving.

Black Beans with Pork
Frijoles Negros con Puerco
LOS ANGELES, CALIFORNIA • YUCATÁN, MEXICO

SERVES 8 TO 10 *I've eaten this traditional Yucatecan dish most often at a friend's home in a little town outside Mérida with the wonderful name of Tixkokob (Teesh-ko-kob). Though Tixkokob is famous as the source of Yucatán's finest hammocks, it is for its food that I return year after year. When Silvio, my friend, serves this dish for a fiesta, he cooks seven pounds of black beans in a pit together with lots of pork, including the hog's head. When we eat, the head is split and set on a huge tray in the middle of the table along with other pieces of meat. Everyone reaches in to spear his morsel of choice. On another platter are grilled pork ribs that have been coated with a paste of Achiote (page 177), spices, garlic, and lime juice, and each person has a bowl of soupy beans to top with a dazzling array of garnishes and condiments, all set out on a tablecloth embroidered by his sister, Concepción. There is guitar music, singing, and dancing—a joyous celebration of the good and simple things in life.*

Rosario Chávez's version is modified for a smaller number of eaters, and she likes to have a sauce of roasted habanero chiles and tomatoes nearby to spoon over the beans and pork for an extra flavor high.

If you serve some hot Corn Tortillas (page 108) with dishes of Red Radish Relish (page 280), shredded cabbage, chopped tomatoes, and avocadoes to scatter on top of the beans, you will have a very typical Yucatecan meal. Or you can have a real fiesta and serve it with Roast Pork Yucatecan-Style (page 178) and finish with Compote of Mango, Papaya, and Strawberries (page 345).

For the Beans and Meat
1 pound dried black beans (about 2 cups)
2 pounds pork butt or boneless country-style
   ribs, cut into 2-inch pieces
½ cup chopped white onion

2 cloves garlic, chopped
2 teaspoons sea salt
1 sprig fresh epazote or 1 teaspoon dried, all
   twigs removed (page 223) (optional)

ingredients continue

For the Tomato Sauce

4 ripe tomatoes, roasted (page 22)

4 tablespoons chopped white onion

1 fresh habanero chile, seeded, or 3–4 serrano
chiles, toasted (page 21) and seeded

1 tablespoon chopped cilantro

sea salt

2 tablespoons safflower or canola oil

For the Toppings

Red Radish Relish (page 280)

2 cups loosely packed shredded cabbage

2 large ripe tomatoes, cut into ¼-inch dice

2 firm but ripe avocados, peeled, pitted, and cut
into ½-inch dice

Rinse the beans thoroughly, picking out any bits of debris or broken beans. Put in a large pot (preferably an earthenware *olla*) with the pork, onion, and garlic. Add at least 2 quarts of water. The water should cover the beans by a good 1 inch. Bring to a boil and lower the heat immediately so that the bubbles barely break the surface. Simmer for 1–2 hours, until the beans are just tender. Add the salt and epazote, and cook another 30 minutes. The beans should be very soft. Add more water if necessary to maintain a brothy liquid.

Place the tomatoes, onion, part of the chiles, and cilantro in a blender or food processor and blend, leaving some texture. Add salt to taste.

Heat the oil in a small saucepan or skillet, and when quite hot, pour in the tomato mixture and cook over medium-high heat about 5 minutes until the sauce has thickened and the flavors have blended. Taste for salt and fire. Blend in a little more chile if you want more heat.

The pork and beans should be served in bowls, with the sauce on the side in another bowl. Use caution when adding the sauce because it has been known to reduce more than a few *macho* persons to tears. Serve with the toppings in separate bowls.

THE AMERICANIZING OF RICE

*F*ollowing the founding of Manila in the Philippines by officers of Spanish ships from Acapulco, the galleons sailed across the Pacific to bring back to Mexico the spices of Malaysia and the islands, and silks, and the medium-grained rice of China. But that's just part of the story. According to historian Judith A. Carney, during the same time period thousands of Africans were being imported across the Atlantic as slaves to work on the sugar plantations of Veracruz and Cuernavaca—many, no doubt, taking with them pocketfuls of rice from their native lands. When they escaped and established fugitive communities outside the Mexican sugar plantation areas in the inland swamps of eastern Mexico, they sustained their families by growing the rice they had brought with them from Africa. Most of the rice used in Mexico today is the starchier medium-grain variety, not the short-grain rice of Spain and Italy.

There is no record of rice being a part of the mule train's cargo in the years of Spain's early settlement of New Mexico, but by the 1800s long-grain rice from Georgia and Carolina was welcomed by the Spanish and Mexican frontiersmen. Before long, settlers on the broad prairie lands of southeastern Texas began growing and selling their own crops of rice, and ever since then rice has been an important part of Mexican-American cooking, calming the aggressive taste of chiles.

Seasoned White Rice
Arroz Blanco
CIUDAD JUAREZ, CHIHUAHUA

SERVES 6   *This simple down-to-earth rice dish is a good balance for the more high-spirited foods found around El Paso and other border communities. As Luis Helio Estavillo and his family well know, it is the kind of dish that can be varied quite easily. Include a handful of chopped blanched chard or spinach, fold in some crumbled cheese, or, as I was once served in southern California, mix the rice with red chile flakes and fresh mint for a flavor that will wake up your senses.*

I think this delicately flavored rice is best served alongside another mild-natured dish that won't override its taste, such as Garlic Chicken (page 153). It can, though, stand up to most moles *and* pipianes, *those traditional dishes with sauces thickened with ground nuts or seeds. Try it with Chicken in a Red Sauce of Pumpkin Seed and Dried Corn (page 158).*

2 tablespoons safflower or canola oil
1½ cups long-grain white rice
¼ medium white onion, sliced or chopped
2 cloves garlic, minced
3 cups Chicken Stock (page 70) or canned
 chicken broth

1 bay leaf
about 1 scant teaspoon sea salt
2 fresh serrano or jalapeño chiles (optional)

Warm the oil in a heavy saucepan over medium heat. When hot, add the rice and stir with a wooden spoon about 10 minutes, until it becomes chalky white and speckled with tan. You will hear the sounds of dry cracking as the rice is cooking. Add the onion and garlic, stir, and cook about 1 minute before adding the broth, bay leaf, salt, and whole chiles. Bring to a boil, lower the heat, and let the rice cook for 5 minutes, stirring occasionally. Cover and simmer over low heat for about 15 minutes so that the rice can absorb the rest of the liquid. Take the pot off the burner and keep it covered for another 10 minutes. Before serving remove the bay leaf and chiles and fluff the rice with a fork.

VARIATION: WHITE RICE WITH PLANTAINS (*ARROZ CON PLÁTANOS*)   In this Veracruz-style dish, strips of 3 roasted poblano or Anaheim chiles are sautéed with the onion and garlic. Add a cup of fresh or frozen corn kernels to the rice at the same time as the broth. While the rice is steaming, fry cubes of 1 ripe plantain or 2 very firm, large bananas in butter and oil over medium-high heat until darkly browned. When the rice is ready to serve, stir in the bananas and ¾ cup of crumbled *queso fresco* (see page 112) or feta cheese.

VARIATION: ELEGANT WHITE RICE WITH POMEGRANATE SEEDS   Val Hermocillo learned this recipe from her uncle who was a priest in a small village in Michoacán with the melodious name of Tzintzuntzan. Cook the rice with the whole jalapeño chiles, and when all the liquid has been absorbed, remove the chiles and stir in ½ cup of thick Mexican *crema* (see page 23) or thinned sour cream, at room temperature or barely warmed; ¾ cup of grated Monterey jack or mozzarella cheese; and ¼ cup of pomegranate seeds. Press the rice into individual lightly oiled molds and reheat, covered, in the oven for 5 minutes. Serve on dinner plates, drizzle on more sour cream, and garnish with a finely chopped jalapeño chile and more pomegranate seeds.

Mexican Red Rice
Arroz a la Mexicana
EL PASO, TEXAS • DURANGO, MEXICO

SERVES 4 TO 6 SERVINGS   *"No chiles for a month!" To Estella Ríos-Lopez, the doctor's remedy for her stomach ailment was terrifying. As we sat eating breakfast, it was obvious that Estella had survived her one-month deprivation since she drastically raised the heat level of her bowl of* menudo *(hominy and tripe soup) with a heavy dose of crushed* chiles de árbol. *Estella's traditional rice dish is mild by comparison but still has the bright flavor of green chiles. In this version I've combined techniques shared by Olivia Dominguez, adding a tomato puree and, to intensify the color and flavor, even more chunks of fresh tomato.*

Often Mexican tomato-based rice is flavored with other vegetables, too, adding even more color. Olivia suggests adding half a cup or so of frozen peas or corn, stirred in with the broth, or a small diced carrot.

Since this earthy rice dish is generously tossed with chiles, its flavor will contrast with a simple grilled steak or Garlic Chicken (page 153), and the addition of a yellow ear of Corn Cooked in the Husk (page 243) will add further brightness to the table.

1 medium ripe tomato, cut into ½-inch chunks, or ¾ cup canned tomatoes, drained

2 tablespoons safflower or canola oil, or a combination of oil and unsalted butter

1 cup long-grain white rice

½ white onion, quartered and cut into ½-inch slices

2–3 cloves garlic, finely chopped

3 fresh long green chiles, Anaheim or New Mexico varieties, roasted (page 21), seeded, and chopped

1¾ cups Chicken Stock (page 70) or canned chicken broth

about ½ teaspoon sea salt

1 ripe plum tomato, chopped into ½-inch pieces

For the Garnish
chopped cilantro or flat-leaf parsley

½ firm but ripe avocado, peeled and sliced (optional)

Puree the tomato in a food processor or blender and set aside.

In a heavy medium-size saucepan or Dutch oven with a lid, heat the oil over medium heat. Add the rice and onion, and toss until the rice turns a toasty golden color and has a nutty aroma. It will take 5–10 minutes, depending on the pot.

Stir in the garlic and continue to cook for 1 minute. Stir in the tomatoes, chiles, and chicken broth, and bring to a simmer. Taste and add salt if necessary. Cover the pan, lower the heat, and cook *without peeking* for 15 minutes, until all the broth is absorbed. Remove the pot from the heat and let it continue to steam, covered, at least 5 minutes more.

When ready to serve, add the plum tomato pieces and toss together in the pot. For even more color, decorate with chopped cilantro or slices of avocado.

Green Rice
Arroz Poblano
CHICAGO, ILLINOIS • MICHOACÁN, MEXICO

SERVES 6 *Priscilla Gomez Satkoff learned how to make this handsome rice dish, speckled with the muted shades of green herbs and chiles, from her mother in Zitácuaro, Michoacán. This area has two special claims to fame: The nearby fir-covered mountains are the annual winter hideaway of more than 100 million monarch butterflies, and it is where Diana Kennedy, one of Mexico's strongest culinary advocates, has lived for close to twenty years. Among the first words of English Priscilla learned when she came to Chicago as a bride were the names of herbs so she could buy the needed ingredients for dishes like this green rice.*

This rice is a colorful companion to a simple plate of fish or Garlic Chicken (page 153).

2 fresh poblano or Anaheim chiles, roasted (page 21), peeled, seeded, and roughly chopped (see Note)

3 cloves garlic, peeled and roughly chopped

1 cup roughly chopped white onion

4 large spinach leaves or 2 outside leaves of romaine lettuce, chopped

1 cup flat-leaf parsley

20 sprigs cilantro plus extra for garnish

2½ cups Chicken Stock (page 70) or canned chicken broth

2 tablespoons virgin olive oil

1½ cups long-grain white rice

sea salt

Put the chiles, garlic, onion, spinach, parsley, cilantro, and ½ cup of the broth together in a blender and blend until smooth. Set aside.

Heat the oil in a medium-size saucepan over medium-high heat until it almost starts to smoke. Add the rice and cook, stirring, for 3–5 minutes, until golden brown. Add the pureed ingredients to the rice and continue cooking over medium heat, stirring gently to incorporate the mixture well into the rice. Add the rest of the broth, salt to taste, and bring to a boil, shaking the pan to mix ingredients together. Turn the heat to low, cover, and cook about 15 minutes, until the rice absorbs all the liquid.

It is ready when the separate kernels of rice are tender but firm and there is no liquid left in the bottom of the pan. Remove the pan from the heat, keep covered, and let it sit for 5–10 minutes more. Fluff the rice with a fork, spoon into a serving dish, and garnish with cilantro.

NOTE: I've enriched the color of the rice with a handful of spinach and roasted the poblano chiles for a sweeter flavor. Anaheim chiles can be substituted but, while tasty, do not give the full rich taste of the poblano. Other cooks may dice the chile instead of pureeing it with the broth.

Lentils and Chorizo
Lentejas y Chorizo
SAN LUIS, COLORADO

SERVES 4 TO 6 *Lentils and sausage make a very Spanish combination, and considering that the roots of Teresa Vigil's family go back to some of the earliest Spanish settlers of southern Colorado's San Luis Valley and that Teresa has traveled extensively in Spain, it is not unusual that this is a favorite family dish. Even the enrichment of olive oil is a Spanish touch. Some of the older people living in the valley that I spoke to recall when lentils were grown there, but now they are only found at R&R Market, the local grocery store that has been owned by members of the same family since 1857.*

This tasty mixture goes well as a side dish with grilled spareribs for a casual supper. The Watercress Salad with Pine Nuts (page 52) is a nice contrast of taste and texture, with a full-bodied red wine to drink. Hot Corn Bread (page 319) is a natural.

2 cups quick-cooking lentils, rinsed

4 cups Chicken Stock (page 70) or canned chicken broth or water

2 cloves garlic, peeled

2 bay leaves

sea salt

coarsely ground black pepper

1 tablespoon olive oil

½ pound chorizo, crumbled (see Note)

½ cup finely diced white onion

½ cup finely diced carrot

½ cup finely diced celery

3 fresh ripe plum tomatoes, chopped

For the Garnish

2 tablespoons chopped flat-leaf parsley

Bring the lentils to a boil in the chicken broth along with the garlic and bay leaves. Simmer until the lentils are just becoming soft, about 20 minutes. Do not overcook. Season with salt and pepper to taste.

Meanwhile, heat the olive oil in a medium-size skillet and lightly brown the chorizo, onions, carrots, and celery over medium heat. Add the tomatoes and simmer until the liquid is partially evaporated and the flavors have blended.

Stir the tomato mixture into the lentils, seasoning, if needed, with more salt and pepper, and simmer another 10–15 minutes, until the carrots are tender. Remove the garlic and bay leaves before serving.

Garnish with the parsley.

NOTE: It is very important to use a good quality chorizo, either one you have prepared yourself (page 170) or freshly made by a butcher. Do not even be tempted to use that prepackaged concoction that is sold under a label of chorizo. Your dish will be greasy and of an unrecognizable flavor. It would be better to substitute hot Italian sausage.

VARIATION: LENTILS WITH BACON AND POTATOES In Albuquerque, Irma Aguilar uses bacon instead of chorizo, substitutes cubes of potatoes for the carrots and tomatoes, and adds 1 tablespoon of pure ground dried New Mexico chile for flavor.

LIVING OFF NATURE: WILD GREENS
Verdolagas and Quelites

Yes, the best things in life are often free. Living in the Northwest, I find that foraging comes naturally. Being a confirmed believer in living off the land and sea, I naturally have an affinity with Mexican cuisine. Through the centuries, the Indians of Mexico often existed only because of their foraging ability. Now such things as tiny sautéed grasshoppers and ant eggs may be as prized as snails and caviar in the finest city restaurants, but it takes only a walk through a Mexican market to see their everyday importance. So it is with the wild greens of spring: Their push through the warming earth is in a rhythm parallel to the season of Lent, with its abstinence from meat.

The most traditional green eaten at Lent is verdolagas (Portulaca oleracea), or purslane, a ground-hugging succulent that grows as a weed in gardens throughout the world. Although the whole plant is good to eat, it is the new leafy tips, with their mild acidic taste, that are prized. They are fresh-picked for salads or lightly steamed and mixed with meats or other vegetables. While you may want to uproot most of these fast-spreading plants, isolate several so you can pinch off the tender tips to enjoy throughout its growing season.

Quelites (Chenopodium album), which is variously called pigweed, goosefoot, or lamb's-quarters, is favored by many Mexican families in the United States, since it seems to be even more abundant than verdolagas. Its spinachlike leaves are picked in backyards from the northern border city of Detroit south to El Paso, and from Florida to my daughter Amy's garden in Washington. Quelites *should* be eaten when young and tender, and, like spinach, just needs to be steamed and wilted, although I find it can use a minute or so more cooking time than cultivated spinach.

Wild Greens with Pinto Beans

Quelites con Frijoles

FAIRVIEW, NEW MEXICO

SERVES 4 *The earthy combination of greens and beans is common in Mexico, but its austerity reminds me even more of the food and land in the upper Rio Grande country of southern Colorado and northern New Mexico. Each spring wherever Mexican families observe the Catholic traditions there will be* quelites, *called lamb's-quarters or wild spinach, served at the table during Lent.*

My husband and I met Sally Borrego one day while she was working in a drugstore near where we were staying in northern New Mexico. During the next week she introduced me to many of the local dishes, including ways to prepare the wild spinach.

At a typical New Mexico or southern Colorado meal, I've been served the greens with a platter of panfried rabbit or chicken with unadorned vine-ripe sliced tomatoes on the side. It is also a good companion dish for Red Chile with Meat (page 174).

9 cups loosely packed, well-washed lamb's-quarters (*quelites*) or 7 cups loosely packed chard or spinach (see Notes)

2 slices bacon (see Notes)

1 tablespoon bacon grease or safflower oil

½ small white onion, cut in half vertically and then thinly sliced into half-moons

3 cloves garlic, thinly sliced

⅓ cup pine nuts (optional)

½ cup cooked pinto beans (page 224) or canned

1 tablespoon chile seeds or caribe chile (page 263)

about ½ teaspoon sea salt

½ teaspoon freshly ground black pepper

Stem the lamb's-quarters or other greens. If you are using chard or spinach, cut the leaves into 1-inch-wide strips.

Bring a pot of water to a boil. Place the greens in a colander and pour the boiling water over them. Cool with cold running water. Squeeze in small handfuls to extract the water. Chop the greens into large pieces and fluff to loosen the leaves. This dish can be prepared to this stage in advance.

Fry the bacon in a large, heavy skillet over medium heat. When it is crisp, remove the bacon and drain on absorbent paper. Pour out all but 1 tablespoon of the grease from the pan; if not using the bacon grease, wipe it all out and add oil.

Reheat the skillet, add the onion, and toss quickly in the pan about 5 minutes until it is almost crisp. Add the garlic and pine nuts, and toss again until they start to color. Add the greens, pinto beans, chile, salt, and pepper. Toss quickly, removing the mixture before the spinach releases its juices.

Serve immediately as a side dish with Flour Tortillas (page 125), although the greens are tasty as a filling for enchiladas with Basic Green Tomatillo Sauce (page 212).

NOTES: Of course, not everyone has wild greens growing nearby, so it makes sense to substitute tender new spinach, kale, or Swiss chard. Any leafy green will work, though the earthy quality of green chard seems to come the closest in taste.

For a Lenten vegetarian dish, eliminate the bacon and use olive oil for sautéing the vegetables.

Green Beans Flavored with Bacon
Ejotes con Tocino
HOMESTEAD, FLORIDA • TAMAULIPAS, MEXICO

SERVES 4 TO 6 AS A SIDE DISH   *Born and raised in Arkansas, Elroy Garza has lived for many years in Homestead, Florida. He and his wife, Maria, both work at a large tropical fruit plant where Elroy supervises the packing of limes and avocados. At home, Maria usually cooks the simpler foods of Tamaulipas, the foods that Elroy grew up eating. Making flour tortillas is part of her daily routine, and the lunches she and Elroy bring to work could typically be a burrito filled with well-fried beans and chopped hard-boiled eggs or just a huge mess of green beans like this wrapped in a flour tortilla.*

The green beans and crispy-fried bacon provide a colorful contrast alongside Garlic Chicken (page 153). I like to accompany it with Corn Bread (page 319).

1 pound fresh or frozen green beans, thawed
4 strips lean bacon
½ white onion, finely chopped
1 ripe tomato, chopped, or 1 cup chopped
  canned tomatoes

pinch of cumin
sea salt and freshly ground black pepper

Cut off the ends of the fresh beans and, if needed, remove the strings. Cut into 1-inch pieces and set aside.

In a large, heavy skillet, fry the bacon over low heat. Remove when crispy and drain on absorbent paper. Pour off all but 1 tablespoon of the fat.

Sauté the onion in the bacon grease over medium heat, and when it is quite dark brown, add the tomato and let the mixture reduce, adding water a little at a time if needed. Add the green beans and cover, stirring occasionally, for about 20 minutes, until the beans are tender. Crumble the bacon and stir most of it into the beans. Save some for garnish. Add salt and pepper to taste. Place the beans on a serving plate and top with the remaining crumbled bacon.

Green Beans, Onions, and Tomatoes Bound with Egg

Ejotes Guisados

TOPPENISH, WASHINGTON

SERVES 4 *By combining egg with tender young green beans fresh from her garden, Toni Tabayoyan creates a substantial side dish that can also be served alone as a quick supper.*

The practice of mixing tomatoes, onions, and garlic with another vegetable is very common to both Mexican and Filipino cooking.

Since Toni's husband is Filipino, she didn't have to make many changes in her cooking habits when she got married—except to cut down the amount of chiles! Both cuisines routinely add small pieces of meat or, as in this dish, egg to vegetable dishes to provide more protein in the meal. Turn this hearty mixture into vegetarian tacos and enliven with Six Chiles Salsa (page 272). This is a dish I like to serve with Cream of Chayote Soup (page 84).

2 tablespoons safflower or canola oil

1 large white onion, quartered and thinly sliced

2 cloves garlic, thinly sliced

1 pound fresh green beans, trimmed and cut into 1-inch pieces, or 9 ounces frozen green beans, thawed

2 large ripe tomatoes, peeled and chopped, or one 14-ounce can tomato pieces

1 tablespoon chopped fresh oregano or 1 teaspoon dried, preferably Mexican

¼ teaspoon ground cumin

sea salt and freshly ground black pepper

2 large eggs

For the Garnish

1 tablespoon chopped fresh cilantro

Heat the oil in a medium-size skillet and add the onion and garlic. Cook over medium-low heat until they just begin to relax. Raise the heat, add the beans, and toss for several minutes to mix thoroughly. Add the tomatoes, oregano, cumin, and salt and pepper to taste. Cook over medium heat, about 10 minutes, until the beans are barely tender, stirring once; cook no more than 5 minutes if using frozen beans. Add a splash of water if the tomato mixture begins to dry out.

Meanwhile, beat the eggs gently in a small bowl. When the beans are the texture you want them, add the eggs to the pan all at once, tossing and stirring until just set, barely a minute. Season again with salt and pepper, garnish with cilantro, and serve immediately.

Corn Cooked in the Husk
Elotes
CORAL GABLES, FLORIDA • MEXICO CITY, MEXICO

SERVES 6   *Although Veronica Litton travels extensively and has quite a taste for fine foods and wine, she still craves the simple street foods of Mexico. One of her favorites is corn on the cob lathered with thick crema instead of butter, the flavor accented with grated cheese and chile.*

While this is traditionally a snack food served by street vendors, Veronica uses it to accompany grilled or barbecued fish or meat. Serve with plenty of napkins. Try it with the King Salmon Grilled in Corn Husks (page 142).

1 cup Mexican *crema* (page 23) or sour cream
  thinned with milk
1 cup finely grated Parmesan or *queso añejo* (see
  page 111)
2 limes, quartered

¼ cup ground pequín or other good-quality chile
¼ cup sea salt
6 ears very fresh corn
2 teaspoons sea salt

Place the *crema,* cheese, and limes in shallow bowls. Place the chile and salt in smaller bowls or in shakers.

Remove the outer layer of cornhusks and discard. Carefully pull back the remaining husks, remove the silk, and return the husks around the corn.

Bring a large pot of salted water to boil. Gently drop the corn into the water and cook 5–10 minutes, just until tender. Drain and serve immediately, letting all unwrap their own ears.

recipe continues

Spread the corn with the *crema*, sprinkle or roll on the cheese, dust with chile, squirt with lime juice, and start eating.

VARIATION: ROASTED CORN (*ELOTE ASADO*) The same general technique can be used with grilling corn, only after removing the corn silk, soak the ears in cold water for 1 hour. Tie the top of each ear with thin strips of the outer husks. Roast over coals, turning frequently, for about 20–25 minutes. If not quite done but the husk is very burned, wrap in aluminum foil to continue cooking. Serve with the same condiments as used with the boiled corn.

Scalloped Chayote and Corn
Chayotes y Elotes Gratinados
SACRAMENTO, CALIFORNIA • MICHOACÁN, MEXICO

SERVES 4 AS A SIDE DISH *The chayote is like a nineteenth-century "romanticized" woman: a bit exotic, always modest, very versatile, and capable of assuming whatever role is needed. Although it is a native of Mexico, its flesh, seeds, flowers, and even the roots of the chayote are relished throughout the tropical world. The chayote is pickled, stir-fried, steamed, creamed, made into soups, or sweetened and used as a pudding or pie filling. In a recipe I found in Belize, it is mixed with dried fruits and dark brown sugar and enclosed in dough and deep-fried. In Louisiana it assumes the alias of mirliton and is cloaked with rich sauces of shrimp and oysters.*

Val Hermocillo likes to serve this humble relative of squashes, the chayote, as an elegant vegetable dish. The golden-crusted surface is punctuated with flecks of green cilantro and kernels of golden corn, and the mild-flavored vegetable is enlivened with bits of feisty serrano chiles.

For Val, this palest of pale green vegetables is just the dish to serve alongside Holiday Stuffed Turkey (page 167), but it also pairs comfortably with Sautéed Fish Fillets with Garlic (page 140).

For the Vegetables
2 large *chayotes*, about 1½ pounds
1 teaspoon unsalted butter
sea salt and freshly ground black pepper

8–9 ounces frozen corn kernels
½ cup grated fat-free mozzarella or Monterey jack cheese

For the Sauce

2 tablespoons unsalted butter

1 teaspoon safflower or canola oil

½ white onion, finely chopped

2 (or to taste) fresh serrano or jalapeño chiles,
 seeded and finely chopped

2 cloves garlic, minced

2 tablespoons flour

1 cup milk, plus more if needed

2 tablespoons chopped cilantro

¼ teaspoon dried oregano, preferably Mexican

about 1 teaspoon sea salt

For the Topping

1 cup dry bread crumbs

½ cup grated Parmesan cheese

2 tablespoons melted unsalted butter

Preheat the oven to 357 degrees F. Peel the *chayotes* and cut into thin slices.

Put a layer of slices on the bottom of a well-buttered 8-inch casserole dish and add salt and pepper liberally. Add a layer of corn kernels, sprinkle with cheese, and continue layering the chayote and corn.

To prepare the sauce, melt the butter mixed with the oil in a small saucepan. Sauté the onion, chiles, and garlic over medium heat and blend in the flour. Remove the pan from the heat and slowly add the milk, blending it in with a fork until smooth. Return to the heat and cook slowly until the sauce is thickened and smooth. Season with the cilantro, oregano, and salt, and pour over the *chayote*. Add enough milk to fill the casserole even with the top layer. The dish can be made to this stage, covered, and set aside for a few hours.

Stir the bread crumbs and grated cheese into the melted butter and sprinkle the mixture over the *chayote* and corn.

Bake for 30–40 minutes, or until the *chayote* is tender when pierced with a fork and the top is crusty and lightly browned. Serve immediately because the dish loses its texture if allowed to sit very long.

Stuffed Chayotes
Chayotes Rellenos
MIAMI, FLORIDA • MEXICO CITY, MEXICO

SERVES 6 *Shaped roughly like a pear, the* chayote *is ideal for stuffing—the way Virginia Ariemna and many other Mexican-American cooks like it best. Virginia was born in New York, but her family returned to Mexico when she was five. She has since lived in both Italy and Germany, and is a painter, has*

a master's degree in philosophy, and, above all, has an exuberant enthusiasm for life. This recipe comes from her mother, Virginia Dominguez, who besides being a busy gynecologist is a good cook.

Stuffed Chayotes is an ideal companion for Sautéed Fish Fillets with Garlic (page 140) or Fiesta Meatloaf (page 184).

3 large *chayotes,* about ¾ pound each

about 2 tablespoons sea salt

For the Stuffing

1–2 tablespoons safflower or canola oil

8 ounces Mexican chorizo, store-bought or
   homemade (page 170) (optional)

⅓ cup chopped white onion

2 cloves garlic, chopped

1 large ripe tomato, chopped

2 tablespoons chopped flat-leaf parsley

sea salt and freshly ground black pepper

For the Topping

1 cup dry bread crumbs

6 ounces *queso fresco* (see page 112) or farmer's
   cheese, crumbled

2 tablespoons melted unsalted butter

Boil the whole *chayotes* in enough boiling salted water to keep them covered until they are tender, about 30–40 minutes. Cut each in half lengthwise and remove the large seeds. Carefully spoon out the pulp, leaving a ¼-inch shell. Chop the pulp (and the seed also, if you want) and reserve for the stuffing.

Preheat the oven to 400 degrees F.

Heat the oil in a medium-size skillet. Stir in the chorizo, breaking it up, and fry until the meat is cooked through but not browned. Add the onion and garlic, and cook over medium-high heat about 10 minutes, until soft and golden. Stir in the tomato and cook another 2 minutes.

Add the *chayote* pulp and parsley to the skillet, stirring occasionally, until the mixture is dry. Add salt and pepper to taste.

Divide the mixture evenly among the shells, heaping and pressing down to make a firm mound in each shell. Set close together in a lightly greased baking dish.

Toss the bread crumbs, cheese, and melted butter together in a small bowl and sprinkle on top of each *chayote* shell. Bake in the oven about 15 minutes until the stuffing is browned and crusty.

NOTE: The large, tender *chayote* seed has a delicious nutty quality. It can be cut out and enjoyed raw by the cook, or, if feeling generous, it can be chopped and added to the filling.

Zucchini Stuffed with Cheese
Calabacitas Rellenas de Queso
ALLEN PARK, MICHIGAN • ZACATECAS, MEXICO

SERVES 3 AS A MAIN COURSE, WITH 2 ZUCCHINI ON EACH PLATE, OR 6 AS A SIDE DISH   *Corn, tomatoes, and zucchini—three colorful vegetables from Mexico that are combined in so many different ways. In New Mexico I ate them fried into almost a stew; in California they were a succotashlike dish called colache; in Texas they were all mixed together and baked in a casserole with cheese. Florencio Perea stuffs his garden-grown zucchini with cheese, fries it in a fluffy egg batter, and tops it with a tomato sauce decorated with bright yellow kernels of corn. All the flavors meld together so well that there is not usually a problem with leftovers, which I find are not as attractive reheated. If you think you will have extra, do not batter the zucchini and bake them, covered, in a 350-degree F. oven for about 45 minutes.*

This is a beautiful dish to serve as an entree. All the meal needs to be complete is Mexican Red Rice (page 235) and perhaps a salad of leafy greens. The stuffed zucchini is also a good side dish for Fiesta Meatloaf (page 184).

6 medium 7- or 8-inch-long, straight-shaped zucchinis

½ pound Monterey jack or cheddar cheese, coarsely grated

For the Sauce
1 pound ripe tomatoes (about 3 medium tomatoes) or one 28-ounce can tomatoes, peeled and drained

½ small white onion, roughly chopped

2 cloves garlic, roughly chopped

1 tablespoon safflower or canola oil

1 tablespoon finely chopped flat-leaf parsley

1 bay leaf

½ teaspoon ground cinnamon (cassia)

½ teaspoon dried thyme

2 cups Chicken Stock (page 70)

about ½ teaspoon sea salt

freshly ground black pepper

For the Batter
4 eggs, separated

pinch of sea salt

peanut or safflower oil for frying

½ cup flour

For the Garnish
½ cup frozen corn kernels, thawed

½ cup *cotija* or feta cheese, crumbled

¼ cup chopped cilantro

Wash each zucchini well and cut in half lengthwise. Cut around the seedy core and scoop it out, leaving a thick shell. In a pan wide enough to hold the zucchinis, bring salted water to a boil and cook the zucchinis about 3 minutes. Remove and cool under cold water. Dry the zucchinis, fill with the cheese, then put them back into their original whole shape and hold together with toothpicks inserted at an angle. Set aside.

In a blender or food processor, puree the tomatoes, onion, and garlic until smooth. In a saucepan, heat the oil over medium-high heat. Add the sauce and cook, stirring until it thickens, about 5 minutes. Add the parsley, bay leaf, cinnamon, and thyme and let the sauce cook another 5 minutes. Add the chicken broth, stir well, and season with salt and pepper. Let the mixture simmer on medium-high heat for about 20 minutes. Taste again for seasoning. Set aside and keep warm.

In a bowl, beat the egg whites with salt until stiff. Lightly beat the yolks, then fold them into the whites. Pour ½ inch of oil into a large skillet and heat over medium-high heat. Roll the zucchini in the flour, then dip in the beaten eggs. Place gently in the hot oil and turn as they begin to color, until golden on all sides. Carefully remove from the oil with 2 large slotted spoons and drain on absorbent paper.

Remove the toothpicks. Place the zucchini on a deep serving platter or on individual plates and spoon on the sauce. Garnish with the corn, crumbled cheese, and chopped cilantro.

Summer Squash Stewed with Corn and Tomatoes
Colache

SERVES 4 Colache *(what a wonderful word!) is the Mexican version of the southwest Indian's succotash. Basically just a hodgepodge of whatever garden vegetables are on hand, it always includes the small summer zucchini, pattypan, or crookneck squash. My dad learned to make* colache *from his Mexican friends in California, and it was one of my favorite ways of eating vegetables when I was a child. I've borrowed a few tricks from Jacqueline Higuera McMahan's recipe in her* Healthy Mexican Cookbook; *she had adapted it from an old recipe of her grandmother's. Jacqueline, a vivacious Mexican-American cook from a many-generations California family that was a recipient of one of the last Spanish land grants in that region, has been very influential in spreading the word that "the real heart and soul of Mexican food is healthy. It's just been bastardized in the translation."*

Colache is a tasty side dish with simple grilled pork and chicken dishes, as well as alongside Fiesta Meatloaf (page 184). Set the vegetable dish on a buffet table featuring enchiladas.

3 teaspoons olive oil

1 medium white onion, chopped

1 red bell pepper, seeded and chopped

1½ pounds zucchini or other summer squash, thickly sliced

2 garlic cloves, thinly sliced

3 mild fresh chiles, Anaheim or New Mexican, roasted (page 21), peeled, seeded, and chopped

1 14½-ounce can tomato pieces with their juice

1 large sprig fresh epazote (page 223), coarsely chopped, or 1 teaspoon dried chopped oregano, preferably Mexican

about ½ teaspoon sea salt

4 small ears fresh corn, about 2 ounces each, cut into 1½-inch rounds

For the Topping

2 tablespoons grated *queso añejo* (page 111) or Parmesan cheese

Warm the oil in a large skillet over medium heat and sauté the onion and red pepper about 5 minutes, until slightly softened. Push the onion and red pepper aside. Add the squash and garlic, and sauté until golden brown, turning often.

Stir in the chiles, tomatoes, epazote, and salt, and bury the corn under the vegetables. After the vegetable mixture is bubbling, cover and simmer on low heat for about 15 minutes, adding more boiling water if the mixture starts to dry out.

Spoon the vegetables into a serving bowl and sprinkle the cheese on top. It will be ready to serve when the cheese begins to soften.

Wild Mushroom Sauté with Guajillo Chile Rings

Hongos al Chile Guajillo

AUSTIN, TEXAS • TAMAULIPAS, MEXICO

SERVES 6 AS A SIDE DISH OR MAKES ENOUGH FILLING FOR 12 TACOS *The bold, earthy flavors of wild mushrooms and chiles are ones that are often combined during Mexico's late-summer rainy season when the mushrooms are abundant. Here in the United States, both native wild mushrooms and other unusual varieties such as shiitake are expensive but are now standard items in most supermarkets. Tomas, the son of the recently deceased Guadalupe Garcia, passed her recipe, pungent with garlic, on to us.*

Serve as a side dish with King Salmon Grilled in Cornhusks (page 142) or any simple meat or chicken dish. The mushrooms are equally as tasty as a filling for tacos or an omelet.

¾ pound wild or cultivated mushrooms
¼ cup olive oil
10 cloves garlic, minced
4 dried guajillo chiles, cut in ¼-inch rings and
   seeds removed

1 tablespoon roughly chopped fresh epazote
   (page 223) (optional)
about ½ teaspoon sea salt

Clean the mushrooms with a soft cloth and, if using the common button mushrooms, stem and leave whole or in large pieces. Chop larger mushrooms into irregularly shaped pieces approximately 1½ inches in diameter.

Warm the oil in a large skillet over medium heat. Add the garlic and cook for 1–2 minutes, until softened. Stir in the chile rings, cook for another minute, and then add the mushrooms. Stir in the epazote if using, and salt to taste.

Cook until the mushrooms are just tender. The time will vary depending on the type of mushroom; it's usually about 5–10 minutes. If using the mixture for tacos, you may need to raise the heat until the mushroom liquid is absorbed.

Yellow Turnips and Red Chile Gravy
Nabos Amarillos en Chile Rojo
SAN LUIS, COLORADO

SERVES 4 AS A SIDE DISH *English frontiersmen from the East brought their well-loved "swedes," or rutabagas, with them when they settled around the military forts in Colorado. It was only a matter of time before these yellow turnips were smothered in red chile gravy and put on the table of Hispanic cooks throughout the San Luis Valley. The strong flavor of the root vegetable is a good foil for the fiery sauce. Turnips and taters mixed are equally good.*

Mary Ann Tafoya was raised in an isolated area of southern Colorado with the strong traditional values of the people. They were always poor, but rich in food that was healthful and cooked with love. Freezing winds come early to the valley, and most homes still have root cellars to protect the food that will last them through the winter. Being sent to the cellar for turnips was no chore for Mary Ann, for she knew that soon her grandmother would have a plate of fried turnips with thick chile gravy on the table for breakfast.

Yellow turnips and red chile gravy go well with any simple pork dish, bacon or sausage for break-fast, or pork chops or a roast at dinner.

2 pounds small yellow turnips (rutabagas), peeled
  and diced into ½-inch pieces
about ½ teaspoon sea salt
2 tablespoons safflower or canola oil
1 small white onion, finely chopped
1 clove garlic, minced
1 tablespoon flour

2–3 teaspoons pure red chile powder, preferably
  New Mexican
¼ teaspoon freshly ground black pepper
1 cup hot Chicken Stock (page 70), or canned
  chicken broth, or water
¼ cup chopped fresh flat-leaf parsley

Boil the yellow turnips in salted water to cover over medium heat for about 15 minutes, or until just tender.

While the turnips are cooking, heat the oil in a heavy, medium-size skillet or Dutch oven over medium heat. Add the onion and cook about 4 minutes, stirring occasionally. Add the garlic and cook another minute.

Add flour to the oil remaining in the skillet and brown slightly. If needed, add a bit more oil. Stir in the chile powder and pepper, and slowly stir in the hot broth. Add the turnips to the gravy and simmer, covered, for 10–15 minutes over low heat, scraping the pan bottom as clean as possible. Add more hot broth or water if needed. Sprinkle with parsley before serving.

VARIATION: TURNIPS AND PORK CHOPS Brown pork chops in the skillet before cooking the turnips. Remove and keep them warm. After adding the turnips to the chile gravy, return the pork chops to the pan to cook with the turnips.

Stuffed Sweet Potatoes
Camotes Rellenos
SANTA MONICA, CALIFORNIA • MEXICO CITY, MEXICO

SERVES 6 *The sweet potato, indigenous to tropical America, has been a staple of the Mexican diet since there were people who were hungry. On one of my first trips to Mexico City, I still remember being startled one evening by an eerie, melancholy wail that dominated all other street noises. When I investi-gated, I found it was a camote vendor, pushing his small cart full of dark-skinned tubers steaming in-*

side a metal drum. The mournful cry was the steam escaping, alerting the neighborhood to the camotero's nightly visit. It was this sweet potato that Ricardo Villareal knew as he was growing up in Mexico City, but instead of being used alongside meat or poultry, it was more apt to be a dessert or stirred into a glass of milk for breakfast or supper.

Although Mexican Americans often use the bigger, sweeter, orange-fleshed sweet potato that is sold in the United States as a yam (the true yam introduced by enslaved Africans in the Caribbean is from an entirely different family and is seldom carried in stores), Ricardo prefers the rather dry, lighter-fleshed ordinary sweet potato because its skin is somewhat tougher and holds up better during baking.

Ricardo uses this comforting dish to round out a festive meal featuring Holiday Stuffed Turkey (page 167), but it goes equally well with simple grilled meats.

6 medium sweet potatoes
4 tablespoons unsalted butter, melted
½ cup firmly packed brown sugar
1 egg, lightly beaten
3 tablespoons cognac or good brandy
½ teaspoon ground cinnamon (cassia)
sea salt and freshly ground black pepper

For the Topping

4 tablespoons unsalted butter
¼ cup firmly packed brown sugar
½ cup chopped pecans, or grated unsweetened
  coconut
pinch of freshly ground allspice

Preheat the oven to 350 degrees F.

Scrub the sweet potatoes well but do not peel them. Poke a few holes in the top with the tines of a fork to let the steam escape while they are baking. Bake the potatoes on a rack in the oven for about 40 minutes, or until they respond to pressure when pressed with towel-wrapped fingers.

When the sweet potatoes are cooked and slightly cooled, make a vertical cut through the top of the skin. Scoop out the flesh, leaving a shell. Place the flesh in a bowl and blend with the melted butter, brown sugar, egg, cognac, cinnamon, salt, and pepper. Spoon the mixture back into the shells and place on a large cookie sheet.

To prepare the topping, melt the butter with the brown sugar and add the nuts or coconut and the allspice. Spoon the topping over the sweet potatoes. Return the potatoes to the oven and bake about 15 minutes, until glazed a deep golden brown.

Griddle-Fried Onions and Chiles

Cebollitas Asadas con Chiles

AUSTIN, TEXAS • SONORA, MEXICO

SERVES 6 TO 8   *One of the simplest and most satisfying accompaniments to tacos, especially those made with grilled meat, are small, fat onions called knob or green spring onions, which are either fried on top of the stove or grilled. The very first time I fixed them was in the side yard of our home in Catalonia, Spain. I was following directions from quite a rudimentary cookbook that started, "Place 3–4 dozen spring onions for each on a bed of dried vine shoots and set fire to the latter." The results were smoky-sweet and delicious, and have been a weakness of mine ever since. There is a tiny taco stand a couple of blocks from the hotel where we stay in Mexico City, and it is the first place I head after I arrive—to order tacos de bistec con queso (beef tacos with cheese) but, more important, a double order of cebollitas.*

Try this recipe of Miguel's as an appetizer or alongside Tacos of Charcoal-Grilled Beef (page 115) or other tacos, perhaps surrounded with thick slices of fresh tomato garnished with basil.

16–24 small knob onions or large scallions (depending on size) (see Note)

¼ cup olive oil

8 fresh whole *güero* or other small yellow chiles, or jalapeño chiles

3–4 tablespoons lime juice

sea salt and freshly ground black pepper

Slice off the root end of each onion and several inches of the green top, and pull off the first layer of the onion skin.

Heat the oil in a large heavy skillet and sauté the onions and chiles over medium-high heat for 6–8 minutes, until brown on all sides. If using smaller onions, they may cook more quickly and can be removed.

Place the onions and chiles in a shallow bowl and sprinkle with the lime juice, salt, and pepper. Toss until well coated.

NOTE: Knob or spring onions are usually available in produce and farmer's markets, with bulbs 1–1½ inches across, in early summer, but if they can't be found, substitute the fattest green onions possible.

recipe continues

VARIATION: GRILLED ONIONS AND CHILES   Lay a double layer of heavy foil over the hottest section of a grill with coals that have burned down until white but still quite hot. Lightly rub the chiles and onions with oil and place on the foil with the white onion bulbs extending directly over the coals. Grill until brown, about 10 minutes, depending on the size of the onions and chiles. Turn frequently and remove them as they are done. Place in a shallow bowl, add a few more drops of oil, and toss with the lime juice, salt, and pepper.

Skillet Potatoes with Green Chiles and Onions

Papas Fritas con Rajas y Cebollas

EL PASO, TEXAS

SERVES 4   *When I told my friends from El Paso that Fredric and I were going to be spending some time there, they said in one mighty voice, "Go to H&H Car Wash and Coffee Shop for breakfast." H&H is a tiny place attached to a large, efficient hand carwash. While your car is being washed, you are free to eat your breakfast at one of the three tables or the short counter. It is like being in someone's home. Everyone knows everyone, or if you're an outsider you are quickly made part of the family. There's lots of conversation and lots of good food, such as these crispy ovals of fried potatoes and green chiles that were served alongside our* huevos rancheros.

These potatoes are ideal served with any style of eggs for a hearty breakfast, or the potatoes can be diced and added to a breakfast burrito.

2 pounds red new potatoes (about 6–8 medium-size or 14 small ones)
2–3 tablespoons safflower or canola oil
½ white onion, thinly sliced
2 fresh long green chiles (New Mexican or Anaheim), roasted (page 21), seeded, and cut into strips, or 2 canned green chiles, cut into strips

pinch of cumin (optional)
sea salt and freshly ground black pepper
4 ounces longhorn cheddar or Monterey jack cheese, cubed (optional)

Place the potatoes in a saucepan, cover with cold water, and bring to a boil. Lower the heat and cook about 5 minutes, until barely tender. Drain, rinse in cold water, and pat dry.

Meanwhile, heat 1 tablespoon of the oil in a large skillet. Sauté the onion and chiles until soft and lightly brown. Remove from the pan and set aside.

Cut the cooled potatoes lengthwise into ¼-inch slices.

If necessary, add more oil to the skillet, raise the heat, and add the potatoes. Fry until they begin to brown and crisp, about 10 minutes, shaking the pan from time to time so they do not stick. Stir in the onion and chiles. Add cumin, salt, and pepper, and mix thoroughly. Taste again for seasoning. Sprinkle in the cubes of cheese and toss them with the potatoes using a fork. Serve very hot.

VARIATION: RANCH-STYLE POTATOES WITH RED CHILE SAUCE AND CHEESE
Instead of using green chiles, Geraldo Reyes in New York makes a red sauce, blending together in a food processor 1 ancho chile and 2 guajillo chiles that have been toasted (page 22), seeded, and soaked in hot water; 1 clove of garlic; and 1 teaspoon of dried epazote or oregano. The sauce is added to the potatoes after they are well browned. Cook another few minutes and add the cheese.

Washington Impressions

Tom Cerna, officially retired from a government job, is still a chile farmer in Washington's Yakima Valley. Up most mornings before the sun, he watches his chile plants—hundreds and hundreds of dumpy, dark green jalapeños, alongside poblano, serrano, and habanero chiles—stretch, flower, and ripen. Even when the fields are blanketed with snow, he stands at the window for long minutes of quiet and thinks about plowing and planting and how year after year one stubborn tomato plant always springs up in the very center of a row of chiles. These are the fourteen acres of fertile land his dad bought in 1945 after years of working in beet fields and ranching in Wyoming and Montana. Tom is on his land to stay, and he has never even been to where his father grew up in Chilchota, Michoacán.

Toni Tabayoyan spent her early years in Wyoming and Nebraska, moving to Washington when she was ten. Every day she helped her mother, who was from Guanajuato, cook the regional dishes from that part of Central Mexico. Toni was seventeen when she married Paul, a handsome Filipino she met when they were both picking tomatoes. Soon *lumpia* (similar to Chinese egg rolls) was on the table, too. Luckily for Toni, the cooking technique was not much different from that used for enchiladas. She was in her fifties before she ever visited Mexico on a vacation. She refers to it as "over there" and had tears in her eyes when she spoke about the poor and hungry families she saw.

Toni's five children are now grown and have families of their own. You would think after fifty years of preparing meals following a day's work she'd be tired of cooking. But although she is now retired and living in a large immaculate mobile home with a garden and a close-up view of Mount Adams, her greatest satisfaction still comes from making her own flour and corn tortillas and being able to can jars and jars of salsa made from freshly picked chiles and tomatoes.

Tom and Toni are typical of the many Mexican Americans I met in eastern Washington's Yakima Valley. Sheltered from the heavy rainfall of Puget Sound by the rugged Cascade Mountains, the valley is blessed with an average of three hundred days a year of sunshine. Its crops—apples, mint, hops, and wine grapes—all require a great deal of hand labor, and it is Mexican migrant workers who from the beginning filled this seasonal demand. They still are needed every year, but more and more have become full-time employees, and a great number have long since moved into other professions, and to other communities across the state.

Michoacán, "the land of the fishes," is very like the state of Washington, no doubt one of the reasons that those from Michoacán have become the majority of the Mexican-American population in this state far to the north. Washington has its rugged Cascade and Olympic mountain ranges; Michoacán has Mil Cumbres (Thousand Peaks). Washington has Mount St. Helens, which erupted in 1980; Michoacán has the Paricutín volcano, which spewed forth its lava in 1944, covering 15 square miles of countryside. They both have beautiful coastlands, lakes, and rivers. And Washington offers work. The migration to the area of the state I live in, Pierce County in South Puget Sound, can be traced to the late 1970s when two brothers, Martín and Raúl Andres, of Tzintzuntzan (pronounced "seen-soon-sahn"), a village of three thousand I know quite well, had jobs picking apples in the Yakima Valley. When the season was over, they headed to the coast where they had heard of work on a farm close to Tacoma. There they stayed, marrying two American sisters. Now, sixteen years later, close to five hundred family members, friends, and acquaintances have joined them to live in Pierce County, working mainly in the nearby Christmas tree farms, in plant nurseries, in construction, in factories, and as musicians. Music is very important to those from Michoacán, and they play regularly at those fiestas celebrating life's passages: baptisms and birthdays, weddings and *quinceañeras,* the traditional coming-out party for 15-year-old girls. Guests dance to the rhythms of a Tzintzuntzan band and enjoy the pork *carnitas* and special tamales from their village in Mexico.

Finishing Touches
Salsas, Relishes, Condiments
Salsas y Encurtidos

They cultivate a great diversity of plants and garden truck of which they are very fond, and these they eat raw as well as in various cooked dishes. They have one—like a pepper—as a condiment which they call chili, and they never eat anything without it.

—NARRATIVE OF SOME THINGS OF NEW SPAIN AND OF THE
GREAT CITY OF TEMPESTITAN, MEXICO
Anonymous conqueror

To test salsa, drop some on the tablecloth. If it fails to burn a hole in the cloth, it is not a good sauce.

—SOUTH TEXAS KITCHEN SAYING

ONE OF THE MOST NOTICEABLE CHARACTERISTICS of Mexican food is that no dish is served unadorned. If it isn't cooked with a sauce, it is served with one. If it isn't red, it's green. Even at breakfast, every table will have a bowl filled with the vibrant colors and flavors of salsas. They go in, or on, just about anything—except dessert. Then there are the pickled vegetables to munch on and, of course, guacamole, that wonderful mixture of chiles, tomatoes, and avocados.

The love of table sauces and spicy condiments is as great in the United States as it is in Mexico. There was hardly one meal I shared while researching this book that didn't include at least one salsa. A few times they came prepared from jars—in fact, several of the families bottled and marketed their own salsas. In most homes, though, it was a relishlike fresh salsa of chopped ripe tomatoes, green chiles, and crisp white onions, all mixed together with pungent cilantro. Some of my other favorites were those made of dried chiles—the anchos, guajillos, and New Mexican red chiles, and those with the aromatic smoked chipotle chiles.

Chiles may be used in many ways besides in salsas, but I can't imagine a salsa without chiles. The type of chile may vary, but that essential pungency is always present. In fact, the pungency is so intense that with most chiles I suggest wearing rubber or plastic gloves when handling them or washing your hands thoroughly with hot soapy water. Be careful not to rub your eyes, especially if wearing contacts.

A FEW FACTS ABOUT CHILES

Since Columbus and his fellow travelers mistakenly misnamed the pods of the chile plant after the similarly piquant black pepper—a seed of an East Indian shrub from an entirely different botanical family—confusion has been part of the chile mystique. All true chiles are a part of the Solanaceae, or nightshade, family, as are other edible plants like the potato, eggplant, and tomato. It is separated from those family members into the genus Capsicum, generally believed to contain twenty to thirty different species. All are native to the New World tropics or subtropics, but only five are regularly cultivated.

It is from the *Capsicum annum* that almost all our common chiles are derived, certainly all those used in the United States, with the exception of the well-known incendiary variety of *C. frutescens,* known as tabasco. All the others, from the bell pepper to the habanero, are cultivars—or even subdivisions of cultivars—of *C. annum.*

Chiles cross-pollinate very easily, so if you have two different cultivars in one small area, there soon may be even more kinds growing there with very different characteristics. In each area of Mexico similar chiles will be locally named and become distinctive flavors in the regional dishes. This diversity is not as evident in the United States, except under controlled conditions, as with the extensive cross-breeding of the long green chile in southern New Mexico.

When Mexican families immigrated across the border before the 1980s, very few of their familiar chiles were available in U.S. markets. They had to improvise and adapt with varying results. In recent years, however, most of the common dried chiles can be purchased easily, and I've seen many varieties of out-of-season fresh chiles in all parts of the country. With this abundance, many Mexican-American cooks are now using for the first time chiles that they had previously only heard of from their parents or grandparents, or had tasted and maybe brought back from a visit to Mexico.

VARIETIES OF FRESH CHILES MOST FREQUENTLY USED IN THE UNITED STATES

I found that by far the fresh chile most commonly used by Mexican Americans is the versatile *jalapeño*. Named for Jalapa, the capital of the state of Veracruz, it is diced and made into salsas or used to flavor almost any dish. Sometimes roasted, sometimes canned or pickled, sometimes stuffed, the moderately hot jalapeño is definitely the chile of choice. The sweeter, more mature red form is eaten less often. More and more, though, in the United States I find the flavor quite inconsistent, with the large ones often bland.

Almost as frequently used are what I call the *long greens,* a rather generic term that includes both the Anaheim or California chile and the various New Mexican cultivars, such as Big Jims and New Mexico #6-4. Although they can be used interchangeably, there are decided differences in flavor and intensity of heat, with some of the New Mexican chiles being the most pungent. Chile aficionados, especially in New Mexico where the green chile reigns supreme, can distinguish between the flavors of the various cross-breedings, much as a wine connoisseur can identify a specific varietal grape with only one sip.

All of these chiles are found both in the green form and as the more mature and sweeter reds. Especially when green, they should be roasted before using in salsas, stews, *rajas,* or stuffed for *chiles rellenos.*

The large, fat *poblano chiles,* named for the state of Puebla where they are still grown extensively, are seldom eaten fresh unless they are first roasted, a process that imparts a decidedly rich and earthy flavor. I have not seen them in salsas, but strips of the roasted chiles—*rajas*—are a traditional condiment or topping for steak, tacos, eggs, and with melted cheese. And when these relatively mild chiles are stuffed, they become transformed into one of Mexico's most distinguished dishes, *chiles rellenos.* Although Mexican Americans grew accustomed over the years to substituting the more available long greens, now that the fatter, easier-to-stuff poblanos often show up in the markets, most prefer to use them, especially for special fiesta dishes such as *Chiles en Nogada* (Stuffed Chiles with Walnut Sauce, page 195).

The fiercely hot little *serrano chiles* can be used as a substitute for jalapeños in salsas, although this should be done knowingly. I become quite irate when a supermarket tosses these two together and labels them something like "little green chiles." The serrano's flavor is usually described as grassy, without the sweeter overtones of the jalapeños, and although smaller and thinner, it packs a mighty punch.

The pale yellow or blond *güero chile* may be common in grocery stores, but I seldom found it used except occasionally when roasted and put in salsas or salads. One farmer in eastern Washington regularly sends me home with Mason jars filled with small pickled ones that have an almost cantaloupe flavor, unlike the more common skinny banana chiles. Since the name *güero* refers to the color and not a variety, they will vary in pungency.

I don't know if it's because "eating hot" is now the in thing to do or if somehow a bit of masochism is involved—or possibly a bit of both—but the wondrous *habanero chile* is now much in demand in the United States. Produce departments seem to be meeting the challenge, and since 1996 I can find them almost any season of the year throughout the country. Ironically, only a few of the Mexican-American families use these hottest of all chiles—just those with ties to the Yucatán Peninsula. This is a very regional chile in Mexico, being grown and used in salsas only in this area.

Green, red, yellow, and orange *bell peppers* (listed in order of ascending price) seem to be used much more frequently in Mexican-American kitchens than in Mexico, probably due to their availability. While even in Mexico the bell pepper is found as an ingredient in a few dishes, such as the Yucatecan *queso relleno,* it should not be substituted for the poblano chile or any of the long green or red chiles.

VARIETIES OF DRIED CHILES MOST FREQUENTLY USED IN THE UNITED STATES
There are many more varieties of dried chiles to choose from in the United States than fresh—although, unfortunately, they are often mislabeled. All have much more complex and distinctive flavors dried than when they are green. It is like comparing grape juice to wine. Grape juice is basically grape juice, but a red wine may be a Chambertin with the big full flavors of the French burgundies or a brash California Zinfandel. It is just as important to pair the chile with the right dish as it is with wine. However, for those Mexican-American cooks who grew up in the Southwest, especially Arizona and New Mexico, these subtle distinctions are almost unknown. Having been isolated for so many years from the central and southern regions of Mexico with their diversity of chiles, the early Mexican and Spanish settlers learned to rely on what they could find or grow locally; the tiny wild *chiltepín* and its cultivated variety, the *pequín chile,* and the dried long New Mexican or Anaheim from California.

Chiltepines, or *tepines* for short—searing little balls of fire—still grow wild, especially on the high desert slopes of Sonora, Chihuahua, and Arizona. *Chiquito pero picoso* (small but hot). I also saw scrawny bushes of them growing in backyards in both Texas and Arizona, and their branches hanging upside down drying inside the houses. The tiny pods are usually crumbled and added to salsas, soups, and other dishes where the intense heat gives an extra kick. Many think that the related but more egg-shaped *pequín chile* has an even more penetrating heat, but luckily in both types of chiles the burning sensation doesn't linger.

It was in northern New Mexico around Española and Chimayó that I first met up with a *dried long green chile,* and I quite enjoyed its light, sweet flavor. Every roadside stand selling these long greens and *ristras* of dried red chiles also has large metal drums for roasting the fresh chiles. Many, for a small fee, will even let you bring your own harvest in to char off the tougher outer skin. After roasting, the chiles are peeled, hung out to dry, and later stored for winter use. The same green chile is also field-ripened until it is scarlet red. When dried, this *New Mexican red chile* is used for making the earthy red chile sauces that are an integral part of the enchiladas, tamales, *pozole,* meat, and egg dishes of the southwestern part of the United States. Used in powdered form, it can be ground in advance from whole chiles or purchased in small jars or sacks. Make sure you check the label to see if you're getting the pure chile powder needed and not one already combined with oregano, garlic powder, or even cumin. It was also in New Mexico that I was introduced to a new chile term—*chile caribe*—which was used, almost interchangeably it seemed, to describe the crumbled red New Mexican chile and a thick sauce or paste made from the same chiles. The red New Mexican chile is used in Arizona and New Mexico in place of the dried red Anaheim used elsewhere.

The *ancho chile,* like its revered fresh form, the poblano chile, is indispensable in cooking the foods of Mexico, and it is the more recent immigrants who seek it out. Its sweet, earthy pungency is essential in a traditional *mole* sauce, and it is used as well in many other cooked sauces. Its most characteristic physical feature is well described by its name, *ancho,* which means wide. This chile is almost as wide as it is long and is a wrinkled brownish red color. Many stores sell it under the name *pasilla,* which is a different chile altogether. The true *pasilla* is longer and skinny, usually little more than an inch across, whereas the *ancho* has shoulders usually three inches broad. Although I didn't find the ancho chile's close relative, the *mulato chile,* as commonly used in the United States as it is in Mexico, where it is another of the important chiles used in *moles,* I mention it here because, like the ancho, it is a type of dried poblano, and they are often confused with each other. The mulato is usually not as broad at the shoulders, and its color is a darker brown. If you hold an ancho to the light, you will see a reddish tone, but the mulato is a blackish brown, and the flavor is shallower and not as fruity as the ancho.

Finding a true pasilla chile may take some searching, but its complex bold flavor can make it worth the hunt. Although the ancho chile is often packaged as a pasilla, the pasilla is the dried form of a chilaca chile, not the fatter poblano chile. No matter that in California and in many supermarkets around the country they may even sell the fresh poblano chiles as pasillas, if you are searching for the dried pasilla chile, you shouldn't have any problem identifying it. It is raisin-colored, hence its name, which means "little raisin." It can be up to six inches long, and quite skinny, with a shiny, rather wrinkled skin. Pasilla chiles are another one of the three chiles used to flavor a traditional *mole.*

The shiny brick-red *guajillo chile* looks something like the dried red New Mexican chile but is a bit smaller and not as twisted or wrinkled. It is a very commonly used chile in Mexico and utilized all over the United States by those who grew up in Mexico. I was driving back one night from the little airport in Santa Fe with one of the airplane mechanics who came from Guadalajara about ten years ago. He was obviously still enraged with the difficulty he encountered whenever he wanted a new supply of guajillo chiles to season his *birria,* a dish of braised goat or lamb. He certainly was not about to substitute the local red chiles for the strong distinct flavor of guajillos.

Another commonly used chile is the tongue-sizzling *chile de árbol*. It looks like a tiny guajillo with its shiny, bright, red-orange skin, and like the guajillo it is closely related to the cayenne. Both are primarily ground and used as seasoning, or diluted in a sauce where it adds an uncomplicated straight chile flavor.

I found the little *cascabel chile*—the name referring both to its shape (like a one-inch rattle) and the sound the loose seeds make when it is shaken—used occasionally in the United States, primarily toasted and blended in meat sauces where its wonderful rich nutty flavor is a welcomed enhancement.

Increasingly popular throughout the United States is the dried and smoked jalapeño known as *chipotle chile*. The only exception was in New Mexico where only a few of the home cooks I spoke with had ever used it. A handful had tried it in Santa Fe's upscale restaurants, but they weren't tempted to include the smoky-sweet flavor in their own dishes. Chipotles are found in their dried form primarily in Mexican markets and are very good, though they require some additional effort to prepare. *Mora* and *moritas* are smaller varieties. The canned chipotle chiles *en adobo* are the most convenient to cook with and the easiest to buy. They also come canned in vinegar, so watch the labels. It was the chipotles *en adobo* blended with their sauce that were most often served to me in very special dishes such as a memorable meal of meatballs in chipotle sauce one night in Florida.

Chunky Fresh Tomato Salsa
Salsa Fresca
ZILLAH, WASHINGTON

MAKES ABOUT 2 CUPS *On the table tops of most Mexican restaurants in Texas, Arizona, and California, this chunky salsa of fresh tomatoes, onions, chiles, and cilantro is the reigning condiment of choice. To confuse things, in many places it may be called* pico de gallo *or* salsa Mexicana, *but what stays the same is its clean fresh taste of raw vegetables.*

Mike Esquivel, a retired educator and now farmer from Zillah in eastern Washington, sparks up his salsa with oregano and cumin. Mike stresses that for the best flavor it is important to use fully ripe tomatoes and that all the vegetables be chopped by hand. This salsa loses its fresh taste and texture after sev-

eral hours, but any left over can be quickly sautéed in a little oil and used as a cooked salsa. If you want a milder sauce, some or all of the chiles can be seeded.

This salsa gives a flavorful nudge to almost any taco. It is especially well suited to Tacos of Charcoal-Grilled Beef (page 115) and Fish Tacos Ensenada-Style (page 118), a Deluxe Breakfast Burrito (page 339), or just scooped up with chips.

1 pound ripe tomatoes, cut in ¼-inch pieces
⅓ cup finely chopped green onion with some of the green tops
¼ cup loosely packed chopped cilantro
2–3 fresh serrano or jalapeño chiles, finely chopped

½ teaspoon dried oregano, preferably Mexican
pinch of cumin
2 or more teaspoons lime juice
sea salt
water or ice cubes, if necessary

Toss the tomatoes, onion, and cilantro together in a glass bowl. Add the chiles a little at a time until it has the heat you like. Add the oregano, cumin, and lime juice. Sprinkle with salt and toss again.

If the salsa is too dry, add several splashes of water or an ice cube. Cover and let set for up to 30 minutes—no more—letting the flavors mingle. Stir, remove any remaining ice, and serve immediately in a small bowl.

Tomatillos and Green Chile Salsa
Salsa Verde
MCMINVILLE, OREGON • MORELOS, MEXICO

MAKES 2½ TO 3 CUPS *Like most salsas, this one from Matha Ruiz Gonzales requires little work. There is a whiff of garlic, and the sweet earthy flavor of the chiles balances the tart taste of the tomatillos.*

Several cooks on the West Coast, where the tart flavor of tomatillos is very popular, use a similar salsa verde as a dressing for potato salad. Just add ½ cup of sour cream or yogurt and several tablespoons of the salsa, and mix with cooked sliced or cubed potatoes, grated carrots, or celery, or whatever raw vegetables you would usually use in a potato salad.

Serve this green salsa alongside Crispy Tortilla Flutes Stuffed with Pork and Nuts (page 122), or

Ranch-Style Fried Eggs (page 328), or with any other dish that might benefit from its sharp, tangy flavor. It is especially good as a topping on Chipotle Crab Enchiladas (page 207).

12 fresh tomatillos, husked and rinsed (see sidebar, page 266)
¼ white onion
2 cloves garlic
sea salt

3 fresh New Mexico green chiles or 2 Anaheim
and 2 jalapeño chiles, roasted (page21), peeled,
and seeded (see Note)
¼ cup finely chopped cilantro

In a saucepan, cover the fresh tomatillos, onion, and garlic with water. Add salt and bring to a simmer over medium hear. Cook, uncovered, about 10 minutes, until the tomatillos are soft. Drain and put in a *molcajete,* blender, or food processor with the roasted chiles. Puree until rather smooth but still with some rough texture. Stir in the chopped cilantro.

NOTE: The New Mexico chiles that Matha prefers to use for this salsa have an intensity to their taste that is lacking in the Anaheim. Living in Oregon, where the California chile is more frequently sold in the grocery stores, she substitutes several jalapeño chiles for one of the Anaheim chiles.

TOMATILLOS
(Physalis philadelphia)

Amy, one of our five daughters, cultivates several acres of flowers and vegetables to sell at local farmer's markets around Puget Sound. Several years ago she planted a row of tomatillos (called green tomatoes or tomates verdes in Mexico, even though quite a different plant), and we still have an abundance of these papery-husked green tomato look-alikes growing in both our gardens; mine are "volunteers" from seeds that came in soil clinging to other plants transferred from her garden to mine. Besides being easy to grow and obviously self-propagating when the fruit is allowed to fall to the ground, tomatillos will last a long time, on the vine or stored in the refrigerator where they will keep for several weeks.

The tart, clean flavor of these small—1- to 1½ inches—fruits combines quite naturally with jalapeño and serrano chiles in green salsas and is great to lighten up a sauce made with the smoked chipotle chiles. Unlike juicy red tomatoes, tomatillos are not usually eaten raw, except in a few salsas. Though they have a richer flavor if roasted and pureed with the charred skin still on, tomatillos are usually prepared by simmering for ten to fifteen minutes in water. In Mexico this cooking water is sometimes added to masa when making tamales, acting rather like a leavening to lighten the dough, and in both Mexico and the United States this water may be used to cook nopales (fresh cactus pads), as their acid helps to reduce the sliminess that the nopales usually produce.

Tomatillos are found fresh and canned in almost all supermarkets. Before using fresh, strip off the papery husks and rinse away the sticky film on the skin. The canned ones taste almost as good as the fresh, so you might want to keep a can or two on hand for emergencies.

Green, Green Salsa
Salsa Verde, Verde
LOS ANGELES, CALIFORNIA • OAXACA, MEXICO

MAKES ABOUT 2 CUPS *Aurelia Lopez prepares this brilliant green salsa from raw tomatillos that grow in her backyard in Los Angeles. Though best fixed at the last minute, the salsa will keep its color and flavor for a couple of days. The idea of using sugar to mellow the tartness of the raw tomatillos was the advice of Aida Gabilondo in El Paso, Texas, who also came up with this very descriptive name.*

The fresh, bright taste of this salsa is a good eye-opener with a breakfast of migas (see pages 336 and 338) or Deluxe Breakfast Burritos (page 339). It also sparks up grilled fish or chicken.

2 cups husked, rinsed, and coarsely chopped
  tomatillos (about 1 pound) (see sidebar, page
  266)
1 cup cilantro leaves

3 fresh jalapeño or 4 serrano chiles, seeded and
  coarsely chopped
1 teaspoon dark brown sugar (optional)
sea salt

Puree all the ingredients in a blender or food processor along with 3 tablespoons of water. Taste and add additional salt if necessary and pour into a small bowl. If you make the salsa in advance, stir it briefly before serving.

Chile de Árbol Salsa with Tomatillos

Salsa de Chile de Árbol con Tomatillo

SAN FRANCISCO, CALIFORNIA • JALISCO, MEXICO

MAKES ABOUT 2 CUPS   *Maria Gallardo left her home in Jalisco twenty years ago, but she still makes many of that region's familiar dishes. This is my adaptation of one of Maria's favorite salsas that includes the searing hot* chile de árbol. *It is used sparingly since Maria, like many Jalicienses, prefers a milder flavor.*

This is the salsa that, to me, was created to perfect Tacos of Crispy Pork Bits (page 116) or Crispy Chicken Tacos (page 121). Spoon it over scrambled eggs, and it's superb on a hamburger.

1 pound tomatillos, husked and washed (see sidebar, page 266)

2 cloves garlic, unpeeled

1–2 dried *chiles de árbol*

¼ teaspoon sea salt

2 tablespoons minced white onion

Heat a medium-size cast-iron skillet or griddle. Add the tomatillos and garlic, and roast over medium-high heat, tossing them until they begin to char on all sides. Lower the heat, place the chiles in the skillet, and toast them briefly, until they begin to blister and change color. Turn often so that nothing burns.

Remove the tomatillos, garlic, and chiles, and let them cool for a few minutes. Peel the garlic cloves. In a *molcajete* (see Note), food processor, or blender, briefly blend the tomatillos and garlic, leaving some texture. Break 1 of the chiles into several parts and add, seeds and all, to the tomatillo mixture. Blend again and add salt to taste and, depending on your heat tolerance, the other chile. If it is too thick, a small amount of water may be needed.

Serve in the *molcajete* or a small bowl, stirring in the onion at the last minute.

NOTE: In Maria's kitchen in San Francisco's Outer Mission District, the *molcajete*—a traditional volcanic mortar—is used to grind all the ingredients (see page 19). A food processor or blender can be used, but the salsa will not have the rough texture that makes it so special.

Japonés Chile Salsa with Garlic

Salsa de Chile Japones

CHICAGO, ILLINOIS • COAHUILA, MEXICO

MAKES 2 CUPS *Even with all the fiery chiles of Mexico, there are times when other chiles are sought to provide a slightly different intensity of heat and flavor. Eduardo Garcia, originally from Zaragoza, Coahuila, worked for many years for an American rancher near Pandale, Texas. This simple salsa with its sharp, fresh taste of japonés chiles and garlic was always on his table at home. And even now, living in Chicago, Garcia grinds the dried chiles in his molcajete.*

The japonés chile is rather a mystery chile to me. Although it can be found, packaged in cellophane bags, in many supermarkets, not much seems to be known about its derivation. One distributor told me it was a dried serrano, and maybe some are, but the ones I examined revealed little resemblance. The long, narrow, pointed pod has an appearance much closer to a small cayenne. In thumbing through Amal Naj's well-researched book Peppers, *I noticed his reference to two small, narrow chiles from Japan that are grown in China and returned to Japan to be dried, crushed, and marketed as Tentaka chiles. It sounds much like the one used for this salsa. Miguel remembers his grandmother making a similar table sauce using the tiny dried chiltepín from the Sonoran Desert. I always have it on the table to add some pungency to Zucchini Stuffed with Cheese (page 247) and Stuffed Chayotes (page 245). To make 1 cup of the recipe from Miguel's grandmother, use 10 to 15 chiltepín chiles, 4 cloves garlic, 8 ounces canned tomato sauce, ¼ teaspoon dried oregano, and salt to taste.*

1 pound canned tomatoes or 3 fresh

4 cloves garlic, roughly chopped

10–15 dried japonés chiles, broken into pieces

¼ teaspoon sea salt

Blend the tomatoes together with the garlic, 10 chiles, and salt, using a *molcajete*, blender, or food processor (see page 19). Add more chiles, depending on the pungency you want in the finished sauce.

Racy Red Tomato Salsa
Salsa Roja Picante
LOS ANGELES, CALIFORNIA

MAKES 4 CUPS   *It was in the heart of Los Angeles's old Mexican district, on Olvera Street, that Miguel's sister, Betty Saenz, discovered the secret of this very quick and very easy salsa. One woman in the market, the owner of the busy food stand, often didn't have the time to utilize the local fresh chiles and tomatoes, so instead she came up with this convenient rendition. It is an ideal all-purpose table salsa when there are no vine-ripened tomatoes to use, and it is much, much better than most of the supermarket versions now so popular.*

There will be salsa to use for several meals. Just stir before serving again. Covered and refrigerated, this will keep for about a week, although the flavor may become a bit harsher. This is a condiment to be used as frequently as salt and pepper. It goes on or in almost any dish that needs heightened flavor.

1 2-ounce can jalapeño chiles *en escabeche* (in vinegar with carrots and onions)
6 green onions, trimmed and cut in 1-inch pieces
1 medium white onion, quartered and roughly chopped

1 28-ounce can whole tomatoes, drained
1 tablespoon dried oregano, preferably Mexican
sea salt to taste

Place the jalapeños, vinegar, and vegetables from the can into the bowl of a food processor. Add all the other ingredients except the salt. Pulse briefly to get a chunky consistency.

Pour into a glass bowl and add salt if necessary.

Chipotle Salsa with Radishes and Two Kinds of Tomatoes
Salsa de Chipotle
NEW YORK CITY, NEW YORK • PUEBLA, MEXICO

MAKES ABOUT 2 CUPS   *The intriguing flavor of chipotle chiles is not commonly found in a salsa on a Mexican table, except in the more southern states of Mexico.*

COCINA DE LA FAMILIA

It was in New York that I met Apolonio Mariano Ramirez (known to his non-Mexican friends as Mario) and where I again tasted a salsa with chipotle chiles. It was made, Mario said, exactly as he remembered his mother grinding and mixing it in their village in southern Puebla. The crisp texture and taste of the radishes adds an unusual dimension to the salsa.

I like this gutsy salsa served alongside any grilled fish or meats, and especially with my Black Bean Soup (page 95).

This intense red salsa is best made with dried chiles but is quite satisfying using the more available canned ones. While the small tomatoes are cooked and blended into the sauce, it is important that the coarsely chopped tomato be added fresh and at the last minute.

10 chipotle chiles, dried or canned *en adobo*

12 ripe cherry tomatoes or 2 ripe plum tomatoes

½ large red onion, finely chopped

1 large field-ripened tomato, coarsely chopped

¼ cup chopped cilantro leaves

2 large radishes, coarsely grated

juice of 1 lime

sea salt

If using dried chiles, gently stew in enough salted water to cover them for 10–15 minutes, or until softened. Drain and put into a blender or food processor with about ¼ cup of the chile water. Process only briefly as there should still be some texture. If using the canned chipotles, scrape off most of the *adobo* sauce from the chiles. It's not necessary to use any water to blend the canned chipotles. Set aside and process later with the tomatoes.

In another saucepan, bring enough water to boil to cover the cherry tomatoes and simmer them for 4–5 minutes. Add to the blender with the chiles and agitate a few pulses.

Mix all together in a small serving bowl with the onion, tomato, cilantro, radishes, lime juice, and salt to taste.

Cover the salsa and let it set for at least 30 minutes before serving. If it is to be kept longer than that, refrigerate and add the hand-chopped tomato just before serving.

Six-Chiles Salsa

Salsa de Seis Chiles

PARK RIDGE, ILLINOIS • MEXICO CITY, MEXICO

MAKES ABOUT 4 CUPS *Brash and brawny, Maria Josepha Concannon's table salsa is made with six different chiles, each adding a different flavor component. The slow cooking helps mellow the flavors, but then the fresh lime juice perks them right back up. The salsa keeps extremely well when refrigerated in a covered jar, and it can be added to virtually any dish that needs a jolt.*

Six-Chiles Salsa adds a wonderful wallop to grilled chicken and perks up simple egg dishes. I also add it to a bowl of Beef and Vegetable Broth (page 89).

1 32-ounce can whole tomatoes with juice
6 ripe plum tomatoes, chopped
3 dried ancho chiles, stemmed
3 dried mulato chiles, stemmed
3 dried pasilla chiles, stemmed
3 dried morita or chipotle chiles, stemmed, or 1
   canned chipotle chile *en adobo*
3 dried *chiles de árbol*, stemmed
2 dried guajillo chiles, stemmed

1 white onion, quartered
1 clove garlic
sea salt
juice of 1 small lime

For the Garnish

1 slice white onion, finely chopped
¼ cup chopped cilantro leaves

Place the tomatoes in a medium-size saucepan with all the chiles. Add the onion, garlic, and water to cover. Simmer over medium-low heat for 10–15 minutes, until the chiles are soft and falling apart.

Pour the mixture into a blender or food processor and puree until smooth. It will be a very thick paste. Thin with water to a lighter consistency and add salt to taste. Right before serving squeeze in a little lime juice.

Serve this spirited table sauce with a garnish of chopped onion and cilantro.

Drunken Salsa

Salsa Borracha

McMINVILLE, OREGON • MORELOS, MEXICO

MAKES ABOUT 1 CUP *Martha Ruiz Gonzalez misses the* barbacoa *of lamb from the central part of Mexico that is wrapped and cooked in the membranes of the maguey leaves (see page 375). It is usually accompanied by a very simple rustic sauce made with* pulque—*the fermented but not distilled sap of the maguey. She now uses tequila instead of pulque for a similar flavor.*

This sauce is wonderful on grilled meat and hamburgers and is even good with Tortilla Chips (page 33) and drinks.

6 dried pasilla chiles, toasted (page 22)
4 large cloves garlic, roasted (page 22)
½ cup orange juice

¼ cup tequila
½ teaspoon sea salt

Put the toasted chiles in a small bowl and soak in very hot water for 10 minutes. Drain the chiles and place in a blender or food processor with the garlic, orange juice, tequila, and salt. Puree until smooth. While this salsa can be used right away, it does improve with age.

New Mexican Green Chile Relish

Chile Verde

SANTA FE, NEW MEXICO

MAKES 1½ TO 2 CUPS *This relish is as simple as its name. It is what Dora Chavez and almost all the traditional Mexican-American home cooks I met with in the upper Rio Gránde region of New Mexico have on their table for breakfast, lunch, and dinner. The only exceptions were in the families that were relative newcomers to the United States; they would chop in a tomato.*

This is traditionally served with grilled meats. When spooned over Soupy Pot Beans (page 224) and served with plenty of flour tortillas, it produces a minor culinary miracle.

My friend and business associate Carmen Barnard Baca, who has lived all her life in Morelia, Michoacán, has many relatives and friends in New Mexico. From them I learned to make green chile and

cheese sandwich, (emparedado de chile verde y queso). Mix half of the chile verde (eliminating the onion) with six ounces of grated Monterey jack or good cheddar cheese and heap it on a slice of whole wheat bread, preferably homemade. Eat for lunch or a late-night snack with a bowl of soup. I enjoy this as a grilled sandwich, but Carmen says, "It is just not done."

6 fresh New Mexican or other long green chiles, roasted (page 21), peeled and seeded

2 cloves garlic, roasted (page 22) and finely chopped or mashed

½ white onion, minced

about ½ teaspoon sea salt

a few drops of olive oil (optional)

Chop the chiles and mix with the garlic, onion, and salt. This can all be done in a food processor, although don't overblend it. This is a relish, not a sauce. Add oil if you want a richer taste and texture.

Let the mixture sit for 30 minutes or so. The individual flavors need time to blend. Store, tightly covered, in the refrigerator for up to 2 days. If the salsa is to be kept any longer, stir in 1 tablespoon of vinegar.

Guacamole
Guacamole
ALLEN PARK, MICHIGAN • QUERÉTARO, MEXICO

*G*uacamole, or ahuacatl molli, *in the Nahuatl language, means avocado mixture.*

MAKES ABOUT 2 CUPS *"This guacamole, the first time I ever made it, provided me with the cost of a good suit." That's how Florencio Perea began his description of his favorite guacamole. As a teenager Florencio left his home in Mexico and struck out on his own for the United States. As a dishwasher in a Dallas restaurant, Florencio volunteered to make rice and guacamole. A well-to-do patron was so enamored with that first batch of guacamole that she insisted on meeting him and tipped him an extravagant $20, which in 1950 was more than a day's wages or "the cost of a good suit." Florencio has made his guacamole the same way ever since. It varies from the traditional Mexican version only by the inclusion of a few drops of good olive oil, which he uses to recall the rich buttery flavor of the avocados from home.*

One of our volunteer testers suggested that if you cover the surface with 1 tablespoon of mayonnaise before covering with the plastic wrap, it will last even longer. She then stirred the mayonnaise into the guacamole before serving. I asked some of my Mexican friends, and they said, "Oh, sure," and "Why not? It keeps it green and may make it taste even better."

Guacamole is more than just a dip. For Mexican Americans it is an essential accompaniment to many dishes, especially egg dishes and tacos. Try it with crispy things like Chimichangas (page 130) or Crispy Chicken Tacos (page 121), and for a party, slit open some pickled jalapeños, scrape out the seeds, and stuff them full of guacamole.

1 medium ripe tomato, finely chopped (optional)
2 tablespoons finely minced white onion
1 fresh jalapeño chile, seeded and finely chopped (optional)
3 very ripe avocados
¼ cup lightly packed, finely minced, cilantro leaves

juice of ½ lime; lemon juice can be substituted
1 teaspoon extra-virgin olive oil
sea salt

For the Garnish
leaves from 1 cilantro sprig, chopped

Place the tomato, onion, and chile in a *molcajete* or a bowl and mash a bit but leave it chunky. Halve the avocados lengthwise, remove the seeds, and scoop or squeeze all the flesh into the tomato mixture. Mix together with the cilantro, lime juice, olive oil, and salt to taste.

Garnish with chopped cilantro and serve at once if possible. The guacamole can be kept at room temperature for up to 1 hour. First clean the sides of the bowl with a damp paper towel, then cover the surface directly with a piece of plastic wrap. It can be stored in the refrigerator for up to 2 or 3 hours, but it's best to wait and mix in the salt and cilantro when ready to serve.

SMASHED AVOCADOS—
A POOR MAN'S BUTTER

*P*robably the best way to eat an avocado is to pick one perfectly ripe from your own back-yard tree, then cut it in half, squirt the buttery flesh with lime juice or sprinkle with salt, and scoop it with a spoon directly out of its own bumpy green-black container. Next best is this wonderfully simple combination of smashed avocado and lime juice—mantequilla de los po-bres. It may serve as an economical substitute for butter where creamy avocados are plentiful and butter is a luxury, but for most of us, this will not be an everyday eating experience. Pre-pare this Poor Man's Butter when you have an abundant supply of avocados or just want to splurge by mashing three ripe avocados with the juice of one large lime and adding salt and pepper. If your avocados are hard, put them in a paper bag to ripen for several days at room temperature.

A grilled steak, profusely spread with Poor Man's Butter, creates a superb eating experience, but it will work its magic with any grilled meat.

Avocado Salsa
Salsa de Aguacate
NORTHBROOK, ILLINOIS • DISTRITO FEDERAL, MEXICO

MAKES 2 CUPS   *These days avocados are used in a variety of other salsas besides the traditional guacamole. I especially like Elaine González's refreshing combination, which includes the tart, tangy taste of tomatillos.*

Think of this avocado salsa as just a thinner version of guacamole, and you will have no problem deciding how to use it. Serve as a dip with Tortilla Chips (page 33) or crunchy wedges of jicama. Put a spoonful of this gutsy salsa over Skillet Potatoes with Green Chiles and Onions (page 254), on an omelet, or use it to liven up a hamburger. For a special treat, warm the salsa over low heat and pour over grilled meat or chicken.

6 fresh tomatillos, husked, or one 12-ounce can with ¼ cup of the liquid (see page 266)

sea salt

2 fresh serrano or jalapeño chiles, roughly chopped

½ white onion, cut in small chunks

2 firm but ripe avocados, peeled and pitted

½ cup coarsely chopped cilantro leaves

For the Garnish

leaves from 1 cilantro sprig, chopped

If using the fresh tomatillos, rinse and place with the chiles into a small saucepan of lightly salted boiling water. Simmer over medium-low heat until the chiles are tender and the tomatillos change color, about 10 minutes. Drain but reserve ¼ cup of the liquid. Skip this step if using canned tomatillos.

Place the tomatillos with their liquid, chiles, and onions into a blender or food processor and blend until smooth. Add the avocado pulp, cilantro, and about ½ teaspoon salt, and process briefly. The texture should remain rather coarse. Taste and adjust the seasoning.

Serve immediately with a few cilantro leaves sprinkled on the surface or cover with plastic wrap, pressed directly on the salsa, and use it in the next hour if possible.

Crunchy Cabbage Salsa
Salsa de Col Yucateca
CHICAGO, ILLINOIS • YUCATÁN, MEXICO

MAKES 4 CUPS   *The Yucatán Peninsula—that fat, flat thumb of Mexico that juts out, separating the waters of the Gulf of Mexico from the Caribbean, is made up of the states of Campeche, Quintana Roo, and Yucatán. It has developed a cuisine very different from that of the rest of Mexico. It has enchiladas, but they are filled with hardboiled eggs; it has tamales, but they are wrapped with chaya, a leafy green; and the salsas are quite the hottest ever tasted. In the United States I found only small isolated pockets of families from the peninsula. By and large, the people are Maya and seem to shrug off the desire to make major changes in their lives. In Chicago, though, my husband, Fredric, met with Carlos Arisque, now working at a major hotel but originally from the small village of Tixkokob, outside of Mérida. Best known to the outside world for its meticulously woven hammocks, Tixkokob is a place with some of the most memorable food I've eaten. This salsa is typical, using both cabbage and radishes to counteract the indescribable heat of the habanero chile and to add a refreshingly crunchy texture. Al-*

though it is best served within hours, I like it so much that I often make a double batch and munch on it for the next day or so.

Serve this salsa as a condiment with grilled fish or chicken or virtually anything that needs a flavor lift. Almost a salad, its crunchy texture is a natural with Fish Tacos Ensenada-Style (page 118) or toss it with canned tuna for a glorified tuna salad sandwich.

1–2 fresh habanero chiles, toasted, peeled, seeded (see Note) and chopped

8 cloves garlic, roasted and peeled

½ head small cabbage, cored and cut into chunks

6–8 large radishes

½ medium white onion, quartered

3 tablespoons fresh lime juice

½ teaspoon sea salt

Finely chop and mix all the ingredients together in a food processor or by hand. There should still be lots of texture. If chopping the vegetables by hand, mix together in a bowl with the lime juice and salt. Set everything aside awhile to combine the flavors.

NOTE: Habanero chiles, quite the fiercest chiles around, were once found only in and around Yucatán. Now these lantern-shaped chiles, in shades of vivid green, red, orange, and yellow, have developed an almost cult following in the United States and even regular supermarkets try to stock them, especially during the summer months. No other chile—except perhaps its cousin, the almost-as-hot Scotch bonnet—has the same fiery intensity and fruity flavor. When making this condiment, start with only one chile and then add a second if wanted. If you try to substitute jalapeños or serranos in this salad, more chiles will be needed, and it just won't taste the same. I recommend waiting and using the real thing.

If possible, use rubber or plastic gloves when handling the habanero chiles and wash thoroughly with hot soapy water any surfaces with which they come in contact. These are potent chiles—around fifty times hotter than a jalapeño—and may even blister your skin. This burning potential lingers for quite a time, so be especially careful where you rub your hands. Eyes and other sensitive parts of your body are especially vulnerable.

CAN YOU TAKE THE HEAT?
ARE YOU HOOKED ON CHILES?

You just took a bite of a chile so piercingly painful that you can't breathe. What should you do? Cold water or cold beer doesn't really help except for a brief second because that burning sensation in your mouth comes from contact with a powerfully pungent chemical compound called capsaicin (cap-SAY-uh-sin)—and capsaicin is not water-soluble. For me, eating rice or a piece of bread is the best remedy.

Capsaicin is located in the placenta—that white spongy membrane in the center of the chile—not in the seeds, so if the seeds or flesh seem hot, it is only because of their close proximity to the placenta. Of the hottest chiles, some like the tiny chiltepín have a very fleeting residual heat, but the fresh habanero's intense fire seems to stay in your mouth for an almost unbearably long time.

I tend to agree with statements by various doctors that chiles can be addicting; I know I am hooked. What bothers me, though, is the rationale. According to some experts, what I am seeking is the high, that rush of pain, to alter my state of consciousness. I'm not sure about this thrill component in my involvement with chiles, but I do have that craving for "just a little bit hotter." I even put black pepper or Tabasco on my oatmeal and pancakes.

Evidently what happens is that capsaicin blocks a natural body chemical that carries pain impulses between nerve cells so that, over time, people who eat a lot of chiles develop a tolerance to the heat. This same phenomenon is being used medically to reduce pain as an aftermath of surgical scars.

Red Radish Relish

Salpicón de Rábano

LYNNWOOD, WASHINGTON • YUCATÁN, MEXICO

SERVES 4   *Radishes, while not indigenous to Mexico, fit right into this country's cuisine, just as this lively mixture of chopped radishes and cilantro adds a crunch and color to tacos. I've eaten similar versions in Tabasco and Campeche to the west of Yucatán where some of Ernesto Pino's family still live.*

It is in Oaxaca, though, that the radish takes on a much more significant role. There a major festival is held in its honor—the Night of the Radish. Since the early 1900s this Noche de Rábanos has been an annual event, held on December 23 in the central plaza of this historic city. Artistic farmers from all over the Oaxacan valley set up panoramic religious and historical scenes carved from gargantuan radishes—many over a foot in length. People come from all over the world to view them and join in the night of merry-making. There is even a fine arts section with prizes given for the finest "serious" radish sculpture.

Spoon this crisp radish relish over the top of soft tacos, where it is an especially welcome addition to Fish Tacos Ensenada-Style (page 118). It is useful as an edible garnish with Roast Pork Yucatecan-Style (page 178) and other Yucatecan dishes, and I like to pair these as a small salad with Sautéed Fish Fillets with Garlic (page 140).

16 large radishes
¼ cup chopped cilantro leaves

sea salt
juice of 3–4 limes

Cut off both ends of the radishes and slice lengthwise into ¼-inch slivers. Mix the cilantro and radishes together in a glass bowl, sprinkle well with salt, and toss with the lime juice. Cover and chill in the refrigerator for about 45 minutes.

Pickled Vegetables with Chiles
Verduras en Escabeche
EL PASO, TEXAS • JUÁREZ AND CHIHUAHUA, MEXICO

MAKES ABOUT 2 QUARTS, ENOUGH FOR 20 AS A COLD NIBBLE   *This tangy mixture of garden vegetables is an ideal way to use up any leftover crudités from a party, though a batch is easy enough to make from scratch. Since they keep indefinitely, you should have a bowl filled with these chunky pickled vegetables on your table every time you serve Mexican food—or anytime just to munch on. Luis Helio Estavillo makes this from a family recipe and serves it at his beautiful Restaurante Casa del Sol in Juárez, just across the border from El Paso. His advice is to keep the garlic heads intact and pull off each teardrop clove when you are eating.*

6–8 canned pickled jalapeño chiles, sliced with enough of its vinegar to make ½ cup

¾ cup olive oil

3 entire heads of garlic, outer covering removed and top ends sliced off

7 medium carrots, peeled and thickly sliced in ½-inch chunks

1 small jicama, peeled and cut into 1- by 2-inch strips

2 medium zucchinis, ends removed and cut into 1-inch pieces

1 medium white onion, peeled and cut vertically into ½-inch segments

3 cups rice vinegar

1 cup cider vinegar

about 2 teaspoons sea salt

1 teaspoon dried marjoram

1 teaspoon dried oregano, preferably Mexican

3 bay leaves

2 teaspoons black peppercorns

1 small head cauliflower, broken into florets

Place the chiles in a gallon plastic or glass container.

Heat the olive oil in a very large, heavy skillet or Dutch oven until quite hot. Add the garlic and cook, turning frequently, for 4–5 minutes. Remove the heads and mix with the chiles. Add the carrots, jicama, zucchinis, and onion, and continue to fry another 5 minutes, still stirring so that nothing scorches. Remove and add to the container with the garlic and chiles.

Add 2 cups of water, rice and cider vinegar, and salt to the oil in the pan, along with the marjoram, oregano, bay leaves, and peppercorns. Bring to a boil and drop in the cauliflower, just barely introducing it to the water—no more than 3–5 minutes. Pour the contents of the pan over the other vegetables and toss together in the container.

Cool and store, covered, in the refrigerator for a day before using. Add more salt if necessary. This will keep stored in the refrigerator for at least several months.

Little Pickled Carrots

Zanahorias en Vinagre

SANTA MONICA, CALIFORNIA • MEXICO CITY, MEXICO

MAKES ABOUT 1 QUART, ENOUGH FOR 12 AS A CRUNCHY ADDITION TO A MEAL *Recipes abound for crunchy pickled vegetables that Mexicans so enjoy. In Santa Monica, Ricardo Villareal fixes one that is quite different and very simple, with carrots as the dominant ingredient. We use tiny whole carrots and pearl onions that can easily be eaten with the fingers.*

Dishes of this colorful medley of vegetables can be served with any meal. The individual carrots, the little onions, and the crisp strips of red pepper also make a perfect garnish for dishes such as Tequila Shrimp and Pasta (page 147).

1 red bell pepper, seeded and cut into ½- by 1½-inch strips

1 teaspoon coarsely ground sea salt

1 pound 2-inch carrots, preferably those prepeeled and in plastic sacks

12 tiny pearl onions, peeled

3 fresh jalapeño chiles, seeded and chopped

4 cloves garlic

1 tablespoon dried oregano, preferably Mexican

3 bay leaves

2 cups white vinegar

about 2 teaspoons sea salt (see Note)

Place the red pepper strips in a small bowl and toss with the coarse salt. Cover and let stand for several hours or overnight, stirring from time to time.

When ready to start pickling the carrots, drain the red pepper strips and place in a large pot. Add the carrots, onions, jalapeños, garlic, oregano, bay leaves, and vinegar, and mix together gently. Pour in enough water to cover—about 1½ cups—and add salt. Bring to a boil over high heat, lower the heat, and simmer for 8–10 minutes, until the carrots are just tender.

Turn off the heat and let everything sit in the pot until completely cool.

Transfer to a glass or plastic container, cover, and refrigerate for at least 8–10 hours. The pickled carrots will keep, refrigerated, for several months.

NOTE: Use only a pure sea salt for these pickled carrots, one without any dextrose additives which may cause discoloration and change the flavor over a period of time.

Pickled Beets

Betabeles en Escabeche

ALLEN PARK, MICHIGAN • QUERÉTARO, MEXICO

MAKES ABOUT 1 QUART   *I don't think I ever thought much about beets when I was growing up. I certainly can't remember ever eating them. But then I went to Mexico, and I've been a disciple ever since. My first introduction was on a cold December morning in Chiapas. Fredric and I were wandering through the hillside market in San Cristóbal de las Casas and trying to identify all the unusual herbs, fruits, and vegetables used in this isolated part of Mexico. Stall after stall was mounded with pyramids of familiar burgundy-colored beets. Later we ate them several times in Chiapas, including at a New Year's dinner where cubed beets mixed with flecks of orange and onion accompanied pieces of the special ham of the region. My most memorable tasting of beets was in La Reina, a bar con restaurante in Mérida. It had superb food . . . and it was free. While the men in the bar spent money drinking and throwing dice, their wives, children, and in-laws were kept content with plate after plate of substantial botanas. I was with Diana Kennedy, and, of course, we had to taste everything. After twenty-five different dishes, we lost count. La Reina's beets, which were always served early in the progression, were addictive, reminding me a bit of that unctuous bittersweet cough medicine my mother supposedly forced on me but which I secretly adored. This version, shared with me by Florencio Perea one day in Detroit, catches a bit of all of these memories. It is best made the day before serving and will last, refrigerated, for several weeks. The recipe can easily be cut in half.*

The earthy flavor of beets makes for zesty nibbling before and during a casual spread of Tacos de San Luis Potosí (page 119) or with Crab Salad Tostadas (page 114).

6 medium beets, with an inch or so of stem attached, if possible	10 whole allspice
1 medium white onion	½ teaspoon dried oregano, preferably Mexican
¾ cup red wine vinegar	¼ teaspoon ground coriander
¾ cup fresh orange juice	several strips of orange zest or peel
16 whole black peppercorns	1 teaspoon brown sugar
	olive oil

Preheat the oven to 325 degrees F.

Wash the beets gently, being careful not to puncture the skin. Place them in a baking pan, sprinkle with ¼ cup or so of water, and cover with aluminum foil. Bake for about 1 hour, until rather soft when pressed. Don't be tempted to push a fork in the beets to test them because they will bleed and dry out. If not quite done, continue to cook another 15–20 minutes. The exact cooking time will vary depending on the thickness, youth, and freshness of the beets. When tender, plunge the beets into cold water to cool enough to handle. Slip off the skins, cut them in ¼-inch slices, and place in a glass bowl.

Slice the onion thinly but use only the inner rings of the same diameter as the beets or smaller. Save the rest for another use. There should be ½ cup of onion, more or less. Add to the beets and pour in the vinegar and orange juice to cover. Add water if needed. Stir in the peppercorns, allspice, oregano, coriander, zest, and sugar. Cover and refrigerate, preferably until the next day. Drain and drizzle with olive oil before serving.

Red Onion Garnish
Encurtido de Cebolla Roja
LYNNWOOD, WASHINGTON • YUCATÁN, MEXICO

MAKES ABOUT 2½ CUPS *Crunchy pickled red onions are traditional to Yucatán where members of Ernesto Pino's family still live. Small bowls of these colorful onions are served at almost every meal in their home and wherever else I've eaten in and around Mérida. While these onions always seem to garnish* cochinita pibil, *the local pit-roasted pork, as well as other Yucatecan specialties, you really don't have to make those dishes as an excuse to serve these deliciously sweet and spicy red onions.*

Red Onion Garnish makes a good addition to tortas *and* tostadas *and as a relish with simple fish and chicken dishes. And it is a necessity with Roast Pork Yucatecan-Style (page 178).*

3 large red onions, thinly sliced
1½ teaspoons sea salt
¼ teaspoon freshly ground black pepper
¼ teaspoon dried oregano, preferably Mexican

juice of 3 large lemons
2 fresh habanero chiles, roasted (page 21) (optional)

Place the onions in a heavy heatproof bowl and cover with boiling water. Soak for 2–3 minutes, or just long enough so they lose some of their crispness but do not become soft. Drain well. Add the salt, pepper, oregano, and lemon juice.

Create a well in the center of the sliced onions, place the chiles in the well, and cover with some of the other onions. Allow to steep for 1 hour, stirring occasionally. Covered and refrigerated, the onions will last for several weeks and will lose some of their crunchiness only at the end.

Before serving, take out the chiles and put them on top of the onions as a decoration. Only the foolhardy should try to eat them.

Michigan Impressions

Florencio Perea's eyes were sparkling and his hands were descriptively rolling and patting in the air as he described how to make *tamales de muerto* of blue-black *masa*—a special *tamal* prepared just for *Día de los Muertos* (All Souls' Day, also called The Day of the Dead). Florencio Perea was so obviously enthusiastic about food that I could have spent days just listening to him talk about the many different meals he had cooked, eaten, and enjoyed. As a retired butcher, he spoke with authority on preparing pickled tongue or a ham-, olive-, and pimiento-studded meatloaf to be served cold almost like a pâté. He told me of his favorite fish and chicken dishes, the salads, and tacos, and ways to cook the familiar greens that grow wild even in the suburbs of Detroit where Florencio and his wife live.

Only seventeen when he left Queretero, a rugged, beautiful state in central Mexico, Florencio still feels the pain of that severance and his father saying to him, "There is not a tortilla tree growing here on every corner." In 1950, Florencio made his way to Dallas. He loved the city, but the wandering urge was with him and he and his brother soon continued farther north, stopping in St. Louis and Toledo, Ohio, before deciding to make Detroit their home. Florencio's father and grandfathers on both sides of the family were butchers, so it was only natural that he would follow the trade, first having to learn the very different ways of cutting meat in the United States. Eventually they owned three butcher shops, but now retired, it is wood he cuts, not steak. His prizewinning carvings are proudly displayed in his dining room; my favorite is an intricately carved group of mariachi musicians.

All I knew about Detroit was that it shared a border with Canada, was the automobile capital of the country, and the local museum sported some exciting murals by Diego Rivera that my husband wanted to see. I'd heard about the auto workers being laid off and the race riots, but not being a person comfortable with big cities, going there was not something I was looking forward to. Since I had been personally invited by the Mexican Town Community Development to open the Mexican Town Mercado, a farmer's market in southwest Detroit, I finally said yes to Maria Elena Rodriguez's repeated requests.

As soon as we arrived, I found a rapport with the city and the people I came to know. The biggest Mexican-American community may be divided now by the I-75 freeway, and many may have moved to surrounding suburbs, but there is a togetherness and cohesiveness among the people that I have seldom seen. And it wasn't just people of one ethnic background but included almost everyone. There was a special afternoon in the crowded Bowen Branch of the Detroit Public Library, where I met with an enthusiastic group of young teenagers who were to act in a short play they had scripted based on Sandra Cisneros' *The House on Mango Street,* a moving collection of vignettes about a young Mexican girl growing up in Chicago. The audience included the usual parents and friends, but there were also many supportive members of the wider community. On another evening we attended a graduation party that was like a laid-back get-together of the United Nations—both food and guests a mélange of ethnic backgrounds. This awareness of their common spirit was the undercurrent I found throughout my stay.

Like Florencio, the people in the Mexican-American community I got to know best were a part of Detroit's vast middle class; teachers, social workers, auto workers, librarians, translators, priests, lawyers, and small-business owners. They were proud of their American heritage, but even those who spoke predominantly Spanish strongly identified with being Detroit Americans. Many were born in Michigan, their parents or grandparents having come to the state prior to World War II, some as early as World War I.

It was the demand for workers in the sugar beet fields that first brought Mexicans to Michigan—even those from urban areas who had never before done stoop labor. Recruited both in Mexico and especially in San Antonio, Texas, they came by the thousands with their families—an inducement by the contractors so they would be more apt to stay. Stay they did, but many moved out of the fields with their deplorable housing conditions into higher paying jobs with the railroads and automobile factories.

The Mexican cooking of these second- and third-generation Mexican Americans has gone through an interesting metamorphosis. The rustic cuisine of the high tableland region in Mexico, where the majority of them were from, is rich with local flavors. Michoacán and Querétaro have their unusual tamales and exceptional cheeses; there is *birria,* the chile-coated, pit-steamed goat or lamb of Jalisco and Zacatecas, and the special tacos and enchiladas of San Luis Potosí, all requiring regional ingredients. When the early immigrants, such as Pablo Escamilla and his wife, Luz, arrived in Michigan in 1924 after fighting in the Mexican revolution, very few of the chiles, herbs, fruits, or even *masa* for making tortillas and tamales were available, and their traditional dishes had to be prepared with whatever substitutes they could find, eliminating many of the distinctive flavors.

Since most of Michigan's first Mexican immigrants usually stopped on the way north in Texas or Arizona, they inevitably picked up some of the border cooking techniques that used simpler combination of ingredients found there. Through the years they modified the foods they had grown up eating and cooking; only the always reliable beans remained unchanged. Today, many of the younger generations have never tasted the traditional flavors of their grandparents' dishes, even though most of the ingredients are now easily available.

Dolores Gonzalez-Ramirez was born in Wyandotte, Michigan. Her family was from Zacatecas and Guanajuato; her grandfather went to Texas, as so many did, to work on the railroads. As Dolores was growing up in Michigan, her mother made tamales and other Mexican dishes, but after she died no one on the family cooked the traditional foods. Now, though, she has been reinspired by trips to her husband's family in Cuernavaca, and she is again cooking Mexican dishes and in turn passing on her knowledge to her teenage daughter. Her most important lesson: "Don't cook unless you are happy. If you are sad or angry, the food will reflect your mood and not taste good at all."

Tamales
Tamales

Hot tamales, three in a shuck. Two of 'em slipped, and one of 'em stuck.

—A DITTY SUNG BY TEXAS TAMAL VENDORS

Al que ha nacido para tamal, del cielo le caen las hojas.
(On him who was born to be a tamal, heaven showers corn husks.)

—A *DICHO,* OR MEXICAN SAYING

"THE FIRST THING TO DO WHEN planning any fiesta," exhorted Angelita Espinosa in her persuasive lawyer's voice, "is to make lots of tamales in advance." Angie went on to describe how she and several other equally busy Detroit professional women found the time to prepare all the food for a huge party she was taking me to the next day. Not only are tamales fiesta food, but making them also becomes a celebration. In many homes it is a lively interlude, with everybody sharing in the work and catching up on what's been happening in their lives. Some cooks, especially the one assigned to make the *masa,* may have performed this same ritual for more than thirty years, but younger family members always join in, so the tradition will pass on to a new generation.

Although more and more in the United States tamales are eaten in conjunction with other foods, it is traditional to serve only one or several different kinds with just a hot beverage. This is a dish for morning or supper, and for most Mexican Americans it is the single food that is inseparable from Christmas.

Rose Archuelta's son, Rudy, who now lives in California, called her in Caldwell, Idaho, one night to say, "Guess what I'm having for supper—your tamales! I brought them with me, and whenever I want something to remind me of home—something special—I take them out of the freezer and steam them. It's almost like being with you."

Rose has her technique down to an assembly-line precision, even using a tortilla press, something I had never seen used in this way before, to flatten the *masa*.

There is a seemingly endless variety of sizes and shapes of tamales. A *tamal* may be wrapped in fresh or dried cornhusks or in banana or other large aromatic leaves, but all are a surprise package waiting to be opened. Some are fat with richly seasoned yellow *masa* (dough of ground dried corn) and little or no filling; in others, just a wisp of dough envelops shreds of chile-infused chicken or meat, or perhaps a spoonful of black beans. None of the ones I sampled were the same, although the most common filling was pork and red chiles—but in many different combinations and occasionally even with the traditional meat of a long-simmered hog's head. With tamales more than any other food, there was a direct generational link to Mexico, an attempt to replicate what their mothers and grandmothers had made with only slight changes along the way. Often high-quality vegetable shortening was used to replace the tasteless commercial lard found in the United States; in New Mexico the *masa* might be of musky blue corn instead of white or yellow corn, and everywhere I found substitutions in the type of chiles used. Air was beaten into the *masa* with electric beaters instead of by hand, but the process and product were essentially the same.

General Instructions for Making and Steaming Tamales

Drain the cornhusks and pat dry. Put some of the torn cornhusks in the bottom of a steamer basket or rack and fill the bottom of a large pot with 2 inches or more of water, but not enough to touch the tamales (page 21). Bring to a low boil.

Arrange the cornhusks, *masa,* and filling in a row. Hold a husk in the palm of a hand with the pointed end on your wrist. Spread 1 heaping tablespoon of *masa* on the upper half, as evenly as possible, leaving a margin on all sides. Put 1 tablespoon of filling in the center of the dough. Fold the sides of the husk over the filling to enclose it and bring up the pointed end of the husk until it is even with the cut end. You can tie the upper end with narrow strips of husk knotted together. It's attractive but not necessary.

Place each *tamal* vertically in the steamer basket with the folded side down. It is easiest to start in the center, propping tamales on a small funnel or can with holes in it, and work circularly, placing the filled tamales around it. Put the steamer basket over the water, cover the tamales with more cornhusks and a clean towel, and cover with a tight lid. Steam, without opening, for 1 hour.

To see if they are done, carefully remove a *tamal* from the pot, unwrap it, let it sit for several minutes, then break into it with a fork to see if the dough is firm. If not, continue to steam. When ready, remove the tamales from the pot and set aside for 5 minutes. Let them cool slightly before unwrapping.

A *tamal*-making tip: Put a coin in the bottom of the steamer, and when the water boils, it will rattle. If it stops, you know it is time to carefully add more boiling water. Just don't pour it over the tamales.

PORK LARD

Yes, I know, lard is a forbidden substance these days—the culinary equivalent of crack. Just remember, though, very good things are made of lard: the lightest of tamales, the flakiest pie crusts, and the rich, traditional biscochitos *(aniseed cookies). A spoonful of fat added to refried beans as they are cooking provides a special flavor and keeps the beans moist and shiny. There is a lot of truth in the Mexican saying,* "La manteca hace la cocina, no Catarina." *It's lard that makes the dinner, not Catherine.*

You may be surprised to learn that butter is said to have more than half again the amount of cholesterol found in lard. If you eat butter, you can use lard. If you're sinning, though, make it worth your while. I never use those flavorless white waxy blocks of lard sold in grocery stores but instead melt my own. It's easy, but if it seems like too tedious a task, find a butcher, especially in an Hispanic neighborhood, who renders his own richly flavored fat.

To make your own lard, ask your butcher for one or two pounds of pork fat and see if he will grind it for you. If not, chop it up finely at home with a knife or in a food processor. Heat the oven to 300 degrees F. Spread the fat in a large baking pan and cook it in the oven for thirty to forty-five minutes, or until most of the fat has melted, leaving behind only small bits of residual solids. If the fat starts to color, lower the temperature.

Let the melted lard cool a bit, then strain it into containers that can be tightly sealed. Put any leftover pieces of browned pork bits, tiny cracklings, in your next pot of beans or scramble them with eggs.

If kept tightly sealed—I put it in a screw-top jar—lard will last several months in the upper part of the refrigerator or about a year in the freezer.

Masa for Tamales

MAKES ENOUGH *MASA* FOR 30 TAMALES   *Not so surprisingly, none of the Mexican-American cooks I interviewed made their tamal masa from scratch, as is frequently done in Mexico. Instead they use commercially prepared fresh masa or make it from masa harina that is more coarsely ground than for tortillas. Either can be used, but those made with fresh-ground masa will be lighter and fluffier.*

Cooks who live near Hispanic neighborhoods are usually able to buy fresh-ground masa that is coarser ground for tamales. Check the yellow pages of the telephone book under Mexican foods or tortilla factories. The finer-ground tortilla masa will just make smoother textured tamales. The masa usually comes in five-pound plastic sacks and can be divided and frozen. Fresh or already frozen and thawed masa will last only three to four days before it begins to sour.

Masa made from masa harina, or flour ground from dried corn, is readily available in almost all supermarkets and can be quickly reconstituted with water. Note: This is not cornmeal but is made with specially processed corn. Mexican grocery stores often carry a masa harina just for tamales, and this coarse-textured corn flour is worth searching for but is not essential.

Basic Tamal Batter using freshly prepared or frozen and thawed masa

⅔ cup lard or vegetable shortening
2½ pounds prepared *masa* (6 cups)
1 cup lukewarm broth or water
1½ teaspoons baking powder
1½ teaspoons sea salt

Beat the lard with an electric mixer about 5 minutes, until fluffy and like thick whipped cream. Gradually add the *masa*, alternating with most of the liquid, and continue beating for at least another 10 minutes. Add more liquid if the batter is too dry. This long beating traps air in the batter, which expands the tamales as they steam, making them light and tender. Stir in the baking powder and salt, and mix well. A spoonful of the batter dropped into cold water should float to the surface.

Basic Tamal Batter using masa harina

4 cups *masa harina*
1½ teaspoons baking powder
1½ teaspoons sea salt, or to taste
3 cups lukewarm broth or water
⅔ cup lard or vegetable shortening

Mix the *masa harina,* baking powder, and salt together in a large bowl and stir in enough of the broth to make a moist batter.

Beat the lard with an electric mixer about 5 minutes, until creamy and fluffy. Mix with the *masa,* adding more water if needed. To make a spreadable batter, continue beating for at least another 10 minutes. Taste for salt and add more if necessary. The batter is ready when a spoonful dropped into cold water floats to the surface.

Pork Tamales with Red Chile Gravy
Tamales de Puerco con Chile Colorado
SACRAMENTO, CALIFORNIA • GUANAJUATO, MEXICO

MAKES 30   *Exquisite porcelains from Germany and Czechoslovakia accented the Italian furnishings throughout the home where I was enjoying the rustic flavor of Lupe Viramonte's tamales. Each tamal is small in size but big with the taste of dried red chiles, both in the filling and in a gravy. The contrast between the food and its surroundings is typical of Lupe's life. Starting school in Sacramento at nine, she spoke no English. Now, after years of living in Europe with her military engineer husband, she speaks English, German, Italian, and Spanish. Lupe still routinely cooks the foods she learned growing up in a Mexican family. The main difference is that the amounts are smaller now, since her children are grown and usually only two are at home for meals.*

Because of the lively chile gravy on the tamales, try these as a supper dish with Well-Fried Beans (page 227) on the side and a cooling Jicama, Melon, and Orange Salad (page 57).

2 pounds pork butt or pork shoulder

3 cloves garlic

about 1½ teaspoons sea salt

5 peppercorns

2 tablespoons pure chile powder containing mixed chiles

3 dried ancho chiles or dried red California or New Mexican chiles, toasted (page 22), stemmed, seeded, and finely ground

1 dried *chile de árbol,* toasted (page 22), stemmed, seeded, and finely ground

¼ teaspoon cumin

1 cup flour

3–4 tablespoons safflower or canola oil or melted pork lard

½ teaspoon dried oregano, preferably Mexican

about ½ teaspoon sea salt, depending on the saltiness of the broth

3 pounds Basic *Tamal* Batter (page 292)

1 pound dry cornhusks

30 narrow strips soaked cornhusks for tying (optional)

Cut the pork into large pieces, place in a large, heavy pot or Dutch oven, and cover with 6 cups of water. Flatten the garlic with the back of a knife and add to the pot with the salt and peppercorns. Bring to a boil and let the meat simmer about 1½ hours, until ready to fall apart. Remove the pot from the heat and let the meat cool in the broth. Remove the meat, reserving the broth, and cut off any fat. Shred the meat with your fingers, cover, and set aside. (If time allows, cook the meat in advance and chill the broth so that the fat congeals and is easier to remove. Otherwise, spoon off as much grease as possible.)

Add the chile powder, ground chiles, and cumin to 3 cups of the broth and mix thoroughly.

Brown the flour in an ungreased skillet until lightly toasted; stir and shake the pan so that the flour doesn't burn. Drizzle in some of the oil until the flour is saturated and continue to stir until it is a deep khaki color. Slowly stir in the chile-broth mixture and cook over medium heat until the gravy thickens. Add the oregano and salt to taste. Stir and taste, adding more chile if necessary.

Stir half of the gravy into the shredded pork meat. Cover the remaining gravy with a layer of plastic wrap placed directly on top and set aside to be reheated later.

Prepare the *tamal* batter according to the instructions for using *masa* or *masa harina*. Rinse the cornhusks and soak them in very hot water for 15 minutes, until pliable. Pat them dry. Cut the narrow strips for tying, if using.

Line up the pile of corn husks, the *masa,* the filling, and the ties, then assemble and steam the tamales following the directions on page 290.

After the tamales have been cooked and removed from the pot, let them set while the remaining gravy is reheated, adding some extra broth to thin it out. Remove the husks, place 1 or 2 on a plate, and pour a spoonful of the heated gravy over the top.

VARIATION: PORK TAMALES WITH CHILE-FLAVORED *MASA*   Some people prefer their tamales without the gravy on top but instead add 1 to 2 tablespoons of pure chile powder to the *masa* and proceed as before, eliminating the final topping. In this case, serve the tamales in their wrappers.

Fiesta Tamales
Tamales de Picadillo con Chile Colorado
TUCSON, ARIZONA • SONORA, MEXICO

MAKES ABOUT 30 *Carmen Villa Prezelski may not appear to be Mexican, and with her last name, few people at the University of Arizona, where she is a professor in historical anthropology, believe her at first, but as she told me,*

> *Believe me, I am definitely Mexican-American. I still remember that first Christmas I ever spent away from home here in Tucson. I had just gotten married, and my husband, who is Polish, took me back to New York City to meet my in-laws. What a disaster. They had prepared a special feast in my honor featuring a large, succulent roast goose, but even before we sat down to eat, I began to cry—and went on crying and crying. All I could explain to my husband as he was trying to comfort me was that it just didn't feel like Christmas. I couldn't smell the tamales.*

Fat with chile-spiced meat, raisins, and olives, these are similar to the traditional Arizona tamales that Carmen Villa Prezelski has to have in order to make her Christmas complete. Only an extra kick from fresh jalapeño chiles has been added.

To serve for a holiday buffet, add Christmas Eve Salad (page 58), hot Christmas Punch (page 382), and plates of Aniseed Cookies (page 362).

1½ pounds beef brisket

½ pound pork butt

2 cloves garlic

about 1 teaspoon sea salt

8 dried New Mexican or California red chiles, toasted (page 22)

1 tablespoon safflower or canola oil

2 cloves garlic, minced

1 tablespoon flour

½ teaspoon powdered cumin

⅓ cup diced black olives

3 fresh jalapeño chiles, seeded and chopped

½ cup black raisins

¼ teaspoon dried oregano, preferably Mexican

about ½ teaspoon sea salt, depending on the saltiness of the broth

3 pounds Basic *Tamal* Batter (page 292)

1 pound dry cornhusks

60 narrow strips soaked cornhusks for tying

For the Garnish

1 cup Mexican *crema* (page 23) or sour cream thinned with milk (optional)

½ cup chopped green onion (optional)

The meat is best cooked 6–12 hours in advance. Place the meat in a large stockpot, cover with 4 cups of water, and bring to a boil over medium-high heat. Skim off any foam and add the whole cloves of garlic and salt. Lower the heat and simmer until the meat is very tender, about 2 hours. Remove the meat, reserving the broth, and when the meat is cool enough to handle, cut half of it into ½-inch chunks and shred the rest, removing all the fat. Cover and refrigerate.

Strain the broth and refrigerate. When the fat has congealed on the surface, lift it off and discard.

Put the toasted chiles in a bowl, pour boiling water over them, and let them soak about 10 minutes, until soft. Puree the chiles in a blender or food processor with 1 cup of water until they are a smooth paste. Add more water if necessary. Set aside 2 tablespoons of the pureed chile to add to the *masa*.

Heat the oil in a large skillet or saucepan. Add the minced garlic and brown lightly over low heat. Sprinkle in the flour and cumin, and stir constantly for 2 minutes, until the mixture begins to brown. Stir in the chile puree and 1 cup of broth, and simmer for 2 minutes. Add the meat, olives, jalapeños, and raisins. Sprinkle with oregano and salt to taste. Simmer for about 15–20 minutes, until the mixture is thick and has a rich aroma. Taste and correct the seasonings. Set aside to cool, then refrigerate, covered, if time allows. The filling improves in flavor if made 1 day in advance.

Prepare the *tamal* batter according to the instructions for using *masa* or *masa harina*.

Rinse the cornhusks and soak them in very hot water for 15 minutes, until pliable.

Beat the 2 tablespoons of chile puree into the *masa* until thoroughly combined. Add more broth or water if needed to make a moist dough.

When you are ready to assemble the tamales, pat dry the softened cornhusks and set out alongside the *masa* and cooled filling. Tear narrow strips from the less perfect husks, knotting them together if necessary to make 60 ties, each 10 inches long.

Follow the directions on page 290 to prepare the steamer and to form and steam the tamales, but use 2–3 heaping tablespoons of *masa* and filling so that each *tamal* is plump and well endowed. Spread the *masa* evenly in the center of the smooth side of a husk, leaving a 1-inch margin at both ends and a smaller one on the sides.

Spread 2 tablespoons of the filling on the inside of the *masa,* leaving a ½-inch frame of *masa* around the outside. Fold 1 side of the husk over the filling, roll it up, and tie on both ends like a party favor. If the husk doesn't completely enclose the *masa,* slip in another smaller piece of husk. Repeat to make the remaining tamales. Steam directly or freeze for later use.

Arrange the remaining tamales flat on the steamer rack, alternating the direction with each layer. Steam for 45 minutes to 1 hour, until the *masa* is firm and pulls away easily from the husk.

These tamales should be eaten warm, with each person unwrapping his own, or the husks can be removed and each *tamal* topped with *crema* and scattered with chopped green onion.

Christmas Tamales with Mole
Tamales Navideños
SAG HARBOR, NEW YORK • PUEBLA, MEXICO

MAKES ABOUT 30 *When Olga Vaquero needs ingredients for tamales and other Mexican dishes, they are brought directly to her front door on the tip of Long Island by Jesus Blanco, a traveling grocer. He has a van outfitted like a small Mexican market, complete with many varieties of fresh and dried chiles, tomatillos, dried epazote and* hoja santa, *as well as canned goods, Mexican cheeses, cecina, and, of course, tortillas fresh from a Brooklyn tortilleria. Any seasonal fresh food requested in advance will be brought out from a central produce market.*

Olga first arrived in Los Angeles when she was only seventeen, sharing living space in an already crowded household of relatives of family friends. Now on each trip back to Mexico with her husband, Isaías, who is the grill chef at the prestigious American Hotel on Long Island, she has added to her knowledge of regional Pueblan cooking. And now with the availability of ingredients she can reproduce most of them in the United States. Complex-flavored moles and tamales, using this same rich sauce, are among the family favorites for the Christmas holidays, usually being served after church on Christmas Eve and at other festive gatherings.

For Christmas Eve, serve this with the traditional cup of Mexican Hot Chocolate (page 386) or Hot Chocolate Atole (page 384). For a more complete meal, add a big green salad or the Vegetable Salad with Pears and Cherries (page 60).

3 pounds Basic *Tamal* Batter (page 292)

1 pound dry cornhusks

2 tablespoons sesame seeds

1 tablespoon unsalted Spanish peanuts

3 cloves

3 black peppercorns

4 each dried ancho, mulato, and pasilla chiles, toasted (page 22) and deveined

1 slice dry white bread or 4 saltine crackers

1½-inch piece true cinnamon bark, broken up, or about 1 teaspoon ground cinnamon (cassia)

ingredients continue

¼ cup melted pork lard or peanut oil

2 cups chicken or pork broth

½ ounce Mexican chocolate, chopped

about 1 teaspoon sea salt, depending on the saltiness of the broth

3 cups poached chicken (page 70), shredded, or cooked pork, shredded

Prepare the *tamal* batter according to the instructions for using *masa* or *masa harina*.

Rinse the cornhusks and soak them in very hot water for 15 minutes, until pliable.

Warm a small ungreased skillet over medium heat and toast the sesame seeds, peanuts, cloves, and peppercorns. Toss for a few seconds until the seeds begin to turn color and the aromas begin to rise from the pan. While still hot, place in a spice grinder, add the chiles, bread, and cinnamon bark, and grind until smooth. This may have to be ground in batches. Do not add liquid at this point.

Heat the lard or oil in a large skillet and stir in the ground chile mixture. Fry over medium heat, stirring constantly, about 5 minutes, until darkened and thick. Stir in the broth, chocolate, and salt, and continue to simmer until thickened. Remove from the heat.

Follow the directions on page 290 to form and steam the tamales. Use a spoonful of the *masa* mixture and a teaspoon of the *mole,* and add some shredded pork or chicken on top of the *mole* in each *tamal*. Fold the cornhusks to form tamales and steam for 1½ hours in a steamer.

To see if the tamales are done, remove 1 tamale from the pot. When it is unwrapped, the dough should be firm enough to come free easily from the husks. If ready, remove the rest of the tamales from the pot and set aside for 5 minutes before serving. Let each person unwrap his own *tamal,* or for a more formal presentation, open them up and serve them on top of their own wrappers.

VARIATION: MINIATURE PARTY TAMALES　Sister Aline María often is called upon to provide party food for large numbers of guests at Mount St. Mary's College in Los Angeles where she is an instructor of languages. Tiny tamales filled with chicken *mole* are reliable standbys because they can be made in advance and frozen. Other fillings can be used as well.

To make about 6 dozen, use the Basic *Tamal* Batter recipe (page 292). The procedures are also the same, but spread only 1 heaping teaspoon of the *masa* in the middle of each husk and use a scant teaspoon of filling. Roll and turn up the long end and tie with a narrow strip of husk. Steam for 30–45 minutes.

Green Chile Tamales

Tamales Vaporcitos de Chile Verde

AUSTIN, TEXAS

MAKES ABOUT 2 DOZEN, SERVING 2 OR 3 PER PERSON *Say "tamales" to most folks, and they think of fat, doughy morsels of* masa *filled with chile-seasoned shredded meat wrapped and cooked in dried cornhusks. The green chile tamales that Miguel makes are quite different from those usually found in Texas and the other border states. The thin layer of* masa *dough wrapped in fragrant banana leaves contains butter and sour cream instead of lard and is filled with vegetables. When unwrapped, the whole thing ends up looking a bit like an oversized ravioli—and what a joy to eat!*

The best thing is that even if you are a novice at tamal making, these are simple. You should be able to find the banana leaves, frozen, in an Asian, Caribbean, or Hispanic market. Defrost overnight in the refrigerator, then unfold and cut out any thick veins. Dried cornhusks, softened in water, can be used in a pinch.

These tamales are wonderful with eggs in the morning, for a light evening snack, or as part of a party buffet. They can be frozen uncooked, then steamed without thawing, or they can be cooked and frozen to be thawed later and steamed or reheated in the microwave.

25 banana leaves, 8 by 7 inches, with extra leaves to line the top and bottom of the steamer rack

6 fresh poblano or Anaheim chiles, roasted (page 21), peeled, and seeded

¾ pound ripe tomatoes (about 2 medium or 5 plum tomatoes), roasted (page 22)

1 white onion, chopped

1 clove garlic, minced

about ½ teaspoon sea salt

2 pounds Basic *Tamal* Batter using *masa* (page 292)

1¼ cups unsalted butter at room temperature

6 tablespoons sour cream

about 1 generous teaspoon sea salt

1–1½ cups Chicken Stock (page 70) or canned chicken broth

Put several inches of water in the steamer and cover. Set it over low heat so that it will be boiling when the tamales are ready to cook. Line the steamer rack with a layer of extra banana leaf pieces.

To soften the cut banana leaves, pass them slowly over a gas or electric burner until they darken and change texture or can be loosely rolled together and steamed, standing vertically, for 30 minutes, until pliable. Tear 1 banana leaf into 24 narrow 10-inch-long ties. They may be knotted together to make longer ties if wanted.

With your hands, squish the chiles and tomatoes together in a medium-size bowl until thoroughly mashed and mixed. Add the onion and garlic. Mix well, salt lightly, and set aside.

Prepare the *tamal* batter according to the instructions for using *masa*. Beat the butter in a large bowl with an electric mixer at high speed until fluffy. It will take several minutes. Add the sour cream, lower the speed to medium, and gradually beat in the *masa* and enough salt to generously season the mixture. Taste to make certain it has the right amount. Add the chicken broth a little at a time until the mixture is like a thick cake batter. (*Tamal* batter varies in absorbency, so very likely there will be leftover broth.) Let the *masa* mixture set for about 5 minutes.

One at a time, lay out a few pieces of banana leaves. Spread a ⅛-inch layer of the *masa* in the center of each piece, leaving about a ¾-inch margin on the larger ends and 2 inches on each side.

Place 1 tablespoon of the filling in the center of the *masa*. Fold 1 of the long sides a bit over the center, then overlap with the opposite side. Flip the ends over to form a 3- by 4-inch packet. Repeat the process until all the tamales are made. While not necessary, it is attractive to complete the packaging of each *tamal* by loosely tying it across the middle, holding the folded end in place.

Layer the tamales horizontally with the seam side up, alternating the direction of each layer. Cook for about 45 minutes, remembering to add boiling water if the level of water gets too low. The tamales are done when the dough is firm and can be separated from the banana leaf.

Remove the tamales from the pot and let stand several minutes before opening and serving. Or let each person unwrap his own.

Tamales of Tiny Vegetables
Tamales Cambray
GIG HARBOR, WASHINGTON • OAXACA, MEXICO

MAKES ABOUT 30   *This is a very special dish for me, and I must admit these tamales are included in this book not because I came across the recipe in the United States but because Susy Torres, my "almost daughter" from Puerto Angel in Oaxaca, had friends make these vegetable-packed tamales for me on my sixtieth birthday.*

Cambray usually refers to tiny whole onions, potatoes, or other small vegetables, but in this case I assume it is because the vegetables are cut in small pieces.

When I have an informal tamal *party, I especially like to make these tamales with vegetable broth and vegetable shortening as an offering to those friends and family members who are vegetarians. For the others there will be a choice of savory ones, perhaps Fiesta Tamales (page 295) and Fresh Corn Tamales (page 302), and then the Sweetened Bean Tamales (page 304) as a contrast. I make some as Miniature Party Tamales (page 298) so that everyone can try all the different kinds. I definitely make these far in advance and freeze them. Different kinds of salads can be added, especially Cactus Salad (page 54) and Jicama, Melon, and Orange Salad (page 57). Serve a big pot of Drunken Beans (page 227) and end with the easy Pineapple Cake with Ginger Icing (page 369). I usually serve both Sangria (page 380) and Hibiscus Flower Water (page 379) and lots of cold beer.*

1 large white onion, roasted (page 22)

1 whole head of garlic, roasted (page 22)

5 medium ripe tomatoes, roasted (page 22)

3 tablespoons safflower or canola oil

½ teaspoon dried oregano, preferably Mexican

sea salt

4 cups Chicken Stock (page 70), or canned
   chicken or vegetable broth

3 tablespoons cornstarch

½ pound red potatoes, cooked peeled, and
   chopped

2 medium carrots, cooked peeled, and chopped

1 large chayote, cooked peeled, and chopped

10 ounces fresh or frozen green beans, cooked
   and chopped

4–8 pickled jalapeño chiles, chopped

½ cup chopped green olives

3 pounds Basic *Tamal* Batter (page 292)

1 pound dry cornhusks

60 narrow strips of soaked cornhusks for tying
   the ends

Chop the onion into chunks and place in a blender or food processor. Take the husk off the garlic and add to the blender with the tomatoes, skins left on, and all the juices. Puree until smooth.

Warm the oil in a large skillet or Dutch oven over medium-high heat and add the tomato puree, oregano, and salt to taste. Cook, stirring frequently, about 5 minutes until darkened and thick. Mix in the chicken broth, turn the heat to medium-low, and simmer gently.

Put the cornstarch in a cup and stir in enough water or broth to dilute it to a thin gravy. Slowly pour into the sauce, mix well, and continue to simmer for 10 minutes. Add all the vegetables, chopped chiles, and olives, and check for seasoning again. After simmering another 5 minutes, remove the pan from the heat and let the mixture cool. The filling can be made in advance to this point, covered, and refrigerated.

Prepare the *tamal* batter according to the instructions for using *masa* or *masa harina*.

Rinse the cornhusks and soak them in very hot water for 15 minutes, until pliable, and cut the narrow strips for tying.

recipe continues

To make the tamales and steam them, follow the instructions on page 290, but since these will be somewhat larger tamales, it helps to roll the *masa* into ½-inch balls, and, with a piece of plastic wrap laid over the top, pat each one down in the center of a cornhusk, working the *masa* almost to the edge.

Put 1 heaping tablespoon of filling in the center of the *masa*. Fold over 1 of the long sides and roll together firmly. Tie each end with thin strips of cornhusks.

Lay each tamale in horizontal layers in the steamer, alternating the direction. Cover tightly and steam for about 1½ hours. Check carefully during the end that the water doesn't boil away. If it is low, pour more boiling water into the bottom of the pot.

VARIATION: VEGETABLE TAMALES WITH CHICKEN   To make my special birthday tamales, poach 1 whole chicken breast, and after coarsely shredding the meat, lay a few pieces on the top of the vegetables before folding and tying each *tamal*.

Fresh Corn Tamales
Tamales de Elote
TUCSON, ARIZONA • SONORA, MEXICO

MAKES 4 DOZEN; 1 DOZEN SERVES 4 TO 6   *Tamales made with ground fresh corn kernels instead of* masa *are treats found in most regions of Mexico, wherever the starchy field corn is harvested. I'd always heard from the experts that the sweet corn grown in the United States has too much moisture in it to become firm enough without adding* masa, *so I was surprised when Adela Bacahui served the first of the tamales she had just made using only local supermarket corn—so sweet and moist it was almost like eating a corn pudding. They were wonderful.*

When I was back in my own kitchen, although I followed Adela's procedures diligently, even to using "three big handfuls of lard," we never could get the numerous batches we steamed to firm up properly. Remembering that cold will convert sugar to starch, I stored the ears of corn in the refrigerator. I used the forlorn leftover corn in the grocery bins thinking it would be starchier. The dough still didn't set up properly. It was finally decided that for consistent good results masa harina *would have to be included. The tamales will still be of a somewhat softer consistency than you might expect, but it is the intense sweet corn flavor that sets them apart.*

The tamales are usually served hot and unadorned, but sometimes with salsa such as Green, Green

Salsa (page 267) or Mexican crema (page 23) on the side. Black beans are a good companion dish. Any extras can be steamed for another meal—unwrapped, sliced in half, and fried in butter with cheese. These tamales freeze well, both before and after steaming, and should not be defrosted before resteaming. If they are frozen, be sure to add 30–45 minutes to the steaming time.

about 1 dozen ears fresh corn

1½ pounds Monterey jack or longhorn cheese, cut into ¼-inch cubes

2 cups *masa harina*, preferably a coarsely ground type

1 cup lard or ¾ cup vegetable shortening plus 4 tablespoons unsalted butter, softened

1 tablespoon baking powder

1 tablespoon plus 1 teaspoon sea salt

16 fresh New Mexican or Anaheim chiles, roasted (page 21), peeled, and seeded

1 large clove garlic, chopped

sea salt

Cut 1 or 2 inches off the pointed tip of each ear of corn and then the base ends. Carefully remove all the leaves, saving the whole leaves and discarding the tiny inner leaves and corn silk. Wash the leaves and drain them. Set the shaggy outside husks aside for lining the steaming pot.

With a sharp knife, scrape the corn kernels off the cob into a large bowl. Be careful to save as much of the corn "milk" as possible. Add the cheese.

Thoroughly process the corn and cheese mixture in small batches in a food processor until the consistency of applesauce.

Using a mixer with a paddle or a food processor, beat the lard until creamy and forming peaks—about 5 minutes. Scrape down the sides of the bowl from time to time so that all the lard is thoroughly beaten.

Add the ground corn to the bowl, a few handfuls at a time, alternating with the *masa harina*, and mix it well with your hands. Stir in the baking powder and salt. The dough should still be quite sticky.

Cut the chiles into small strips, ¼ by 1½ inches, and place in a small bowl with the garlic.

To form a *tamal*, hold a leaf open in one hand and place a heaping tablespoonful of the ground corn mixture in the center of the leaf. If there are not enough large leaves, overlap several smaller ones. Place 5–6 strips or a small spoonful of chopped chiles on top, leaving a wide margin of dough on all sides. Fold both sides over the filling, then fold the pointed end over, leaving the straight end open.

Line a steamer pot with some of the unused leaves. If you don't have a steamer, put the corn cobs on the bottom of a large pot, then add a layer of leaves. Stand each *tamal* upright in the steamer with the open side to the top. Add water to the bottom of the pot. Top with additional leaves and a damp kitchen towel, and cover tightly. Bring the water in the steamer to a slow boil and let the tamales steam for about 1 hour, although they may require another 15–30 minutes. Make sure the pot never boils dry; add more boiling water if necessary.

To check, remove a *tamal* from the pot and let it cool for a few minutes, allowing the *masa* to set. Unwrap to see if it is firm and no longer sticks to the cornhusk. If the dough is still sticky, rewrap and return it to the pot and continue steaming.

VARIATION: FRESH CORN DUCK TAMALES　　Add 2 cups of cooked and shredded duck or chicken to the chile filling for the tamales.

Sweetened Bean Tamales
Tamales Dulces de Frijol
McMINVILLE, OREGON • SINALOA, MEXICO

MAKES ABOUT 30　　*As Maria told me:*

> *When my mother was preparing tamales for Christmas—usually using the leftover turkey from Thanksgiving—she would occasionally run out of filling but still have* masa *left over—an event we all hoped for. When this happened, she would sweeten the* masa *with piloncillo (brown sugar) and add some walnuts and raisins, along with some allspice. Then she would make a filling from* refritos *[refried beans] to which she added more brown sugar, raisins, allspice, cinnamon, nutmeg, and ginger—or just some pumpkin pie spice. The little sweet bean tamales were made somewhat smaller than the meat ones and wrapped like a little bundle, with the ends tied, then steamed. This was a special treat for us and is now a special treat for our grandson, Aidan.*

I didn't get to try these wonderful and unusual tamales when I was at Maria McRitchie's, but Miguel and I followed her instructions closely and came up with these, which we think are great and now are a special treat for my children and grandchildren.

These sweet tamales are often served alongside a plate of another type. Just make sure they are wrapped differently so they can be told apart. They are a wonderful treat for a special breakfast or brunch and equally good for supper. Hot chocolate or atole is the traditional beverage to drink with tamales.

COCINA DE LA FAMILIA

For the Tamales

1 pound dry cornhusks

30 narrow strips of soaked cornhusks for tying

3 pounds Basic *Tamal* Batter (page 292)

½ cup brown sugar

½ cup finely chopped walnuts

½ cup raisins

½ teaspoon ground allspice

For the Filling

2 cups Well-Fried Beans (page 227) or one 16-ounce can refried pinto beans

⅓ cup raisins

2 tablespoons brown sugar

1½ teaspoons ground cinnamon (cassia)

½ teaspoon ground nutmeg, preferably freshly ground

½ teaspoon ground ginger

½ teaspoon ground allspice

Rinse the cornhusks and soak them in very hot water for 15 minutes, until pliable, and cut the narrow strips for tying.

Prepare the dough and put it in a large bowl. Stir in the brown sugar, nuts, raisins, and allspice.

To make the filling, in a medium-size bowl, stir together the beans, raisins, and brown sugar. Add the cinnamon, nutmeg, ginger, and allspice, and mix well.

Pat the cornhusks dry. For each tamale, lay a cornhusk flat with the smooth side up. Spread about 1 tablespoon of the batter on the center of each husk, leaving the edges bare. Spread 1 teaspoon of the filling on the dough. Fold the sides of the husk lengthwise over the center so they overlap. Bring up the pointed end until it is even with the cut end. Using narrow strips of another husk, tie the end tightly. If needed, knot 2 strips together to make the strip long enough to tie. (The tamales should be somewhat smaller than the usual meat ones and wrapped like a little bundle with the one end tied.)

Prepare the remaining tamales and follow the directions on page 290 to steam them.

Sweet Pumpkin Spice Tamales

Tamales Dulces de Calabaza

BURBANK, CALIFORNIA, AND EL PASO, TEXAS

MAKES 12 TO 14   *Serving a sweet spicy tamal is not as unusual as it sounds. It is an ideal partner for morning coffee or hot chocolate, as well as an evening snack. Roberto Cortez, Jr.'s tamales have no filling at all. The pureed pumpkin and ground spices are instead part of the masa and give the* *tamales a rich, autumnal flavor. Roberto, a second-generation Mexican American, learned the basics for his Mexican cooking from his grandmother and supplemented them with ideas and techniques learned from Diana Kennedy's and Patricia Quintana's cookbooks. Now a professional cook, he often draws on his Mexican culinary heritage and adapts recipes, but he makes very few changes in traditional recipes such as these tamales.*

30 large dry cornhusks

1 cup unsalted butter at room temperature

⅔ cup sugar

1 teaspoon sea salt

1 teaspoon ground cinnamon (cassia)

¼ teaspoon ground cloves

1¼ cups freshly prepared *masa* or from *masa harina* (page 108)

1 cup canned pumpkin puree

2 teaspoons baking powder

⅛–¼ cup milk

Rinse the cornhusks and soak them in very hot water for 15 minutes, until pliable.

In a mixer with a paddle attachment or food processor, cream the butter and sugar on medium-high for 12 minutes. Add the salt, cinnamon, and clove after the first few minutes. Scrape the sides of the bowl when needed.

Meanwhile, mix the *masa*, pumpkin puree, baking powder, and milk in a separate bowl until thoroughly combined. Add this mixture, ¼ cup at a time, to the creamed butter. When it is all incorporated, check to see if it is light enough by placing a small ball in a cup of cold water. If it floats, it is ready. If it sinks, continue to beat in more air until a ball will float.

Follow the directions on page 290 to form and steam the tamales. For each *tamal*, spread about 2 tablespoons of the batter on the center of a softened cornhusk. If the husks are small, use additional husks to extend the size. Fold the sides of the husk lengthwise over the center so they overlap, then bring up the pointed end until it is even with the cut end. Repeat the process to make 12–14 tamales. The remainder of the cornhusks can be used to line the steamer.

Steam the tamales, standing upright in the steamer, for 45 minutes. They are done when the dough is firm and no longer sticks to the husks.

VARIATION: SWEET TROPICAL TAMALES   Beatriz Esquivel, a Detroit language teacher, eliminates the spices and substitutes for the pumpkin ½ cup of drained, crushed pineapple and ½ cup of shredded coconut.

Florida Impressions

The Spanish spoken by 13 percent of Florida's population is not a new language to be heard in this tropical landscape. The first documented landing by a European in what would become the United States two centuries later was on April 2, 1513, by the Spaniard Juan Ponce de León. He was thought to come ashore at a little inlet near what is now Daytona Beach. Observing that the surroundings were lush and green, he named the region La Florida (Flowering Land) and claimed it all for the Spanish crown. A little more than fifty years later, Spanish colonists arrived and settled to the north in St. Augustine, the first permanent European settlement in North America and still a fascinating city to visit.

In Miami these days, it is easy to understand the city's title as the de facto capital of Latin America—more than 50 percent of its residents are Hispanic, many middle- and upper-class Cuban exiles but also thousands of Puerto Ricans, Guatemalans, and transplants from South America. What I hadn't realized was that Florida also has a sizable Mexican-American population—in fact, it has the fifth highest percentage of any state in the country, even without counting the many migrant and seasonal workers who travel up and down the East Coast.

In Miami and the sprawling residential regions surrounding the city, I discovered a very different type of migrant—sophisticated world travelers who for one reason or another have visited many parts of the globe. Rose María Trevino has lived in Indonesia, Virginia Ariemma in Berlin and Naples, and Veronica Litton leads wine aficionado groups to Italy and Chile. And the cooking of all of them reflects this international influence, as does the strong Cuban presence in the city.

I met ninety-four-year-old Eva Celayo de Garcia at the home of her granddaughter, Veronica Litton, in Pembroke Pines. Señora Garcia is a woman with a palate still amazingly acute. After arriving in Florida five years before, she was eating at an upscale Mexican restaurant when she determined with only a few bites that the chiles and seeds had not been toasted in the *mole* she was served. The chef had to admit she was right, and undoubtedly he hasn't taken that shortcut again.

Señora Garcia, married at thirteen to the twenty-eight-year-old National Railroad superintendent, traveled all over Mexico in his private railroad car. When they were living in Mexico City, her husband began to lose his sight and was not able to work. Eva opened several boardinghouses in the center of the city and soon was cooking every day for fifty or more businessmen, who appreciated the care with which she prepared her food. In this way, Eva kept busy, until 1991, when in her late eighties she came to live in Florida with her daughter.

I found a different world after leaving Miami and heading south on Highway 997 toward the Florida Keys. This is flat land, bordered on one side by the Everglades and on the other by the Straits of Florida. The torpid hot air is enervating, with only the freeway traffic and the occasional swallow-tailed kite soaring overhead to remind you to pay attention to your driving. I was to spend several days talking to workers at Brooks Tropicals, outside of Homestead, probably the premier supplier of tropical fruits and vegetables in the country. While Cubans dominate Miami, Homestead and its surrounding agricultural lands are where thousands of Mexican Americans and Mexican immigrant laborers live and work, helping to cultivate and process the tomatoes and tropical fruits for the U.S. consumer.

Elroy Garza, the plant supervisor of the huge lime and avocado packing division, was born and raised in Arkansas; his folks were from Río Bravo, right across the border from McAllen, Texas. His wife Maria's parents came from Guadalajara. As Elroy and I talked, seated in the back of the huge warehouse, he described to me how they had adjusted their cooking and eating schedule to fit a family with three teenagers and two working parents. Breakfasts are filling: eggs, potatoes, *chilaquiles* and on weekends maybe *huevos rancheros*. Since Maria makes flour tortillas every day, they bring a burrito filled with chopped hard-boiled eggs and refried pinto beans or some other stuffing to work for lunch. Suppers are simple and usually include a salad, refried or soupy beans, and always flour tortillas. It's on Sundays that the family enjoys getting together at the table for large meals that combine the border cooking of Elroy's family, those more elaborate dishes from Jalisco, and the simplified cooking techniques available in the United States.

Chile-red *menudo,* made with canned hominy or *pozole blanco,* thick with chopped cabbage, onion, and radishes, is a favorite for a late breakfast. Later that day perhaps a chunky vegetable stew, enriched with beef or a chicken *mole* would be served by using commercially prepared *mole* paste, and microwaving store-bought corn tortillas in the bag to soften them. Occasionally her mother will make Guadalajara's regional specialty, *birria,* though she may have to use lamb instead of the more traditional goat for the mildly chile-spiced meat.

Bread and Breakfast
Pan, Pan Dulce, y Huevos

Seguro que el pan para la mañana.
(As sure as the bread in the morning.)

—A SAYING INSCRIBED AT THE FORMER FOUR-CENTURIES-OLD
CONVENT OF SANTA CATALINA, NOW THE CAMINO REAL
HOTEL, OAXACA, MEXICO

"EL CIELO HUELE A PANADERÍA." Heaven smells like a bakery. If so, there is no Mexican-American community without its bit of heaven, whether a suburb of San Francisco, a barrio near the center of Chicago, or a sparsely populated town in Texas. In the mornings, the yeasty smell wafting out of bakery doors makes it hard to pass by without entering, picking up tongs, and choosing two or three of the most tempting from the array of freshly baked sweet breads. Then there are other flaky pastries to be eaten with *café con leche* for a late supper or *bolillos* to accompany dinner. For those who do not have access to a Mexican bakery or, like me, just love to bake, we have included a few of the most familiar recipes.

Traditionally in Mexico and still in some farming communities in the United States, *desayuno,* the first meal of the day, is a cup of coffee or chocolate, maybe fresh juice, and always some sweet breads or tortillas just to break the fast of the night. Later, especially on weekends, the family gathers to share *almuerzo,* the enormous morning meal of festively prepared eggs and meats, enlivened always with salsas and served with stacks of tortillas and more breads. Sometimes a hearty bowl of *pozole* or *menudo* is served, sometimes tamales, or some *carne con chile* from the day before.

Whether frugal or elaborate, breakfast is a filling meal—one to give stamina and zest for the coming day.

Crusty Bread Rolls
Bolillos

MAKES ABOUT 16 ROLLS   *In the small Oregon town of McMinville is one of the West Coast's best Mexican restaurants. Owned by Claire and Shawna Archibald, Cafe Azul has customers driving regularly from Portland and even points farther away.*

Claire's version of Mexico's hard bread rolls has the same distinctive shape as the classic bolillo, *a pudgy oval with tapered ends, but the addition of a bit of corn meal and of* masa harina *gives it a delightful crunchy texture.*

I must admit I like to eat these crusty rolls best just out of the oven, when the interiors are soft and porous, just right for absorbing the butter as it melts. Ordinarily they are served in a basket as dinner rolls, but they may be hollowed out, filled with Well-Fried Beans (page 227) to become the rustic breakfast dish Molletes *(page 327), or sliced and stuffed with layers of meats, cheeses, and condiments to become a* torta, *Mexico's famous sandwich.*

1 tablespoon sugar
2 packages (½ ounce) active dry yeast
2½ cups warm water
½ cup lard (page 291) or olive oil
1 tablespoon sea salt

7 cups all-purpose flour
½ cup *masa harina* (page 108)
½ cup white cornmeal
1 teaspoon sea salt

Place ½ cup of warm water in a small bowl. To make sure it is the correct temperature, test a drop on the inside of your wrist. It should be comfortably warm. Sprinkle in the sugar and then the yeast. Stir and let the yeast mixture proof until it becomes foamy—about 5 minutes.

In a large bowl, mix together 1½ cups of warm water, lard, salt, 2 cups of the flour, and the proofed yeast mixture. Stir well with a wooden spoon to create a creamy batter. Add the remaining 5 cups of flour, a little at a time, along with the *masa harina* and cornmeal. Continue stirring until the dough pulls away from the side of the bowl and is rather firm.

Turn out the dough onto a floured surface and knead, sprinkling more flour onto the board if the dough becomes sticky. Continue to knead about 4 minutes, until the ball of dough is firm, resilient, and satiny smooth.

Butter or oil a large bowl and turn the ball of dough in it so that all sides of the dough are covered by a film of butter. Cover with a towel or plastic wrap and let rise in a warm place for 1 hour, or until doubled in bulk.

Turn out the dough on the lightly floured surface and knead for 2 minutes. Divide the dough into 4 equal portions and cover 3 of them. Divide the piece of dough into 4 rolls. Form each into a flat oval, pinching the ends to form a spindle shape. Repeat the process with the remaining dough.

Place on unbuttered baking sheets, cover, and let rise again in a warm place for 30 minutes. Meanwhile, preheat the oven to 375 degrees F.

Mix ¼ cup of water with the salt and lightly brush over the surface of the rolls. Pinch the ends of the rolls again. Bake the rolls for 20–30 minutes; lower the heat to 350 degrees F. if they appear too brown. When the rolls turn a pale golden color and sound hollow when tapped, remove from the oven and cool on a rack.

THE DAY OF THE DEAD
Día de Muertos

One year, at the end of October, I tried to get last-minute airline tickets to Mexico, but my plans were almost stymied for lack of seat space. At that time I was unaware of the annual tide of generations of Mexican Americans returning south to renew their alliance with family members—both living and dead. The Reverend Thomas Belleque, priest of Saint Andrew's Catholic Church in Sumner, Washington, said of his large Mexican congregation, most of whom came north from Michoacán during the last ten years, "I can't think of ever burying anybody here. We always have the funerals here, then the bodies are shipped back. Their heart, their soul, who they are, is Mexican."

In Mexico, especially in the central and southern states, the first and second days of November belong to the dead, and friends and relatives gather to share the pleasures of living—favorite foods, drink, and music—with the deceased. It is not macabre at all, for here death is not an end but a stage in a constant cycle. It is an ebullient time for it is thought that at this time

continued

the souls of those who have died can continue to participate in the fiestas they enjoyed so much during their lifetime.

Those unable to return home often send money to their families in Mexico, helping to provide a bit of the gaiety honoring their ancestors. In the United States the Catholic churches may hold special masses, and many immigrants, such as Tita Cervantes in Detroit, who left Michoacán forty years ago, will decorate a home altar with photos of the departed, flowers, and candles. When family members are buried in the United States, flowers are taken to the cemeteries, and along the border festively decorated Styrofoam crosses are put on the graves and the children eat candy skulls. But it isn't the same as in Mexico.

There, the Day of the Dead is one of the most important and joyful holidays of the year, and it is still celebrated much the same way that it was centuries ago. In some areas, such as Oaxaca and Pátzcuaro, Michoacán, it is a three-day fiesta of music, parades, fireworks, and candlelight processions to the cemetery. In the homes and some public buildings, altars are set up and laden with the favorite food, drink, or even cigarettes for each expected visiting spirit. Flowers, especially a strong-smelling brilliantly colored type of marigold, adorn the altar, because it is thought the aroma leads the dead back to their place among their family and friends. Fanciful breads are set out and, according to their means, moles, tamales, napkin-wrapped tortillas or a treat of mezcal or tequila are added as the special time approaches.

In the cemeteries, the tombs and gravestones are repainted in bright colors and families bring armfuls of flowers. Everyone congregates on one night, usually November 1, and a feast is held at the graveside with all the wonderful foods that the deceased enjoyed during life. Again, care is taken that the aroma of the food is pungent and strong enough to guide the dead back.

> The living do not eat of the feast until the dead have left. They sit up all night with the little dead ones (invisible human beings) as if at a wake—a Mexican wake; singing, praying, drinking, making a little love—the tombs are turned into banquet tables similar to those at home. The food is put upon them, heavy purple wild blossoms and the yellow pungent cempalxochitl—ancient sacred blooms. *

*Anita Brenner, *Idols Behind Altars* (Boston, Mass.: Beacon Press, 1970).

Bread of the Dead

Pan de Muerto

TOPPENISH, WASHINGTON

MAKES 1 LARGE ROUND LOAF OR 2 SMALLER ONES AND SERVES 8 TO 12 *Festive loaves of sweetened eggbread play an important part in the observances of All Souls' Day. Loaves of this rich sweet bread are always included in the offering to the dead. Sometimes they are round with a suggestion of a skull and bones baked on top or with painted porcelain heads impaled in the dough. I've even seen the dough elaborately shaped into the form of a skeleton and decorated with colored sugar. Traditionally, families also take this bread to the cemetery in the evening to "feed the spirit" of their departed.*

Definitely a soul-satisfying treat, this version is similar to one that Paula Solis used to make. I've simplified the process as well as substituted butter for lard and included orange flower water, a strong flavoring that, used sparingly, adds a delicate perfume and taste to the bread. It is common in Middle Eastern cooking and is sold in specialty food stores.

Señora Solis, now eighty-six years old, had a bakery for twenty-six years in Lubbock, Texas. Left a widow at thirty-four, with eight children, she supported herself making her sweet breads, conchas, and seasonal specialties such as this rich egg bread. Orphaned at thirteen, Paula learned to cook from the nuns who had raised her. She eventually moved to live with her children in the Yakima Valley.

For the Dough

2 tablespoons aniseeds

2 packages (½ ounce) active granulated yeast

1 cup (2 sticks) unsalted butter, melted, or vegetable shortening

½ cup sugar

6 egg yolks, lightly beaten

2 eggs, lightly beaten

1½ teaspoons orange blossom water (optional)

1 tablespoon finely grated orange peel

½ teaspoon sea salt

4–5 cups unbleached all-purpose flour, plus extra for the work surface

about 1 tablespoon oil

For the Glaze

1 egg, lightly beaten with 1 tablespoon water

For the Topping

2 tablespoons unsalted butter, melted

¼ cup sugar

Boil ¼ cup of water and pour over the aniseeds in a small heatproof bowl. Steep until cool, about 15 minutes.

Pour ½ cup of warm water in a large bowl and sprinkle on the yeast. Let it sit until the yeast dissolves and puffs up.

Strain the aniseeds and pour the cool flavored water into the yeast. Add the melted butter, sugar, egg yolks, eggs, orange blossom water, grated peel, and salt. Stir in 3 cups of the flour and beat well for several minutes. Gradually add the rest of the flour, a handful at a time, until the dough begins to pull away from the side of the bowl and forms a slightly sticky ball.

Turn the dough out onto a floured surface and knead about 10 minutes, add more flour, a little at a time, until the dough is smooth and elastic. The amount will vary depending on the flour.

Wash the bowl, dry thoroughly, and rub with oil or butter. Place the dough in the bowl and turn it around so that all sides are coated. Cover the bowl with a sheet of oil-coated plastic wrap or a tightly woven damp towel and let the dough rise in a warm place until doubled in bulk, about 1½ hours. It can be set aside to rise overnight in the refrigerator and brought to room temperature before proceeding.

Turn the dough out onto a lightly floured surface, punch down, and divide into equal parts or leave as 1 large loaf. Pinch off about ¼ of each part to make the decorative attachments. Coat a large baking pan for each loaf, using either oil or butter.

For each loaf, shape the larger piece of dough into a round ball. Flatten the ball with the heel of your hand into a circle about 1 inch thick and put it on the baking pan. Form part of the remaining piece of dough into a 1½- or 2-inch ball and the rest into a long strip. Pinch off 4 to 6 pieces of the strip, depending on the amount of dough left, and shape into small ropes with knobs to resemble bones. Make an indentation in the center of the large circle, elongate the bottom of the small ball into a point, and press into the indentation, arranging the "bones" in a spokelike pattern. Repeat the process for each loaf. Allow the bread to rise for 45–60 minutes in a warm place, covered lightly.

Toward the end of the final rising period, preheat the oven to 375 degrees F. When the bread has almost doubled in size, brush the top of the bread with the egg wash and bake for 25–30 minutes. The surface should be well browned. The larger loaf may take closer to 45 minutes. Remove the bread from the baking sheets and place on a rack. Brush with melted butter, sprinkle immediately with the sugar, and let the bread cool.

VARIATION: CANDIED FRUIT BREAD   Pieces of candied fruit are a festive addition to the bread. Follow the directions but omit the aniseeds, and after the first rising, knead in 3 cups of various chopped candied fruits. Candied orange or citron peel, pineapple, and figs are the most common.

Three Kings Bread
Rosca de Reyes
BAKERSFIELD, CALIFORNIA

MAKES 2 RING-SHAPED LOAVES   *On January 6 in Mexico, it is the custom to commemorate the three kings who welcomed the baby Jesus with gifts of gold, frankincense, and myrrh. A ring-shaped cake, rich with candied fruits, is baked, and in it is hidden a tiny porcelain or plastic doll. To me finding a doll that won't melt when baked is the real challenge. The old five-and-dime stores had them, and I have found them in Mexican markets. The person who finds the doll in his or her portion must host another party on February 2, which is El Dia de la Candelaria (Candlemas Day). Some families include several large beans to designate the helpers for the upcoming party.*

This recipe is taken in part from a version by Socorro Muños Kimble and Irma Serrano Noriega, two California women who, because they felt that the sweet side of Mexican cooking had received only passing attention, wrote Mexican Desserts, *an excellent little book. Socorro and Irma usually embellish this festive bread with a sherry-flavored icing, but it is just as good when an equal amount of orange juice is substituted for the wine. In either case, stud the top with strips of candied or dried fruit.*

Three Kings Bread is usually served with Mexican Hot Chocolate (page 386).

For the Dough

2 packages (½ ounce) active granulated yeast
1 cup (2 sticks) unsalted butter, melted
½ cup sugar
6 egg yolks, lightly beaten with 3 tablespoons water
2 eggs, lightly beaten
½ teaspoon orange blossom water (optional)
1 tablespoon finely grated orange peel
1 tablespoon finely grated lemon peel
½ teaspoon sea salt
4–5 cups unbleached all-purpose flour, plus extra for the work surface
about 1 tablespoon oil

1 cup chopped candied fruit
¾ cup dark raisins
½ cup chopped pecans
2 tiny porcelain or nonmeltable plastic dolls

For the Glaze

1 egg, lightly beaten with 1 tablespoon water

For the Topping

2 cups sifted powdered sugar
⅓ cup medium-dry sherry or orange juice
6 sun-dried or candied figs, cut in strips (optional)
strips of candied orange peel (optional)
strips of other candied fruits or nuts (optional)

Pour ½ cup of warm water in a large bowl and sprinkle on the yeast. Let it sit until the yeast dissolves and puffs up.

Add the melted butter, sugar, egg yolks, eggs, orange blossom water, grated orange and lemon peels, and salt. Stir in 3 cups of the flour and beat well for several minutes. Gradually add the rest of the flour, a handful at a time, until the dough begins to pull away from the side of the bowl and forms a slightly sticky ball.

Turn out onto a floured surface and knead. Add more flour, a little at a time, until the dough is smooth and elastic, about 10 minutes. The amount will vary depending on the flour.

Wash the bowl, dry thoroughly, and coat with oil or butter. Place the dough in the bowl and turn it around so that all sides are coated. Cover the bowl with a sheet of oil-coated plastic wrap or a tightly woven damp towel and let the dough rise in a warm place until doubled in volume, about 1½ hours. It can be set aside to rise overnight in the refrigerator and brought to room temperature before proceeding.

Coat 2 baking sheets with oil or butter. Turn the dough out onto a lightly floured surface, punch down, and divide in half. Add half of the candied fruit, raisins, and pecans to each piece of dough and knead only until they are evenly distributed. Form the dough into 2 long, thick rolls and join the ends together firmly to make a ring. Push 1 doll into the dough of each circle, far enough so that they do not show, and place a circle on each baking sheet. To preserve the circular shape, insert a 3- or 4-inch ovenproof bowl or soufflé dish that has been buttered on the outside in the center of each ring so that it fits snugly. Allow the bread to rise until almost doubled in size, 45–60 minutes, covered lightly.

Toward the end of the final rising period, preheat the oven to 375 degrees F. When the bread has almost doubled in size, brush the tops with the egg wash. Bake for 25–30 minutes. The surface should be golden brown. Remove the bread from the baking sheets and place on a rack.

Mix the powdered sugar with the sherry or orange juice and drizzle over the bread while it is still hot. Garnish with the fruits and nuts, and let the bread cool before eating.

Pumpkin and Pine Nut Yeast Rolls
Semitas de Calabaza y Piñones
FORT GARLAND, COLORADO

MAKES ABOUT 24   *I heard about these autumn gold yeast rolls studded with pine nuts one morning from Teresa Vigil in San Luis, Colorado. I couldn't get the exact recipe because her source, Eliza Garcia, had been deceased for some years, but after talking to other locals and doing some experimenting, I came up with this version.*

The early Spanish and Mexican settlers of the upper Rio Grande Valley, in what is now northern New Mexico and southern Colorado, had a harsh existence that was sustained only by what they grew or obtained by foraging, hunting, and fishing. Today homes may boast an electric stove, but they still use their wood stove for most of their cooking. Rolls like these, using fresh pumpkin and pine nuts gathered from the Colorado piñon tree, were always favored.

In the small remote communities that dot the valley and perch on the sides of the mountains, social life revolves around family, church, and community-run activities. In Fort Garland, where Eliza Garland and her husband lived, everyone looked forward to the monthly dances in the community hall. He played the violin, and Eliza would bring food.

These rolls go especially well with Harvest Vegetable and Pork Casserole (page 190), and I like to serve them with Holiday Stuffed Turkey (page 167).

2 packages (½ ounce) active granulated yeast
1 tablespoon dark brown sugar
½ cup warm water
3 tablespoons melted unsalted butter, cooled
1½ teaspoons salt
2 eggs, lightly beaten

3 cups unbleached white flour and ½ cup extra if needed
¾ cup mashed cooked pumpkin
1 teaspoon ground cinnamon (cassia)
½ teaspoon nutmeg, preferably fresh ground
½ cup shelled and lightly toasted pine nuts
oil or butter for coating the bowl

Sprinkle the yeast and sugar over the warm water in a large bowl. Stir once and let sit for 5 minutes. Add the butter, salt, and eggs to the yeast mixture and stir until well blended or use a heavy-duty electric mixer. Add the flour, a little at a time, alternating with the pumpkin. The dough should still be soft. Sprinkle the cinnamon, nutmeg, and pine nuts over the dough and knead until well combined. Turn the dough out onto a lightly floured surface and knead for several minutes. Add more flour if necessary to keep it from sticking to the surface, although the dough will remain quite soft. When it is springy after being pushed with your thumb, shape it into a ball.

Oil or butter a large bowl, place the dough in it, and turn it around so that all sides are coated. Cover the bowl with plastic wrap and let sit in a warm place until doubled, about 1 hour.

When the dough has risen, punch it down and reshape it into a large ball. Pull off pieces to form 1½- to 2-inch balls and place them 2 inches apart on an oiled cookie sheet. Cover lightly with a damp towel and let rise until doubled in bulk.

Preheat the oven to 375 degrees F. When the rolls have completed rising, transfer the pan to the hot oven and bake until golden brown and they sound hollow when tapped, about 15–20 minutes. Remove the rolls from the oven and let cool on a rack.

VARIATION: SAVORY ORANGE-PUMPKIN ROLLS WITH PINE NUTS In a less traditional Colorado version of these dinner rolls, toast the pine nuts until deep golden brown and they give off an intense aroma. Omit the cinnamon and nutmeg, and substitute 1 teaspoon of finely crushed coriander seeds and the zest from 1 whole orange. If using a special zester, it will remove the rind in very thin, narrow strips. If you use a vegetable peeler, be careful to remove only the colored top rind, not the bitter white pith. Slice the skin into thin strips.

Sweet Aniseed Buns
Molletes de Anís
SANTA FE, NEW MEXICO

MAKES ABOUT 2½ DOZEN *Though this is my version of a recipe for the sweetened yeasty egg roll made by Spanish cooks throughout the Southwest, it comes from a tiny self-published recipe collection by Lucy Delgado entitled* Favorite Holiday Recipes. *It is similar to many others I tried in New Mexico, where it has long been a favorite treat flavored with aniseed or the wild safflower. As with other regional foods, similar rolls may be called by a different name, most commonly* bolletes, *but even more confusing, many families who come from Oaxaca or states in central Mexico will toast a split* bolillo *or hard roll and spread it with beans and cheese for breakfast, also calling it a* mollete.

While it is definitely not typical, I enjoy pairing these aniseed-flavored rolls with Carrot Soup (page 73) for a surprising flavor contrast.

1 package (¼ ounce) active granulated yeast	2 teaspoons aniseeds
¼ cup warm water	pinch of sea salt
1½ cups milk	2 beaten eggs
4 tablespoons unsalted butter	4–6 cups all-purpose flour
1 cup sugar	½ cup melted unsalted butter

In a small bowl, sprinkle the yeast over the warm water. Let it set until the yeast dissolves and becomes puffy.

Heat the milk with the butter over low heat until the butter melts. Pour into a large mixing bowl and stir in the sugar, aniseeds, and salt. When the mixture is lukewarm, gently mix in the yeast and eggs.

Gradually add just enough flour so the dough is soft but not sticky. Place the dough on a lightly floured surface and knead until smooth, about 4 minutes. Add more flour if necessary.

Oil or butter a large bowl, place the dough in it, and turn it around so that all sides are coated. Cover the bowl with plastic wrap or a slightly damp towel and let it set in a warm place until doubled in bulk, about 1 hour.

Punch it down and knead again for several minutes, still in the bowl. Cover and let rise again for 30 minutes.

Punch the dough down again and form into balls about 1½ inches in diameter. Place several inches apart on an oiled baking sheet and press down with the palm of your hand to slightly flatten the dough. Brush the top of the rolls with melted butter, cover, and let rise for another 45–60 minutes, until doubled in size. While they are rising, preheat the oven to 350 degrees F.

Bake the rolls until golden or until they sound hollow when thumped, about 30 minutes. Serve warm with lots of butter and with tea, coffee, or hot chocolate. The rolls can be wrapped in foil and reheated. They also freeze very well.

Corn Bread
Pan de Elote
GARDEN CITY, MICHIGAN • NUEVO LEÓN, MEXICO

MAKES 1 LOAF TO BE CUT INTO 12 TO 14 SLICES *Maria Petra Vasquez loves to bake, and she is often asked to make this rich corn bread for various fiestas. The day I visited at her home in the outskirts of Detroit, she had recently served it for an event honoring the Mexican consul for Costa Rica.*

Although her mother made her corn bread with lard, Petra uses butter and often margarine. You can use low-fat sour cream, but no-fat sour cream doesn't work. It is best if the corn has slightly lost its moist tenderness.

It is customary to set out a bowl of softened butter and honey for slathering onto the still warm corn bread, but it is equally good with dishes such as Steak and Potato Stew (page 92). Petra sometimes makes it in advance and serves it as a coffee cake for a midday or evening snack.

2 cups frozen corn kernels, slightly thawed, or kernels cut from about 3 large ears of fresh corn

1 cup all-purpose flour

1 cup milk

4 tablespoons melted unsalted butter

½ cup sour cream

2 eggs, well beaten

2 teaspoons baking powder

1 teaspoon grated onion (optional)

1 teaspoon sea salt

butter and flour for coating the pan

Preheat the oven to 325 degrees F.

Mix all the ingredients together in a bowl. Butter the sides and bottom of an 8½- by 11-inch baking pan and lightly dust with flour, shaking off any excess. Pour the batter into the pan and bake for about 45 minutes, or until crusty brown and a toothpick inserted in the center comes out clean.

Let the bread cool for 5 minutes before slicing.

Corn and Green Chile Bread

Pan de Elote y Chile

PHOENIX, ARIZONA

SERVES 6 TO 8 *Dina Mendival Lansdale's moist corn and chile bread is quite different from the conventional corn bread of our southern United States and closer to Mexico's* budín, *or corn torte, which is usually served with a sauce as a side dish or separate course. I found similar versions throughout Arizona and California.*

Serve with plenty of butter or with the sauce from a main dish, such as Chicken in a Piquant Tomato Sauce (page 152).

1 cup cornmeal

1 cup flour

1 cup sugar

1 tablespoon baking powder

1 teaspoon sea salt

1 14-ounce can creamed corn

½ pound grated Monterey jack and longhorn cheddar cheese mixed together

1 cup large-curd cottage cheese, drained

1 4.5-ounce can green chiles, finely chopped, or 6 canned jalapeño chiles, finely chopped

¼ cup corn or safflower oil or melted unsalted butter, cooled

1 egg, well beaten

Preheat the oven to 400 degrees F.

Mix the cornmeal, flour, sugar, baking powder, and salt together in a mixing bowl. In a larger bowl, stir together the creamed corn, cheese, cottage cheese, chiles, oil, and egg. Add the dry ingredients to the corn and cheese mixture, a little at a time, and stir until well blended.

Pour into a greased 9- by 13-inch pan and bake for about 30 minutes. It is done when a toothpick inserted in the bread comes out clean and the top is puffy and golden.

Tail-End Sweet Bread
Colitas de Pan
GARDEN CITY, MICHIGAN • NUEVO LEÓN, MEXICO

SERVES 8 TO 12 *"Habiendo hambre no hay pan duro." Being hungry, there is no hard bread. This popular dicho, or saying, is very much a way of life for Maria Petra Vasquez, who saves the heels and other slices of stale bread until she has enough to make this moist cakelike bread. Don't think of this as a bread pudding; the bread crumbs create a texture similar to a moist, chewy corn bread.*

Petra serves this at room temperature with coffee or as an after-school snack for her grandchildren, but it is equally good hot out of the oven with whipped cream or a scoop of vanilla ice cream.

12 slices mainly white bread, including ends
½ cup (1 stick) unsalted butter plus some for
  greasing the pan
1 teaspoon flour
2 cups milk
1 cup brown sugar

pinch of sea salt
1 egg and 1 egg white
2 teaspoons ground cinnamon (cassia)
½ cup raisins
½ cup coarsely chopped walnuts
½ teaspoon baking powder

In advance, tear apart the bread and allow to dry out in a warm oven or overnight. When ready to prepare the sweet bread, crumble the bread into tiny pieces and put in a large bowl. The food processor works very well for this but leave some texture. There should be about 10 cups of coarse, irregular crumbs.

Preheat the oven to 325 degrees F. Coat a 9- by 12-inch pan with butter and then sprinkle on the flour, shaking off any excess. Pour the milk into a medium-size saucepan, add the sugar, butter, and salt, and warm it over very low heat until the sugar dissolves and the butter melts.

recipe continues

Beat the egg and egg white in a small bowl until frothy and add to the bread. Add the cinnamon, raisins, walnuts, and baking powder, and toss thoroughly. Pour the milk mixture into the bread mixture, fully combining the liquid with the other ingredients.

Spoon everything evenly into the buttered and floured pan. Bake, uncovered, about 30 minutes, until light brown. Remove from the oven and let cool slightly before cutting into squares.

Spanish Fritters

Churros

NORTHBROOK, ILLINOIS

MAKES ABOUT 20, 4 INCHES LONG *Elaine González, a passionate and knowledgeable chocolate enthusiast, has built her career around the multiple uses of cacao beans. In the morning or after a long day, Elaine likes to drink a cup or two of piping hot chocolate, and into it she dunks the thin, crispy* churros *that are so loved throughout Spain and Mexico. I was lucky to persuade Elaine to share her mother's recipe with me. Elaine uses a* churrera, *a specially made metal squirt gun found in Spain for making* churros, *but a decorating bag works equally well if you use a large ½- or ⅜-inch fluted or star tube.*

I don't really like sweets, but it's no exaggeration to say I adore churros. *Elaine is the only home cook that I know who makes these special snacks, but I've tried them from street vendors in Chicago, New York City, and Los Angeles. The problem is that, like other fritters, they must be eaten freshly made and be still quite hot to touch, something that is seldom found in the United States, where they are usually fried in one place and only kept warm at the stands.*

½ cup water
½ cup milk
¼ teaspoon sea salt
1 tablespoon safflower or corn oil

1 cup all-purpose flour
1 large egg
peanut or safflower oil for frying
½ cup sugar

Place the water, milk, salt, and oil in a 1½-quart saucepan over medium-high heat and bring it to a boil. Add the flour all at once, lower the heat, and mix vigorously with a wooden spoon until it forms a stiff, dry ball.

Transfer the dough to the large bowl of an electric mixer and let it cool for about 5 minutes. Beat it on medium-high speed for 1 minute, or until the dough softens and becomes more malleable. Add the egg and continue beating. At first the dough will be in pieces, but as you continue to beat it, it will come together to form a smooth mixture. Set it aside to cool.

Meanwhile, heat at least 1 inch of oil in a deep 8- or 9-inch skillet until it reaches 350 degrees F. If the oil is not this hot, the *churros* will brown on the outside but remain raw on the inside. Cuff the top of a 12-inch decorating bag and insert a large star or fluted tube (½-inch opening). Fill the bag with half of the dough, uncuff the top, push the dough down toward the tube end, and twist the top of the bag closed. Hold the opening of the bag perpendicular to the skillet, about 3 inches above the surface, and squeeze out a 3- to 4-inch length of dough directly into the hot oil. Cut off the flow of the dough with a knife. Squeeze out 2 or 3 more lengths of dough depending on the size of the skillet. Fry each *churro* until golden brown on one side before flipping it over to the other side to brown. Drain on absorbent paper, sprinkle with sugar, and serve at once.

Thin Fritters with Syrup

Buñuelos

FIFE, WASHINGTON • MICHOACÁN, MEXICO

MAKES EIGHT 8-INCH OR TEN 6-INCH FRITTERS *The holidays are a time of both expectation and remembering; and for Mexican Americans many of the memories of Christmas involve* buñuelos, *the thin, crispy rounds of fried dough drenched in hot syrup. The eating is always a treat, but it is gathering together and watching them being made that makes them so special. The dough is first s-t-r-e-t-c-h-e-d over the cook's knee (usually a grandmother, as years of practice are needed to make the dough so transparent that you can almost see through it). Each flimsy circle is then slipped into a large cauldron of rippling hot oil, to emerge puffy and crisp.*

I first learned to make buñuelos *from two sisters in Morelia, Michoacán, who used the dried husks of tomatillos as a natural leavener instead of baking powder. One day when I was with a group of women from another smaller town in Michoacán, who with their families moved to Washington's Puyallup Valley, we began to discuss* buñuelos, *and I was pleased that they use almost the identical ingredients and methods that I do. This is my adaptation. I never can attain the perfection of their delicate sheets of fried dough, but I have a good time trying.*

Miguel likes an anise-flavored syrup as a topping, but they are equally good just dusted with a mixture of cinnamon and sugar, a common practice in the southwestern United States.

Some people insist on eating their buñuelos very crisp and with just enough of the hot syrup to make them sticky, while others prefer them broken into pieces and soaked in the syrup until soft. A spoon comes in handy then. A cup of Mexican Hot Chocolate (page 386) or Hot Chocolate Atole (page 384) is the traditional accompaniment.

For the Dough
10 tomatillo husks, rinsed, or ½ teaspoon baking powder (see Note)
½ cup (1 stick) unsalted butter or shortening
2 cups unbleached all-purpose flour
½ teaspoon sea salt
1 egg, lightly beaten

For the Syrup (optional)
1 tablespoon aniseed
1 pound dark brown sugar or crushed *piloncillo* (page 25)
1 cup fresh orange juice

For Frying
enough peanut or safflower oil for a deep fryer or 1 inch in a large deep skillet

For Topping (optional)
ground cinnamon (cassia)
granulated sugar

Place the husks in a saucepan and add 1 cup of water. Bring to a boil, lower the heat, and let simmer for 10 minutes. Stir occasionally and push the husks back under the water. After removing the husks, add the butter to the water. It will melt as the water cools.

Place the flour in a mixing bowl, mix in the salt, and form a well in the center. Slide in the egg and add the cooled tomatillo water, a few splashes at a time. Toss in a bit of the flour from the sides until the flour is completely absorbed. The dough should be moist but not sticky.

Turn the dough out on a lightly floured surface and knead vigorously until smooth and elastic. Oil or butter a mixing bowl, place the dough in it, and turn it around so that all sides are coated. Cover the bowl with a dry towel and let the dough rest for 30 minutes.

While the dough is resting, put the anise in a small saucepan with 1 cup of water and boil for 3 minutes. Strain, reserving the water. Reheat the anise-flavored water with the sugar and orange juice. Simmer over medium heat about 8 minutes, until it thickens and forms a light syrup or until the syrup reaches 210 degrees F. on a candy thermometer. Remove from the heat and rewarm later if necessary.

Depending on the size *buñuelos* that you want to make, form balls of dough 1½- to 2 inches in diameter. To form the *buñuelo:* Flatten each ball of dough between the palms of your hands. Then, holding by the edge, turn the dough and, with your fingers, work from the center to ease the dough out until it forms a thin 4- to 5-inch round. It will stretch quite thin, and if holes appear, they can be pinched together.

Lay the flattened dough on the lightly floured work surface and, working with the palm of your hand, flatten out the edges of the circle. Make the dough as thin and transparent as possible without tearing it, although a few holes are to be expected. Repeat with the rest of the dough and let the *buñuelos* rest for 20 minutes. This will help prevent bubbles from forming when the dough is fried.

Heat the oil over medium-high heat until very hot but not smoking (375 degrees F.). To test, drop in a small piece of dough; it should immediately sputter and become golden. Have absorbent paper spread out on a tray near the stove. Cook the *buñuelos* 1 at a time. Lay a circle of dough in the hot oil. It will puff up in little balloons and turn a light golden color. Turn over with 2 slotted spatulas and fry the other side for a few seconds. Remove from the oil and drain. When all the *buñuelos* are fried, serve immediately, dusted with cinnamon and sugar. Or traditionally, dribble the hot syrup over the hot *buñuelos* and serve in a wide bowl.

NOTE: If you prefer to stay with baking powder, simply mix in one-half teaspoon of the flour, rub softened butter or lard into it, and add the water.

Puffed Fry Bread

Sopaipillas

ALBUQUERQUE, NEW MEXICO

MAKES ABOUT 50 SMALL OR 25 LARGE ONES   *Think of the* sopaipillas *of New Mexico as a hybrid between the fry bread of the Pueblo Indians and the* buñuelos *of Mexico and Spain. At any meal in the upper Rio Grande Valley you can expect baskets of dough puffs in a variety of geometric shapes—triangles, squares, rectangles. Although* sopaipillas *are often served solo with honey and butter, or sliced and stuffed with beans, usually on the table is the triumvirate of* sopaipillas*, fiery chile stew, and sweet honey on the side to soothe the taste buds. Others prefer them as a dessert sprinkled with sugar and cinnamon or with caramel syrup. Farther south, the* sopaipillas *are apt to be smaller, like this* *version by centenarian Miguel Baca, who lived with his son on a small farm on the outskirts of Albuquerque. Pilar, one of his granddaughters, told me:*

> *My Abuelito [grandfather] Miguel, who worked for the railroad for many years, had large work-gnarled hands that stoked a pipe, cracked black walnuts on rocks behind the house, and cooked wonderful New Mexican foods, such as enchiladas New Mexican-style, chile (green New Mexican chile, that is), and sopaipillas. I remember Abuelito teaching us how to make sopaipillas like this. He'd walk into the kitchen, after taking off his Panama hat, roll up his sleeves, and don an apron. He would describe what he was doing, call me "mi hijita" and let me help him fix the food for the meal.*

While the sopaipillas are hot, wrap them in a napkin and set on the table in a basket, with a small pitcher of honey close by. Even if you are making the larger sopaipillas and fill them with Well-Fried Beans (page 227) and shredded cheese or Red Chile with Meat (page 174), keep the honey nearby, along with chopped lettuce, tomato, and Guacamole (page 274). The New Mexican Green Chile Relish (page 273) is another welcome addition.

4 cups all-purpose flour
2 teaspoons baking powder
1¼ teaspoons sea salt

4 tablespoons vegetable shortening or lard
about 3 cups peanut oil for frying

Sift the flour, baking powder, and salt together in a large mixing bowl. Using 2 knives or a pastry cutter, cut the shortening into the dry ingredients until a coarse meal is formed. Add just enough lukewarm water, about 1 cup, to soften the dough. Mix it in with a fork or your fingertips until it forms a sticky dough.

Turn the dough out on a lightly floured surface and knead and turn about 40 times. The dough will still be soft but no longer sticky. Roll into 4 balls, cover with a clean towel or plastic wrap, and let it rest for 20–30 minutes. The dough can be refrigerated for several hours if needed, but bring to room temperature before continuing.

One at a time, roll each ball of dough on a lightly floured work surface into a circular shape ⅛ inch thick. Cut out diamond-shaped wedges about 2 or 3 inches long on a side. Or if you want, the dough can be cut in other shapes or in a larger size. Since it's best not to rework the dough because it makes it tough, any extra-large pieces can be cut into other small, irregular shapes. Loosely cover the *sopaipillas* while forming the others.

In a large, heavy skillet or electric frying pan, heat 1 inch of oil to 400 degrees F. It will take several minutes. Test a small scrap of dough by dropping it into the hot oil. It should sizzle and puff up immediately. When the oil is hot enough, place the *sopaipillas*, a few at a time, into the oil and hold them under with a slotted spoon until they balloon, or spoon some hot oil over the top. Turn over after a few seconds and fry the other side. When light golden brown, lift them out with a slotted spoon and drain on absorbent paper. The bread can be kept warm in a 200-degree F. oven while frying the remainder, or they can be reheated at 350 degrees F.

Toasted Open-Faced
Bean Sandwich with Cheese
Molletes
SAN DIEGO, CALIFORNIA · MICHOACÁN, MEXICO

SERVES 4   *If you have refried beans on hand, this open-faced sandwich is a quick and unusual morning snack. They also come in handy for an informal autumn brunch. In New Mexico, molletes always referred to a sweet roll, usually flavored with aniseed. Elsewhere they were similar to the ones I've eaten in both Oaxaca and Michoacán—a crunchy bolillo or hard roll mounded with beans and melted cheese—although the ones from Texas were mighty hot, owing to an almost lethal amount of chopped jalapeño chiles.*

Ana Rosa Bautista, who manages the family guacamole business in San Diego, likes to put slices of avocado on top of the melted cheese. You also can mix fried Mexican Chorizo (page 170) with the beans, as I was served in El Paso.

Serve molletes *immediately with Chunky Fresh Tomato Salsa (page 264) or, if there are no ripe tomatoes available, Racy Red Tomato Salsa (page 270).*

1 tablespoon safflower or canola oil
½ white onion, thinly sliced
2 cups Well-Fried Beans (page 227) or canned
1–2 tablespoons pickled jalapeño chiles, chopped (optional)
Crusty Bread Rolls (page 310) or sourdough or other hard rolls

2 tablespoons melted unsalted butter or safflower or canola oil
4 ounces Monterey jack or cheddar cheese, grated

Preheat the oven to 375 degrees F.

Heat the oil in a medium-size skillet and sauté the onion over medium heat until golden. Add the beans and jalapeños, and stir until heated through.

Cut the rolls in half and scoop out most of the insides. Brush with butter and toast for 5 minutes on a cookie sheet. Fill the rolls with the bean mixture, sprinkle with grated cheese, and continue to bake until the rolls are crisp around the outside and the cheese is melted.

Ranch-Style Fried Eggs
Huevos Rancheros
PHOENIX, ARIZONA

SERVES 4   *This is one of the many egg dishes that Miguel remembers eating for* almuerzo—*the very big mid-morning meal—on Saturday or Sunday mornings, when he didn't have to go to school. This is how he recalls his role in the preparation:*

The whole family would sit together and eat—my grandfather, Don Miguel, at one end of the table, and my grandmother, Lupe, at the other. Sometimes we were fifteen people at the table at one time. My grandmother would always prepare the main dish. I remember my job was to make café con leche *(page 386) and iced tea or fruit drinks.*

Serve with Well-Fried Beans (page 227), fresh fruits, and café con leche *for a very traditional Mexican breakfast. The salsa ranchera used in this dish also is used frequently in other dishes, such as with beef, pork, and chicken.*

For the Salsa Ranchera
2 pounds ripe tomatoes (about 4 tomatoes)
  roasted (page 22), with skin left on
2 cloves garlic, roughly chopped
6 fresh serrano chiles, stemmed and roasted
  (page 21)
sea salt

2 tablespoons safflower or canola oil
2 tablespoons chopped white onion

For the Eggs
¼ cup safflower or canola oil
8 store-bought corn tortillas
8 eggs
sea salt

4 tablespoons Mexican *crema* (page 23) or sour
  cream thinned with milk

4 tablespoons crumbled *queso añejo, queso fresco,*
  or feta cheese

4 tablespoons chopped cilantro

Put the tomatoes, garlic, chiles, and salt in a food processor or blender and briefly puree, leaving some texture.

Heat the oil in a medium-size saucepan or skillet over medium-high heat. Add the onion and cook about 3 minutes. Pour in the tomato mixture and cook 4–5 minutes over high heat, until the sauce is somewhat thickened. It should reduce to about 1½ cups of sauce. Keep warm while the eggs are being prepared.

Heat the oil in a skillet over medium-high heat and fry the tortillas about 2 seconds on each side. Drain on absorbent paper, wrap in foil, and keep warm in a very low temperature oven.

Lower the heat under the skillet and fry the eggs as you like them, adding salt to taste. (The eggs can be poached instead; just start the water to boil before frying the tortillas.)

Overlap 2 tortillas on each plate, then top with 2 eggs. Spoon the *salsa ranchera* over the eggs, then the *crema*. Sprinkle on the crumbled cheese and cilantro, and serve.

Eggs Motul-Style with Ham, Peas, and Well-Fried Beans
Huevos Motuleños
LYNNWOOD, WASHINGTON • YUCATÁN, MEXICO

SERVES 4 *This colorful layered egg dish is a great favorite throughout the Yucatán Peninsula, but it was created many years ago by the owner of a restaurant in the little town of Motul, north of Mérida. It is only natural that huevos motuleños is a favorite breakfast dish of Ernesto Piño because Motul is where one part of his father's family lived. Ernesto prepares these eggs almost like a sandwich, with a tortilla both above and below the fried egg. For a less filling dish, the top tortilla can be omitted.*

The potent habanero is the chile of choice for flavoring this egg dish, but it should remain in the sauce only while it is cooking and then tossed away. If you use serrano chiles, they will become part of the sauce.

For the Sauce

2 tablespoons safflower or canola oil

1 white onion, diced

6 ripe medium tomatoes, roasted (page 22)

1 habanero chile, quartered, or 1–2 serrano or
jalapeño chiles, roasted (page 21) and peeled

about ½ teaspoon sea salt

For the Garnish

2 ripe plantains or firm bananas

6 ounces good-quality ham, julienned or
chopped

1 cup small frozen peas, partially defrosted

1 cup crumbled *queso fresco* or grated Monterey
jack cheese

Mexican *crema* (page 23) or sour cream thinned
with a little milk (optional)

For the Eggs

safflower or canola oil

8 store-bought corn tortillas

1½ cups Well-Fried Black Beans (page 227) or
canned

8 eggs

sea salt

Preheat the oven to 200 degrees F. to warm the plates and keep various foods warm.

To prepare the sauce, warm the oil in a medium-size skillet and fry the onion until golden. Place the roasted tomatoes—with all but the most charred parts of their skin—into a blender or food processor. If using serrano or jalapeño chiles, add just 1 to the blender and coarsely puree. Taste and add another chile if needed, and again briefly puree. Add the tomato mixture to the onion, and salt to taste. If using the habanero, stir it into the sauce. Cook over medium-low heat about 10 minutes, until the sauce thickens. Remove the chunks of the habanero chile and discard. The sauce can be made in advance and reheated.

Peel the plantains and cut in ¼-inch slices. In a large skillet, heat 2 tablespoons of oil over medium heat. Lay the plantain slices flat in the skillet and fry about 4 minutes a side until darkly browned. Remove with a slotted spatula, drain on a baking pan lined with absorbent paper, and keep warm in the oven along with the ham and peas. Put the cheese and cream in small bowls.

In the same skillet, over medium-high heat, fry the tortillas briefly, about 30 seconds, just to soften. Drain them on absorbent paper and keep warm.

Heat the beans. Lay 4 of the tortillas on warm plates and spread with a large spoonful of beans. Keep the tortillas warm while the eggs are frying.

In the same pan used for the tortillas, heat 1 tablespoon of oil and fry 2 eggs sunny-side up or, if you prefer, over lightly. (I prefer them with the yolk still soft but not as runny as I usually fix them.) Salt to taste.

Place 2 eggs on each of the bean-covered tortillas, spoon on a little sauce, and top with a second tortilla. Repeat with the remaining eggs and tortillas.

Pour the remaining sauce over the top tortillas and sprinkle with ham, peas, and cheese. If you want, add a spoonful of *crema* in the middle. Place the plantain slices around the edge of the plates.

Poached Eggs in Chile-Tomato Broth
Huevos "Rabo de Mestiza"
VICTORIA, BRITISH COLUMBIA, CANADA • MEXICO CITY, MEXICO

SERVES 2 WITH 2 EGGS APIECE   *The colloquial name for this egg dish loosely translates as "the rags and tatters of the daughter of a Spaniard and an Indian," but no one quite knows why. It is still served today in Mexican-American households in quite the same manner that it was prepared through the centuries in Mexico. This is my version of a very similar recipe by Maria Elena C. Lorens, who likes to serve* Rabo de Mestiza *as a principal dish for brunch. This can be increased for a small group.*

3 fresh ripe tomatoes, roasted (page 22), and
  coarsely chopped with the peels on
2 tablespoons butter, safflower, or canola oil
½ medium white onion, finely chopped
2 fresh poblano or Anaheim chiles, roasted (page
  21), peeled, seeded, and cut into strips

sea salt
4 large eggs

For the Garnish
1 cup Mexican *crema* (page 23) or sour cream
  thinned with milk
4 tablespoons crumbled *queso fresco* or feta cheese

Place the tomatoes in a blender with ½ cup of water and process until smooth. If the mixture is still dry, add a few more tablespoons of water.

Melt the butter in a medium-size skillet over medium-low heat and fry the onions about 3 minutes, until softened. Add the chile strips and cook just a few more minutes.

Add the tomatoes and salt to taste. Turn up the heat to medium and continue to cook about 5 minutes, until the sauce is thickened and well flavored.

Crack each egg into a small cup or custard dish and very carefully, so as not to break the yolks, slip gently into the sauce. Cook about 4 minutes, spoon some of the sauce over the egg as it cooks, until the yolk just begins to firm up. Remove the eggs from the sauce with a slotted spoon and slide onto warmed shallow bowls. Spoon the sauce around the eggs, add a dollop of *crema*, and sprinkle with the cheese. Serve immediately, accompanied by warm tortillas.

Mexican-Style Scrambled Eggs
Huevos a la Mexicana
AUSTIN, TEXAS

SERVES 4   *Along with* huevos rancheros, *this is the most common way—scrambled with chiles, onions, and tomato—that Mexicans and Mexican Americans prepare their breakfast eggs. Miguel makes his in the classic manner. About all that might be different is the type of fresh chile used.*

Well-Fried Beans (page 227), a few hot tortillas, and an extra fillip of Tomatillos and Green Chile Salsa (page 265), and you have one of Mexico's most satisfying breakfasts.

3 tablespoons safflower or canola oil, lard, bacon
   grease, or unsalted butter
½ medium white onion, finely chopped
1–2 fresh serrano or jalapeño chiles, finely chopped
2 medium ripe tomatoes, chopped
8 eggs, lightly beaten
about 1 teaspoon sea salt

For the Garnish
crumbled *queso fresco* or feta cheese (optional)
½ firm but ripe avocado, peeled and cut into ½-
   inch cubes

Heat the oil in a medium-size skillet over medium heat. Sauté the onion and chiles until just soft, add the tomatoes, and cook for 3–4 minutes.

Pour the eggs into the skillet and let them set for a minute, then sprinkle with salt and stir gently with a fork or wooden spoon. Lower the heat if they are cooking too quickly. The eggs should be folded together with the tomato mixture until softly set but not dried out. Serve quickly, with a sprinkle of crumbled cheese and avocado.

VARIATION: SCRAMBLED EGGS WITH EPAZOTE OR CILANTRO   Add 2 cloves of chopped garlic to the onion and chiles when they are frying and mix a chopped sprig of fresh epazote or 2 or 3 sprigs of cilantro and a pinch of ground cumin into the eggs before they are scrambled.

Scrambled Eggs with Cactus and Chorizo

Huevos Revueltos con Nopales y Chorizo

SACRAMENTO, CALIFORNIA

SERVES 4   *This is one of those dishes that is exceedingly simple, yet very special. Lupe Viramontes, whose recipe this is, likes to add chorizo, but be certain it is freshly prepared by the butcher or use your own. Patricia Flores in Tucson uses a big handful of cheese in her eggs. Some cooks add oregano, some fresh jalapeños. Lupe's version is the way my husband, Fredric, likes to prepare them for a Sunday breakfast.*

For an unusual breakfast or supper dish, Maria McRitchie in Oregon likes to wrap the eggs and cactus in huge warm flour tortillas. You can have them available along with a bowl of your favorite salsa. The flavors of Green, Green Salsa (page 267) will complement and not overwhelm the eggs.

2 cups canned cactus, drained and well rinsed, or 2 pads fresh cactus, cooked (page 54–55)

1 tablespoon safflower or canola oil

¼ pound (about 2 links) freshly prepared Mexican Chorizo, store-bought or homemade (page 170)

½ medium white onion, finely chopped

8 large eggs

1 teaspoon dried chile flakes (optional)

sea salt and freshly ground black pepper

For the Garnish

1 tablespoon chopped cilantro

Thoroughly rinse the cactus to wash away the *baba* (saliva). If needed, chop into ½-inch pieces. Drain and pat dry.

Heat the oil in a large, heavy skillet and fry the chorizo over medium heat until well browned. Add the onion and sauté until transparent. Stir in the cactus and continue to fry 2–3 minutes more.

While the chorizo, onion, and cactus are cooking, beat the eggs lightly in a small bowl with the chile flakes, salt, and pepper. Pour the eggs into the skillet, let set a moment, and cook to taste, gently stirring from time to time. Serve immediately, topped with a sprinkle of cilantro.

Sonoran Cheese Omelet

Omelette con Queso Estilo Sonora

SUMNER, WASHINGTON • SONORA, MEXICO

SERVES 1   *Tina Aguilar and I have been friends for many years. Tiny and vivacious, she works in administration at the University of Washington but still has the energy to help her husband in his continuing efforts on behalf of the Mexican community. Ernie was one of the founders of the Washington State Hispanic Chamber of Commerce, and is currently president of the Centro Mexicano del Estado de Washington.*

This extremely satisfying omelet is one of their favorite weekend breakfast dishes, and I serve it for supper with Caesar Salad with Chipotle Chile (page 50). To prepare a perfect omelet, it helps to have an 8- or 9-inch special omelet pan with sloping sides and a nonstick finish.

Chilaquiles (page 215) are Tina's usual choice to pair with the spicy omelet, but Well-Fried Beans (page 227) or Pureed Beans with Cheese and Ancho Chiles (page 229) also match well. Serve a platter of fresh fruit to start.

2 eggs
1 tablespoon chopped fresh jalapeño chile
1 tablespoon finely chopped white onion
1 tablespoon chopped ripe tomato
a scant ½ teaspoon sea salt
1 tablespoon unsalted butter or safflower or
  canola oil
1 tablespoon shredded Monterey jack cheese

For the Topping
1–2 tablespoons Mexican *crema* (page 23) or sour
  cream thinned with a little milk (optional)
1 teaspoon chopped flat-leaf parsley (optional)

Break the eggs into a small bowl and beat lightly with a fork. Add 1 tablespoon of water if you want a fluffier omelet. Add the salt.

Melt the butter in a small skillet over medium heat. When it is bubbly, stir in the chile, onion, and tomato and cook about 2 minutes. Raise the heat and pour in the egg mixture. Continually shake the pan. Lift up the edges of the egg and tip the pan so that the uncooked egg will slide underneath.

When the egg is almost cooked through, sprinkle with the cheese. Tilt the pan and roll or fold the omelet away from you.

To serve, hold a plate next to the pan and carefully slide out the omelet. If you want, drizzle with *crema* and sprinkle with parsley.

VARIATION: *CHORIZO OMELET* Substitute 2 tablespoons of cooked Mexican Chorizo (page 170) for the cheese and chopped jalapeño chile.

Spanish Potato Omelet
Tortilla Española de Papa
CHULA VISTA, CALIFORNIA

SERVES 6 TO 8 *A tortilla is not always made of ground corn or wheat. All it has in common with its Spanish counterpart is its name, both being derived from its Latin root—*torte*—meaning a round cake. In Spain it is an omelet, and the all-time popular choice is a simple one made of potatoes and usually eaten at room temperature as a* tapa, *or appetizer.*

When Carmen Mesto has black beans left over from a meal, she prepares her youngest son's and her husband's favorite egg dish—a Spanish omelet topped with pureed black beans and crema.

This omelet is much more apt to show up as a supper dish than for breakfast, but it is very versatile. I like to pair it with garden-ripened sliced tomatoes or a big green salad, such as Watercress Salad with Pine Nuts (page 52), or for a buffet at room temperature in wedges with just a favorite salsa.

¾ cup olive oil

2 whole cloves garlic

1½ pounds red-skinned potatoes, about 6, peeled, then sliced in half lengthwise and cut into ⅛-inch slices

1 large yellow onion, thinly sliced

sea salt

8 eggs

1 4½-ounce can chopped green chiles, drained

freshly ground black pepper

For the Garnish

1½ cups black beans mashed with bean broth

1 cup Mexican *crema* (page 23) or sour cream, thinned with milk

Warm the oil in a 9-inch nonstick or cast-iron skillet. Flatten the garlic with the back of a knife, add to the oil, and sauté. When golden brown, remove and discard. Add the potatoes in a single layer, then the onion, salting each layer lightly. Cook over medium heat for about 20 minutes, until the potatoes are tender but not brown. Turn them from time to time so they do not stick together.

Remove the potatoes and onions with a slotted spatula and put them on absorbent paper to drain off any excess oil. Discard all but 2 tablespoons of the oil, scraping off any stuck pieces of potatoes. The bottom of the pan should be very clean and smooth.

Whisk the eggs in a large bowl and add salt and pepper to taste. Add the potatoes and green chiles, pressing down so that the eggs thoroughly coat them.

Reheat the oil in the skillet over high heat. Spread the potato and egg mixture evenly over the bottom of the pan. Turn the heat to low, cover, and cook until about 1 inch around the edges of the eggs is set, but the eggs are still liquid in the center. Uncover, lift the edges with a spatula, and tilt the pan so that the uncooked eggs run underneath.

Heat the beans in a small saucepan and keep warm, but don't let them dry out.

When the egg mixture begins to brown on the bottom, invert a large flat plate or rimless baking sheet over the pan and flip the skillet over so that the omelet is on the plate. Another spoonful of oil may be needed in the skillet before sliding the omelet back into the pan, cooked side up. This can be repeated several times until both sides are brown but the center is still moist. Slide the omelet onto a warm serving platter, cut into wedges, and serve hot with the beans spooned on top and dollops of *crema*. Accompany it with hot Crusty Bread Rolls (page 310) or other hard rolls.

Broken-up Tortillas Scrambled with Bacon and Eggs
Migas con Tocino y Huevos
DETROIT, MICHIGAN • NUEVO LEÓN, MEXICO

SERVES 2 OR 3   Migas, *the Spanish word for crumbs, are a universal favorite with Mexican Americans almost everywhere I went in the United States. In Spain, where this dish originated,* migas *are made with crispy cubes of golden-fried bread and tossed with ham or bacon instead of tortillas. I've never eaten it either way in Mexico, but it is certainly a "kissing cousin" to chilaquiles (page 215). Frugal cooks combine broken-up old tortillas with eggs, some onions, garlic, chile, and a chopped tomato, to create a filling and economical meal. As Bettie Lee Taylor in Sacramento told me, "This way my great-aunt could feed eight people on just three eggs." I particularly like this version from Beatriz Esquivel, a* *bilingual teacher in Detroit. She adds both jalapeño chiles and red bell peppers to heighten the flavor, along with a big pinch of cumin. Making* migas *invites creativity, so experiment with other additions.*

The melted bacon fat can be used as part or all of the oil for frying the tortilla bits. It will add flavor but, of course, will also raise the cholesterol count.

This hearty breakfast dish can be doubled or even tripled to serve for a casual brunch, although it would be best to prepare the bacon and tortillas in advance and cook the eggs in batches. Set the migas *out in an earthenware or pottery casserole dish. Add a pitcher of freshly squeezed juice, Spiced Pork and Apple Turnovers (page 44), a Jicama, Melon, and Orange Salad (page 57), and a pot of Cowboy Beans (page 226), and nobody will go away hungry.*

The migas *can be served with Chunky Fresh Tomato Salsa (page 264) or other fresh tomato salsa and a large spoonful of Well-Fried Beans (page 227) on the side. Silvia Sosa's children like their* migas *covered with ketchup.*

2 thick slices bacon	½ red bell pepper, seeded and finely chopped (optional)
3 tablespoons safflower or canola oil	6 ripe plum tomatoes, coarsely chopped
6 leftover corn tortillas, slightly dried and torn into 1- to 1½-inch pieces	½ teaspoon cumin
½ medium white onion, finely chopped	4 eggs, lightly beaten
3 cloves garlic, minced	½ cup grated Monterey jack or white cheddar cheese
2 fresh jalapeño chiles, seeded and finely chopped	sea salt and freshly ground black pepper

Place the bacon in a small cold skillet and cook slowly until it is crispy. Remove the bacon strips and drain on absorbent paper. The bacon can be fried in advance and set aside.

In a large, heavy skillet, warm the oil over medium-high heat and quickly fry the tortilla pieces—about a handful at a time—until very lightly gold. They should be rather crispy but still chewy. Remove and drain them on absorbent paper. Continue cooking in batches until all the tortilla bits are fried. The tortillas can be fried ahead and set aside.

Add the onion, garlic, chiles, and bell pepper, and cook until the onions are slightly yellow and the chiles are tender. (It may be necessary to add more oil.) Crumble the bacon and stir it in along with the tomatoes and cumin. Cook several minutes, then add the tortilla pieces, mixing in thoroughly.

Pour the eggs over the tortilla mixture and stir in the cheese and salt and pepper to taste. Continue to stir gently until the eggs are just set and the cheese has melted. Serve immediately.

Easy Migas
Migas Fáciles

SANTA ANA, CALIFORNIA • CHIHUAHUA, MEXICO

SERVES 4 TO 6   *Instead of waiting until she has leftover tortillas, María Gonzáles de Herrera likes migas so much that whenever she wants a quick supper, she buys a bag of unsalted corn tortilla chips. Fifteen minutes later her meal is ready to eat. Now a new grandmother, María will have the opportunity to introduce yet another child to this satisfying heap of chewy tortilla chips and eggs.*

To make this dish even easier, substitute 1 cup of your favorite salsa for our fresh version.

Serve with Well-Fried Beans (page 227) and your favorite salsa.

2 tablespoons safflower or canola oil
½ cup chopped white onion
3 fresh serrano or jalapeño chiles, seeded and
  chopped
2 cloves garlic, minced
6 ripe plum tomatoes, chopped
sea salt and freshly ground black pepper

For the Migas

8 eggs
50 unsalted tortilla chips (about a 10-ounce bag),
  slightly broken up
2 tablespoons unsalted butter
¼ cup shredded *queso añejo* or Parmesan cheese

Warm the oil in a medium-size skillet and sauté the onion and chiles over medium-high heat. Add the garlic, cook for 1 minute, and add the tomatoes. Lower the heat and simmer for 10 minutes. Add salt and pepper to taste, and keep warm.

In a large bowl, beat the eggs lightly and carefully fold in the tortilla chips.

Melt the butter over medium heat in a large, heavy skillet or earthenware casserole. Pour in the egg mixture and cook very briefly, stirring constantly, until the eggs are set but not dry. Remove from the heat and fold in the sauce. Taste and add more salt or pepper if necessary. Scatter the cheese over the top before serving.

Deluxe Breakfast Burrito

Burritos para el Desayuno

HOMESTEAD, FLORIDA • TAMAULIPAS, MEXICO

MAKES 4 *Along the Mexican border and in Florida I found various versions of these burritos being served not only for breakfast but also throughout the day. Elroy Garza often brings these to work, filled with scrambled eggs and wrapped in aluminum foil. For brunches, serve bowls of different fillings, a plate of tortillas wrapped with a cloth, and some warmed chile sauce, red or green, to suit everyone's taste.*

Serve with lots of Chunky Fresh Tomato Salsa (page 264) and a small scoop of Well-Fried Beans (page 227).

4 Flour Tortillas (page 125) or store-bought, 7–8 inches in diameter

4 thick slices bacon

½ white onion, chopped into ½-inch pieces

¾ pound new potatoes, boiled and cut into ½-inch dice

⅛ teaspoon ground cumin

sea salt and freshly ground black pepper

3 eggs, lightly beaten

¼ cup chopped canned green chiles

¼ cup shredded Monterey jack cheese

½ ripe avocado, peeled and cut into ½-inch dice

Wrap the tortillas in foil and warm in a 250-degree F. oven.

Fry the bacon in a heavy skillet or nonstick sauté pan over medium-high heat. Remove the pieces when crispy, drain on absorbent paper, and crumble. Add the onion to the skillet and sauté until softened. Stir in the potatoes and sprinkle with cumin and salt and pepper to taste. Fry for about 10 minutes, until the potatoes are nicely browned. You may have to scrape the bottom of the pan with a spatula so that the potatoes do not stick. Lower the heat and stir in the eggs and green chiles. Scramble gently with a fork until the eggs are thoroughly set but still moist. Remove from the heat and stir in the cheese and crumbled bacon.

Spoon ¼ of the mixture across the middle of each warmed tortilla, leaving room for folding. Sprinkle on some diced avocado and fold down. Turn in each side of the tortilla, slightly overlapping the filling. Fold up the bottom side to cover more of the filling, then roll into a cylinder.

VARIATION: NEW MEXICAN BREAKFAST BURRITO Most New Mexican chefs seem to crave their burritos smothered with a red chile sauce and baked with grated cheese. When the cheese is just melted, Mexican *crema* (page 23) is squiggled over the top, and the burrito is then decorated with finely chopped green onions.

New York Impressions

Mexican villages nestle within the confines of this big city, jostling and rearranging themselves around the shapes of other established neighborhoods. In the past few decades, according to the Mexican consul's cultural attaché, at least 93,000 Mexicans have streamed into all the city's five boroughs—establishing barrio-like communities throughout. Most of the new families are from Mexico, the majority from the towns and villages of Puebla, Guererro, Oaxaca, and Morelos, a contiguous pocket of states southwest of Mexico City.

Some of the earliest Mexicans to settle in New York were wealthy landowners from Yucatán. After the revolution ended with only a few of its goals realized, the country, in 1934, elected Lázaro Cárdenas, the former governor of Michoacán, as president. An honest and reform-minded leader, he set out to accomplish by law what guns had not achieved: raising the living standards of the working class and redistributing millions of acres of land that had been formerly appropriated into large haciendas, including those in Yucatán dedicated to hemp growing. For some of these families, New York City became their new home.

World War II brought the next wave—men and later their families from the central Mexican states of Jalisco and Michoacán. In Brooklyn's Sunset Park and around Union Avenue, sidewalk stands proclaim the famous Michoacán *helados,* or ice creams, and the numerous restaurants dish up the traditional meat specialties from these two regions: *carnitas* from Michoacán and Jalisco's *birria.*

Following the familiar pattern of immigrants to New York, many of the families I talked with have moved out of the city. While continuing to work in the Bronx or Manhattan, they now live in nearby suburbs on Long Island or in Westchester County.

Apolonio Mariano Ramirez was fourteen years old when he left his village of Huehuepiaxta, Puebla, for New York City to join his father. When his father became ill and returned to Mexico after less than a year, Apolonio—who by then was calling himself Mario—stayed and began his culinary career. Mario longed for many of those special *poblano* flavors he couldn't find in New York City and planned one day to have his own Mexican restaurant—but not until he could provide the missing ingredients to make the dishes taste the way they had when his mother, Imelda, prepared them. When he had saved enough money for a down payment, he purchased a fifty-acre plot of land in upstate New York, and there he began to grow *pápalo, hoja santa,* epazote, cilantro, and other hard-to-find herbs, chiles, vegetables, and fruits—even the proper corn for his handmade tortillas.

Finally, Mario opened Rinconcito Mexicano on West Thirty-ninth Street, a block or so from the Port Authority bus terminal. A handsome, midsize man now probably in his late thirties, his dark eyes sparkle and his whole face radiates excitement when he talks about the dishes he had learned to prepare at home and was now cooking in his home and restaurant kitchens—*moles* and other unusual meat and vegetable dishes that I'd never seen outside of Puebla.

Mario is expanding both his restaurant and his menu, but one item that will never appear on it is tamales. Mario walked over with me to Eighth Avenue, about one hundred feet from Rinconcito Mexicano, where every afternoon and early evening Mexican women sell tamales from motorized cooking wagons. "That is their livelihood," he told me. "I don't take business away from my people."

Sweet Endings
Postres

I am trying to think of something my father enjoyed. Sweets.
Any kind of sweets. Candies. Nuts. Especially the gore oozing from the
baker's wreath. Carlyle writes in The French Revolution *about the*
predilection of the human race for sweets; that so much life is unhappiness
and tragedy. Is it any wonder that we crave sweets? Just so did my father,
who made false teeth, love sweets."

—RICHARD RODRIGUEZ, *DAYS OF OBLIGATION:*
AN ARGUMENT WITH MY MEXICAN FATHER

WHEN I ASKED ABOUT DESSERTS, Teresa Vigil started talking about "the embroidered set of white tea towels we all grew up with—'Monday for washing' through to Friday being 'pie day.' We always made pies on Friday for the coming weekend, and almost always from fruits we had gathered or grown ourselves. When you don't have, you improvise."

Teresa, a former nurse and the local authority on the herbs and wild plants of the area, described to me how she returned to the isolated valley of San Luis in southern Colorado after spending twenty-eight years growing up in San Francisco. This valley was where her grandparents and many generations of her mother's family were born, and they were baptized in the same church where she now works.

All around the headwaters of the Rio Grande grow squawberries, or *garambuyos*, somewhat like fat orange or black currants. They are picked by the bushel basket and used to make pies. For Teresa, these are a familiar favorite, and in the colder months, pumpkin and dried fruits take the berry's place.

During my crisscrossing of the country, I had many opportunities to sample the sweet endings to family dinners. Since I was often company, some member of the family would usually spend the extra time to make a pie or one of the more classic Mexican desserts with their obvious Spanish heritage—a flan, rice pudding, or custard.

One of the most welcomed contributions of United States technology to those desserts has been canned sweetened and condensed milk, followed later by evaporated milk. Lack of refrigeration was an early reason for their popularity with Mexican cooks; now they have become a tradition.

Except for holidays, feast days, and special family or company dinners, not much is served at the end of a meal except fresh fruit, ice cream, and perhaps a few cookies. Gelatins are an exception to the rule, as popular among Mexican Americans as they are in Mexico. Mostly made with plain gelatin and then flavored with everything from tequila and wine to coffee and various fruit juices, they become very intriguing and original desserts. But for those celebrations that commemorate special occasions—baptism; a daughter's *quinceañera*, that special fifteenth birthday; weddings; and holidays such as Christmas and Easter—time-honored sweets of Mexico are brought to the table. Desserts provide the final sweet touch for all times of rejoicing.

QUINCEAÑERAS

*T*he small Catholic church in Mountain Home, Idaho, was festive with green and white balloons. Six guitarists accompanied the singer; her words expressed how wonderful it was for a young woman to become fifteen. After all the friends and family were seated, down the center aisle walked a few dozen teenagers—the girls in green party dresses, the young men in tuxedos—and with them was Veronica Marie, about to publicly profess that she accepted the Christian way of life in which she had been raised.

A traditional quinceañera like this is one of the major events in the religious and social lives of Catholic Mexican females. It is a celebration that often eclipses even the wedding day, for it is their day alone. It is so important that all the friends of the family financially support the festivities; one donating the music, one the dress, and another the decorations. The accompanying excitement seemed just as evident in the United States, as I became aware while listening to Josephina Lopez in Los Angeles and Marisol Dominguez in Chicago, and later by participating in Veronica's quinceañera. The event means they have come of age and are ready to go out into the world. Not long ago in Mexico the average life span for a woman was forty years, and by the time she was sixteen, she was expected to have a husband and be raising a family. One mother told me, "We were always dressed as brides at our quinceañeras in case we ran off with a man before we were officially married."

The times have changed. As the priest said to Veronica, "Times are very different now. We know you need a longer time to mature and to make the decisions that will shape the rest of your life." But then, when padrino and madrina (godfather and godmother) and many sponsors came forward to attest to Veronica's goodness and to present her with gifts—among them a crown, ring, necklace, and earrings—the ceremony could just as easily have been one hundred years ago.

After the ceremony comes the party, usually in a rented hall, with music, dancing, and always heaping platters of food. Frijoles charros share the tables with mashed potatoes, mole negro with sliced ham, tortillas and rolls, every kind of salad, and always lots of punch and plates and plates of cakes, cookies, and other sweets.

Compote of Mango, Papaya, and Strawberries
Frutas en Almíbar
ALLEN PARK, MICHIGAN • QUERÉTARO, MEXICO

SERVES 6   *It may seem strange to combine strawberries with such tropical fruits as mangoes and papayas, but it is very natural for Florencio Perea. Querétaro, where he grew up, lies high on a vast plateau north of Mexico City. The strawberries that grow in its fertile valleys are famous throughout Mexico, but even though the climate is too temperate for mangoes and papayas, they flourish in the hot, humid weather in neighboring Veracruz. Served plain, this mixture of fruits was a frequent breakfast starter,* and in our version a simple syrup made of honey and sweet wine transforms it into the perfect dessert to follow a heavy meal.

The mangoes and papayas found in U.S. supermarkets are often still green and hard. If so, don't be afraid to substitute another combination of fruit. I particularly like peaches, and I've used pineapple when truly ripe.

This compote is a very nice ending to a meal featuring a mole. For special meals try the fruit alongside slices of Pine Nut Torte (page 368), served with more of the slightly sweet gewürztraminer.

1 cup gewürztraminer wine
½ cup orange blossom or another aromatic
 honey
juice of 2 oranges

¼ cup orange liqueur (optional)
3 ripe mangoes, peeled
1 small ripe papaya, peeled and seeded
16 large ripe strawberries, hulled

Mix the wine, honey, and orange juice in a small saucepan and bring the mixture to a simmer. Pour into a bowl and, when cool, add the orange liqueur. Slice the mangoes and papayas into ¼ by 1-inch pieces directly into the syrup. Cover and chill for several hours or more so that the flavors meld. The compote can be prepared to this point up to 12 hours in advance.

About 1 hour before serving, slice the strawberries and mix with the other fruit. Return the compote to the refrigerator until ready to serve.

Creamy Coffee Liqueur Gelatin
Gelatina de Licor de Café
BRITISH COLUMBIA, CANADA • MEXICO CITY, MEXICO

SERVES 4 *Every region of Mexico produces its own special liqueurs: sweet or astringent liquors flavored with the fruits, herbs, or nuts from their particular area. Raisin-based* pasita *from Puebla, served with a small cube of white cheese;* xtabentún, *Mérida's liquor of anise and honey; and* xanath *from Veracruz's vanilla are all well worth seeking if you are traveling to Mexico.*

It is the coffee liqueurs, though, such as Kahlua, that most people associate with Mexico; indeed, these are even more popular in the United States than in Mexico. We combined strong coffee with condensed milk to heighten the flavor of Maria Elena Lorens's deliciously light dessert. Chocolate-covered coffee beans are available in many gourmet food shops.

This gelatin is simple enough to follow a hearty meal of Meatballs in Chipotle Sauce (page 182) and has enough elegance to complete a dinner featuring Chicken with Spicy Prune Sauce (page 154).

1 envelope unflavored gelatin

1 14-ounce can sweetened condensed milk

2 heaping teaspoons instant espresso coffee granules

3 egg yolks

¼ cup milk

½ cup coffee liqueur

For the Garnish

1 cup heavy cream, whipped

16 chocolate-covered coffee beans (optional)

4 sprigs of mint (optional)

Sprinkle the gelatin over ¼ cup of water in a small bowl and let it stand about 2 minutes until absorbed and "fluffy."

Combine the condensed milk, the coffee granules, and 1 cup of water, in a medium-size pan. Heat over medium heat until the mixture just begins to boil. Remove the pan from the heat and stir in the gelatin until completely dissolved. Cool.

In a separate bowl, beat the egg yolks and milk together. Add to the gelatin along with the coffee liqueur.

Strain the mixture into dessert glasses and refrigerate for 4 to 12 hours, or pour into lightly oiled individual molds or a large 4-cup mold. To unmold, dip in very hot water for several seconds, then turn over onto a chilled serving plate.

Garnish the gelatin with a dollop of whipped cream and a chocolate-covered coffee bean or a sprig of mint.

Gelatin of Three Milks with an Orange Prune Sauce

Gelatina de Tres Leche con Salsa Dulce de Naranja y Ciruela Pasa

CHICAGO, ILLINOIS • GUANAJUATO, MEXICO

SERVES 4 TO 6 *It's not a coincidence that whenever Pamela Díaz de León has time to cook, she turns out wonderful sweets and pastries. Although now an active young Chicago businesswoman, her earlier years were spent in Celaya, Guanajuato, a candy-making town famed equally for soft, caramel cajeta made of rich goat's milk and for its strawberries, which are as sweet as any I've ever eaten. Every*

Monday, Pamela's grandmother played cards, and it was Pamela's responsibility to prepare the dulces, or sweets, for the ladies to eat. They had to be not so heavy as to put them to sleep but with enough sweetness to give the ladies energy for another hand of bridge, so gelatins were often the solution.

This shimmering milk-white gelatin is imbued with three different types of milk, each adding its own flavor and consistency. The result is a very refreshing dessert with a pale color and silky texture that give it a special elegance. It is delicious just dusted with ground cinnamon and topped with crushed or sliced mangoes or strawberries, or it can be drizzled with chocolate syrup. I like to prepare a sauce for the gelatin that is a special mixture of liqueur-marinated prunes and oranges. I adapted this from a recipe given to me by a friend of mine in Mexico City, María Dolores Torres Yzábal. It will need to be made several days in advance so the prunes become properly tipsy.

While usually made as a molded dessert, this is equally attractive served directly out of a crystal parfait glass or wineglass. Just eliminate the oiling of the container and the unmolding. Add a few crispy Aniseed Cookies (page 362) on the side of each plate when presenting this distinctive dessert. Together they make a festive ending to a meal of Meatballs in Chipotle Sauce (page 182).

For the Sauce

12 large pitted prunes, cut into strips
1 cup amaretto or an orange liqueur
zest or peel from ½ orange, cut in 1- to 2-inch
    narrow strips

For the Gelatin

2 envelopes unflavored gelatin
1 12-ounce can evaporated milk
1 ½ cups whole or 2% milk
1 14-ounce can condensed milk
1 tablespoon vanilla extract
1 tablespoon rum or brandy (optional)

Place the prunes in a 1-quart jar with a lid and cover with boiling water. When the water cools, pour it off and replace it with the liqueur, covering the prunes completely. Add the orange peel and let it all infuse for several days or up to 2 weeks if possible. The prunes do not require refrigeration.

Lightly oil 4 to 6 small individual serving molds, each holding 1–1½ cups.

Sprinkle the gelatin over 1½ cups of cold water in a small saucepan. Let stand without stirring for 1 minute. Place over low heat until the gelatin is completely dissolved and is crystal clear. Don't let it come close to boiling. Remove the saucepan from the heat and set aside to cool slightly.

Using a hand or electric beater, slowly blend the 3 milks together, starting with the evaporated milk, then the whole or 2% milk, and finishing with the condensed milk. Try not to create many bubbles as you beat.

Stir gelatin into the milk mixture, add the vanilla and rum or brandy, and pour into the mold(s). Refrigerate for a minimum of 2 hours and unmold when ready to serve.

When unmolding, cut around the edge of the mold with a warm knife to allow air to enter. Shake gently to loosen the gelatin. Cover the mold with a chilled dessert plate, turn upside down, and lift off the mold. If the gelatin doesn't come sliding out, tap or shake it lightly. If all else fails, dip the mold quickly into hot water and repeat the process.

Place the plates of gelatin in the refrigerator until time to serve, then spoon the orange-prune sauce over the top and around the edge of the gelatin. If serving in individual parfait glasses or wineglasses, spoon the sauce on top.

Mexican Eggnog Gelatin
Gelatina de Rompope

SERVES 4 *Hidden away among a stack of notes Miguel and I had collected on desserts, I found a small sheet of yellow-lined paper with the recipe for this delightful gelatin—one made with thick Mexican eggnog called* rompope. *Rich and creamy on the tongue, it tastes of cinnamon with a lick of brandy. I am only sorry that I can't acknowledge the source.*

Rompope, another of those egg-rich creations of the Mexican convents, is far better when you make it yourself. Since it keeps a long time in the refrigerator, I always like to have some on hand. A pre-made version can, however, be purchased in Hispanic grocery stores that sell alcoholic beverages and in some liquor stores.

This sweet is equally at home on a rustic menu that might include Cascabel Chile-Sauced Tacos (page 119) or with more sophisticated dishes of moles.

For the Rompope (makes 1 quart)
4 cups milk
1 cup sugar
3 inches cinnamon bark
¼ teaspoon baking soda
12 egg yolks
½ cup brandy

For the Gelatin
2 cups milk
¼ teaspoon baking soda
¼ cup sugar
4 inches true cinnamon bark or cinnamon stick
  (cassia)

ingredients continue

1½ envelopes unflavored gelatin
½ cup heavy cream

fresh berries or frozen berries

In a medium-sized saucepan over medium heat, mix together the milk, sugar, cinnamon bark, and baking soda. When it begins to boil, lower the heat and simmer about 20 minutes. Set aside to cool, and strain to remove the cinnamon bark.

Place the egg yolks in a mixing bowl and whisk or beat with an electric mixer about 5 minutes, until thick and lemon yellow. While still beating slowly, pour the cool milk mixture into the yolks. Return to the saucepan and cook over low heat, stirring constantly, until the mixture thickens and lightly coats the back of a wooden spoon.

Remove from the heat and stop the cooking by pouring the *rompope* into a bowl (preferably metal) that is resting on ice in a large bowl. Stir until cool. Gradually stir in the brandy and it's ready to serve, or it can be tightly covered and stored in the refrigerator.

When ready to make the gelatin, bring the milk to a boil in a medium saucepan over medium-high heat, then immediately remove from the heat and add the baking soda, sugar, and cinnamon bark. Bring to a boil again, then set aside to cool. Remove the cinnamon bark.

Soak the gelatin in ⅓ cup of cold water. Add to the milk mixture with the *rompope*, stirring until the gelatin is completely dissolved.

Whip the cream in a bowl until it stands in peaks. Fold the whipped cream into the gelatin and pour into a lightly oiled 1-quart mold or 4 individual molds. Chill for at least 3 hours before unmolding. This can be made up to 1 day in advance.

Turn the mold out onto a chilled serving plate and cut into wedges to serve, or put the 4 molds on individual dessert plates. Spoon a few berries on the top and around the side of the gelatin.

Almond Meringue Pudding
Almendrada
TUCSON, ARIZONA

SERVES 6 TO 8   *It's difficult to describe the* almendrada *of Arizona. A bit like* natillas, *those custards lightened with fluffy egg whites that are found in other parts of the Southwest and Mexico, the* almendrada *has custard that is used more as a sauce, on top of an uncooked meringue stabilized with gelatin. We found this traditional dessert quite a few places in Arizona, but in Tucson it was at its most* *spectacular, with the meringue tinted green, white, and red, the colors of the Mexican flag. Our version is based on the very first almendrada that my husband, Fredric, and I tasted while eating lunch one day with Carlotta Flores at her El Charro Café.*

Instructions for making this delicate almond dessert are invariably accompanied by the admonition to "beware of the mal de ojo, or the evil eye." It is definitely not to be made if you are angry or distraught or, some even say, if you are a male or a pregnant woman. Don't worry too much. It's really not that temperamental. The important thing is to have the eggs at room temperature and the bowl and beaters chilled. Break the eggs carefully so that when you separate them, no yolk mixes with the egg whites.

I like to serve this dessert after a main dish of Chicken Breasts in Green Sauce (page 155).

For the Meringue
peanut oil
1 envelope unflavored gelatin
6 egg whites at room temperature
½ cup sugar
½ teaspoon pure almond extract
½ teaspoon vanilla extract
1 cup finely chopped toasted almonds

For the Custard Sauce
6 egg yolks, lightly beaten
3 tablespoons sugar

⅛ teaspoon sea salt
2 cups scalded milk
½ teaspoon vanilla extract
½ teaspoon almond extract or 1 tablespoon almond or hazelnut liqueur (optional)

For the Garnish
slivered almonds
fresh whole strawberries or fresh fruit (optional)
sprigs of mint (optional)

About 1 hour in advance, lightly oil a 9- by 5- by 3-inch glass loaf pan or 6-cup mold and chill. Also chill a large mixing bowl and beaters.

In a small bowl, sprinkle gelatin over ¼ cup of cold water and let sit for about 5 minutes, until all the water is absorbed. Add ½ cup of boiling water, stir until dissolved, and set aside to cool.

In the chilled bowl, beat the egg whites until they just form stiff peaks. Gradually beat in the sugar, alternating with the gelatin. Add the almond and vanilla extracts, and beat until frothy. Fold in the chopped almonds.

Spoon or carefully pour into the cold pan and chill several hours or until firm. If not using right away, cover with plastic wrap when chilled.

To prepare the custard sauce, heat water in the lower half of a double boiler until barely at a simmer. Put the lightly beaten egg yolks in the top section of the boiler with the sugar and salt. Gradually add the milk, stirring slowly with a wooden spoon, until the mixture begins to coat the spoon—about 15 minutes.

When thickened, remove from the heat, pour into a bowl, and cool. Stir in the vanilla and almond extracts or liqueur. Cover and chill.

The meringue and sauce can be made in advance and assembled when it is time to serve. To serve, unmold the almond meringue onto a serving plate and drizzle the custard sauce over the top. Sprinkle with the slivered almonds and arrange the berries and mint around the outside. The *almendrada* can also be served individually, sliced in ¾-inch-wide portions, and then drizzled with the sauce and garnished.

VARIATION: PATRIOTIC ALMENDRADA   When making the meringue, after adding the almonds and flavorings to the beaten egg whites, place ⅓ of the mixture into a bowl and blend in several drops of red food coloring. In another bowl, tint ⅓ of the mixture with green food coloring, and leave the remaining ⅓ white. Spoon the red mixture into the loaf pan first, then spread the plain white, then finish with the green. Chill for 2 hours, or until firm, and continue with making the custard sauce. This variation is especially appropriate for a Mexican patriotic holiday such as Cinco de Mayo.

VARIATION: *ALMENDRADA DE CAFÉ Y CHOCOLATE*   In *Mexican Desserts* by Socorro Muñoz Kimble and Irma Serrano Noriega there is a recipe for *Almendrada de Chocolate.* Miguel adapted it to make this very different *almendrada.*

Fold 3 tablespoons of cocoa or instant coffee into half of the basic meringue, then carefully spoon first a chocolate or coffee layer and then a white layer into a 6-cup mold. Repeat with 2 more alternating layers. Sprinkle the chopped almonds on top of each layer instead of mixing throughout. For this version we like to use a coffee liqueur as a flavoring and add 2 tablespoons to both meringue and the custard, although rum can also be used.

Rum-Spiked Bread Pudding

Capirotada

ZILLAH, WASHINGTON

SERVES 8 TO 10 *"Most people have a family tree. I just seem to have a woodpile,"* said Mike Esquivel. *He explained that his mother died when he was born, leaving him to be raised by an assortment of aunts and family friends in Utah.*

This holiday bread pudding was one of his special favorites. In Mexico it is traditionally served at Easter time, but Mike makes it every Christmas for his family, using apples from the surrounding Yakima Valley orchards. During my travels I discovered that capirotada *takes many forms; the most common variation, especially in New Mexico, includes thick layers of melting cheese, maybe Monterey jack, cheddar, or even yellow American cheese. Aída Gabilondo in El Paso includes tomatoes, green onions, orange peel, and cilantro in her syrup, which is amazingly good.*

This homey dessert is best served warm, topped with whipped cream or a scoop of rich vanilla ice cream. It's good the second day, too, and makes a special breakfast treat when drenched in cold milk. Since capirotada *is traditionally served during the Lenten season, it is natural to use it to follow another Lenten dish, such as Salt Cod with Raisins and Macadamia Nuts (page 149) or Cheese Fritters with Chile and Fruit Sauce (page 203). It is also very good after a bowl of Hominy and Pork Soup (page 99), or Meatball Soup (page 90).*

For the Rum Syrup

1½ cups dark brown sugar

2 cups apple juice or water

5 whole allspice

1 4-inch piece true cinnamon bark or 1 cinnamon
  stick (cassia)

1 tablespoon aniseeds

2 tablespoons rum or to taste

For the Bread Pudding

8 ½-inch slices French bread (if time allows, let
  the bread slices sit out a few hours to dry)

3 eggs, beaten

5 tablespoons milk

1 teaspoon ground cinnamon (cassia)

1 medium apple, pared, halved, seeds removed,
  and thinly sliced

½ cup chopped walnuts or pecans

½ cup sliced almonds toasted

½ cup raisins

1 cup crumbled *queso añejo* or feta cheese

2 tablespoons butter, cut into small pieces

Heat the oven to 350 degrees F. Lightly oil a low baking dish, just big enough so that 2 layers of 4 bread slices each will fit snugly.

Combine the sugar, apple juice, allspice, and cinnamon bark in a medium-size saucepan. Bring to a boil, then lower the heat and simmer. Place the aniseeds in a tea strainer or tie in a square of cheesecloth, immerse in the simmering syrup for 10 minutes, then remove and discard. If you prefer a more pronounced flavor, leave it until the syrup is done. Continue simmering the syrup until slightly thickened, about 10 minutes more.

While the syrup is simmering, lightly toast the bread slices in the oven. Place 4 of them in an even layer in the baking dish.

Mix the eggs, milk, and cinnamon together in a small bowl. Dribble half of the mixture over the bread. Add a layer of apple slices. Sprinkle with half of the nuts, raisins, and cheese. Dot with half of the butter. Place the 4 remaining slices of toast in the pan, dribble on the rest of the egg mixture, evenly distribute the remainder of the nuts, raisins, and cheese, and dot with the remaining butter.

Remove the syrup from the heat. Discard the cinnamon bark, allspice, and aniseed if still left in. Add the rum.

Pour the syrup very slowly over the *capirotada*, letting the bread on top absorb the syrup and become thoroughly coated. Bake, uncovered, for 20–30 minutes, until the top is slightly browned.

Chocolate Rice Pudding
Arroz con Leche Achocolatado
NORTHBROOK, ILLINOIS

SERVES 6 TO 8   *Across the United States, almost as popular as* capirotada—*the classic Mexican bread pudding—is rice pudding, a direct transplant from Spain. The very best of its kind is said to come from Asturias, in that country's far northwestern corner. Rich and creamy, it requires large quantities of milk, the use of plump small- or medium-grain rice, and over an hour of slow, carefully monitored cooking. I find it is well worth the time, though, to create such a delicious, satisfying dessert.*

Both of Elaine González's parents and her grandmother were born in Asturias and settled first in Mexico and then in Indiana and Illinois. Her grandmother's recipe clearly reflects its Spanish roots, but with a delicious difference.

I especially like this pudding after a large bowl of Beef and Vegetable Broth (page 89) but it also follows nicely in the wake of other comfort dishes, such as Gloria's Red Chicken Enchiladas (page 204).

2 quarts milk

1 ounce coarsely chopped unsweetened chocolate

1 cup plus 1 tablespoon sugar

1 4-inch piece true cinnamon bark or 1 cinnamon stick (cassia)

½ cup imported short-grain or California pearl rice

2 large egg yolks

For the Garnish

cocoa for dusting each serving

In a large, deep saucepan over medium heat, bring the milk, chocolate, 1 cup of sugar, and the cinnamon bark to a boil, stirring frequently. Lower the heat and add the rice. Stir frequently with a wooden spoon to prevent the grains of rice from sticking together. Don't be concerned if the milk appears speckled with chocolate at first; this will change as the cooking progresses.

Simmer, uncovered, over gentle heat for about 1 hour, stirring the mixture and every 5 or 10 minutes, removing the film of albumin that forms on the surface. When ready, a grain of rice squeezed between the fingers should feel tender.

Whisk the egg yolks and the remaining 1 tablespoon of sugar in a small bowl until well mixed. Add ½ cup of cooked rice to the beaten yolks and mix vigorously with a fork to avoid scrambling the eggs. Add the warm yolk mixture to the cooked rice all at once and cook, stirring, for another 5 minutes. The pudding should be the consistency of soft custard, thickened but still somewhat loose. (It will continue to thicken as it cools.) Discard the cinnamon bark.

Transfer the pudding to a bowl and set aside to cool, stirring occasionally. When it is room temperature, chill in the refrigerator for several hours. Dust with cocoa powder and serve cold, with lots of hot coffee.

Eggnog and Raisin Ice Cream
Helado de Rompope
LOS ANGELES, CALIFORNIA • OAXACA, MEXICO

MAKES ABOUT 1½ QUARTS   *Before the War of Independence in the early 1800s closed the numerous convents in Mexico, the nuns had devised many uses for the hundreds of egg yolks left over after using the egg whites to glaze the gilded altars and murals inside the churches. One of the most delicious is an eggnoglike liqueur created by the sisters of a convent in Puebla, where it is still bottled and sold. I* *always bring this* rompope *home when I am there because it will keep indefinitely in the refrigerator. Since I think it is too thick and sweet for an after-dinner drink—its traditional use—I pour it over berries, simple cakes, or ice cream. Aurelia Lopez makes an ice cream from the* rompope. *We've added raisins and thick cream for further enrichment.*

Only a special dinner should finish with a dessert as rich as this. It is at its best after a main course of the spectacular Stuffed Chiles with Walnut Sauce (page 195), or it can even be served next to a sliver of pumpkin pie following a Thanksgiving Day turkey. To accompany the ice cream, serve a fine cognac along with coffee, or a tequila añejo *such as Tres Generaciones.*

½ cup raisins
¼ cup brandy
1½ cups whole milk
1 cup sugar

1 4-inch piece true cinnamon bark or cinnamon
    stick (cassia)
4 egg yolks
1 cup heavy cream

If possible, soak the raisins in the brandy for 3 or 4 hours in advance, then strain and set aside in a small bowl. Reserve the brandy to use later.

Place the milk, ½ cup of sugar, and the cinnamon bark in a medium-size saucepan and bring to a slow boil over medium heat. Lower the heat and let simmer for 15 minutes.

Beat the egg yolks in a bowl with the remaining ½ cup of sugar until thickened. Gradually stir in the hot milk. Return the mixture to the saucepan and continue cooking about 15 minutes, until thickened. Stir in the cream and the brandy and pour through a strainer into a bowl. Cover and put in the refrigerator to chill.

Every ice-cream maker is different, so process according to the manufacturer's specific directions. When is it half-frozen, add the brandy-soaked raisins, then continue the freezing process. Keep the ice cream in the freezer until ready to serve, but don't wait for more than a few days.

Raspberry Bombe
Bombe de Frambuesas
LOS ANGELES, CALIFORNIA • MEXICO CITY, MEXICO

SERVES 12   *Sister Aline Marie Gerber calls this frozen dessert displaying Mexico's patriotic colors, her "Mexican bomb."*

Sister Aline Marie may be listed in the catalogue of Mount St. Mary's College in Los Angeles as a French language teacher, but for many her claim to fame is the cooking she has done for the elaborate Cinco de Mayo fiestas held for all the students during the last thirty years. According to Sister Aline Marie, her mother was considered the "Mother Teresa of Mexico" and also figured prominently in many of Elizabeth Barton Treviño's novels—books that are well worth reading for the glimpse they give of an earlier era in Mexico.

This colorful creation fits into all sorts of menus, from a special dinner party to a casual meal of tacos or enchiladas, especially following on the heels of the Chipotle Crab Enchiladas (page 207).

20 store-bought packaged macaroons
1 cup Kahlua or other coffee liqueur
1 quart French vanilla or Cinnamon Ice Cream
   (page 358), slightly softened
1 quart store-bought or homemade Raspberry
   Ice (recipe follows), slightly softened

For the Toppings
10 sprigs of mint (optional)
20 chocolate-covered coffee beans (optional)
1 cup fresh raspberries (optional)

Chill an attractive 2½-quart metal mold or bowl. Crumble the macaroons in a bowl, pour Kahlua over them, and mix until thoroughly soaked.

Scoop a layer of ice cream into the mold, spread, and rechill. When solid, add a layer of raspberry ice and rechill.

With a spatula, spread a layer of the Kahlua-soaked macaroons, then continue layering and rechilling, ending with raspberry ice. Cover the filled mold with lightly oiled wax paper and seal tightly.

Refreeze for at least 4 hours or overnight. When ready to serve, dip the mold very briefly in hot water, run a knife around the inside rim, and turn out onto a chilled serving plate. The bombe can be made up to 1 week in advance. If not to be served immediately, cover with a larger bowl and foil or plastic wrap and keep in the freezer. Decorate with the mint sprigs and chocolate-covered coffee beans or fresh raspberries.

recipe continues

RASPBERRY ICE (*NIEVE DE FRAMBUESAS*)   This easily made ice adds an especially refreshing flavor to the bombe, but try it sometime just by itself with a mint garnish.

⅓ cup sugar
1 pint fresh raspberries or one 10-ounce package
  defrosted frozen raspberries
¼ cup fresh orange juice

Dissolve the sugar with ¾ cup of water in a saucepan and bring to a fast simmer. Continue to cook for 5 minutes, and when syrupy, remove from the heat.

Puree the raspberries with the orange juice in a food processor or blender. Strain through a fine-meshed sieve and stir into the syrup. When cool, process in an ice-cream maker according to the manufacturer's directions.

If you do not have an ice-cream maker, pour the raspberry mixture into ice cube trays and place in the freezer. When partially frozen, scoop the mixture from the trays into a bowl and beat thoroughly with a whisk or hand mixer set on low speed until smooth. Return it to the trays and again freeze. Repeat the process twice more, then freeze the sherbet covered in a container until firm but not hard.

Cinnamon Ice Cream with Ice Coffee
Helado Blanco y Negro
SAN FRANCISCO, CALIFORNIA

SERVES 4 TO 6   *Not just a dessert, not just a beverage, but a truly delightful indulgence. This came to our attention after we made a request for recipes in major Spanish-language newspapers throughout the country. There was no return address accompanying this recipe, just a scribbled note—"¡Buen Provecho!"—and the signature of Ana Elena. So thank you, Ana Elena, wherever you are.*

This very refreshing afternoon treat can be served alone or perhaps with delicate Cinnamon Sugar Cookies (page 359). Also consider it as a finish to a festive meal of Stuffed Chiles with Walnut Sauce (page 195), or a simpler supper with Poblano Chile–Stuffed Crêpes (page 201).

For the Ice Cream

2 cups heavy cream

2 cups whole milk

¾ cup sugar plus 1 tablespoon

1 6-inch true cinnamon bark or cinnamon stick
  (cassia)

1 large vanilla bean, split lengthwise

peel of 1 lemon

4 egg whites

1 squeeze of lemon juice

For the Topping

2–3 cups strong black coffee, chilled

3 tablespoons coffee liqueur (optional)

ground cinnamon (cassia)

Mix the cream, milk, and ¾ cup of sugar in a heavy saucepan and bring to a slow boil. Add the cinnamon bark, vanilla bean, and lemon peel. Lower the heat and simmer for 15 minutes, stirring occasionally. Remove from the heat and let cool. Cover with plastic wrap and refrigerate until cold.

In a small bowl, beat the egg whites until they form stiff peaks. Gradually add the lemon juice and remaining tablespoon of sugar. Remove the lemon peel, cinnamon bark, and vanilla bean from the cold milk mixture. Scrape the seeds from the bean into the milk mixture and slowly fold it into the egg whites.

Pour the mixture into an ice-cream maker and process according to the manufacturer's instructions. It can be frozen, tightly sealed, in a metal bowl or ice tray in the freezer. When ready, the consistency should still be somewhat soft.

Chill parfait glasses or large wineglasses, and when ready to serve, scoop the ice cream into the glasses. Mix the iced coffee and coffee liqueur together and pour over the top. Sprinkle with the cinnamon and serve with both a spoon for eating and a straw for sipping.

Cinnamon Sugar Cookies
Polvorones con Canela
PHOENIX, ARIZONA • SONORA, MEXICO

MAKES 3 TO 4 DOZEN   *How can something so simple taste so good? Arabic in origin, the recipe was transplanted intact to Mexico by the Spaniards. Except in New Mexico and southern Colorado where biscochitos are the cookie of choice, I seldom spoke with a Mexican-American cook in the United States who didn't rate this as his favorite sweet snack. The only disagreement was the question of using all butter, all lard, or a combination of both. This recipe from Miguel's mother Amelia Galbraith, makes* *a cookie with a very fine, flaky texture and is so small that it can be popped in the mouth and eaten in one bite. Polvorones are a favorite sweet to be served at weddings and other celebrations, festively wrapped in multicolored tissue paper.*

Serve on a contrasting colorful dish alongside a glass of Cinnamon Ice Cream with Iced Coffee (page 358). These are also a good partner of hot tea—or try them with a glass of sherry.

1 cup (2 sticks) unsalted butter at room temperature or ½ cup butter and ½ cup vegetable
  shortening (see Note)
1½ cups sifted powdered sugar
1 tablespoon vanilla extract or brandy

2 cups flour
¼ teaspoon sea salt
⅔ cup finely ground pecans or walnuts
1 teaspoon ground cinnamon (cassia)

Preheat the oven to 325 degrees F.

Beat the butter in a bowl with an electric beater until creamy. Add the ½ cup of powdered sugar and vanilla, and continue beating until light and fluffy.

Mix in the flour and salt very gradually—a tablespoon at a time—until thoroughly incorporated. Add the nuts with the last of the flour. Cover tightly with plastic wrap and chill thoroughly.

Using your hands, form the dough into ¾-inch balls. Place on an ungreased baking pan about 1 inch apart. Bake in a moderate oven about 15 minutes, or until the edges turn pale gold.

Place the remaining cup of sugar in a shallow bowl or plate with the cinnamon. Remove the pan from the oven and, while still hot, carefully roll the cookies in the powdered sugar mixture. Set aside until cooled completely and roll them again in the sugar, shaking off any excess. The cookies can be eaten fresh or stored between layers of wax paper in an airtight tin for several weeks, although then the powdered sugar tends to be absorbed into the cookies. They also freeze well in airtight plastic bags.

NOTE: Since butter plays an important flavor role in these small cookies, it is important that newly purchased butter be used, not some that has been in the refrigerator for a while. For health reasons and as a substitute for the more traditional lard, Maria Petra Vasquez in Michigan substitutes vegetable shortening for half of the butter.

CHRISTMASTIME

*T*he Christmas season in New Mexico is an unabashedly joyous time, starting on December 12 with the Feast of Guadalupe, a celebration commemorating Mexico's first saint. In the clear, crisp air of night, luminarias light up the centuries-old adobe buildings of Santa Fe and outline the streets. Everywhere nacimientos are displayed, those simple crèche scenes carved of wood, molded from clay, or constructed from other natural or man-made materials. The manger in the crèche is usually left empty until Christmas Eve, when a child's doll representing the Infant Jesus is added.

As in Mexico, groups of friends and family in many other Mexican-American communities still conduct the traditional posada (lodging), reenacting Mary and Joseph's search throughout Bethlehem for an inn to stay in the night that Jesus was born. Participants go from house to house in a song-filled candlelight procession, at first being refused admission but at the last home being joyfully welcomed with food and drink. Hot ponche and chocolate are served, along with biscochitos and panes dulces. There are always colorful piñatas in fanciful shapes, filled with candies, fruits, and little toys. These clay or papier-mâché figures extravagantly decorated with tissue paper are suspended on a rope, just waiting to be whacked by a blindfolded child wielding a long stick. Everyone gathers around, clapping and shouting while the children take turns batting at the piñata. Eventually someone bursts it open, spilling out its surprises which are collected by all in a frenzied scramble.

For the many Spanish-speaking Catholics I met in New Mexico, these activities are only the prologue to La Noche Buena or Christmas Eve. Then all the families—children, parents, grandparents, and other relatives—come together and attend midnight mass—or, as I was told, La Misa del Gallo in remembrance of the rooster who announced the birth of the Christ Child with its crowing. Afterward, everyone returns home for a celebratory meal that undoubtedly includes tamales.

Mexican families hold similar celebrations throughout the United States, and in many cities and communities there are public festivities. In Los Angeles's Olvera Historical District,

continued

on the nine nights before Christmas everyone joins in the posadas, winding their way by candlelight between the old adobe and brick buildings. A jubilant three-day Fiesta Navideña is celebrated in San Antonio's El Mercado, complete with music, folk dancing, and even Pancho Claus, and the city's famed Las Posadas along the Riverwalk is truly spectacular, being lit by thousands of lights and luminarias.

Aniseed Cookies
Biscochitos
CHIMAYÓ, NEW MEXICO

MAKES 6–7 DOZEN *There can't be a Christmas gathering in New Mexico without biscochitos. Every cook I met made them in quantities and kept them on hand throughout the holiday season. They may make other cookies as well, but the cookie with the place of honor on the serving plate will always be these rich biscochitos laced with the subtle licorice flavor of aniseeds. Nolia Martinez likes to use pure lard, as do most of the local cooks, but we've substituted part butter, which gives a nice flavor.*

Many cooks who like crisper cookies roll the dough ¼ inch thick or less and bake them at 375 degrees F. Nowadays the dough for biscochitos is cut out in fancy shapes with small cookie cutters no more than 2 inches in diameter or is cut into diagonal strips about ¾ inch wide and 2 inches long, with a triangular wedge taken out of the narrow ends to look more like the emblematic iris. What I was looking for was the true fleur-de-lis shape that I had read was the older, traditional fashion. Finally, someone remembered an aunt who had a friend who made them. The secret is to roll the dough a bit thinner and cut them twice as wide. On one end, cut 3 narrow strips an inch long, pull them a bit apart and curl back into a spiral. They are more work, but the results are impressive.

For the Cookies

1 cup (2 sticks) unsalted butter at room temperature

1 cup shortening or lard at room temperature

1 cup sugar

2 eggs

2–3 tablespoons aniseeds

6 cups all-purpose flour

3 teaspoons baking powder

1 teaspoon sea salt

¼ cup Amontillado sherry, sweetened wine, brandy, or orange juice

¼ cup sugar

1 teaspoon ground cinnamon (cassia)

Cream together the butter, shortening, and sugar, beating vigorously until light and fluffy. Mix in the eggs and aniseeds.

Sift together the flour, baking powder, and salt. Add to the creamed shortening mixture, with just enough sherry to make a firm dough. Do not beat the dough but gently stir it. Divide the dough into 4 portions and chill, tightly wrapped, for 30 minutes.

Preheat the oven to 350 degrees F. Roll out the dough on a lightly floured surface to about ¼- to ½ inch thick and cut into small shapes. Try to handle the dough as little as possible.

Place the *biscochitos* on ungreased baking sheets and bake in the oven for 10–15 minutes, until a light golden brown.

Mix the sugar and cinnamon together in a wide, shallow dish or plate. When the *biscochitos* are done, remove from the oven and let them cool in the pan for 3 minutes. When they can be easily handled, dredge in the sugar mixture and cool completely on a rack. Store in a tightly sealed container or bag. If not eaten immediately, they will last for several weeks.

Pumpkin Turnovers

Empanaditas de Calabaza

PHOENIX, ARIZONA

MAKES ENOUGH FILLING FOR 3 DOZEN 3-INCH *EMPANADITAS* OR 1 DOZEN 5-INCH EMPANADAS   *Sweet little empanaditas can be filled with almost anything you enjoy. Instead of pumpkin pies, I shared miniature turnovers filled with spiced pumpkin as holiday favorites in New Mexico and Arizona, as well as in Detroit. Here's a version from Miguel's mother, Amelia Galbraith.*

These can be served with Spiced Pork and Apple Turnovers (page 44), along with Christmas Punch (page 382). For a dessert after a festive meal, accompany with a goblet of Eggnog and Raisin Ice Cream (page 355).

1 recipe Savory and Sweet Empanadas—the Dough (page 43)

For the Filling

2 cups pureed canned or cooked fresh pumpkin or squash

½ cup brown sugar

2 teaspoons pumpkin spice (see Note)

½ teaspoon ground cinnamon (cassia)

¼ teaspoon ground nutmeg

2 teaspoons brandy (optional)

For the Glaze

1 egg, lightly beaten with 1 teaspoon water

For the Topping

2 teaspoons granulated white sugar

Preheat the oven to 350 degrees F.

Prepare the dough according to the directions in the recipe.

Place the pumpkin, sugar, and spices in a medium-size saucepan and mix well. Bring to a boil over medium heat, then set aside to cool. Stir in the brandy if using.

Roll the dough out on a lightly-floured surface until it is less than ¼ inch thick. Divide the dough in half and roll again to at least ⅛ inch thick. Cut into 3-inch circles and place about 2 teaspoons of filling in the center of each circle.

Fold one side over the filling and seal tightly with your fingers. Crimp the edges with the tines of a fork.

Brush the tops with the egg wash and place on a lightly greased baking sheet. Bake for about 15 minutes, until lightly browned. Remove from the oven and, while still hot, sprinkle with the sugar.

NOTE: If you don't have pumpkin spice, double the amount of cinnamon and nutmeg and add ½ teaspoon each of ginger and allspice.

Ancho Chile Flan
Flan de Chiles Anchos
AUSTIN, TEXAS • MEXICO CITY, MEXICO

SERVES 8 TO 10   *This unusual flan used to be the favorite dessert of Nushie Chancellor's grandmother. In those days ancho chiles were used only to make sauces or in adobos, but the ever-creative Virginia Coutlolenc de Kuhn, admiring the chile's rich, sweet flavor, so reminiscent of chocolate, made the chiles the focus of a flan. Nushie never was given the actual recipe but recreated it from memory and added the sauce as her own personal touch.*

The flan is an especially good ending to a meal featuring Chicken in a Piquant Tomato Sauce (page 152).

1 cup sugar
8 eggs and 4 egg yolks
2 cups whole milk
2 cups evaporated milk
2 cups sweetened condensed milk
¾ cup fresh or frozen orange juice
2 teaspoons pure vanilla extract
½ cup dark brown sugar
2 dried ancho chiles, seeded, deveined, and cut
  into thin strips

For the Sauce

1 cup fresh or frozen orange juice
½ cup dark brown sugar
1 ancho chile, seeded, deveined, and broken into
  pieces
4 tablespoons grated orange rind
1 teaspoon cornstarch, dissolved in ¼ cup water

Place the sugar in a small skillet or saucepan with ½ cup of water. Stir with a wooden spoon over medium heat until the sugar dissolves, then let the liquid boil down, becoming an amber-colored syrup.

Pour the hot syrup into an 8-cup flan mold, tipping it to lightly coat the entire bottom and most of the sides. Let it cool and harden.

Preheat the oven to 350 degrees F. and set a pot of water on to boil.

Beat together lightly the eggs and egg yolks. Add the whole, evaporated, and condensed milk and blend together. Stir in the orange juice and vanilla extract. Mix in the dark brown sugar, stirring until it dissolves. Fold in the chile strips and pour the mixture into the caramelized mold. Place the mold in a large baking pan on the middle rack of the oven. Carefully pour the hot water into the pan—enough to reach halfway up the sides of the flan mold. Bake for 1½–2 hours, until a toothpick inserted in the center comes out clean. Add more hot water if necessary.

Remove the pan with the flan from the oven. Let it cool for at least 1 hour, then refrigerate, covered, for 8–10 hours.

To make the sauce, blend the orange juice, dark brown sugar, and ancho chile together in a blender or food processor. Pour into a small saucepan, bring to a boil over medium heat, and simmer for 10 minutes. Add the orange rind, remove from the heat immediately, and stir in the dissolved cornstarch. Set aside to cool.

To serve, loosen the sides of the flan with a knife and invert onto a large, round serving plate. Drizzle the sauce over the top.

Cajeta Cheesecake
Pastel de Queso con Cajeta
EL PASO, TEXAS

SERVES 12 TO 16   *There is a little Mexican restaurant in El Paso called L & J Cafe that has been around a long, long time. Back in the 1930s when it was called Tony's Place, the owner, Antonio Flores, had false walls constructed within this old adobe building at the edge of town to conceal the bootlegging and slot machines that were a good part of the restaurant's trade in those days. Movie stars, politicians, and other celebrities flocked there, and when prohibition came to an end, they kept returning, by then hooked on the food. Now Tony's grandson, Leo Duran, with his wife, Fran, serves basically the same traditional dishes in the very same building, including a cheesecake like this, with its satiny ribbons of sweet cajeta.*

The rich character of this cheesecake makes it best to follow a lighter entree, such as Shredded Beef Salad (page 64) with its mildly piquant flavor.

For the Crust
4 tablespoons unsalted butter, melted
1 cup graham cracker crumbs
¼ cup chopped pecans

For the Filling
2 pounds cream cheese (not low-fat) at room
    temperature

½ cup sugar
4 large eggs
1 teaspoon finely grated orange zest
2 teaspoons vanilla extract
¼ cup heavy cream
¼ cup sour cream
1 cup *Cajeta* (page 367) or store-bought

Heat the oven to 350 degrees F.

Mix the melted butter, crumbs, and chopped pecans together in a small bowl. Sprinkle the mixture into the bottom of a 9-inch springform pan and pat evenly over the bottom and most of the sides of the pan. Chill the crust in the refrigerator while preparing the filling.

Beat the cream cheese in a bowl with an electric mixer. Beat in the sugar. Add the eggs and blend just until smooth. Scrape down the sides and bottom of the bowl so the cheese is thoroughly mixed. Stir in the zest, vanilla, cream, and sour cream with a large spoon, blending well.

Warm the *cajeta* and, with a knife, gently stir it into the cream cheese filling so that it just streaks the filling.

Bring a large pot of water to a boil. Remove the crust from the refrigerator and cover the outer bottom and sides of the springform pan with heavy foil. Slowly pour the filling into the crumb-lined pan.

Set a roasting pan on a rack in the middle of the oven and place the filled cake pan in the center. Pour in enough boiling water to come halfway up the sides of the cake pan. Bake for 55–60 minutes. The center should still be somewhat soft and jiggly. Leave the oven door open, turn off the heat, and let the cake remain there for another hour.

Remove from the water bath and set on a wire rack to cool completely. Remove the circular rim of the pan and refrigerate until well chilled. This can be refrigerated up to 3 days.

Cajeta
Cajeta
CHICAGO, ILLINOIS • GUANAJUATO, MEXICO

MAKES ABOUT 2 CUPS *Pamela Díaz de León lived for years in Celaya, Mexico, a small town given over almost entirely to the confecting of cajeta. Originally, this thick goat's milk caramel syrup was made with different fruits and nuts and was so dense it could be packed in little wooden cajetes, or boxes, from which the name of the sweet is derived. Pamela still prefers the rich taste of this homemade version to that now sold all over Mexico and the United States in glass jars.*

Use the largest, heaviest pot you have. The mixture will foam up, so it needs to be large enough to hold double the volume of the syrup. Copper is the usual choice in Mexico. I've also used a large cast-iron Dutch oven and a porcelain enamel-coated steel casserole with sloping sides that worked well.

1 quart goat's milk
1 cup sugar
¼ teaspoon baking soda

2 teaspoons cow's milk
1 teaspoon vanilla extract or 1 tablespoon brandy

Stir the goat's milk and sugar together in a large pot and bring to a simmer. In a cup mix the baking soda together with the cow's milk until completely dissolved. Remove the simmering milk from the heat. Pour the baking soda mixture into the hot goat's milk while still stirring. It will foam up, so be very careful.

Return the pot to the stove and let the milk continue to simmer over medium heat, stirring quite often, for about 30 minutes. As the mixture thickens and darkens in color, lower the heat and stir constantly until the *cajeta* becomes a dark caramel color and coats the back of a wooden spoon—another 20–30 minutes.

Pour the *cajeta* into a bowl, and after it has cooled a bit, stir in the vanilla or brandy and then cool completely. It can be used immediately or stored in a tightly covered jar in the refrigerator for months.

Pine Nut Torte
Torta de Piñones
SANTA FE, NEW MEXICO

SERVES 10   *The ochre pink of northern New Mexico's dry hillsides are broken high up by spinneys of juniper and weathered piñon pine. For centuries the local Indians have gathered the ripe nuts in the fall. After slowly roasting them, they were stored for winter eating as snacks. The nuts were also ground into heavy flour and used to add to breads and to thicken stews. These pine nuts were nothing new to the early Spaniards who eked out their existence in this formidable country, and they were eagerly added to the diet, where they were mixed with wild greens or an occasional braised chicken or wild rabbit.*

During the harsh depression years of the 1930s, condensed milk was used as both sweetener and liquid in this intensely pine nut–flavored torte, an idea that works as well today. This extremely fast and easy recipe was given to us by a young woman we met at a concert in Santa Fe who said it belonged to her aunt, Bernadette Garcia, whose family had homesteaded there years ago.

This torte is very light in texture—almost custard-like. If a denser consistency is preferred, just blend the ingredients together for a shorter period of time. To toast the pine nuts, spread them on a heavy cookie sheet or baking pan and bake in a preheated 275-degree F. oven until very aromatic and slightly flecked with brown, about 5 minutes. Stir frequently so they toast evenly.

An extremely versatile dessert, Pine Nut Torte can follow almost any main course except maybe moles, which share a nut-thickened base. I especially like it after spirited dishes such as Chicken and Vegetables Flavored with Pickled Jalapeño Chiles (page 156), Drunken Chicken (page 151), or Sea Bass Baked in a Spicy Red Sauce (page 138).

⅔ cup toasted pine nuts

12 ounces canned sweetened condensed milk

2 large eggs

1–1½ tablespoons freshly grated orange peel

powdered sugar for dusting

COCINA DE LA FAMILIA

Preheat the oven to 350 degrees F. Lightly butter or oil an 8-inch square baking pan, line with aluminum foil or wax paper, and butter again. Lightly dust with flour, shaking out any excess.

Finely grind the pine nuts in a spice/coffee grinder and put in a blender. Pour in the condensed milk, scraping out the thick milk still clinging to the sides of the can. Add the eggs and orange peel, and blend on high speed for about 5 minutes to create a light, airy batter. Scrape down the sides several times with a spatula so that the mixture is thoroughly blended.

Pour the mixture into the cake pan and bake for 45–50 minutes, or until a toothpick when inserted in the center comes out clean. Allow the torte to cool on a rack for 10 minutes. Run a knife around the inner edge of the pan and turn the torte out on a plate. Remove the paper, then turn the torte back onto a serving plate.

Sift a light dusting of powdered sugar over the top before serving.

Pineapple Cake with Ginger Icing
Pastel de Piña
PHOENIX, ARIZONA

SERVES 12   *Pineapple—that queen of New World fruits—is the symbol of welcome and hospitality. Amelia Galbraith, Miguel's mother, often bakes this dense but delicate pineapple cake and serves it with a cream cheese and candied ginger icing, which picks up the sweet flavor of the pineapple. Since this cake has the texture of a carrot cake and will stay moist for several days, Amelia likes to keep it on hand to welcome guests, both old friends and new, to her home.*

This cake pairs perfectly with Compote of Mango, Papaya, and Strawberries (page 345) after a Mexican-style brunch or to follow a simple supper of tacos or enchiladas. It is a welcome dessert at potlucks and to serve alongside a cup of tea or coffee at any time of day or night.

2 cups sugar

2 cups flour

2 teaspoons baking soda

2 eggs, lightly beaten

½ cup chopped pecans

2 20-ounce cans crushed pineapple, undrained

1 teaspoon vanilla extract

For the Icing

4 tablespoons unsalted butter at room temperature

8 ounces cream cheese, at room temperature

1 teaspoon vanilla extract

1 teaspoon lemon juice

2 cups sifted powdered sugar

1 tablespoon thinly slivered candied ginger

recipe continues

Preheat the oven to 325 degrees F. Butter a 9- by 13-inch Pyrex pan. (It's important to use a Pyrex pan for baking this cake because the acid in the pineapple will react with a metal one.)

Stir together the sugar, flour, and baking soda in a large mixing bowl. Add the eggs, pecans, pineapple, and vanilla, mix well, and then pour into the baking dish. Bake for 35–40 minutes, until a toothpick inserted in the center comes out clean.

Beat the butter, cream cheese, vanilla, and lemon juice in a bowl until smooth. Gradually beat in the powdered sugar. Add the candied ginger. Spread on top of the cake while it is still hot.

Oregon and Idaho Impressions

Though I lived many places while I was growing up, the center of my life was always Caldwell, Idaho, and the farming and ranching community of the surrounding Boise Valley and eastern Oregon.

While the Hispanic presence in this inland region is relatively recent, nearly four centuries ago Spanish explorers sailed north along the Oregon coast and up as far as southeast Alaska, mapping and naming many locations. Cape Blanco and Cape Sebastian on Oregon's southwest coast bear the oldest European place names in the state. In the 1800s, Mexican *vaqueros* came up from California as trail riders and settled on ranches in southeastern Oregon around Steens Mountain and the Owyhee brakes.

It was, however, during World War II that thousands of Mexicans were recruited to come to the Northwest to relieve the critical farm crisis. Unlike Canada and the United States, Mexico played a neutral role in the war, and for the huge number of people suffering from the disastrous economic situation in that country, this was a welcomed opportunity. All was not easy for these *braceros*. These were men separated from their families, many for the first time in their lives (no women or children were allowed in this governmental program). Few spoke any English or were even literate in Spanish. They lived together in farm labor camps, often six workers in sixteen-by-sixteen-foot tents, furnished only with a cot and a blanket.

During the summer, the temperature often rises into the 100s in the Snake River Valley where I lived. I know it was hot that Sunday when I drove with my dad to a nearby labor camp to visit some of the workers he had gotten to know. There was a fiesta going on; the main thing I remember about that day was the pig they had evidently butchered earlier—I found evidence of its unused remains. It was my first ever meal of *carnitas,* crisp brown bits of pork drenched in a freshly made tomato salsa made with green chiles grown in coffee cans nailed to the side of their dilapidated wood quarters. And I remember how very, very hot it was. No trees, only sand, sticker bushes, and the late afternoon shade on the side from the buildings.

By the time the war was over in 1945, the Mexican workers were more than ready to go home, though some returned later with their families as part of the increasingly important labor force of migratory farmworkers. These are the men and women I got to know best as I worked beside them in the fields and packing sheds.

Rose Archuleta and her family lived in a labor camp outside Caldwell for twenty-nine years. Coming from a small town in Colorado with only one other Hispanic family, Rose didn't learn to cook Mexican food or even eat a taco until she was in the labor camp. For some years now she has made her home up on Canyon Hill, an area outside Caldwell where I used to pasture my horses. It is now a suburban development complete with winding roads and cul de sacs.

Her family raised, today Rose Archuleta cooks mainly the same way as her Anglo neighbors do, though occasionally she still makes flour tortillas, *pozole,* or *capirotada,* and at Christmas, always tamales.

On the other hand, Mexican dishes regularly appear on the table of María Andrea Berain and her husband, Jesse, who live in a big old house in one of Boise's quiet neighborhoods. Jesse has been teaching cooking classes for the last twenty years at the local college—a sideline he sees as a natural outgrowth of his father's occupation as a hotel restaurant chef. His main job is as the adviser to the governor of Idaho on state Hispanic initiatives such as jobs, housing, and education. Cooking is now mainly a sideline for Jesse. His wife handles all the daily meals and the special holiday cooking, but he likes to keep his hand in with favorite dishes like beans and chorizo.

Along the Willamette Valley corridor stretching south to the California border, Oregon's Mexican-American population continues to grow. In a few towns like Woodburn, the residents are predominantly bilingual, the store signs are in Spanish, and the restaurants, such as Luis's Tacqueria, serve only Mexican food. Though many families are originally from Michoacán, this was one of the few states where I met people from Yucatán—the part of Mexico that is the farthest in miles from Portland. These Mayan families, encouraged by a few earlier immigrants, now work primarily in the valley's plant nurseries and vineyards.

Not too long ago Mexican Americans were only pass-through seasonal workers, but, this has changed, especially since the 1960s. They have bought their own homes, found more rewarding jobs, and bought small businesses. Marco Rodriguez in Nyssa, Oregon, manages a very successful family bakery that his mother and father started in 1964; their sugar-topped *conchas* and other pastries are favorites even in Idaho.

In both Idaho and Oregon, the Mexican Americans have come to stay. They may still not be as totally accepted in the smaller conservative farming towns as they are in the populous urban areas, but their presence is now woven into the fabric of these communities.

And to Wash It All Down
Bebidas

Para todo mal mezcal, para todo bien tambien. (For any sickness mescal, for health, also mescal.)

—A POPULAR MEXICAN SAYING

NO MATTER THE TIME OF DAY, whenever I went to someone's home to talk about Mexican cooking, I was without fail offered something to drink, usually a cup of American coffee or a bottled soft drink—Coke, Pepsi, or an orange soda, those *refrescos* (carbonated drinks) that in Mexico appear to be fast replacing the traditional and healthier *aguas frescas*. Yet despite the shift to the popular omnipresent American drinks, many of these familiar naturally flavored waters have not been forgotten. In Los Angeles there was *tepache,* a lightly sour fermented pineapple drink; in a little restaurant in Woodburn, Oregon, I drank two glasses of refreshing *horchata,* a beverage flavored with sweetened ground rice and coconut water with just a taste of cinnamon. In my travels I sipped crimson *jamaica* water made of dried hibiscus blossoms, molasses-brown *tamarindo,* and fresh limeade. The most refreshing surprise of all came in Florida on a day so hot that even the turkey vultures were listless and feeling the heat. I had gotten totally lost driving down one of the back roads close to the Keys, so eventually I turned around and stopped for directions at a fruit stand operated out of the back of a truck. That wonderful woman there not only put me on the right road, but she gave me a huge glass of watermelon pulp crushed with ice and freshly squeezed lime juice.

TIME FOR A BEER
Except for children and teetotalers, beer is the drink of Mexico, and some of the best as well as a good number of the most insipid Mexican beers are available in the United States.

It was from Germany, which boasts more breweries than anywhere else in the world, that Mexico's brewmasters came, bringing with them their distinctively light golden Pilsner-style beers and the amber red Vienna-style lager.

In these days of microbreweries and their bolder beers, the more lighthearted golden lagers may be out of favor in the United States, but not with Mexican Americans. All three of Mexico's leading brewing companies, Modelo, Cuahtémoc, and Moctezuma, export these thirst-quenching beers. The best of the pilsners are, I think, the well-balanced and fragrant Superior, and Bohemia, another very pleasant beer. Other labels in what is considered the clear-bottle class are produced primarily as cheap thirst quenchers, with the malt often lightened by rice or a high percentage of corn. Typical are Chihuahua and Sol Especial. Corona, Modelo's offering in this category, though with an almost cult following in the United States, is still, to me, bland and insipid, more like a vaguely hop-flavored sparkling water than a beer. Another very popular brew of this type, the rather dry Tecate, is marketed in a can and invariably accompanied by salt and a wedge of lime.

On the other side of the beer spectrum, the dark Negra Modelo is well worth seeking. Creamy in body, I find it a satisfying companion to most Mexican meals, especially those with complex chile sauces. The other excellent dark beer, rich and full-bodied, is Noche Buena (loosely translated as Holy Night), released by Moctezuma only during the Christmas holiday season. If you like dark beer, make sure your supermarket stocks it.

To many drinkers of Mexican beer though, Dos Equis XX is the choice for both casual imbibing with friends and to share the table with the best of Mexican cooking. Its malty and rich, very slightly sweet taste and aroma, and its clear copper color, make for a good all-around beer. Don't confuse this with the also popular but lighter, somewhat overcarbonated Dos Equis XX Special Lager.

Decide on the type and brand of beer you like best for different occasions. Buy it cold (beer is perishable), store it cold, and drink it after the chill is off a bit, to best appreciate the flavor.

A SIP OF WINE

Despite its long Spanish and French ties, Mexico is still not a country associated with wine. The root stock of the grapes brought by the Spanish was nurtured primarily for sacramental purposes. Although the soil and climate around Aquascalientes, Querétero, and Baja California Norte were accommodating, the rulers in Spain were not: Wines grown for pleasure were prohibited and were brought by ship from Europe. Only in the last few decades have Mexican vineyards been producing wine of any reasonable quality at all, and only much more recently can any be considered notable. Wine, however, is a suitable complement to Mexico's foods. In fact, every year, Santa Fe, New Mexico, promotes a major Wine and Chile Festival, which demonstrates just how compatible different wines can be with a chile-laced dish. Veronica Litton, originally from Mexico City and now manager and wine consultant of Crown Wine Merchants in Coral Gables, Florida, shared some of her recommendations with me, which I've included along with Miguel's and my suggestions.

In general, with most of Mexico's complex-flavored dishes, look for wines with equally concentrated flavors. We drink California's fruity zinfandels, dense and rich, and some full-bodied red wines from Spain and Italy. The wonderfully spicy shiraz from Australia is a favorite, as is the similar California Petite Sirah and a fruity Pinot Noir. There are some merlots, especially from Washington, with a subtle chocolaty tinge that matches well with many *moles*. For foods emphasizing the tartness of tomatillos, a crisp sauvignon blanc stands up well, including some from Chile, though if you are looking for a white wine for red-chile-infused dishes, I prefer a softer-focused dry gewürztraminer or a Riesling. We in Washington have some excellent fruit wines, as I'm certain other states do, too. I've served a pear wine with *picadillo*-stuffed poblano chiles and rhubarb wine with shrimp. The main thing is to understand that wine pairs well with most Mexican food.

THE SPIRIT OF MEXICO

While chocolate may be considered the drink of the gods, the traditional drink of the people certainly comes from the heart of the maguey.

With its fierce swordlike leaves—the very same as the century plant that grows throughout the arid Southwest—maguey is officially an agave, one of a large genus of similar plants. Although every species has useful qualities, different kinds have been used in the past for fiber, fences, and fuel, as well as other products, and, in fact, almost all the essentials for a basic life existence. It is the very center of the plant that makes the maguey so valuable today—the mother lode, so to speak, of mezcal and its most distinguished version, tequila.

Mezcal is almost Mexico's national drink, especially in the semiarid regions of the country where maguey thrive. There is one village in Oaxaca that I visit, Matatlán, where virtually every family is engaged in making mezcal, still using homemade copper stills and horses to pull monotonously around and around the huge circular grindstone that crushes the roasted *piña*, or heart of the *maguey*. (It takes up to ten years for most of these *piñas* to mature and ripen, often at a weight of one hundred pounds.) Mezcal may not be as smooth as tequila, but the distinctive smoky flavor, like that of chipotle chiles, grows on you. Mezcal is now increasingly available in U.S. liquor stores, although in a somewhat subdued version. Still, it's worth a try.

Tequila is the drink most equated with Mexico. Made famous when included by a border bartender in a mixed drink named a Margarita (many must have come up with the idea at the same time, to judge by the number of self-proclaimed originators), tequila has assumed its own place of honor in recent years. In Mexico this liquor is distilled from just one distinct species of the blue agave, *A. tequilania Weber,* and has always been consumed straight, with perhaps a lick of salt, a suck of lime, or a swallow of *sangrita,* a chaser with a life of its own. Sharing a small glass of their coveted favorite tequila, the liquid soul of Mexican hospitality, was my ultimate welcome as a guest in the Mexican-American homes I visited.

In the 1990s tequila came into its own in the United States, fired perhaps by the intense interest in Mexican cuisine by chefs and food aficionados alike. The word has gone out, and the result is that many of the best restaurants and bars now offer a wide assortment of fine 100 percent agave tequilas to be savored straight up, just like a premium gin, vodka, bourbon, or scotch. Here are a few of the best, including Miguel's and my favorite tequilas that are available in the United States. Most distilleries market four very distinct styles, which vary greatly in both taste and cost. Look for them, ask for them, and then enjoy again and again those you prefer.

White tequila: Labeled either *blanco* or *plata* (silver), this is pure, usually unaged tequila with only the addition of water allowed. Like a premium vodka, it can be very elegant. Look for Cuervo's almost sweet Dos Reales Plata or Patrón Silver with its refreshing slightly peppery taste, and my usual choice, Herradura Silver, which I find very dry, and herby, with a wondrous smooth finish.

Gold tequila: This popular yellow tequila, sold with a gold label, seems to be more a U.S. marketing gimmick than anything else. It is an unaged clear tequila that has been colored and flavored with additives such as caramel and is best used for margaritas and other mixed drinks. Sauza Tequila Especial and Cuervo Especial Premium Tequila set the lead.

Tequila Reposado: This is the connoisseur's tequila of choice, as both an aperitif and a drink during a meal. To produce it, a high-quality silver tequila is "reposed," or rested, for two to twelve months in oak barrels—sometimes the same barrels used to age Kentucky's bourbon—tempering but not controlling the assertive rambunctious flavor of the agave. Two of the very best are the exquisitely light Don Julio and, with its rich oak tones, Cuervo 1800, a super-premium blend of *reposado* and *tequila añejo.* A choice for very special occasions.

Tequila Añejo: Sipping Mexico's mellow oak-aged tequilas can be a wonderfully luxurious experience with a harmonious complex and mellow flavor, but at the low end, as with brandy, there are those that leave such a harsh feeling in the mouth, you will wish you had never tried it. This is a drink to savor at the end of a meal for its aroma as well as for its taste. The two most often served are both from Sauza: Commemorativo and the velvety cognac-like Tres Generaciones, which like cognac is usually served in a small snifter.

COMFORTING OR BRACING HOT BEVERAGES

Two of Mexico's most esteemed hot drinks, the comforting *atoles* and *chocolates,* in the United States seem to be saved primarily for the holiday ritual of eating tamales or for drinking by the very young or infirm. It is unfortunate because they have long been a vital part of Mexico's history.

The origin of the cacao bean and how it came to the hot, wet country of southern Mexico is a legend entwined in the past of the Mexican people. As a gift from the god Quetzalcoatl, its first recorded use was as a sacred drink consumed only by priests and nobles. Even part of its scientific name, *theobroma,* means "food of the gods." At first the chocolate was mixed only with water, but the Indians soon sweetened it with wild honey, and with the Spaniards came sugar and milk. Today, many Mexicans still prefer the sweetened chocolate mixed with water, but the flavor and texture of Mexican chocolate combined with milk is incomparable, truly worthy of being a drink of the gods.

Atole, another nourishing beverage from Mexico's past, is nothing more than ground dried corn (*masa harina*) thinned with water or milk and usually flavored with fruits, chocolate, or, my favorite, chiles. I found it virtually unknown in the United States except by older generations—those born in Mexico during the early 1900s—or more recent immigrants, though several times in New Mexico I was served *atole* made of blue corn. Much more common in New Mexico is *pinole,* made of either roasted cornmeal or wheat combined with milk, sugar, and spices, and served cold as well as hot.

Drinking coffee, on the other hand, seemed to be everyone's favorite way to start and end a day, and almost all the Mexican Americans with whom I shared a cup of coffee preferred to drink it strongly brewed and then tempered with milk. It was only on special occasions that I encountered Mexico's familiar *café de olla,* coffee cooked in a pot, sweetened with dark sugar, and redolent with cinnamon and other spices.

Whatever the beverage served, the act of offering something to drink is a sign of hospitality, and the variety of possibilities among Mexicans and Mexican Americans is as great or greater than anywhere in the world.

Fruit Shakes
Licuados

SERVES 1 GENEROUSLY   *As part of the daily ritual in getting her active family off to school and work in Chicago's Mexican Pilsen neighborhood, Olivia Dominguez starts their day with these nourishing drinks combining milk with whatever ripe fruit she has handy. It is an ideal way to use up extra ripe fruit, but even a can of drained fruit cocktail will do. The flavor seems better, however, if two different fruits are mixed together, keeping in mind the aesthetics of the resulting color combination. Some favorites are bananas with blackberries and cantaloupe with strawberries. Peaches and mangoes are also good additions. To make it more nutritious, Olivia often adds egg whites to the licuado when she is blending it, and others like to thicken it with one-half cup of yogurt. The fruit smoothy, an identical beverage, is now "in" with the health-conscious of California, paying an unrecognized compliment to the influence of their large Mexican population.*

For more servings, the amounts can be increased proportionally. If the drink must be made in advance, pour it into a pitcher, cover, refrigerate, and stir well before serving. It's best, though, just to have the fruit prepared and blend it at the last moment.

1 cup cold milk

1 cup ripe fruit, peeled, seeded, and cut into
  chunks

1 tablespoon honey (optional)

juice of 1 lime (optional)

dash of ground cinnamon (cassia) or nutmeg, or
  a sprig of mint, depending on the fruit used

Puree the milk, fruit, honey, and lime juice together in a blender or food processor until thick and smooth. If the drink is too thick, thin with more milk or try orange juice.

Pour into a tall glass with ice cubes or even crushed ice. Sprinkle a little cinnamon or nutmeg on top, or garnish with the mint, and serve.

VARIATION: *AGUAS FRESCAS*   Some fruit mixtures, especially those that use a fruit that is acidic, such as pineapple, seem to taste better with water instead of milk, making them less of a breakfast drink than a drink to be served with other meals. Another we especially like combines cantaloupe or watermelon with strawberries in equal amounts, thinned with diluted frozen orange juice concentrate and a good squeeze of lime juice.

Hibiscus Flower Water
Agua Fresca de Flor de Jamaica
DENTON, TEXAS • OAXACA, MEXICO

MAKES ABOUT 7 CUPS CONCENTRATED FLOWER WATER *Soda pop now appears to be the drink of choice for most of the second- and third-generation Mexican-American families I met, replacing natural* aguas frescas *such as this beautiful drink. Some of the more health-conscious have "discovered"* jamaica *water or, as it is often labeled, hibiscus flower tea, and are surprised to learn that it is the same neon red beverage ladled out of glass barrels by street vendors all over Mexico and in Mexican neighborhoods in the United States. The dried flowers, high in vitamin C, can be found in Hispanic grocery stores and in most health food stores. Aurora Cabrera Dawson's version of this classic beverage has the subtle flavor of orange and spice. For an even more pronounced taste of orange, Valerie Hawkins-Hermocillo in Sacramento suggests diluting the flower water with fresh orange juice. Do be aware that* jamaica *is a diuretic and may have an effect on one's kidneys.*

2 ounces dried hibiscus flowers (about 2 cups)
½ cup honey or sugar
peel of 1 orange
1 clove

1 3-inch piece true cinnamon bark or cinnamon stick (cassia)
2 tablespoons lime or lemon juice

Bring 6 cups of water to a boil. Add the dried flowers, honey, orange peel, clove, and cinnamon bark to the boiling water and stir. Simmer for 5 minutes. Remove from the heat and allow to stand for 1 hour.

Strain the water into a pitcher. Add the lime juice. Taste for sweetness and tartness, and adjust if necessary. Cover and refrigerate.

When serving, dilute with as much water, orange juice, or sparkling water as you like, then pour over ice.

VARIATION: *JAMAICA SANGRIA* For this spirited drink, use less sweetener and mix with 24 ounces of a dry, fruity red wine and ¼ cup of mixed fresh orange and lime juice. Taste and add more sugar or juice if needed. Refrigerate several hours or overnight. When very cold, pour into tall glasses. A cup of sparkling water can be added right before serving. Serves 10 to 12.

Cucumber Cooler
Agua Fresca de Pepino

VICTORIA, BRITISH COLUMBIA, CANADA • MEXICO CITY, MEXICO

SERVES 4 TO 6 *The expression "cool as a cucumber" is so appropriate for this refreshing drink that Maria Elena Lorens serves during summer days on Vancouver Island. I've adapted the recipe from one in her book,* Mexican Cuisine.

2 large cucumbers, peeled, seeded, and roughly
   chopped
juice of 3 limes
6–8 tablespoons sugar

For the Garnish
sprigs of mint or long sticks of cucumber (optional)

Blend the cucumber, lime juice, sugar, and 2 cups of cold water in a blender until frothy. Pour into a glass pitcher and add 4 additional cups of cold water. Taste for sugar and lime, adding more if needed. If not drinking immediately, store in a refrigerator, covered, for no more than 2 hours. Before serving, put ice cubes into tall glasses, stir in the cucumber water, and pour. For a special touch, add a garnish of mint or cucumber.

VARIATION: SPIRITED CUCUMBER COOLER Add 1 cup of good-quality tequila, vodka, or gin to the pitcher just before stirring or add an appropriate amount to each glass before adding the cooler.

Sangria
Sangria

GIG HARBOR, WASHINGTON • VERACRUZ, MEXICO

SERVES 6 *I've frequently shared a glass of the familiar Spanish wine drink sangria with my Mexican friends in the United States, but most of their versions include frozen limeade, which I think changes the taste from a beverage with sparkling fresh fruit flavors to something more ordinary—more like a bottled wine cooler. This is my own way of making sangria. It evolved during the years we lived*

in Catalonia, Spain, and includes some variations I learned in Veracruz. It is so refreshing, Mexican-American friends who have tasted it have asked me for the recipe.

This recipe can be increased by any amount and even served in a punch bowl. Traditionally, though, the sangria would be served in pitchers.

½ cup freshly squeezed lime juice
½ cup freshly squeezed orange juice
½–⅔ cup sugar
1 bottle dry red wine
2 tablespoons orange liqueur, such as triple sec or
  Grand Marnier (optional)

1 small orange, thinly sliced
1 lime, thinly sliced
1 cup club soda or mineral water
vodka (optional)

In a pitcher stir together the lime and orange juices and sugar until the sugar dissolves. Add the wine, orange liqueur, and sliced orange and lime. Chill for several hours. Add the club soda just before serving.

Serve over ice cubes in a large bowl-shaped wineglass or in a tall, clear glass, with a straw. In Mexico it is common to pour an ounce or so of vodka into each glass before adding the *sangría*. The drink will be clear on the bottom and have a dense layer of red on top. Before drinking, mix it all together with the straw.

TAMARIND
(*Tamarindus indica*)

A passion for the soft sour taste of tamarind was acquired long ago by the Mexicans. The brittle brown tamarind pod, looking quite like an elongated dried-out pea pod, came with the Spaniards to the New World but had its origin somewhere in Southeast Asia or Africa. It is probably best recognized as the fruity sweet-sour flavor in Indian cuisine, where it shows up in all sorts of curries, pilaus, chutneys, and dipping sauces. If you think you haven't ever tasted tamarind, just check the back of a bottle of Lea & Perrins Worcestershire sauce.

Tamarind pods and already prepared paste or concentrate can almost always be found in Latin American or Indian grocery stores, as well as in many well-stocked supermarkets.

Christmas Punch
Ponche de Navidad
MIAMI, FLORIDA • GUANAJUATO, MEXICO

SERVES 16 TO 20   *Memories of Christmases in Mexico almost always include a simmering punch, darkly fragrant with exotic fruits and spices, rather like a liquid fruitcake. Virginia Ariemma uses a family recipe from her mother, Virginia Domínguez, and she is fortunate to be able to find the intensely aromatic guavas in Florida where she lives. If they are not available, substitute a can of guava nectar. The sugarcane can be found in many Filipino or Hispanic markets. Silvia de Santiago, up north in Chicago, makes almost the identical punch to celebrate the Fiesta de Navidad.*

For holiday entertaining, serve plates of cookies, including the traditional Aniseed Cookies (page 362).

½ pound tamarind or 6 tablespoons tamarind paste or 2 tablespoons tamarind concentrate

2 cones of *piloncillo* (page 25), chopped (about 1 pound) or 2 cups raw sugar

1 cup chopped and pitted dried prunes

2 feet fresh sugarcane, peeled, quartered, and cut in 3- or 4-inch pieces (optional)

½ cup raisins

1 6-inch piece cinnamon bark or 3-inch cinnamon stick (cassia)

8–10 fresh or canned guavas, blossom end trimmed off and cut in half (optional)

1 small orange spiked with 10 whole cloves

1 cup dried hibiscus flowers

1 apple, chopped

2 pears, peeled and chopped

juice of 2 oranges

brandy or rum to taste

If using the tamarind pods, soak them for several minutes so that the brittle shell can be removed more easily along with the 3 fibers that run the length of the pod. Place the peeled pods in a bowl and cover with 2 cups of boiling water. Let them soften for 1–2 hours. Using your fingers or a spoon, scrape all the pulp off the large seeds. Strain the pulp and water into a container, pressing to extract as much of the tamarind flavor as possible. This may be done in advance and stored, tightly sealed, for up to 1 week in the refrigerator. (The premade tamarind paste or concentrate need only be diluted with 2 cups of water.)

Place the *piloncillo* in a large pot with 4 quarts of water and bring to a boil over medium-high heat, stirring until the sugar dissolves. Add the 2 cups of tamarind water, prunes, sugarcane, raisins, cinnamon bark, guavas, and clove-studded orange, and simmer for 1 hour.

In a separate pan, bring 6 cups of water to a boil and add the hibiscus flowers. Remove from the heat, allow to steep for 20 minutes, and strain the water into the punch. Mix well, add the chopped apple and pears and the orange juice, and continue to simmer.

Ladle the hot punch into cups with some of the fruit. Add the brandy or rum at the last minute.

Spicy-Sweet Chaser for Tequila
Sangrita

MAKES 3 CUPS *Tequila is not just an ingredient of margaritas, a drink created for and beloved by U.S. tourists in Mexico. Like a fine scotch or a premium gin, a quality tequila is best enjoyed on its own. If ordering a brand tequila in Mexico, it would come in a squat shot-style glass accompanied by a plate of limes, a bowl of salt, and another small glass filled with a vibrant red chaser of* sangrita. *You can lick a bit of salt off the side of your hand, suck on a wedge of lime, and take a sip of* sangrita, *or do a ritualistic combination of all three. In general, the better quality of tequila used, the less need there is of any distracting flavor.*

Some of the commercially prepared sangrita *is pretty ghastly stuff, but properly prepared it provides a spicy sweet balance that many enjoy with tequila. Much of the flavor and the red, or "little blood," coloring of the chaser emanates from dried chiles, pomegranate or grenadine syrup, or tomatoes, depending on who prepares it. When serving tequila at home, Miguel prefers using wonderfully ripe tomatoes, sweetened just a bit, and a contrasting bite of onion, lime juice, and chiles.* Sangrita *will keep, sealed, in the refrigerator for about 1 week.*

2 pounds very juicy tomatoes, peeled and seeded (about 6 tomatoes)
1 cup orange juice
¼ cup lime juice
¼ cup chopped white onion
1 teaspoon sugar
about ¼ teaspoon sea salt
3–4 fresh serrano chiles, seeded and chopped, or ½–1 teaspoon ground *pequin*, *tepin*, or cayenne

Place all the ingredients in a blender or food processor, adding the chiles in small amounts, tasting as you go. Blend until quite smooth and as spicy as you like. It may have to be done in several batches. Put the *sangrita* in a jar or other container, cover, and chill for at least 1 hour.

When you are ready for your tequila drinking to begin, pour the *sangrita* into very small glasses, holding 2–3 ounces each, and serve with a good-quality tequila poured into other small glasses similar to shot glasses. Take a sip of the tequila, then *sangrita*, with an occasional suck on a lime wedge between sips.

Hot Chocolate Atole
Champurrado
DETROIT, MICHIGAN • MICHOACÁN, MEXICO

MAKES 3 CUPS *Petra Cervantes, who went to Detroit from Zamora, Michoacán, twenty years ago, always prepares this traditional rich chocolate drink thickened with masa to serve with her tamales at Christmas time. Miguel remembers that when he was too sick to eat, his grandmother made a similar champurrado just for him. But you don't have to wait until you don't feel well to try this warming drink. It is wonderful for breakfast on cold mornings.*

Mexican chocolate is made into different shapes, depending on the brand, and the amount of sugar and spices included in the chocolate mixture varies. Taste the atole as you add the sweetening.

⅓ cup *masa harina* (page 108)

2 cups milk

¼–½ cup dark brown sugar or 2–4 small cones piloncillo (page 25)

¼ teaspoon ground cinnamon (cassia)

3–4 ounces Mexican chocolate

¼ teaspoon ground nutmeg, preferably freshly ground

Add about 4 tablespoons of warm water to the *masa harina*, enough to dampen it thoroughly. Spoon it into a blender or food processor with 2 cups of water and blend thoroughly. Pour into a medium-size pot and bring to a simmer over medium heat, stirring so that any lumps will be broken up. The mixture will have the familiar look of cream of wheat. Add the milk, sugar, cinnamon, and chocolate, and when it starts to bubble again, lower the heat as far as possible. Simmer, stirring from time to time, until the mixture begins to thicken and the chocolate is melted.

Whisk or beat with a hand mixer until foamy. Pour into sturdy cups or mugs, sprinkle with nutmeg, and serve immediately. If the *champurrado* sits for a few minutes, it may become too thick. Whisk in a little more hot milk.

VARIATION: FRESH FRUIT *ATOLE* For 3 or 4 servings, puree 1½ cups of peeled and cubed fresh pineapple, apricots, or peaches with 1½ cups of water. If using strawberries, substitute milk for the water. Pour into a saucepan with ½ cup of sugar. Bring to a slow boil and simmer for 5 minutes. Dissolve ½ cup of *masa harina* in a little water and mix into the fruit. Cook, stirring frequently, for another 5 minutes.

Sweet Spiced Coffee
Café de Olla
PHOENIX, ARIZONA

SERVES 4 TO 6   Café de Olla, *that wonderfully dark-roasted coffee brewed in a traditional earthenware pot with spices and sugar, is just as much a favorite way to end a meal in the United States as it is in Mexico, and Miguel's version is quite typical. It can also be served iced.*

As Miguel told me,

> I think I was about nine years old when my grandfather, Don Miguel, gave me my first coffee-making class. To me it was a big thing because it was a sign of growing up. You have to remember that Mexican coffee is brewed without a coffeepot. My grandfather also had his little tricks, like using an eggshell in the coffee to settle the grounds, even though the grounds do eventually sink to the bottom. No matter, my grandmother had to have her coffee strained, and he let me know not to forget. Somehow my grandfather also happened to have a clean handkerchief in his pocket just for that reason, to use as a strainer. Anyway, after I served the coffee, I would look at Don Miguel to get the sign that my coffee was good. His sign of approval was a big smile and a wink of the eye.

1 6-inch piece cinnamon bark or 1 cinnamon stick (cassia)

½ cup dark brown sugar or 4 small piloncillo cones, chopped (page 25)

3 cloves

7 tablespoons dark roasted coffee, medium to coarse ground

In an earthenware pot or saucepan, heat 1 quart of water. Add the cinnamon, sugar, and cloves, and cook over medium-high heat until the sugar has dissolved. Add the coffee and bring to a boil, cover, turn the heat off, and let the coffee steep for 10–15 minutes before serving.

recipe continues

Very carefully pour into coffee mugs or strain through a fine-meshed sieve or a piece of cheesecloth.

VARIATION: *CAFÉ CON LECHE* In a small pot, bring 2 cups of milk to a simmer while the coffee is steeping. When ready to serve, pour the milk and coffee into each cup, using more or less milk as you wish, and add sugar if you need more.

VARIATION: ICED SWEET SPICED COFFEE Miguel reminded me that when he had lived in Arizona with its blistering heat, they often served their *café de olla* and *café con leche* over lots of ice for a cooling drink. Just strain and let cool before pouring over the ice.

Mexican Hot Chocolate
Chocolate ala Mexicana
AUSTIN, TEXAS

MAKES 4 CUPS *Holidays and hot chocolate went together in Miguel's family whenever tamales were being made. Being so hot where he lived in Arizona, his grandmother often served the chocolate drink cold, contrary to custom.*

Mexican chocolate is widely available in many U.S. grocery stores. It comes sweetened and is usually flavored with cinnamon. Ibarra is a familiar brand, and Miguel still uses Popular, the same kind his grandmother always bought. Check the label, but one section of chocolate is usually the amount needed for one cup of the drink.

Hot chocolate can be served anytime you want a soothing drink, but if you plan to make tamales, this drink should be its companion.

4 cups milk
3–4 ounces Mexican chocolate

In a medium-size saucepan, warm the milk and chocolate over low heat stirring continuously, until the chocolate melts. When the chocolate milk begins to simmer, beat it vigorously with a whisk or a hand mixer until the mixture is thick with foam.

Serve hot in mugs. If serving the drink cold, let it cool to room temperature before adding ice cubes.

Selected Bibliography

The flavor of this cookbook is derived from the social, political, and culinary history of the Mexican people now living in the United States. With the assistance of public, university, and museum libraries throughout the country, I consulted sources far too numerous to list. The following are recommended books that should be available to the interested reader.

Acuña, Rodolfo. *Occupied America: A History of Chicanos*. 3rd ed. New York: Harper & Row, 1988.

Andrews, Jean. *Peppers: The Domesticated Capsicums*. Austin, Tex.: University of Texas Press, 1984.

Arnold, Sam'l P. *Eating up the Santa Fe Trail*. Niwot, Colorado: University Press of Colorado, 1990.

Baker, Richard. *Los Dos Mundos: Rural American Americans, Another America*. Logan, Utah: Utah State University Press, 1995.

Bayless, Rick, with Deann Groen Bayless. *Authentic Mexican*. New York: William Morrow, 1987.

Bayless, Rick, with Deann Groen Bayless and JeanMarie Brownson. *Rick Bayless's Mexican Kitchen*. New York: Scribner, 1996.

Bermúdez, María Teresa. *Mexican Family Favorites Cookbook*. Phoenix, Ariz.: Golden West, 1995.

Casas, Penelope. *The Food & Wine of Spain*. New York: Alfred A. Knopf, 1982.

Chapman, Charles E. *A History of California: The Spanish Period*. New York: Macmillan, 1946.

Chipman, Donald E. *Spanish Texas, 1519–1821*. Austin, Tex.: University of Texas Press, 1992.

Clark, Amalia Ruiz. *Amalia's Special Mexican Dishes*. Oracle, Ariz.: Gila River Design, 1979.

Cook, Warren L. *Flood Tide of Empire: Spain and the Pacific Northwest*. New Haven, Conn.: Yale University Press, 1973.

Dent, Huntley. *The Feast of Santa Fe*. New York: Fireside, 1985.

Dondero, Carlo Andrea. *Go West: An Autobiography of Carlo Andrea Dondero, 1842–1939*. Eugene, Ore.: Garlic Press, 1992.

Ellis, Merle. *Cutting-up in the Kitchen*. San Francisco, Calif.: Chronicle Books, 1975.

Fontana, Bernard L. *Entrada: The Legacy of Spain and Mexico in the United States*. Tucson, Ariz.: Southwest Parks and Monuments Association, 1994.

Gabilondo, Aída. *Mexican Family Cooking*. New York: Fawcett Columbine Cook, 1986.

Gamboa, Erasmo, and Carolyn M. Buan, eds. *Nosotros, the Hispanic People of Oregon*. Portland, Ore.: Oregon Council for the Humanities, 1955.

Garza, Lucy. *South Texas Mexican Cookbook*. Phoenix, Ariz.: Golden West Publishers, 1982.

Gilbert, Fabiola C. *Historic Cookery*. Las Vegas, Nev.: La Galeria de los Artesanos, 1970.

———. *The Good Life: New Mexico Traditions and Food*. 2nd ed. Santa Fe: Museum of New Mexico Press, 1982.

Grebler, Leo, Joan W. Moore, and Ralph Guzmán. *The Mexican-American People: The Nation's Second Largest Minority.* New York: Free Press, 1970.

Hardwick, William. *Authentic Indian-Mexican Recipes.* P. O. Box 1109, Fort Stockton, TX 79735, 1972.

Hutson, Lucinda. *The Herb Garden.* Austin, Tex.: Texas Monthly Press, 1987.

———. *Tequila.* Berkeley, Calif.: Ten Speed Press, 1995.

Jamison, Cheryl Alters, and Bill Jamison. *The Border Cookbook.* Boston, Mass.: Harvard Common Press, 1995.

———. *The Rancho de Chimayó Cookbook.* Boston, Mass.: Harvard Common Press, 1991.

Jaramillo, Cleofas M. *The Genuine New Mexico Tasty Recipes.* Santa Fe, N.M.: Ancient City Press, 1981.

Kay, Elizabeth. *Chimayo Valley Traditions.* Santa Fe, N.M.: Ancient City Press, 1987.

Kennedy, Diana. *The Cuisines of Mexico.* New York: Harper & Row, 1972; rev. ed., 1986.

———. *Mexican Regional Cooking,* rev. ed. New York: Harper & Row, 1984.

———. *The Art of Mexican Cooking.* New York: Bantam Books, 1989.

Kimble, Socorro Muñoz, and Irma Serrano Noriega. *Mexican Desserts.* Phoenix, Ariz.: Golden West Publishers, 1987.

King, Shirley. *Fish: The Basics.* Shelburne, Vt.: Chapters Publishing, 1996.

Loranzo, Ruben Rendon. *Viva Tejas, the Story of the Mexican-Born Patriots of the Texas Revolution.* San Antonio, Tex.: The Alamo Press, 1936; reissued with new material by Mary Ann Noonan Guerra, 1985.

Lorens, Maria Elena C. *Maria Elena's Mexican Cuisine.* Victoria, British Columbia: General Store Publishing, 1989.

Magoffin, Susan Shelby. *Down the Santa Fe Trail and into Mexico: The Diary of Susan Shelby Magoffin, 1846–1847,* ed. by Stella M. Drumm. New Haven, Conn.: Yale University Press, 1926.

Martinez, Ruben. *The Other Side: Notes from the New L.A., Mexico City and Beyond.* New York: Vintage Departures, a division of Random House, 1992.

Martínez, Zarella. *Food from My Heart.* New York: Macmillan, 1992.

Meir, Matt S., and Feliciano Ribera. *Mexican Americans/American Mexicans—from Conquistadors to Chicanos.* New York: Hill & Wang, rev. ed., 1993.

Muller, Frederick R. *La Comida: The Foods, Cooking, and Traditions of the Upper Rio Grande.* Boulder, Colo.: Pruett Publishing, 1995.

Naj, Amal. *Peppers.* New York: Alfred A. Knopf, 1992.

Ortiz, Elizabeth Lambert. *The Encyclopedia of Herbs, Spices, and Flavorings.* London: Dorling Kindersley, 1992.

Parkes, Henry Bamford. *A History of Mexico.* Boston, Mass.: Houghton Mifflin, 1969.

Peyton, James W. *La Cocina de la Frontera, Mexican-American Cooking from the Southwest.* Santa Fe, N.M.: Red Crane Books, 1994.

———. *El Norte: the Cuisine of Northern Mexico.* Santa Fe, N.M.: Red Crane Books, 1990.

Preston, Mark. *California Mission Cookery.* Albuquerque, N.M.: Border Books, 1994.

Quintana, Patricia, with Jack Bishop. *Cuisine of the Water Gods.* New York: Simon & Schuster, 1994.

Rodriguez, Richard. *Days of Obligation: An Argument with My Mexican Father.* New York: Penguin Books, 1992.

Ronstadt, Fedrico José María. *Borderman: Memoirs of José María Ronstadt,* ed. by Edward F. Ronstadt. Albuquerque: University of New Mexico Press.

Sanchez, George J. *Becoming Mexican American.* New York: Oxford University Press, 1993.

Simmons, Helen, and Cathryn A. Hoyt. *Hispanic Texas: A Historical Guide.* Austin: University of Texas Press, 1992.

Simons, Marc. *New Mexico: An Interpretive History.* Albuquerque: University of New Mexico Press, 1988.

Weber, David J. *Myth and the History of the Hispanic Southwest.* Albuquerque: University of New Mexico Press, 1988.

West, John O. *Mexican-American Folklore.* Little Rock, Ark.: August House, Inc., 1988.

Zelayeta, Elena. *Elena's Secrets of Mexican Cooking.* Garden City, N.Y.: Doubleday, 1968.

———. *Elena's Famous Mexican and Spanish Recipes.* San Francisco, Calif.: self-published, 1944.

Product Sources

The best sources of Mexican fresh produce and the dried and canned goods necessary for cooking Mexican dishes are usually those available closest to home. Most supermarkets carry fresh and dried chiles, fruits, and vegetables such as avocados, tomatillos, mangoes, plantains, jicama, *chayote,* and *nopales.* If they don't, they are in their catalogs and can be ordered. Just ask for them. Mexican and Latino markets are found in most cities and towns that have any appreciable Hispanic population. Check the Yellow Pages for their locations. Most will carry freshly ground *masa* and always *masa harina.* The mail-order sources listed are ones we know through personal experience and recommend for sometimes difficult-to-locate products. For herbs, it is always best to grow your own and use fresh.

GROW IT YOURSELF

J. L. Hudson, Seedsman
P. O. Box 1058
Redwood City, CA 94064
Zapotec seed collection. Seeds of Oaxaca. Unique food plants, including chiles and unusual herbs, *chilacayote* (squash with superb edible seeds), and amaranth.

It's About Thyme
11726 Manchaca Road
Austin, TX 78748
512-280-1192
512-280-6356 fax
A good selection of Mexican plants. Two species of Mexican so-called oregano (the common *Poliomintha longiflora* and the sweeter *Lippia graveolens*), *hoja santa,* and epazote.

Native Seeds/Search
2509 North Campbell #325
Tucson, AZ 85719
602-327-9123

Seeds for epazote, chiles, tomatillos, and other Mexican herbs and plants.

Seeds of Change
P. O. Box 15700
Santa Fe, NM 87506-5700
505-438-8080
505-438-7052 fax
Heirloom seeds of many essential Mexican herbs and plants, including *quelites,* epazote, and traditional beans and corn.

GENERAL MEXICAN PRODUCTS

Don Alfonso Foods
P. O. Box 201988
Austin, TX 78720
800-456-6100
800-765-7373 fax
An excellent source of dried chiles, pure ground chiles, dried and canned Mexican ingredients, cooking utensils—including *mol-*

cajetes, tortilla presses, and *tamal* steamers—
and Mexican cookbooks.

The CMC Company
P. O. Box 322
Avalon, NJ 08202
800-262-2780
A wide selection of dried and canned chiles,
avocado leaves, *masa harina,* achiote paste,
Mexican herbs, dried shrimp, *piloncillo,* and
Mexican chocolate; also cooking utensils, in-
cluding *comales* and *molcajetes.*

Dean and DeLuca
Catalog Department
560 Broadway
New York, NY 10012
800-221-7714
Mexican and other Latino products, including many varieties of unusual dried beans,
chiles, and herbs. Also dried *pozole,* pumpkin
seeds, and *masa harina.*

Santa Cruz Chile and Spice Company
P. O. Box 177
Tumacacori, AZ 85640
602-398-2591
Producers of Arizona chile products. Very
helpful, but no credit cards are accepted.

Santa Fe School of Cooking
116½ West San Francisco Street
Santa Fe, NM 87501
505-983-4511
505-983-7540 fax
Specialists in New Mexican cooking products.

Elizabeth Berry
Gallina Canyon Ranch
P. O. Box 706
Abiquiu, NM 87510
Wide selection of heirloom beans. For a cat-
alog, send one dollar and a self-addressed
business-size envelope.

Peter Casados
P. O. Box 852
San Juan Pueblo, NM 87568
The special ingredients of New Mexico.

Gazella Mexican Chocolate
3200 Corte Malposa No. 108
Camarillo, CA 93012
800-445-7744
Various blends of Oaxaca-style Mexican chocolate.

Herbs of Mexico
3903 Whittier Boulevard
Los Angeles, CA 90023
213-261-2521
Many, many dried Mexican herbs.

Mozzarella Company
2914 Elm Street
Dallas, TX 75226
800-798-2954
Fresh handmade Mexican cheeses, including
queso blanco and Oaxacan-style *quesillo.* Also
ancho-chile and epazote-flavored cheeses.

Permissions Acknowledgments

page 31: Reprinted with permission of Macmillan Publishing Company USA, a Simon & Schuster Macmillan Company, from *Food from My Heart,* by Zarela Martinez. Copyright © 1992 by Zarela Martinez.

page 44: Museum of New Mexico Press from *The Good Life,* by Fabiola Cabeza. Copyright © 1949 by Fabiola Cabeza.

page 48: Reprinted with permission of the Garlic Press from *Go West: Autobiography of Carlos Andrea Dondero, 1842–1939,* by Carlos Andrea Dondero. Copyright © 1992.

page 49: Reprinted by permission of HarperCollins Publishers, Inc., from *The Cuisines of Mexico,* by Diana Kennedy. Copyright © 1972 by Diana Kennedy. Illustrations copyright © Harper & Row, Publishers, Inc.

page 60: Reprinted by permission of Front and Center Press, Inc., from *Healthy Mexican Regional Cooking,* by Lotte Mendelsohn. Copyright © 1995 by Lotte Mendelsohn.

pages 83 and 351: Self-published, from *El Charro Café,* by Carlotta Flores. Copyright © 1989 by Carlotta Flores.

page 105: "Tortillas Like Africa" from *Canto Familiar,* copyright © 1995 by Gary Soto, reprinted by permission of Harcourt, Brace & Company.

page 137: Reprinted, by permission, from *The Florentine Codex: General History of the Things of New Spain,* by Fray Bernardino de Sahagún. Book 8—Kings and Lords, p. 39. Translated by Arthur J. O. Anderson and Charles E. Dibble. Copyright 1954 by the School of American Research, Santa Fe. Retranslated from the Aztec by Michael Coe.

page 158: Reprinted by permission of the Seton Press, Santa Fe, from *New Mexico Tasty Recipes,* by Cleofas M. Jaramillo. Copyright © 1942 by Cleofas M. Jaramillo.

pages 199, 331, 346, and 380: Recipes reprinted by permission of General Store Publishing House, from *Maria Elena's Mexican Cuisine,* by Maria Elena Lorens. Copyright © 1989 by Maria Elena Lorens.

page 221: Self-published, from *Elena's Famous Mexican and Spanish Recipes,* by Elena Zelayeta. Copyright © 1944 by Elena Zelayeta.

page 259: Mitford House, from *Narrative of Some Things of New Spain and of the Great City of Tempestitan, Mexico,* by an Anonymous Conqueror, copyright © 1972.

Index

INDEX

Metric Equivalencies

LIQUID AND DRY MEASURE EQUIVALENCIES

Customary	Metric
¼ teaspoon	1.25 milliliters
½ teaspoon	2.5 milliliters
1 teaspoon	5 milliliters
1 tablespoon	15 milliliters
1 fluid ounce	30 milliliters
¼ cup	60 milliliters
⅓ cup	80 milliliters
½ cup	120 milliliters
1 cup	240 milliliters
1 pint (2 cups)	480 milliliters
1 quart (4 cups)	960 milliliters
	(.96 liter)
1 gallon (4 quarts)	3.84 liters
1 ounce (by weight)	28 grams
¼ pound (4 ounces)	114 grams
1 pound (16 ounces)	454 grams
2.2 pounds	1 kilogram
	(1000 grams)

OVEN-TEMPERATURE EQUIVALENCIES

Description	°Fahrenheit	°Celsius
Cool	200	90
Very slow	250	120
Slow	300–325	150–160
Moderately slow	325–350	160–180
Moderate	350–375	180–190
Moderately hot	375–400	190–200
Hot	400–450	200–230
Very hot	450–500	230–260